Worlds Gone Awry

Worlds Gone Awry

Essays on Dystopian Fiction

Edited by JOHN J. HAN,
C. CLARK TRIPLETT
and ASHLEY G. ANTHONY

McFarland & Company, Inc., Publishers
Jefferson, North Carolina

ISBN (print) 978-1-4766-7180-2
ISBN (ebook) 978-1-4766-3377-0

LIBRARY OF CONGRESS CATALOGUING DATA ARE AVAILABLE

BRITISH LIBRARY CATALOGUING DATA ARE AVAILABLE

© 2018 John J. Han, C. Clark Triplett and Ashley G. Anthony.
All rights reserved

*No part of this book may be reproduced or transmitted in any form
or by any means, electronic or mechanical, including photocopying
or recording, or by any information storage and retrieval system,
without permission in writing from the publisher.*

Front cover illustration by Victor Zastolskiy (iStock)

Printed in the United States of America

*McFarland & Company, Inc., Publishers
Box 611, Jefferson, North Carolina 28640
www.mcfarlandpub.com*

Table of Contents

Acknowledgments — vii

Introduction
    John J. Han, C. Clark Triplett *and* Ashley G. Anthony — 1

Part One: Classical Dystopian Fiction

Feminine Subterfuge in Margaret Atwood's *The Heart Goes Last*
    Megan E. Cannella — 15

"Forget sad things": Kurt Vonnegut's Dystopian Short Fiction as Social Critique
    Ashley G. Anthony — 28

"A secure but partly demented society": Reconsidering Human Depravity in William Golding's *Lord of the Flies*
    Natasha W. Vashisht — 40

Streets of Spectrality: Kevin Barry's Dystopian *City of Bohane*
    Deirdre Flynn — 56

Interrogating Utopia: On Colin MacInnes' *Absolute Beginners*
    Andrew Hammond — 69

"What if I said that he's a god?": Messianism in Cormac McCarthy's *The Road*
    Wes Yeary — 88

"Maps and mazes": Mapping as Metaphor in Postsecular America
    Harold K. Bush — 100

Part Two: Popular Dystopian Fiction

Unmasking the Deception: The Hermeneutic of Suspicion in Lois Lowry's *The Giver*
  C. CLARK TRIPLETT *and* JOHN J. HAN — 111

Ending Dystopia: The Feminist Critique of Culture in Suzanne Collins' *Hunger Games* Trilogy
  JANE BEAL — 122

Commodifying the Revolution: Dystopian Young Adult Literature and Cultural Critique
  JILLIAN L. CANODE — 139

Dystopia, Competition and Reality Television Tropes in *The Bachman Books*: "The Long Walk" and "The Running Man"
  ALISSA BURGER — 150

Stranger Than Fiction: Locating the Digital Dystopia in Contemporary Fiction
  ROBYN N. ROWLEY — 163

Disembodied Heads and Headless Philosophies: C.S. Lewis' Aesthetic Rejoinder to Dystopian Utility in *That Hideous Strength*
  MATTHEW BARDOWELL — 178

The Creation of the Future from Remnants of the Past: Order from Disorder in William Gibson's *All Tomorrow's Parties* and Neal Stephenson's *Snow Crash*
  MELANIE A. MAROTTA — 196

The Future Is White, the Future Is Undead: Reframing the American Vampire Dystopia in Guillermo del Toro and Chuck Hogan's *The Strain Trilogy*
  SIMON BACON — 210

Here's Looking at You, Kids: The Urgency of Dystopian Texts in the Secondary Classroom
  MICHAEL A. SOARES — 225

About the Contributors — 245

Index — 248

Acknowledgments

We would like to thank all the scholars who submitted their respective essays to this volume. Without their participation, cooperation, and gracious patience, this book would not have come to fruition. Special thanks go to McFarland's two blind peer reviewers who provided us with invaluable suggestions for revising and improving our manuscript. Matthew Bardowell, one of the contributors and our colleague at Missouri Baptist University, kindly volunteered to assist us during the process of re-conceptualizing and restructuring the materials in this volume. We also appreciate the assistance of Rebecca Klussman and Mary Ellen Fuquay for copyediting the manuscript and Krista Krekeler for proofreading the essays.

Introduction

JOHN J. HAN, C. CLARK TRIPLETT
and ASHLEY G. ANTHONY

The Development and Popularity of Dystopian Fiction

Since the turn of the twenty-first century, new dystopian fiction has gripped the attention of the reading public, and some classical dystopian novels have seen their popularity resurge. Popular dystopian authors such as Cormac McCarthy (*The Road*), Suzanne Collins (*The Hunger Games* series), and Veronica Roth (the *Divergent* trilogy) have garnered critical acclaim. As Alexandra Alter notes in her 2017 *New York Times* article, sales of dystopian novels also dramatically rose after the inauguration of U.S. President Donald Trump; after the November election, 100,000 new copies of Margaret Atwood's *The Handmaid's Tale* (1985) were published, and George Orwell's *Animal Farm* (1945) and *Nineteen Eighty-Four* (1949) also saw dramatic increases in sales ("Uneasy"). In a more recent *New York Times* article, Alter reviews several new dystopian novels—Omar El Akkad's *American War*, Lidia Yuknavitch's *The Book of Joan*, Zachary Mason's *Void Star*, Michael Tolkin's *NK3*, and Kim Stanley Robinson's *New York 2140*—identifying the common theme of these "doomsday books" as "[t]hings may seem bad, but they might become much, much worse" ("Boom"). Peter Firchow rightly argues, "[M]ost of the memorable utopian fictions of our time are largely pessimistic—not of course about the future, but really about the present" (5).

Whether the election of the new U.S. president portends the rise of a dystopian society will elicit different answers depending on one's political viewpoints. What is certain is that people who live in today's society are increasingly concerned about the future of the world. Literature reflects the concerns and anxieties of readers, and dystopian literature focuses particularly on the potential problems humans face, such as totalitarianism, political anarchy, technological oppression, environmental disasters, global war, resource shortage, and widespread disease, among many others. The new television adaptation of *The Handmaid's Tale* reflects the existential angst among contemporary citizens, who fear the rise of a dystopian nightmare.

Dystopian fiction has proven especially popular among young adult readers and moviegoers. Even earlier dystopian novels have received renewed interest, such as Lois Lowry's 1993 book *The Giver*, which was adapted into a movie in 2014. *The Giver* is just one of several dystopian films based on their novel counterparts, as *The Maze Runner*, *Divergent*, and *The Hunger Games* series have proven to be successful film adaptations.

What is it about these works that appeals to the young adult reader? Perhaps the themes embodied in dystopian literature provide young people with something more relatable as they struggle in their lives. Not surprisingly, common elements found in most dystopian novels include the pressure to conform and a lack of individual freedom (Scholes and Ostenson). Young people tend to relate to the ongoing stress of fitting in with their peers; they harbor a constant anxiety and fear of being the one who stands out. On the other hand, young adults often feel that their individual freedom is being stifled by authority, most often by their parents. Dystopian literature portrays a world much like, yet much unlike, the currently known world, and since young adults are often the protagonists and guiding forces in these texts, it provides space for young people to imagine themselves in dangerous, world-changing situations. It is not just the young adult who is invited to change his or her own ideas or actions; instead, he or she is invited to be a catalyst for change in an imaginary world. As the reader follows along with each story, there seems to be a constant question of "How would you act in this situation?" If the world were destroyed and the current authorities were out of control and immoral, would you rise up to the challenge of resisting, even if no other person, adult or otherwise, stood with you? Young adults are able to see themselves as protagonists and world changers in these texts and films, as opposed to leaving this challenge to the adults.

Another facet of dystopian fiction that young adult readers may connect with is the rapidly growing rate of technology emphasized in many novels. Today's young adults were born into a digital age; specifically, young adults may identify with feelings of social isolation in these novels due to their largely disconnected social lives. Most of contemporary young adults' encounters with friends are online rather than face-to-face, a phenomenon that contributes to a declining sociability among peers. In addition, young adults are beginning to face the harsh realities that come with rapid advances in technology. While some technologies make daily life more efficient, others are largely unnecessary, making readers imagine a day when technology itself could outsmart humans.[1]

Although dystopian fiction—both classical and popular—has seen a dramatic increase in recent decades, it has a long history. Before the idea of an imperfect society came about, there was first speculation about a potentially perfect one. While Thomas More's *Utopia* (1516) sparked the birth of dystopian fiction, there are some classical and Christian precedents for More's text. The notion of an ideal place appears in ancient, medieval, and other early modern texts, such as the book of Genesis in the Hebrew Bible, Plato's *Republic*, and St. Augustine's *City of God*. In his 2011 article "The Meaning of Utopia," Yves Charles Zarka, a philosophy professor at the Sorbonne, points out that *utopia* should be understood in terms of the impossibility of the existence of an ideal place: "[U]topia can be thought of only when the relationship is reversed, when the real appears overloaded and offers no way out of war, violence, cupidity, exploitation, hunger and injustice. Faced with a reality which is overloaded in this way, we have to look for an elsewhere." He cites a well-known passage in the first chapter of More's *Utopia*, in which the traveler Raphael Hythloday and More himself debate on the merit of common ownership as practiced on the island of Utopia. According to Zarka, conceiving an ideal society demonstrates that human society is not ideal and that an ideal society conceived by utopian thinkers exists outside the human realm—a place "[n]o one knows precisely where, but somewhere other than here and now." Along Zarka's lines, one might then say that the meaning of the word *utopia* already conceives the idea of dystopia. Indeed, More coined the word, a term that reflects the tension between plausibility and possibility. As a Latin pun, utopia signifies an imagined space, "ut-topos," as well as an ideal place, "eu-topos."

From More's initial work, the term *utopia* shifts to describe an emerging genre of texts steeped in historical and political contexts, such as the English Civil War, the Interregnum period, and the Restoration. Scholars have begun to note a nationalistic tendency within utopian fiction. Additionally, a strain of utopian works by female authors began to emerge during the Early Modern period. In keeping with More's pun, these texts often merge the imagined concerns with contemporary concerns.[2] Looking slightly ahead, the Golden Age of Elizabethan England reveals interesting observations about how political commentary has shifted over time.

The eighteenth century marks the beginnings of dystopian literature as a counterpart to utopian literature. Jonathan Swift's *Gulliver's Travels* (1726) played an important role in popularizing the genre of dystopian fiction, and his novel included a dystopian twist—according to his social critique, humans in contemporary society were no better than the savage Yahoos. However, most classical dystopian novels appeared in the twentieth century. Notable texts from this period include Franz Kafka's *The Trial* (1925), Aldous Huxley's *Brave New World* (1932), George Orwell's *Animal Farm* (1945), and Margaret

Atwood's *The Handmaid's Tale* (1985). All of these novels were inspired by some unpleasant, ominous historical events. For instance, Joseph Stalin's dictatorship inspired Orwell to write *Animal Farm*, in which the author portrays the threat of ubiquitous government control. The rise of Nazi Germany and McCarthyism motivated Bradbury to write *Fahrenheit 451*, which examines censorship policies. In *The Handmaid's Tale*, Atwood envisioned a dystopian society in which society is controlled by Christian theocracy. Finally, two recent events, the post–9/11 War on Terror and the rise of right-wing populist politics, have played a large role in the dramatic increase of readers who turn to dystopian fiction—both classical and new—to better understand the possibly disastrous consequences of "utopian" societies.

Dystopian Fiction as a Form of Critique

Dystopian critique aims at different targets including the social and political order, technological sufficiency, and/or the hope or promise of a utopian future. In light of the present-day artifice and pretense that surround and sometimes overwhelm the average person with such an onslaught of ideas and opinions delivered through digital and visual means, it is even more important to understand the value of this form of critique. Through the use of fascinating and absorbing stories, the reader is provided with a counter-narrative that creates a level of suspicion about the surface of the so-called realities they experience on a daily basis in the modern/postmodern world.

Although dystopian literature can be classified as "popular" literature, most works of dystopian fiction widely read—or re-read—today are not simply works of entertainment. As this collection of critical essays shows, the authors of dystopian fiction convey their sense of urgency about the ominous signs of catastrophic disasters that may await humankind in the future. There is a diversity of themes and trends in dystopian fiction as is made evident in this collection. Regardless of whether the discussion is on recent young adult renditions, such as *The Hunger Games* and *The Maze Runner* (2009), or more classical novels such as *Fahrenheit 451* and *Nineteen Eighty-Four*, it is difficult to find a single thread that pulls together the broad range of concerns and interests addressed within the corpus of dystopian fiction. Many literary scholars would agree, however, that some aspect of critique is at least implicit within all types of dystopian works, whether aimed at political manipulation, cultural power, governmental control, or technological sufficiency.

In some dystopian works, the ongoing discourse of the narrative is constantly being challenged not only by the reader but also by the characters within the story itself. The text continuously raises suspicions about whether something is being revealed or hidden. The story becomes a vehicle for questioning and challenging the way the reader understands his or her own social and political life-world and the ways in which contemporary discourse and social interactions may be filled with subterfuge.

Perhaps it is too much to expect middle and high school students who read young adult dystopian novels—such as *The Hunger Games*, *The Maze Runner*, or the *Divergent* series—to seriously consider the critical function of these popular stories, but many do recognize the message about the dangers of power and subterfuge in political and social systems. Most, of course, simply read these novels as a form of entertainment that tell a compelling and interesting story of survival and discovery. However, it is important to understand how these compelling stories might provide a framework for critical discussions among both younger and older adults about the often hidden hazards and concerns related to ideological systems which have been accepted as normal in today's strange political and cultural climate. Interestingly, some dystopian writers, including Lois Lowry, actually provide discussion questions at the end of their books for open-ended discourse about the implications of their texts in contemporary society.

Utopian Desire and the Dystopian Impulse

In this section, we consider how new, popular dystopia fiction demonstrates a continuity with the impulses of utopian fiction and should be brought into the fold of the older, more literary dystopian fiction. Contemporary dystopian fiction has been differentiated by some critics into categories of classical and popular young adult forms. A number of critics argue that although young adult versions of dystopian literature have gained recognition and acceptance in popular culture, themes and content of works such as the *Divergent* series, *The Maze Runner*, and *The Hunger Games* do not warrant the same level of serious scholarly consideration as do more classical literary works such as Orwell's *Nineteen Eighty-Four*, Atwood's *Handmaids Tale*, and/or Bradbury's *Fahrenheit 451*, even though these novels were originally considered novels that appealed to a mainstream audience with subsequent film productions. Critics argue that classical dystopian literature, however, provides underlying questions about specific social and political concerns that elicit critical discourse on these issues in contemporary culture. Young adult dystopian literature, on the other hand, tends to appeal to popular adolescent issues such as self-identity, thrill-seeking, and romantic angst. Some scholars would tend to compare these novels with comic books and graphic novels. The series of essays in this volume, however, demonstrates that such distinctions are arbitrary and that the intent of both classical and popular young adult dystopian works have similar trajectories and elicit critical inquiry that is more complex than is evident *prima facie*.

The relationship between classical and popular dystopian fiction might be better understood in the context of critical discussions on the important connection between utopian and dystopian impulses. Several scholars emphasize that it is difficult to understand the dystopian intent without appreciating an underlying utopian desire. Fredric Jameson, for example, argues that "the critical dystopia is a negative cousin of utopia proper, for it is in the light of some positive connection of human social possibilities that its effects are generated and from utopian ideals it's politically enabling stances derive" (198). Jameson makes the case that rather than characterizing dystopian fiction as the product of a disaffected society, it makes more sense to view it as an idealistic contingent arising within a disaffected culture. Dystopia is not strictly a rejection of the mores of a repressive hegemony; rather it is a method in which writers continue to hold to some deeply loved "positive conception of human social possibilities" (198). Dystopian fiction, as with utopian literature, begins with a desire for the good life and firmly held vision of human flourishing that makes the bleak imagery of the dystopian narrative even more vivid. The literary trajectory differs from the utopian desire only as it occurs over a historical time period. In other words, once the notions of a particular utopia have been tried and found wanting, it is then the intent of the dystopian writer to cast light on the nature of this failure and reassert the vision that motivated utopian thinking in the first place.

Tom Moylan, in his densely written critical work *Demand the Impossible: Science Fiction and the Utopian Imagination*, elaborates more precisely on this connection between utopian and dystopian literature. Moylan observes that utopian desire is "at heart, rooted in the unfulfilled needs and wants of specific classes, groups, and individuals in their unique historical contexts" ("Introduction" 1). This utopian desire "negates the contradictions in a social system by forging visions of what is not yet realized either in theory or practice" (1). According to Moylan, both utopian desire and dystopian critique arise in opposition to the status quo, but at different points in the formation or reformation of society. Utopian literature points to a vision of an imagined future, while dystopian literature explores the limitations of that vision. Moylan uses the term "critical utopia" to describe the perspective of dystopian works. While on the surface, the narrative seems anti-utopian, at a deeper level there is an alternative utopian vision that is a corrective to the existing system. So although the dystopian narrative serves a critical function, there is a counter narrative that is implicitly communicated. Ildney Cavalcanti has argued for this double action of the text—both critical and visionary—by suggesting that feminist utopias include "utopian potentials" (271) that offer an alternative path for the future of society.

While it would be mistaken to assume that all dystopian stories are really about utopia in disguise, it is possible to make the case that there is some continuity between dystopian critique and utopian desire. Both seem to clearly seek the ultimate good of society, but dystopian fiction, in particular, offers a necessary corrective to the boundlessness of the utopian imagination. This double movement of both critique and revision emerges in each of the essays presented in this volume. It is also clear that the possibility of serious critique is conspicuous in each of the works represented in this collection regardless of whether they are examples of classical dystopian fiction or popular young adult fiction. It is evident that even in contributions such as *The Giver* and *The Hunger Games* the ideas of both critique and revision or reimagination are the primary intent of the narrative and although the literary quality of the works reviewed may vary, these two elements are clearly manifest.

Essays at a Glance

Considering the insufficient scholarly resources on this emerging field, we have collected 16 scholarly essays on dystopian themes in fiction since 1925. The contributions in this collection attempt to lift the facile veil of contemporary ideologies that are often portrayed in dystopian literature. To this end, we offer two sections that utilize the categories of "classical" dystopia and "popular" dystopia to show that at root these apparent dissimilarities belie an essential relationship to each other: "Classical Dystopian Fiction" and "Popular Dystopian Fiction," respectively. These two parts reflect the fact that dystopian literature demonstrates a continuity with the impulses of utopian fiction.

Part One consists of seven essays. In "Feminine Subterfuge in Margaret Atwood's *The Heart Goes Last*," Megan E. Cannella borrows Dunja M. Mohr's concept of the "transgressive utopian dystopia" in analyzing *The Heart Goes Last*, a story that complicates what is popularly understood as the utopian-dystopian binary. At the same time, Cannella views the dystopian world of Consilience through the lens of female activism in a society surrounded and controlled by a patriarchal social structure. Cannella asserts that Atwood criticizes traditional gender roles through the representation of the main characters as empowered and independent women while also undermining traditional dystopian fiction by incorporating elements of utopia. Cannella argues that, by challenging these norms, Atwood creates a new way of understanding both speculative fiction and the world.

Meanwhile, in "'Forget sad things': Kurt Vonnegut's Dystopian Short Fiction as Social Critique," Ashley G. Anthony analyzes autobiographical elements of Kurt Vonnegut's writing, such as references to war, his dysfunctional family, and PTSD. Vonnegut specifically uses his dystopian fiction to criticize parts of mainstream society with which he is dissatisfied. While many dystopian writers express a fear of what the future holds, Vonnegut expresses his discontent and mistrust of the events in his own lifetime. Anthony argues that Vonnegut urges his readers to delve deeper into current issues rather than continuing to live their lives in ignorance.

Natasha W. Vashisht's essay, "'A secure but partly demented society': Reconsidering Human Depravity in William Golding's *Lord of the Flies*," presents dystopian revelations in the text through an examination of Golding's view that mankind is morally diseased. Man's debauchery and egocentricity forced Golding to review his utopian vision of the world. Vashisht analyzes the pessimism and cynicism that shine through in Golding's critique of mankind, particularly focusing on his criticism of wars, destruction of ecosystems, and other crises modern humanity causes. She specifically discusses the four central characters along with traditional dystopian elements, such as apocalypse, that appear in Golding's novel.

In "Streets of Spectrality: Kevin Barry's Dystopian *City of Bohane*," Deirdre Flynn examines the uniquely hybrid nature of *City of Bohane*. According to Flynn, Barry breaks down the traditional binary opposition of dystopia/utopia with his mix of Lyotardian eclecticism and uncanny depictions. Unlike the technological takeover that takes place in many YA dystopian novels, technology becomes obsolete in Barry's work, making readers encounter a perspective they have likely never considered before. Flynn praises the eccentric nature of the novel that combines traces of cyberpunk, steampunk, and postmodernism, along with other references, to criticize the regression of nations around the world toward violence and away from the tradition of their culture and identity of their pasts.

Andrew Hammond, in "Interrogating Utopia: On Colin MacInnes' *Absolute Beginners*," focuses on the text's deconstruction of the political idealism common in 1950s Britain. Opposing Paula Derdiger's view that *Absolute Beginners* is "irreverently optimistic" and "undeniably utopian," Hammond maintains that MacInnes' piece of speculative writing challenges the preoccupation with future possibilities by creating fear surrounding current realities. Hammond commends MacInnes' critique of consumerism, individualism, and ethnocentrism, adding that, while *Absolute Beginners* reflects some of the discriminatory attitudes of the period, the novel's problematization of conservative ideologies is a radical move in post-war British literary culture.

Meanwhile, in "'What if I said that he's a god?': Messianism in Cormac McCarthy's *The Road*," Wes Yeary explores the text's various connections to Christianity. In a post–apocalyptic world, he argues, there are overt spiritual references, the portrayal of a Christ-like figure within the main character, and a strict adherence to a moral code. While acknowledging and analyzing these references, Yeary asserts that this is not necessarily a case of messianism, but rather a story of a boy with a strong and inherent sense of morals that prevent him from turning to savagery.

In the final essay of Part One, "'Maps and mazes': Mapping as Metaphor in Postsecular America," Harold K. Bush describes the significance of the map symbolism in Cormac McCarthy's *The Road*. He asserts that, in an increasingly lost society, the map serves as a symbol of hope and calling as we wander through the maze of life. He believes that this symbol has spiritual implications: the map represents a guide from God, leading us on our own journey through life and ultimately revealing our callings to us and showing us the way forward. He criticizes the lack of interest in spirituality in America today, especially in English departments, which graze over significant symbols such as the map described in *The Road*.

Part Two of this volume includes nine essays. In the opening essay, "Unmasking the Deception: The Hermeneutic of Suspicion in Lois Lowry's *The Giver*," C. Clark Triplett and John J. Han approach Lowry's dystopian narrative in light of the philosophy of Paul Ricœur, whose hermeneutic of suspicion provides a tool for critical analysis. Ricœur's critical method is carried forward by the work of Rita Felski at the University of Virginia, who argues for the place of suspicion in literary studies in order to ask the right kinds of questions that might produce new insights about the text. In examining *The Giver*, Triplett and Han consider whether the text is not only an underlying critique of culture, but also presents critique as an essential component of the narrative itself. The co-authors observe that, as the story makes clear, the retrieval of memory does not necessarily guarantee a utopian experience, but it does bring an expanded scope of reality that makes life rich.

In the next essay, "Ending Dystopia: The Feminist Critique of Culture in Suzanne Collins' *Hunger Games* Trilogy," Jane Beal considers the subgenre of feminist dystopia in her analysis of Suzanne Collins' popular speculative fiction trilogy. Beal focuses on the transformation of some traditional elements of utopian satire—such as classical learning, Christian ethics and morality, and the discovery of a new world articulated in a conversation between male characters—in feminist dystopian fiction. Contrasting Thomas More's *Utopia* with *The Hunger Games* trilogy, she notes that the conversation to critique culture is internalized in the female protagonist, Katniss Everdeen, and externalized in interactions between both male and female characters. Ultimately, she identifies that Collins critiques modern warfare and manipulative media while focusing on the human rights of women, especially the right to life, the right to freedom of the will, mind, heart, and body, and the right to self-determination in relationships and roles in the world. Beal emphasizes that these ideas connect back to the responsibility of American citizens—including the readers of the trilogy—who live in the real dystopia of the present day: we must learn from our past using our new knowledge to end wars and prevent a dystopian future.

In her essay "Commodifying the Revolution: Dystopian Young Adult Literature and Cultural Critique," Jillian L. Canode focuses on the underlying criticism of the consumer-driven, capitalist Western society in YA dystopian literature through analysis of M.T. Anderson's *Feed* (2002), Scott Westerfeld's *Uglies* (2005), Elaine Dimopoulos' *Material Girls* (2015), and Alexander London's *Proxy* (2013). Considering that humans today dehumanize themselves through excessive consumption and waste, dystopian YA fiction can provide the initial impetus in moving the young adult population to create change in the world around them for the sake of empathy and hope. Canode notes that YA books are powerful tools for promoting global engagement, social awareness, and critical thought.

In "Dystopia, Competition and Reality Television Tropes in *The Bachman Books*: 'The Long Walk' and 'The Running Man'," Alissa Burger presents dystopia through the scope of a reality television competition. Themes include surveillance, intrusion of privacy, and dehumanization, all of which lead back to Stephen King's criticism of an increasingly demoralized and technological society that enjoys watching death for the entertainment factor. Ray Garraty and Ben Richards both live the most painful moments of their lives under scrutiny for the entertainment of the watching masses as they are abused, exploited, and destroyed. Each enters into the competition as an act of desperation, hoping for some alleviation of poverty and a struggling existence, in the full knowledge that they stand little to no chance of making it out alive.

Meanwhile, in "Stranger Than Fiction: Locating the Digital Dystopia in Contemporary Fiction," Robyn N. Rowley analyzes three texts: Alena Graedon's *The Word Exchange* (2014), Dave Eggers' *The Circle* (2013), and M.T. Anderson's *Feed* (2002). Rowley discusses the need for a new subgenre in dystopian fiction that she dubs "the digital dystopia." According to her, these authors parody the contemporary world while commenting on the potential state of the future world as technology continues to advance at an alarming rate. Eggers, Anderson, and Graedon's novels help tease out latent concerns regarding the implementation of technologies by encouraging readers to think more deeply about real-world implications of extant technologies that inspire the digital dystopia. Additionally, the ability to glean important insights from this literature when it is placed alongside the discourse of critical digital studies supports the notion that genre writing should not be viewed merely as a mode of writing that seeks to entertain, but as literature that can offer valuable critical insights.

In his essay, "Disembodied Heads and Headless Philosophies: C.S. Lewis' Aesthetic Rejoinder to Dystopian Utility in *That Hideous Strength*," Matthew Bardowell discusses C.S. Lewis' use of dystopian themes to raise moral questions in modern society. According to Bardowell, C.S. Lewis criticizes a rapidly industrializing society from the perspective of aesthetic value. Lewis' dystopian vision is one in which no meaningful relationship exists between people and the objects and individuals that surround them; it is a vision in which all interactions are reduced to use. To remedy this condition, Bardowell argues, Lewis appeals to aesthetic judgments, such as the kind presented in Immanuel Kant's Third Critique, which can help those who render them engage the world more justly.

In "The Creation of the Future from Remnants of the Past: Order from Disorder in William Gibson's *All Tomorrow's Parties* and Neal Stephenson's *Snow Crash*," Melanie A. Marotta primarily uses ecocriticism to demonstrate the connection among technology, the environment, and identity formation in the two texts. She examines the authors' use of elements of cyberpunk and postcyberpunk in their efforts to express the significance of using the "lone wolf" protagonist in dystopian fiction. According to Marotta, these texts criticize mainstream society's ignorance of unconventional and alternative communities that have become the norm in dystopian fiction; the "lone wolf" protagonists eventually become part of communities throughout their journeys. Marotta notes that contained within the works of the two heralded science fiction writers is the notion that utopian constructions can originate from dystopian conditions.

In "The Future Is White, the Future Is Undead: Reframing the American Vampire Dystopia in Guillermo del Toro and Chuck Hogan's *The Strain Trilogy*," Simon Bacon demonstrates how *The Strain Trilogy* brings together many of the disparate threads from other contemporary dystopian apocalyptic vampire books and series. According to Bacon, this trilogy is a social commentary on the current state of racial politics and immigration in the United States. He asserts that, in these novels, a true twenty-first century dystopia is actually the American mindset of closing off its borders to those who are culturally different while simultaneously attempting to force its own nationalistic identity on the rest of the world.

In the final essay of Part Two, "Here's Looking at You, Kids: The Urgency of Dystopian Texts in the Secondary Classroom," Michael A. Soares stresses the importance of teaching dystopian literature in all secondary schools. According to the author, dystopian fiction will equip students with strong critical thinking skills that will allow them to create change in the world. He asserts that, because students are captivated by the dystopian genre's rising popularity, it is the teacher's responsibility to encourage its reading in the classroom. In his own classroom, Soares connects dystopian themes directly to current events so that he can empower students to be quick and open-minded thinkers with an ability to apply practical knowledge outside the classroom.

Last Words

Over the past few decades, several scholarly books on dystopian fiction have appeared. Mary Elizabeth Theis' main concern in her *Mothers and Masters in Contemporary Utopian and Dystopian Literature* is motherhood in twentieth-century dystopian literature. While built in a sound theoretical framework, Tom Moylan's *Scraps of the Untainted Sky: Science Fiction, Utopia, Dystopia* mainly discusses Kim Stanley's *Robinson's Other California*, Octavia Butler's *Parables*, and Marge Piercy's *Tale of Hope*.

An important analysis of modern dystopian fiction is M. Keith Booker's *The Dystopian Impulse in Modern Literature: Fiction as Social Criticism*. Published more than two decades ago, Booker's work analyzes several twentieth-century dystopian novels as political critiques of totalitarianism, Stalinism, capitalism, and fascism. The primary texts the author covers are Zamyatin's *We* (completed in 1921), Huxley's *Brave New World*, Orwell's *Nineteen Eighty-Four*, the bourgeois dystopia after World War II, the contemporary Communist dystopia, and Western postmodernist dystopias. In addition, Booker briefly references or summarizes other well-known dystopian texts, including Bradbury's *Fahrenheit 451*, Fyodor Dostoyevsky's *Notes from Underground*, and Lewis' *It Can't Happen Here*.

The editors believe that the present collection is unique in that it examines dystopian themes in both classical and more contemporary texts. It combines the analysis of classics such as Lewis' *That Hideous Strength* and Golding's *Lord of the Flies* with more contemporary texts such as Suzanne Collins' *The Hunger Games* (2008), Lois Lowry's *The Giver* (1993), Guillermo del Toro and Chuck Hogan's *The Strain Trilogy* (2009–2011), Kevin Barry's *City of Bohane* (2011), and Margaret Atwood's *The Heart Goes Last* (2015). Not only does *Worlds Gone Awry* consider newer texts, it also explores more contemporary forms of dystopian fiction, such as digital dystopia and dystopian young adult literature. Throughout the volume, constant attention is paid to the role of dystopian fiction as a form of social critique.

This collection of essays focuses on what is arguably one of the most popular and fascinating genres of our time. It has captured the interest and imaginations of countless readers as they consider what it might be like to live in a devastated world eerily similar to their own. It is easy to be deeply affected by this genre, but it can be more difficult to pinpoint what about it is so affecting. So, why are both lay readers and academics fixated on this genre? In this volume, we uncover new insight into the dystopian genre by considering the critical function of dystopian literature. Finally, the volume brings not only an international flavor, but also a unique angularity to the discourse on contemporary dystopian fiction. The novelty of perspectives reflects the diverse cultural and intellectual backgrounds of the contributors. This diversity opens up a fresh conversation on a number of questions related to dystopian fiction, which is an important area of study for a variety of disciplines, including literary studies, sociology, and political science.

Notes

1. Considering the popularity of dystopian fiction among young adults, it is not surprising that this particular genre has found its way into the middle and high school English curriculum. A challenge to secondary English courses nationwide is finding a genre that will interest and engage even those students who vehemently dislike reading. Teachers understand that incorporating dystopian fiction into their curricula is an effective way to engage all students. On their part, students can easily relate to the realistic plight of the dystopian protagonist at its core, challenging the establishment and questioning why things are the way they are. As Caitrin Blake notes, they can relate to "societal fears that are often represented by government control, totalitarianism, surveillance and violations of privacy"—the fears that indeed pervade all forms of modern literature.

Dystopian literature is taught extensively at the college level as well. Searching "dystopian literature syllabus" on a web search engine will generate many syllabi from across the United States. Some courses address dystopias only, while others discuss dystopias alongside utopias. The description of Bradley Birzer's course "Dystopian Literature and the Moral Imagination" at the University of Colorado offers an idea of how a dystopian literature course is taught in the context of intellectual history and interdisciplinary studies. Specifically, the course examines "the power of imagination, the essence of words and language, the fears of conformity, the deadliness of ideologies (right, left, capitalist, communist, fascist) and fundamentalisms, the dignity and complexity of the human person; and the realities of equality and hierarchy in the social as well as the political spheres of life […]." Meanwhile, Jennifer Atkinson at the University of Chicago offers an English course titled "Utopia & Dystopia," in which students approach eleven texts from Thomas More's *Utopia* (1516) to Hakim Bey's *T.A.Z.: The Temporary Autonomous Zone* (1991) with an emphasis on not only their essential literary elements but also human nature and human institutions as reflected in the texts. In particular, the course explores the ways in which "various texts have negotiated the problems of labor, leisure, the family, property relations, pleasure and desire, class, gender, race, science and technology, nature, primitivism, membership and exclusion, escapism and politics, nostalgia and futurism, anxiety and hope." The two course descriptions above clearly indicate that dystopian fiction can be a useful tool for not only teaching the fundamentals of literary analysis but also discussing some of the social, political, economic, technological, and ecological issues that have challenged humanity since the Renaissance.

2. For a feminist and gender study of the utopian imagination in the Early Modern period, see Nicole Pohl's *Women, Space and Utopia 1600–1800* (New York: Routledge, 2006).

Works Cited

Alter, Alexandra. "Boom Times for the New Dystopians." *New York Times* 30 Mar. 2017. Web. 16 May 2017.

_____. "Uneasy About the Future, Readers Turn to Dystopian Classics." *New York Times* 27 Jan. 2017. Web. 16 May 2017.

Atkinson, Jennifer. "ENGL 229: Utopia & Dystopia, Spring 2006." *University of Chicago*. Web. 16 May 2017.

Birzer, Bradley. "SEWL 1020-172R: 'Dystopian Literature and the Moral Imagination.'" *College of Arts & Sciences, University of Colorado Boulder*. Web. 16 May 2017.
Blake, Caitrin. "Why Are YA Dystopian Novels So Popular with Students?" *Concordia University Nebraska Professional Resources*. 2 Sept. 2014. Web. 16 May 2017.
Booker, M. Keith. *The Dystopian Impulse in Modern Literature: Fiction as Social Criticism*. Westport, CT: Greenwood Press, 1994. Print.
Cavalcanti, Ildney. "Very Inspiring—and Still Highly in Demand." *Demand the Impossible: Science Fiction and the Utopian Imagination*. Ed. Raffaella Baccolini. Bern, Switzerland: Peter Lang, 2014. 270–74.
Firchow, Peter Edgerly. Introduction. *Modern Utopia Fictions from H.G. Wells to Iris Murdoch*. Washington, D.C.: Catholic University of America Press, 2007. 2–17.
Jameson, Fredric. *Archaeologies of the Future: The Desire Called Utopia and Other Science Fictions*. London: Verso, 2007. Print.
Moylan, Tom. "Introduction: The Critical Utopia." *Demand the Impossible: Science Fiction and the Utopian Imagination*. Ed. Raffaella Baccolini. Bern, Switzerland: Peter Lang, 2014. 1–11. Print.
_____. *Scraps of the Untainted Sky: Science Fiction, Utopia, Dystopia*. Boulder, CO: Westview Press, 2000. Print.
Scholes, Justin, and Jon Ostenson. "Understanding the Appeal of Dystopian Young Adult Fiction." *The Alan Review* 40.2 (Winter 2013). Web. 16 May 2017.
Theis, Mary Elizabeth. *Mothers and Masters in Contemporary Utopian and Dystopian Literature*. Bern, Switzerland: Peter Lang, 2009. Print.
Zarka, Yves Charles. "The Meaning of Utopia." *New York Times* 28 Aug. 2011. Web. 19 Dec. 2017.

PART ONE: CLASSICAL DYSTOPIAN FICTION

Feminine Subterfuge in Margaret Atwood's *The Heart Goes Last*

MEGAN E. CANNELLA

Dystopian literature has become an increasingly enduring part of popular culture. Gone are the idyllic Jetson-esque views of the future, where our beds would place us onto a conveyer belt that takes us through a carwash of hygiene and daily preparation. Current views of the future trend toward zombie-riddled, post-apocalyptic dystopias, where we can only hope that the odds will be in our favor. Margaret Atwood is unquestionably a powerful force in the world of dystopian literature. Perhaps best known for her *MaddAddam* series and *The Handmaid's Tale*, Atwood offers audiences a new type of dystopian near-future in her novel, *The Heart Goes Last*.[1] In this novel, Atwood creates a dystopian future full of the crime, exploitation, and despair that has become synonymous with the beginning of almost every post-apocalyptic and/or dystopian narrative. However, the beacon of hope in this otherwise hopeless world is the community of Consilience. Consilience offers a complete escape from the dystopic realities and hells that have consumed everyday life. Upon entering Consilience, the newcomer signs a contract. Once a resident is accepted into this community, there is no leaving, and there is no communication with the outside world. But that is a fair exchange for a better, safer, more stable quality of life, isn't it?

Participants enter Consilience, a new community and ultimately a new social order, to regain a better quality of life that is all but entirely elusive in the outside world. The caveat to life within Consilience is that one's time must be split between voluntary incarceration and a traditionally domestic setting. Every other month, individuals leave their domestic lives and enter Positron Prison. At this point, the other half of the population, which had been voluntarily incarcerated for the previous month, takes over the domestic lives and jobs in Consilience. This model is designed to ensure that everyone has a comfortable standard of living. Everyone is employed. Everyone has a home. No one falls prey to social welfare or crime, because everyone is spending six months out of the year in prison in order to establish the quality of their freedom. Jobs are assigned, and alcohol consumption, music, and television are regulated so as to control the violence within the community. Ultimately, through many layers of control and protocol, residents' personalities are more or less sculpted to fit the Consilience lifestyle.

By juxtaposing the seemingly utopic twin cities of Consilience and Positron with the dire, dystopic realities of the outside world, Atwood creates a narrative which is best understood through Dunja M. Mohr's concept of the "transgressive utopian dystopia" (Mohr 3). In her book, *Worlds Apart: Dualism and Transgression in Contemporary Female Dystopias*, Mohr argues for a recategorization of texts like Atwood's with strong utopian *and* dystopian themes, and she suggests "calling these hybrid texts transgressive utopian dystopias for two reasons. First, they incorporate within the dystopian narrative a utopian undercurrent. Second, these utopian strategies criticize, undermine, and transgress the established binary logic of dystopia" (3). Through the creation of a transgressive utopian dystopia, *The Heart Goes Last* complicates what is popularly understood as the utopian-dystopian binary. However, while Atwood destabilizes the binary typical for speculative fiction, she also uses her female characters—specifically Charmaine and Jocelyn—to deconstruct representations of dystopic femininity, further undermining the patriarchal dystopia in which they live.

Regardless of the fact that Atwood's novel is destabilizing and deconstructing many of the pervasive speculative fiction/dystopic fiction norms, with so many representations of dystopias within popular culture, it can be difficult to navigate how a represented dystopia relates to current conditions. In her article, "'Time to Go': The Post-Apocalyptic and the Post-Traumatic in Margaret Atwood's *Oryx and Crake*," Katherine V. Snyder discusses the overlaps between current society and dystopian literature, asserting, "Dystopian speculative fiction takes what already exists and makes an imaginative leap into the future, following current socio-cultural, political, or scientific developments to their potentially devastating conclusions" (470). This is the case in *The Heart Goes Last*, but the novel goes further in its exploration and representation of femininity. To this end, Mohr argues that this seemingly utopic community is actually a hallmark of feminist utopias, as she explains:

> Thematically, feminist utopias shift the focus to female reality and to everyday life; they restructure the distribution of power within society and family and reject sex-segregated labor. They particularly emphasize gender equality, communitarian goals, decentralized, consensual decision-making, cooperation, education, and ecological

issues, and they discard the classical utopian notion of growth and domination nature. These non-aggressive, and nonhierarchical, and hence classless future societies challenge patriarchy [24].

Superficially, the twin cities of Consilience and Positron seem emblematic of Mohr's assessment of the feminist utopia. Work is evenly and equally distributed. While the population is divided by gender within Positron, that is simply presented as part of the prison lifestyle and certainly not indicative of a larger system of control. In contrast to the devastatingly dystopic nature of the outside world, Consilience appears to be the egalitarian answer to all the problems Charmaine and her husband Stan are faced with in their current lives.

As with most dystopian societies, in order to promise safety, there must be a radical degree of control. Eliminating choice eliminates autonomy, and in a society void of autonomy, safety does not exist. The controlled setting produces a controlled product, and it is assumed that the results are acceptable. Snyder reminds us that "the imaginative effects of dystopian literary speculations depend precisely on their readers' recognition of a potential social realism in the fictional worlds portrayed therein. These cautionary tales of the future work by evoking an uncanny sense of the simultaneous familiarity and strangeness of these brave new worlds" (470). As Consilience strives to reclaim an idealized, simpler time free of crime and discontent, life begins to look more like a 1950s sitcom, with strong, traditional, patriarchal tones pervading every aspect of this new community. The world that Atwood creates in Consilience is essentially adults playing house, by way of government edict, consumed by traditionally defined gender roles. Though overt displays of humanity and individuality are officially verboten, they prove to be indomitable time and again throughout the novel.

While the patriarchal gaze and control of Consilience is undeniable and seemingly inescapable, the quest—overt or not—for autonomy is equally persistent. Given this framework, it seems as if Atwood's novel will follow the claims Raffaella Baccolini makes in her article "Gender and Genre in the Feminist Critical Dystopias of Katharine Burdekin, Margaret Atwood, and Octavia Butler," when she writes, "Contemporary science fiction texts written by women increasingly foreground the interaction of gender and genre [...] contribut[ing] to the creation of a "new" genre, such as the 'critical dystopia' [...]. Critical or open-ended dystopias are texts that maintain a utopian core at their center, a locus of hope that contributes to deconstructing tradition and reconstructing alternatives" (13). Despite the controlling patriarchal and dystopian powers in place, Charmaine and Jocelyn's relationship is foregrounded in the novel, providing the platform for their successful acts of subterfuge. Charmaine and Jocelyn are each other's alternates—meaning that when Charmaine and her husband are in Positron Prison, Jocelyn and her husband are living in the house that Charmaine and Stan inhabit during alternating months. Alternates are forbidden from interacting—yet another protocol put in place to keep Consilience calm, sedate, and conflict free, yet another form of oppression by which Charmaine and Jocelyn will not be restrained (Atwood 47).

Despite the stifling control of Consilience, Atwood positions her female characters as the only true rebels within this world of voluntary submission. Regardless of this positioning, in *Strategies for Identity: The Fiction of Margaret Atwood*, Eleanora Rao asserts, "The self-division that marks Atwood's female character is reduplicated by her marginality, by her condition of being part of and yet excluded from the hegemonic discourse. Woman is located both within Nature and within Culture: a cultural speaking subject, she is at the same time, by means of her reproductive capacities, aligned with Nature" (132). This is clearly demonstrated as Charmaine assumes a second identity as Jasmine when she enters into an affair with her husband Stan's alternate. She carries on this affair in direct violation of Consilience's code of conduct. During her time inside Positron Prison, she administers lethal injections to prisoners who must be eliminated. She has a great amount of power in this position, yet she risks it all to disobey the rigid social structure and carry on an affair as Jasmine. Jasmine is the exact opposite of Charmaine, who is docile, proper, and often described by her husband as dull—basically the perfect Consilience woman. Despite her outward appearance, Charmaine is not fulfilled by this prescribed, "utopic" life. Explaining Atwood's motive with this type of character development, Rao argues,

> Womanliness tends to be portrayed in many of Atwood's novels as a mask, a disguise that stubbornly resists interpretation; woman's adornment becomes merely a simulation to please a masculine scopic economy of pleasure [....] Female subjectivity emerges in the texts as having been appropriated by the "masculine," a process that denies woman any specificity in her relationship with the imaginary and with her own desires. Opaque, inert matter, she is there to offer man his own specularized self-image: like the moon, she only gives reflect light [Rao 132].

Charmaine/Jasmine functions within the Madonna/whore paradigm, offering a divisive depiction of femininity—both submissive to male dominance in overlapping yet unique ways. The innumerable rules and regulations that accompany life in Consilience often automatically situate Charmaine/Jasmine and Jocelyn as subordinates to the reigning masculine power. Nevertheless, both women work to supplant the dominating patriarchal rule of this community to establish autonomy and subvert the community controls that continually evolve into more menacing iterations.

The power Charmaine harnesses as Jasmine is amplified in Charmaine's true alternate, Jocelyn. Jocelyn does not have Jasmine's beauty or allure, but she has the kind of power that both Charmaine and Jasmine desire. While

Charmaine/Jasmine asserts her power through the deviancy of either her sexual withholding or her sexual abandon, Jocelyn uses the system of Consilience to undermine itself. When she discovers her husband's affair with Charmaine/Jasmine, Jocelyn takes matters in her own hands and starts to systematically undermine the status quo of Consilience. To this end, Rao posits, "In focusing on a female identity, Atwood's novels point at those crucial "moments" in women's lives which generate certain roles (such as, for example, the institution of marriage, as well as other structures of social pressure)" (132). Charmaine and Jocelyn are, without a doubt, both at turbulent, unfamiliar points in their lives. It is through their perspectives and the ways in which each woman handles the turmoil thrust upon her that Atwood "look[s] at the process by which stereotyped or imposed representations are interiorized or behavioral strategies are established. Her novels, however, also focus on the female subject's different forms of resistance to these pressures" (Rao 132). Regardless of the efforts and intentions of Consilience to victimize and subordinate Charmaine, Jocelyn, and virtually all of its residents, through these women, the reader sees an untraditional form of resistance played out in an eerily possible setting.

Consilience is a construct of the patriarchy. Egalitarian appearances aside, incarcerated women are designated to "women's work," and while living their domestic lives, women are relegated to traditionally domesticated female roles and behaviors. While this may read as a one-note example of gendered oppression, Mohr asserts, "Feminist discourses—whether informed by postcolonialism, poststructuralism, liberalism, or Marxism—need to embrace this plurality and diversity of female voices and must abandon notions of the monolithic coherent feminism" (58). By offering the reader the distinct, individual voices of Charmaine, Jasmine, and Jocelyn, as the narrative progresses Atwood easily showcases the subterfuge accomplished through femininity within this dystopia—highlighting how only these uniquely equipped female characters have the power to accomplish such societal deconstruction.

Ultimately, the reason that this dystopian society can be regulated and changed through feminine activism—despite a fundamentally patriarchal social structure—is found in Édouard Glissant's understanding of root and relation identities. Glissant asserts,

> Identity as a system of relation, as an aptitude for "giving-on-an-with" [*donner-avec*], is, in contrast, a form of violence that challenges the generalizing universal and necessitates even more stringent demands for specificity. But it is hard to keep in balance. Why is there this paradox in Relation? Why the necessity to approach the specificities of communities as closely as possible? To cut down on the danger of being bogged down, diluted, or "arrested" in undifferentiated conglomerations [Glissant 142].

What Glissant is explaining here is exactly what Charmaine and Jocelyn struggle with both during their time in Consilience and when they attempt to leave. Atwood makes it clear that it is unreasonably easy to become consumed by the concept and comfort of Consilience. The utopian promise of Consilience allows for the identities of its residents to become "diluted" in the "undifferentiated conglomeration" of this community. It is not until later in the novel, after she thinks Stan is dead, that Charmaine begins to question the veracity and authenticity of her life in Consilience. It is Charmaine's doubt that truly enables Jocelyn's subversive orchestration to gain momentum.

In this way, Charmaine and Jocelyn become clear depictions of Glissant's root and relation identities. Glissant explains, "Root identity therefore rooted the thought of self and of territory and set in motion the thought of the other and of voyage. [...] Relation identity exults the thought of errantry and of totality" (144). Atwood situates these two very different women—quiet, docile, subservient Charmain and strong, assertive, dominant Jocelyn—as not only alternates within the Consilience community but also alternatives within the narrative as a whole. As Jocelyn's root identity is ever-present and unfailing, regardless of external considerations, Charmaine's root identity is defined entirely by her relation identity, continually defined by external forces. Given their different strengths, both of these women are necessary to subvert and deconstruct the patriarchal controls and framework of the community in which they live.

Atwood structures the novel so that neither woman has the upper hand; neither can succeed on her own. The episodic nature of the novel, a carryover from this story's serial origins, prevents the reader from being too entrenched in or committed to any one character. The episodic structure that Atwood employs throughout the novel serves to amplify the characters' experiences with constraint and restriction, making the experiences almost tangible for the reader. Despite these structural and narrative restrictions that have been put in place for the reader, it is undeniable that Charmaine's problematic relation identity and Jocelyn's unwavering root identity are the forces that drive this novel, ultimately destabilizing and redefining the dystopic experience.

Lusting for Security

In the novel's opening scene, the dynamics of Charmaine and Stan's marriage are readily apparent; Stan is in control, and neither Stan nor Charmaine trust Charmaine enough to attempt to change this dynamic. "[Stan] has to be in the front in order to drive them away fast in an emergency. He doesn't trust Charmaine's ability to function under those circumstances: he says she'd be too busy screaming to drive" (Atwood 1). Charmaine's need to be protected and the assumption that she has no ability to protect herself is a large part of what drives her and Stan to sign the contract with Consilience. It is not until they are already living their new Consilience lives, spending every other month in prison and generally living unremarkable, sterile lives, that Charmaine starts to develop as a character. When she has the built-in, seemingly impenetrable security of Consilience, she becomes free to explore her true capabilities and capacities.

Within the walls of Consilience, Charmaine begins to explore and expand the dimensions of her relation identity. Glissant explains that the relation identity "is linked not to a creation of the world but to the conscious and contradictory experience of contacts among cultures; [...] does not devise any legitimacy as its guarantee of entitlement, but circulates, newly extended" (Glissant 144). This becomes exceedingly true for Charmaine, as her life becomes increasingly complex and extraordinary in the wake of her affair with Max.[2] Charmaine's willingness to assume the alter ego of Jasmine and carry on an illicit affair with her husband's alternate becomes a sort of gateway drug, making the rest of the novel possible. This one relatively pedestrian indiscretion sets the stage for the rest of the systematic undermining of the dominating, patriarchal, militant control that Consilience represents. The narrator highlights this fact when educating the reader on how Charmaine is able to switch from Stan's mundane, prudish wife into Max's sultry, sexy lover every switch day.[3]

This torrid, illicit affair is only possible on switch day, because it is the only time when Charmaine can skirt the rules and employ a modicum of deception with relative ease. Max and Charmaine/Jasmine meet in abandoned buildings, with locations for the next rendezvous established in person, before they switch for the month, as all other forms of communication can be intercepted. After all, "[t]he whole town is under a bell jar: communications can be exchanged inside it, but no words get in or out except through approved gateways. No whines, no complaints, no tattling, no whistle-blowing" (Atwood 51). Despite the precautions taken by Consilience to ensure that its residents follow its protocols and no sign of weakness or dissention is visible, Charmaine cannot be dissuaded. She is obsessed with Max, and her sexual, passionate relationship with him is the exact opposite of every other aspect of her life, making this affair the first clear act of subversion in the novel.

Stan eventually finds a note that Charmaine leaves for Max under their shared refrigerator, in their shared home, in anticipation of switch day. It reads, "*Darling Max, I can hardly wait till next time. I'm starved for you! I need you so much. XXOO and you know what more—Jasmine*" (Atwood 46; italics in original). The note also has a fuchsia kiss print on it. Stan instantly becomes obsessed with the idea of Jasmine—the woman who he is sure is his own wife's alternate, never imagining Charmaine could be capable of producing such a note. He laments, "Charmaine has never worn a lipstick that colour. And she's never written him a note like that" (46). Embittered by his lustless and virtually sexless marriage, Stan begins to fantasize about the lust-filled marriage that that their alternates must enjoy, thinking, "What a slut, that Jasmine. Flaming hot in an instant, like an induction cooker. He can't stand it" (48). Just as Stan almost obsessively fanaticizes about Jasmine oozing the sexuality that his wife Charmaine is incapable of, Charmaine grapples with the dichotomy that this affair creates within her. She reflects on the note she left for Max, thinking,

> And that lipstick kiss was so tawdry. She keeps the lipstick in her locker, she's only ever used it on that one note. Stan would never put up with her wearing a garish hue like that—Purple Passion is its name, such bad taste. Which is why she bought it: that's how she thinks of her feelings toward Max. Purple. Passionate. Garish. And, yes, bad taste. To a man like that for whom you have feelings like that, you can say all sorts of things, I'm starved for you being the mildest of them. Words she never used before. Vandal words. Sometimes she can't believe what comes out of her mouth; not to mention what goes into it. She does whatever Max wants [54].

Jasmine, with her Purple Passion lipstick and innately profane personality, is the perfect embodiment of how steeped in her relation identity Charmaine is capable of becoming. She is not just using an alias to ensure the anonymity of her affair; Charmaine is constructing an entirely new relation identity, meant to exist in a completely separate reality from the one in which Charmaine exists. Regardless of Charmaine's attraction to Max and Jasmine, she cannot relinquish Stan or her distinctly Charmaine-esque behaviors, as they represent the safety and security that Consilience offers in this dangerous, dystopic world. Charmaine's love for Stan is "trusting, sedate"—just like the life they are living in this new, controlled community.

Naturally, Charmaine's affair is detected by the Consilience administration, prompting Charmaine's relation identity to morph again—this time into that of a loyal soldier. This is important to the feminine subterfuge that propels all parts of Atwood's narrative. Baccolini argues, "The critical dystopia, then, stresses the connection between imagination and utopia as well as between utopia and awareness" (30). Though Charmaine's awareness is obscured by her blind loyalty and obedience, "[e]mpowerment, resistance, utopian imagination, and awareness, when combined, are the tools of the critical dystopia with which women can dismantle the master's house" (30). Were it not for Charmaine's submissive tendencies disguised as loyalty, Jocelyn would not have been able to disassemble the "master's house" as efficiently. Once Charmaine's affair is discovered, Jocelyn, through her position as a Consilience administrator, detains Charmaine in Positron Prison for an extra month—time Jocelyn uses to convince Stan to be a part of an elaborate plan to expose the hidden evils of the twin cities of Consilience and Positron. To do this, Stan must get out of Consilience, a daunting task in and of itself. It is here that both Charmaine and Jocelyn's different versions of "empowerment, resistance, utopian imagination, and awareness" facilitate the destabilization and undermining of the false hope and security that the controlled state of Consilience perpetuates.

Allusions of Death and Resurrection

Within Positron Prison, Charmaine dutifully works administering lethal injections to prisoners that need to be eliminated. Jocelyn counts on Charmaine's sense of duty when she arranges for Stan to be Charmaine's next patient. To smuggle Stan out of Consilience without suspicion, they must produce the illusion that he is dead. Though Jocelyn has arranged for the injection to be a benign tranquilizer, there is no way for Charmaine to know that. When she receives her procedure assignment for the day, Charmaine is told that this will be a test of her loyalty, and "[t]oday, this time, you may encounter a situation that you find challenging. Despite this, the Procedure must be carried out. Your future here depends on it. Are you ready for that?" (Atwood 149). When faced with either resigning from her post in Medications Administration or completing the procedure assigned to her, Charmaine shows her loyalty to Consilience and indicates that she can go through with the procedure, at which point she is given an ominous warning: "You have now chosen. There are only two kinds of people admitted to the Medications Administration wing, those who do and those who are done to. You have elected the role of those who do. If you fail, the consequences to yourself will be severe. You may find yourself playing the other role" (150). While this easily seems like a direct threat to Charmaine's life, to both Charmaine and the audience, it is indicative of the larger roles Charmaine and Jocelyn play within the novel.

Up until this midway point in the novel, it is largely understood that Consilience is a safe place, a much-preferred alternative to the dystopic disarray of the world outside of Consilience's walls, with only negligible drawbacks. Still, little by little, the façade of security that Consilience clings to begins to fall away. The two types of people in the Medications Administration wing are merely an extension of the compliance-defiance binary established throughout the novel. While Charmaine continually travels between these polarities given her liminal engagement in relation identities, Jocelyn's steadfast root identity is what ultimately fuels the acts of feminine subterfuge throughout the novel.

Jocelyn, calm and controlled in both her sense of self and her purpose, guides Charmaine and Stan throughout the rest of the novel. She choreographs the exposure of Consilience through the news media and takes active steps to make sure that Charmaine and Stan stay married and happy in their lives after Consilience. Ed, the head of Consilience, is sexually obsessed with Charmaine, and Jocelyn uses this knowledge to facilitate Stan and Charmaine's escape from Consilience. However, to free Charmaine completely from Ed's sexual obsession, Jocelyn explains that Charmaine needs to go through a neurological procedure, which Ed thinks will ensure Charmaine's eternal devotion and attraction to him. Regardless of her orders from Ed, Jocelyn arranges for the subject of Charmaine's attraction and admiration to be Stan.

Jocelyn's actions seem to simultaneously undermine the patriarchal authority of Ed and Consilience while also ensuring a happy ending for Charmaine and Stan. When *The Heart Goes Last* opens, Charmaine and Stan's marriage is handicapped by the dystopic challenges they endure both before and during their lives in Consilience. Once Jocelyn restores hope by destroying the claustrophobic patriarchal system of control, Charmaine and Stan believe that they are now fated to a happy marriage. Both believe Charmaine has been neurologically altered to ensure their happiness. In the wake of her procedure, once she has settled into her new life with Stan, "Charmaine is so happy. The dark part of herself that was with her for so long seems to be completely gone. It's as if someone has taken an eraser and erased the pain of those memories" (Atwood 292). She attributes this restoration to the procedure: "It must have been something the doctors did when they were fixing the inside of her head so she would love Stan, only Stan, and nobody else. It was the other Charmaine, the Charmaine of darkness, who'd wandered away from him, and that Charmaine is gone forever. It's so amazing what can be done with lasers!" (Atwood 292).

Just as Jocelyn works tirelessly to deconstruct the false of utopia of Consilience, in the last moments of the novel, she dissolves the false utopia that has become Charmaine's marriage. Jocelyn visits Charmaine to deliver a wedding gift to her and Stan, which Jocelyn explains is not an object but rather "a piece of information, about [Charmaine]" (305). Jocelyn prefaces the gift, warning, "You can choose [...] to hear it or not. If you hear it, you'll be more free but less secure. If you don't hear it, you'll be more secure, but less free" (305). Opting to hear the information, Jocelyn reveals that Charmaine never had the operation that would ensure she loved only Stan for the rest of her life. Jocelyn accounts for the couple's renewed love, explaining, "The human mind is infinitely suggestible" (305). While it would be understandable for Charmaine to be upset that she was lied to, her fickle relation identity rears its head once again, and she is more upset about the fact that she now has the choice of whether or not to stay with Stan.

Her closing exchange with Jocelyn about whether it is better to have the choice to love Stan or to be controlled by compulsion becomes a sustaining micro version of the macro challenges these women endure throughout the novel. Once again, Charmaine clings desperately to this newest iteration of her relation identity, while Jocelyn, stalwart as ever, stays unflinchingly true to her root identity as the two women confront the dystopic reality of Charmaine's neurological state and marriage. In this way, the novel approaches the arc of Atwood's writing style, as Rao asserts, "A focus on the male desire for mastery and possession is emphasized in her early fiction and collections of poetry. In later works, however, this is accompanied by the search for a new dialectics between the sexes. Despite the presence of conflictual heterosexual relations, one notes a parallel tendency to re-think difference so that it appears in some cases, devoid of antagonism and opposition" (Rao 133). As *The Heart Goes Last* seems to end with the erasure of all forms of antagonism and opposition, both in general and in terms of gender, Jocelyn destroys that allusion.

Atwood positions Jocelyn to continually destabilize the system, even at the very end of the novel. Because of this, the reader has no way of knowing if Charmaine really had the operation to turn her into Stan's love slave. Charmaine accepts Jocelyn's word that the operation had never taken place just as readily as she accepted that she had the surgery and was automatically devoted to Stan as a result. By fundamentally unsettling Charmaine's marriage at the end of the novel, Atwood reminds both Charmaine and the reader that a utopian existence is not realistic, and as Jocelyn preaches, "Nothing is ever settled. Every day is different. Isn't it better to do something because you've decided to? Rather than because you have to?" (306). This question at the end of the novel synthesizes the larger goals of *The Heart Goes Last*.

By once again presenting Charmaine with the task of deciding to take the route of the unknown as opposed to having her life and future decisions determined for her, Atwood highlights the fact that as we stare into the potential dystopic abyss, we are in charge of our own destinies, whether we choose to be blindly controlled or not. She shows how, through many dystopic iterations, the root identities of each woman remains her greatest asset, even when it is also a liability—Jocelyn's remains unwavering, ultimately dictating her relation identity, while Charmaine's is hopelessly dependent upon her relation identity.

Going Last...

At the end of *The Heart Goes Last*, the authenticity of Charmaine and Jocelyn's current situation and future remains unclear. Regardless of the obscurity of each woman's future or happiness, the novel ends on a fairly hopeful note. Both women are free and appear content with their new lives outside of Consilience. Whether optimism is warranted here remains unclear, because as Roxanne J. Fand argues in *The Dialogic Self*, "The hope in Atwood's tales is not explicit, but implied mostly by way of cautionary emphasis. 'Progress' for her protagonists is usually minimal or nonexistent, and ambiguous in any case. [...] Atwood's hope lies in 'a new way of seeing' for the victim, the way of being a 'creative non-victim' by imagining positions between the voices of power and victimization" (157). While we cannot be sure whether or not Charmaine's brain has been altered, she has found a way to live a non-victimized life, providing a sense of progress and closure in a still unresolved reality.

By destabilizing not only the genre of dystopic fiction but also the gender roles within that genre, Atwood creates a new way of understanding speculative fiction, the world around us, and the world that we are creating for our future. *The Heart Goes Last* not only becomes a platform for defining our concepts of a future in terms of power, community, and resources, it also offers a critique of our potential for an autonomous future, giving serious attention to the ways in which the concepts of gender limit or foster these autonomous goals. As David W. Sisk explains in his study of language in modern dystopias, "Atwood is among the first writers—if not the first—to publish a critically successful and popular dystopia in which women are oppressed more than men and the narrative is centered within a woman's perceptions" (108). The critical takeaway from *The Heart Goes Last* is not the oppression, marginalization, or objectification of women; the strength in this novel is the representation of women and the power each woman in this novel harnesses. Jocelyn, Charmaine, and Charmaine's alter ego Jasmine, along with the other women in this novel, all have specific goals and perspectives. Some are more ambitious and entrepreneurial than others. Nevertheless, Atwood's narrative requires collaboration between these women to destabilize the patriarchal oppression that the Consilience-Positron community represents. It is this diverse community of feminine power, represented primarily by Jocelyn and Charmaine, that allows for a comprehensive and totalizing deconstruction not only of the patriarchal community structure but also of the patriarchal figures in the novel.

NOTES

1. Originally, *The Heart Goes Last* started as the *Positron* series through *Byliner* over the course of 2012–2013 (Atwood 308).

2. Max's real name is Phil. Phil is Jocelyn's sex addict husband and Stan's alternate. For the purposes of this essay, he will only be discussed in relation to his affair with Charmaine/Jasmine and, therefore, will only be referred to here as Max.

3. Switch day is the day when the prisoners at Positron Prison replace those who are living civilian lives in Consilience and vice versa.

Works Cited

Atwood, Margaret. *The Heart Goes Last*. New York: Doubleday, 2015. Print.
Baccolini, Raffaella. "Gender and Genre in the Feminist Critical Dystopias of Katharine Burdekin, Margaret Atwood, and Octavia Butler." *Future Females* (2000): 13–34. Web. 22 April 2017.
Fand, Roxanne J. *The Dialogic Self: Reconstructing Subjectivity in Woolf, Lessing, and Atwood*. Cranbury, NJ: Associated University Presses, 1999. Print.
Glissant, Édouard. *Poetics of Relation*. Trans. Betsy Wang. Ann Arbor: University of Michigan Press, 1997. Print.
Mohr, Dunja M. *Worlds Apart?: Dualism and Transgression in Contemporary Female Dystopias*. Jefferson, NC: McFarland, 2005. Print.
Rao, Eleonora. *Strategies for Identity: The Fiction of Margaret Atwood*. Bern, Switzerland: Peter Lang, 1993. Print.
Sisk, David W. *Transformations of Language in Modern Dystopias*. Westport, CT: Greenwood Press, 1997. Print.
Snyder, Katherine V. "'Time to Go': The Post-Apocalyptic and the Post-Traumatic in Margaret Atwood's *Oryx and Crake*." *Studies in the Novel* 43.4 (2011): 470–89. Web. 22 April 2017.

"Forget sad things"
Kurt Vonnegut's Dystopian Short Fiction as Social Critique

Ashley G. Anthony

Introduction

Anyone who has read Kurt Vonnegut or listened to one of his interviews recognizes the difficulty of synthesizing the writer's opinions and fiction. Often, this writer's comments are contradictory and do not seem to quite fit his written works, which sometimes carry over into the absurd; however, that Vonnegut includes a part of himself in his literature is almost indisputable. Jerome Klinkowitz, who was one of the first to take Vonnegut's literature seriously, highlights the start of this self-inclusion: "Beginning in the late 1960s and corresponding with his first serious recognition, Vonnegut had introduced more discursive elements in his work, references to a history he had shared and which the reader could reliably recognize" (3). While some writers attempt to remove themselves completely from their writing, to read Vonnegut's works is to get to know Vonnegut himself. While a reading of Vonnegut's fiction might produce an interesting analysis, that analysis would undoubtedly be incomplete without considering his personal life. When reading Vonnegut's longer and more popular works, such as *Cat's Cradle* (1963) and *Slaughterhouse-Five* (1969), autobiographical elements are particularly glaring. War, disjointed family life, and PTSD are just a few of the themes that Vonnegut pulls directly from his own experience, and he writes about them almost exactly as he seemed to have experienced them. With some of his shorter fiction, there are fewer autobiographical parallels, but Vonnegut the writer is still very much a part of his writing in his insertion of opinion and critique. This is particularly true with his shorter dystopian fiction.

Often, because of Vonnegut's unique writing style and inclusion of somewhat bizarre elements, his orthodox views become muddled and hard to decipher. For example, in his most popular work *Slaughterhouse-Five*, he shares anti-war sentiments with which many readers would probably agree. Throughout his text, Vonnegut alludes to the meaninglessness of the bombing in Dresden—and thus the meaninglessness of the loss of life—which Vonnegut actually experienced after he was drafted and which he tried to communicate within his text. In an interview, Vonnegut explained, "The destruction of Dresden was my first experience with really fantastic waste. To burn down a habitable city and a beautiful one at that [...] I was simply impressed by the wastefulness, the terrible wastefulness, the meaninglessness of war" (NPR.org). While this seems like a reasonable assertion, he links this belief with Tralfamadorians, sex with a pornographic actress, and time travel, making it difficult for readers to pinpoint meaning and purpose in his novel.

Vonnegut's dystopian fiction differs from the modern, young adult dystopias with which many readers are acquainted. In the more recent and popular dystopias, the protagonist successfully rebels against a controlling society, proving that there is something special about the protagonist that others might not have. This is evident in series such as *The Maze Runner*, *Divergent*, and *The Hunger Games*. The hidden intent behind the strong, usually likeable protagonist seems to be the desire to be unique and to be an agent of radical change. There is certainly some amount of ambiguous critique of controlling rulers in these dystopias, as it points to what government could possibly become if it became too powerful and desired to make everyone absolutely equal. Unlike this futuristic critique, Vonnegut uses his dystopian fiction to criticize specific aspects of culture with which he is unhappy. A closer look at two of his dystopian short stories, "Welcome to the Monkey House" and "Harrison Bergeron," reveals an evident distrust not of a future, fictitious government, but of the current government and other issues that were occurring during Vonnegut's lifetime.

"Welcome to the Monkey House"

In "Welcome to the Monkey House," Vonnegut presents and scrutinizes a sexually oppressive, carefully controlled society. The society uses misleading language, authority, and the removal of sexual pleasure to prevent the world's population from growing too quickly. The dystopian elements are evident, even though Vonnegut's message to readers might be a little harder to identify because of the unorthodox presentation he employs: Billy the Poet, with the help of his "band of merrymen," kidnap and rape women so that they will begin to desire sexual pleasure.

The controlling authorities in "Welcome to the Monkey House" stand in contrast to other dystopian governments, which are often either competent or mysteriously absent. For example, in *The Hunger Games* and *Divergent* series, the governments are a constant force of control, and strong, antagonistic leaders (President Snow and Jeanine Matthews) hold them together. In Margaret Atwood's *The Handmaid's Tale* (1985), the government seems to be a mysteriously absent yet always represented entity; very rarely do you see a government leader enacting punishment or enforcing orders, yet they are always in control. Conversely, in Vonnegut's short story, the government is always referred to, but it is represented by incompetent muscle in the form of Sheriff Pete Crocker. The sheriff is not an unlikeable character, but he plays the court jester, which is most apparent in his interaction with the hostesses. While he tries to appear in control of a hectic situation and protect the hostesses from knowledge about Billy the Poet, the girls are offended and quickly call him out. One of the hostesses, Nancy, is especially antagonistic and threatens to beat him up:

> "If you'd like to find out how helpless we are, just come toward me, pretending you're Billy the Poet."
> The sheriff shook his head, gave her a glassy smile. "I'd rather not."
> "That's the smartest thing you've said today," said Nancy, turning her back on him while Mary laughed" [32].

The sheriff proves to be virtually unnecessary, since the hostesses show they are willing to uphold the sanctions of the World Government with or without his authority. The muscle of the World Government is not needed since the majority is willing to abide by government ruling on its own.

The society is controlled primarily by the "World Government," which uses misleading and religious language to ensure the citizens follow its rules. While Vonnegut seems to use the language as a message to readers, suggesting that the message perpetuated by the government is ridiculous, citizens regurgitate the government's message thoughtlessly, further displaying the inappropriately controlling nature of the language. The World Government's main concern is the supposed overpopulation of the earth, and it uses different propaganda to spread the message. For example, when people are encouraged to visit suicide parlors to help lower the population, these suicides are described as putting "people to sleep" (31) and allowing them to "[die] peacefully" (34). The birth control taken is described as "compulsory"—which sounds better than "forced"—and also "ethical" (31). In contrast, anything not supported by the government is branded negatively. When a suicide parlor worker describes a rebel, she calls him a "nothinghead," which is someone who disobeys the government's order to take birth control (30). Any birth control besides the one supported by the government is designated "unnatural and immoral" (31). In both of these examples, negative opinions are based solely on the government's regulations as opposed to one's own reasoning. Characters perpetuate the government's language and thus the government's regulations.

Similar to what we will see in "Harrison Bergeron," "Welcome to the Monkey House" features a satiric outlook on egalitarianism and television: "Most people looked twenty-two, thanks to anti-aging shots they took twice a year" (35). Concerning the media and citizens' job situations, Vonnegut snidely writes,

> Most people didn't [have jobs]. The average citizen moped around home and watched television, which was the Government. Every fifteen minutes his television would urge him to vote intelligently or consume intelligently, or worship in the church of his choice, or love his fellowmen, or obey the laws—or pay a call to the nearest Ethical Suicide Parlor and find out how friendly and understanding a Hostess could be [34–35].

The correlation of joblessness, television, and governmental control is made here. Citizens are not just jobless; they are lazy, evidenced in their watching of television instead of participating in something productive. The government controls television programming, and television programming controls the actions of the citizens. While Vonnegut's wording suggests that the programming encourages individual, critical thought and freedom of choice, the citizens are lawfully able to act only within the confines of the government's control. Since the average citizen regurgitates governmental mandates and reasoning, it is logical that citizens will vote, consume, worship, love, obey, and die only as they government allows.

Perhaps this is most clearly seen in the measures the World Government takes to regulate the sexuality of its citizens. The ethical birth control mandated by the government is unique in that it prevents pregnancy by suppressing sexual pleasure altogether. The effects and reasoning are described in the text:

> Most men said their bottom halves felt like cold iron or balsa-wood. Most women said their bottom halves felt like wet cotton or stale ginger ale. The pills were so effective that you could blindfold a man who had taken one, tell him to recite the Gettysburg Address, kick him in the ball while he was doing it, and he wouldn't miss a syllable.
> The pills were ethical because they didn't interfere with a person's ability to reproduce, which would have been unnatural and immoral. All the pills did was take every bit of pleasure out of sex.
> Thus did science and morals go hand in hand [31].

The foolishness of the birth control is further revealed when a disguised Billy the Poet recites the history of its creation. After acknowledging that the pills were not originally designed to be taken by humans, Billy says, "[J. Edgar Nation] and his eleven kids went to church one Easter. And the day was so nice and the Easter service had been so beautiful and pure that they decided to take a walk through the zoo [...]. [They] saw a monkey playing with his private parts! [...] J. Edgar Nation went straight home and he started developing a pill that would make monkeys in the springtime fit things for a Christian family to see" (36). In an effort to show the absurdity of these government regulations, Vonnegut takes what he believes is simplicity in an animal's nature, in this case a monkey's sex drive, and sets it before the religiously pious in his ivory tower. The animal is not projected as perverse for exuding his sexuality, but the Christian is for attempting to suppress it.

While many might understand Vonnegut's reprehension of such an absurd society, the high level on which he places sexual freedom is difficult to support. Even though Vonnegut describes Nancy's introduction to sexual pleasure as a "deflowering," it becomes evident that Billy the Poet is not a gentle hero who will coddle her into her newfound sexuality. Nancy is kidnapped at gunpoint by Billy the Poet, and she is shoved forward several times during their walk to his hiding place and threatened that Billy would "blow her fucking head off" if she tried to get away (40). When they finally arrive, Nancy realizes that Billy has committed followers, and when she asks how they could violate their oaths, "she was promptly hurt so badly that she doubled up and burst into tears" (42). After the pills wear off, she is bathed, dressed in a white nightgown, and told to walk down five steps into Billy's chamber. While she takes these steps on her own, the door is promptly closed and locked behind her, making it clear that even though she took the steps, it was not because she was in control of her situation. In the midst of this struggle between Nancy's desire to continue taking the birth control pills and Billy the Poet's desire to free her from them, we see the climax of the short story, when Billy gets ready to deflower Nancy. Despite the violence thus far, the room itself is set up as if for a date for two consenting parties. There are champagne and candles on the table, and Billy attempts to compliment her, welcoming her and then kindly admiring her beauty. The room itself stands in contrast to the treatment Nancy has received so far from Billy, but the violence continues when Nancy refuses sex:

> "So I think your idea of happiness is going to turn out to be eight people holding me down on that table, while you bravely hold a cocked pistol to my head—and do what you want. That's the way it's going to have to be, so call your friends and get it over with!"
> Which he did [47].

It quickly becomes apparent that even though Billy's intention is to free Nancy from her birth control pills and the authority of the World Government, the only way he achieves this freedom is to subject her to his own authority.

It is evident that, according to Vonnegut, a woman's identity can be found in her sexuality. Perhaps this is why rape by Billy the Poet is acceptable and even championed: the end justifies the means. This viewpoint is most available in Billy and Nancy's conversations. At one point, Billy claims that "a woman's not a woman till the pills wear off," to which Nancy replies, "You certainly manage to make a woman feel like an object rather than a person" (36). Billy brushes off this comment by saying, "Thank the pills for that" (36). Nancy is not objectified because Billy has just forcibly kidnapped and will soon rape her; Nancy is objectified because her sexual pleasure and interest have been removed when she takes her pills. Additionally, Nancy's womanhood is in question as long as she is unable to feel sexual pleasure. This is clearly seen before the rape when she is injected with a truth serum by one of Billy's henchmen. When Nancy is asked how it feels to be a virgin at sixty-three, she simply replies, "Pointless" (44). Despite her outward show of conformity to the government's mandate and allegiance to her job in the suicide parlor, when she has to answer honestly, she, of course, confirms what Billy the Poet has suggested all along. Without sex, her sixty-three years of life have been a waste of time. With this idea in mind, Billy the Poet becomes a hero to all of his rape victims: not only is he returning each woman's womanhood, but he is also providing them with a regenerated identity and purpose. The women enter Billy's charge as the World Government's unknowing, sexless slaves, but they leave transformed. That Billy's purpose is to rescue these women and not satisfy his own sexual pleasure is evident in a conversation before Nancy and he have intercourse:

> "And what about *my* happiness?" [Nancy asked.]
> The question seemed to puzzle him. "Nancy, that's what this is all about" [46].

Nancy simply thinks that Billy is subjecting her to his own fantasies, but really, he is providing her with the means to happiness at the expense of his own. Afterward, Billy is described as "terribly depressed" and apologetically expresses, "Believe me, if there'd be any other way—" (47). Vonnegut is showing Billy's deep remorse for his own actions because to Vonnegut, the real misfortune is society's mutilation of Nancy's sexuality and not Billy's rape. To Billy, it is not that he has just raped Nancy because of his own lusty happiness, but he has raped Nancy because it is necessary for her happiness.

Published during the same year as *Humanae vitae* (*Of Human Life*), which was issued by Pope Paul VI and included the prohibition of all forms of artificial birth control, "Welcome to the Monkey House" seems to be Vonnegut's perceived future of the world if this edict was fulfilled. Karol Wojtyla, who interpreted and analyzed the encyclical, explains the crux of the prohibition of birth control in her essay: "The respect due to the body, particularly in its procreative functions—functions rooted in the whole specific somatic quality of sex—is respect for the human being, that is, for the dignity of the man and the woman" (745). In other words, man is not identified just by one or two aspects of his person as if they exist independently; rather, man should be identified in light of the "supreme unity of man" (746). Vonnegut's perceived importance of a woman's sexuality being what defines her as a woman conflicts with the encyclical's view that sexuality is just a component of man that needs to be considered in light of the entirety of man. To Vonnegut, actual birth control that women continue to use is necessary in order for a woman to achieve happiness through sexual pleasure. At the end of the short story, in an almost holy moment of intense honesty and realization, Billy the Poet suggests that he has loved Nancy in his deflowering of her and then he dramatically offers her a bottle of artificial birth control pills. The label on the bottle reads, "Welcome to the Monkey House." With this action, Billy has fulfilled his entire duty as hero to Nancy, and it is assumed that Nancy can indulge in all of the sexual pleasure she desires without the distress of pregnancy.

The bottle's label acts as the punch line of the short story. Before Billy the Poet kidnaps Nancy, when he recites the history of J. Edgar Nation and his visit to the monkey exhibit at the zoo, he showed just how ridiculous Nation was to believe that a monkey "playing with his private parts" in his own natural habitat was inappropriate. The label on the bottle suggests that the monkey's sexual satisfaction was just a part of its nature, just as avoiding pregnancy so one can indulge in sexual pleasure is just as natural a desire. According to Vonnegut, by taking a woman's right to sex without consequences (i.e. sex with a birth control pill), the government is essentially taking away a woman's identity.

"Harrison Bergeron"

One of Vonnegut's more popular short stories, "Harrison Bergeron" is fittingly named after the heroic protagonist, Harrison Bergeron. The opening lines of the short story immediately orient the reader to the society and Vonnegut's distaste for it:

> The year was 2081, and everybody was finally equal. They weren't only equal before God and the law. They were equal every which way. Nobody was smarter than anybody else. Nobody was better looking than anybody else. Nobody was stronger or quicker than anybody else. All this equality was due to the 211th, 212th, and 213th Amendments to the Constitution, and to the unceasing vigilance of agents of the United States Handicapper General [7].

Here, readers learn that equality was achieved through a laughable number of amendments to the Constitution and the suggested brutal control of the agents of the U.S. Handicapper General. While it may seem reasonable that equality is sought for everyone, the equality presented is that everyone would be "perfectly average," reduced to the simplest of this society's citizens. In an effort to overthrow the government, Harrison Bergeron stages a coup on television, but before it has time to affect anyone, he is shot dead, and the revolution is over.

It is the understanding of this equality and how it is achieved that helps show Vonnegut's negative view toward it. Although still alive, the people within this society have a very poor quality of life. All the things that seem to make life good for them have been taken away or controlled. This is perhaps best seen in the ballerinas and musicians, who have been chosen to perform publically but wear handicaps so they remain what the government considers average. The ballerinas wear birdshot and sash-weights so "no one ... would feel like something the cat drug in" (8) in comparison. Similarly, the musicians also wear handicaps that do not allow them to play as well as they are able. While the musicians and ballerinas probably pursued their craft based on talent or interest, they are unable to truly enjoy what they do. While having talent reduced to average might not seem unbearable, the government's idea of average is problematic. George Bergeron, who has an above-average intelligence, is forced to wear a sound transmitter that forcefully scatters his thoughts so he cannot think very long or hard on anything; by wearing this, he has the same attention span of his wife, who is described as "perfectly average," which means that she can "only think about things in short bursts" (7). Throughout the short story, no one experiences joy or other human experiences that make life enjoyable, and what they love is taken away from them. If Hazel and George Bergeron are an indication of the rest of society, their lives center around the television and programming that they cannot even remember.

Vonnegut employs media, and particularly television, as the lens through which readers experience the climax of Harrison Bergeron's revolution. The short story is actually set in the house of Harrison's parents, Hazel and George, who have recently had their son taken away from them for undisclosed reasons. While tragic, the narrator muses, they cannot remember that he was taken away because of George's handicap and Hazel's average intelligence. As Harrison's parents are watching the television, a news report claims that Harrison is on the loose, and seconds later, Harrison appears on the screen. He begins ordering the musicians and dancers to take off their handicaps so that they can play according to their talent, chooses a dancer to become his partner, and starts dancing. To say that the dancing was extraordinary would be an understatement:

> Not only were the laws of the land abandoned, but the law of gravity and the laws of motion as well.
> They reeled, whirled, swiveled, flounced, capered, gamboled, and spun.

> They leaped like deer on the moon.
> The studio ceiling was thirty feet high, but each leap brought the dancers nearer to it.
> It became their obvious intention to kiss the ceiling. They kissed it.
> And then, neutraling gravity with love and pure will, they remained suspended in air inches below the ceiling, and they kissed each other for a long, long time [13].

While the year 2081 seems far into the future, until this point, the society itself seems identical to what would be experienced today. There are no advanced technologies or creative worlds, but this scene is the first that ventures into the unbelievable or fantastical. In this moment, the two dancers become otherworldly; it becomes an opportunity for even the completely average to realize that something out of the ordinary is happening, something that should change the way they think, believe, and live. The government has forced them to view all people and events as "completely average," but in this scene, citizens experience joy and beauty.

Moments later, still separated by the television, Harrison and his partner are shot dead by the Handicapper General, who orders the musicians and dancers to put on their handicaps or they will be next. Orders are obeyed, and then the television goes blank. Once again, readers are returned to the Bergerons' living room and have the opportunity to see what the death of these martyrs has accomplished. Surely, if their deaths have affected anyone, it will begin with Harrison's parents:

> Hazel turned to comment about the blackout to George. But George had gone out into the kitchen for a can of beer.
> George came back in with the beer, paused while a handicap signal shook him up.
> "Yup," she said.
> "What about?" he said.
> "I forget," she said. "Something real sad on television" [14–15].

They had just witnessed the death of their son, but there is no remembrance, even for a few minutes. Harrison's revolution and death are immediately forgotten, so readers are left to assume that life in this society will continue with no hope of even the smallest ripple effect. In an ironically morbid attempt to console his wife, George responds to his wife's sadness with the simple exhortation to "Forget sad things," to which she replies, "I always do" (15). Of course, George cannot remember that his son has just been brutally murdered on television, so he assumes that his wife had just witnessed programming undeserving of her attention. The perversity that Harrison's death has already been forgotten by his parents and that they are able to converse as if they were watching an entertaining television program is jarring.

In a 2003 interview, Vonnegut described some of his thoughts on the government's sanction of war and the people subjected to the government: "The government satirizes itself. All we can wish is that there will be a large number of Americans who will realize how dumb [war] is, and how greedy and how vicious" (The Progressive). Vonnegut clearly shows his distaste for the government and its wartime decisions, with which most readers are probably already familiar, but he continues his thoughts about government with the following comments on media: "Such an audience is dwindling all the time because of TV. One good thing about TV is, if you die violently, God forbid, on camera, you will not have died in vain because you will be great entertainment" (The Progressive). Even though Vonnegut is talking about American war-related deaths, it obviously parallels the death of Harrison. His death has no lasting effect on its viewers; in fact, his death is not even remembered, so it does not even make "great entertainment." If readers are hopeful that the death of Harrison will begin a revolution, they hope in vain. Just as Vonnegut believes that his fellow Americans will not be moved to act by the deaths of real men and women on television, he creates a similar, exaggerated society where not even parents are moved to remember the brutal death of their son, Harrison. Vonnegut has simply taken his perception of his current society and applied it to his fictitious one. For Hazel and George, there is no progress or movement as characters; they remain stagnant, entirely equal to each other and everyone else in their society, partially because of the numbing effects of television but also because of the brutal control of the government.

Despite the seeming absurdity of the government's control throughout the short story, Vonnegut seemed to provide, in an interview, confusing information concerning his intent for the short story's meaning: "I can't be sure, but there is a possibility that my story 'Harrison Bergeron' is about the envy and self-pity I felt at an overachievers' high school in Indianapolis quite a while ago now" (Hattenhauer 388). It seems that, based on this remark, Vonnegut might actually support the brutal pursuit of personal egalitarianism displayed in his short story. In fact, several critics applied this statement to find meaning in Vonnegut's short story, one critic concluding that perhaps "most important is the underlying point that a society does not necessarily suffer from its mediocrity" (Stuckey 89). If this is the case, the Handicapper General is the keeper of peace while Harrison really is an insurgent, intent on disrupting perfected equality amongst people. The handicaps are actually necessary, despite seeming nonsensical and absurd. In the controlled society, women with pretty faces wear hideous masks, and because of Harrison's strength, he is forced to wear 300 pounds of scrap metal, and his appearance is described as "Halloween and hardware" (11). The illogical nature of the handicaps alone make this reading unlikely, but the last part of Vonnegut's quotation, which is sometimes overlooked or forgotten, seems to continue the idea of this as a misreading: "Some people never tame those emotions. John Wilkes Booth and Lee Harvey Oswald and Mark David Chapman come to mind. 'Handicapper Generals,' if you like" (Hattenhauer 388). As a self-proclaimed Humanist, Vonnegut would probably not consider the murders committed by these men heroic.

Conclusion

Vonnegut experienced much during his lifetime, and it is apparent that he did not enjoy all that he saw. Part of what he witnessed was the effect that humanity had on each other and the world. Some of these elements are found in "Welcome to the Monkey House" and "Harrison Bergeron," as Vonnegut exaggerated the negative elements of humanity: religious control, governmental control, war, and media were just an addition to the detriments of society Vonnegut observed.

While Vonnegut's longer works include bits and pieces of his past and experiences, in these two shorter works, he puts forward social critique in an attempt to show readers the implications of current events. In "Welcome to the Monkey House", Vonnegut shows that while the *Humanae vitae* might seem harmless now, if religious authorities are given the ability to make decisions regarding sexuality for all of humanity, then it will end disastrously. In "Harrison Bergeron," he attempts to show readers the effects of a society addicted to television and willing to yield control to government. In reference to Vonnegut's narrators, Jerome Klinkowitz writes, "Far from being a simple storyteller, Vonnegut's spokesperson is a witness to something that defies reductive explanation. Instead, he must expand upon the subject, taking it beyond the confines of rational intelligence and into realms where empathy and emotion can fill in the blanks" (30). As Vonnegut observed circumstances with which he disagreed, such as the institution of *Humanae vitae* or a government that instituted too much control, he used his writing as a place to show others what might happen if they remained silent or unresponsive. Since he took his observations to the extreme, as seen in the dystopian short stories from this essay, many critics categorized him as a science fiction writer; however, Vonnegut was not interested in technological advancements. Instead, he created a place within his fiction where readers could begin to recognize real-world problems they had not been motivated to confront previously.

WORKS CITED

Hattenhauer, Darryl. "The Politics of Kurt Vonnegut's 'Harrison Bergeron.'" *Studies in Short Fiction* 35.4 (1998): 387. *Academic Search Complete.* Web. 21 Feb. 2016.
Klinkowitz, Jerome. *Vonnegut in Fact: The Public Spokesmanship of Personal Fiction.* Web. 5 July 2016.
Stuckey, Lexi. "Teaching Conformity in Kurt Vonnegut's 'Harrison Bergeron.'" *Eureka Studies*

in *Teaching Short Fiction* 7.1 (2006): 85–90. *Education Research Complete*. Web. 21 Feb. 2016.
Vonnegut, Kurt. "Harrison Bergeron." *Welcome to the Monkey House: A Collection of Short Works by Kurt Vonnegut*. New York: Delta Trade, 2011. 7–14. Print.
____. Interview with David Barsamian. *The Progressive* 12 June 2003. Web. 15 May 2016. <http://www.progressive.org/mag_intv0603>
____. Interview with Tom Vitale. *NPR*. 31 May 2011. Web. 18 May 2016. <http://www.npr.org/2011/05/31/136823289/kurt-vonnegut-still-speaking-to-the-war-weary>
____. "Welcome to the Monkey House." *Welcome to the Monkey House: A Collection of Short Works by Kurt Vonnegut*. New York: Delta Trade, 2011. 30–50.
Wojtyla, Karol. "The Anthropological Vision of Humanae Vitae." *Nova Et Vetera (English Edition)* 7.3 (2009): 731–50. *Academic Search Complete*. Web. 6 July 2016.

"A secure but partly demented society"

Reconsidering Human Depravity in William Golding's Lord of the Flies

Natasha W. Vashisht

The advent of the twentieth century ushered in an age that shook modern man's notions about his place in the material and spiritual world. For all its technological and intellectual advancements, the age not only helped man fathom the mystery of both his own evolution and that of the human race, but also provided a glimpse of who or what he could turn into. The resolute conviction of the Enlightenment, the searing individualism of the Romantics, and the nineteenth-century realist project of representing the truth as the truth was reduced to rubble during the First World War. Humanist philosopher Pico della Mirandola's recondite thoughts on the freedom of choice bequeathed to man as the "maker and molder" of whatever "thou shalt prefer" resurfaced in the modernist period as a menacing analogy of giving a matchbox to a child in a room full of firecrackers and candles. This brave new world was one where Mirandola's impression of desiring "to be reborn into the higher forms of life, which are divine" was willfully supplanted with man's weakness towards degenerating "into lower forms of life, which are brutish" (Cassirer et al. 223). Darwin had upset centuries-old theories of evolution, Nietzsche was busy killing God, Freud had demonstrated how the child was, in fact, the father of man, and Marx had debunked the illusion of Capitalism and the dreary dependence of art on material conditions. Three decades later, a tall boy and a fat man established a peril that made torpedoes, airships, metal detectors, radars, barbed wires, and dynamites look like a dumb show. The shredding and splintering of preconceived notions and the multiplicity of contradictions necessitated a need for an artistic sensibility that would attempt to come to terms with the chaos and catastrophe of modernity.

William Golding's appetite for tracing evil in the world back to the defects of human nature and his courage in debunking the idea of modern culture as a "lie" in having constructed "an illusion of a society worthy of human beings" (Adorno 55), are a telling dystopian response to the *zeitgeist* of the great war era. For Golding, man is essentially fallen, his nature diseased, and evil inherent from birth itself. His fall lies in his willed separation from a wholeness, and, in choosing to fracture himself through his limited perception of things, he creates what Nietzsche calls a "life denying" condition and a universe that is hostile to him. Golding's choice of adolescent schoolboys as his protagonists enhances his bleak prophecy in its attempts to dislocate evil as an adult formation and instead present it in juvenile terms. At its core, the boys' society represents that of civilized adults, corroborating that evil exists from birth and is primed to manifest its might at a favorable occasion. The virginal setting of the island and an absence of a state apparatus have a deleterious effect on the psyche of the boys. They enhance viciousness and depravity as a natural product of their consciousness and lay bare an irremediable paradox between innocence and corruption, nature and culture, primitivism and civilization. Their brief spell on the island is a disturbing vignette of a far poorer canvas of life waiting for them when they will return to civilization.

Golding admitted that it had taken him more than half a lifetime, two world wars, and many years among children to realize that man had become physically hardened and morally coarsened. Stating the theme of his novel as being that of "Grief. Sheer grief, grief, grief, grief," Golding furthers his cynical thesis in *The Hot Gates*: "The boys try to construct a civilization on the island; but it breaks down in blood and thunder for the boys are suffering from the terrible disease of being human" (163, 89). The boys conspire, betray, kill, and transform the pristine ecosystem into a barren wasteland.

Within a Christian-existentialist framework, dystopian visions are discernible in Golding's insistence on portraying the boys as morally diseased creatures, in his deliberate blighting of faith in their potential for goodness, and in professing despair in the remotest possibility of a restored state of being. Piggy's painful cry, "What are we? Humans? Or animals? Or savages?" falls like a whiplash and demands a considered response (99).[1] The cruelty and bloodlust displayed by the boys goes beyond Calvinist philosophy and necessitates an attempt to expand Golding's thesis into incorporating Freud's instinctivist theory of aggression and Darwin's theory of the biological basis for human violence and competitive behavior. Nevertheless, if Freud justifies human violence as a consequence of the malaise of modern civilization, and if biologically adaptive aggression serves life by preserving the fittest and destroying the weakest, then how can such intense sadism and aggression displayed by the boys be justified?

It would therefore be useful to measure the complex behavioral divergences as a consequence of human potential—one that is malignant and rooted essentially in the depraved "human condition." In *Anatomy of Human Destructiveness*, Erich Fromm writes that malignant aggression constitutes the real problem and poses a threat to man's existence as a species; that it is specifically human and not derived from animal instincts and hence not ineradicable:

> What is unique in man is that he can be driven by impulse to kill and to torture, and that he feels lust in doing so. He is the only animal that can be a killer and destroyer of his own species without any rational gain, either biological or economic [218].

It is this biologically non-adaptive aggression that creates an "existential contradiction" resulting in a state of "constant disequilibrium" that distinguishes him from the animal, which lives, as it were, in harmony with nature (Fromm 225). Nevertheless, whether viciousness is a product of original sin and atrophied spirituality or of biological theories of evolution and/or the human condition, reading *Lord of the Flies* almost sixty years after its publication reveals a disturbing insight: that there is basically no way out. Perhaps, like Sisyphus, we cannot go back to an original state of harmony with nature, and we really do not know where will we arrive if we go forward.

"Civilization ... was in ruins"

Golding was well aware of being diagnosed as a "pessimist" and "dystopist" after the publication of the novel, and he confessed that this dystopian vision was shaped a good deal by the Second World War, in which he participated as an officer in the British Royal Navy. *Lord of the Flies* was published at a time when British society was trying hard to hold on to the last vestiges of dignity consequent to the crumbling of its colonial empire and its mute complicity in the destruction inflicted by the war's genocide and holocaust on the psyche of man and the fabric of modern culture. The impact of the Second World War was considerably worse than the disillusionment inflicted on European sensibilities by the First World War, the failure of the Russian Revolution, and the rise of authoritarian regimes and narcissistic dictators. The core values of civilization were ripped apart when the Nuremberg Trials revealed the apocalyptic "Final Solution" meticulously planned by the Third Reich. The corruptibility of ethics surfaced when the world shockingly realized that Stalin's gulags in Siberia were replicas of Hitler's camps in Europe. The planet woke up to a lunar landscape of a fouled ecosystem: cities gutted due to land offensives, polluted waterways, psychological maladies, physiological defects, shattered prisoners of war, and refugee crises. As a result of the evolution of the species, the enlightened man had revolted against his creation and creator, becoming a "prosthetic God" (Freud 39), an unruly legislator.

In *A Moving Target,* Golding summarized the effect of violence on British sensibility as such: "Really, it seems as though both World Wars have fused and become a foundation on which all our assumptions are based. Life goes on at the conscious level, frivolous, worried, cynical, anxious, amused, but beneath in some deep cavern of the soul we are stunned" (99). The "great war" (1914–18) challenged cultural discourses on heroism and nationalism. But the "war to end all wars" (1939–45) eclipsed all others with its scale of destruction. It established a diffuse sensibility of cultural disenchantment with political and intellectual leadership. The moral ambiguity circling the notion of bad things being done for a good cause (the firebombing of Berlin, Tokyo, Hamburg, Hiroshima, and Nagasaki; war crimes in Nazi Germany and Fascist Italy; and Britain's Imperialist overdrive) irrevocably shattered the promise of a progressive western culture.

Man's debauchery forced Golding to review his utopian vision of the world and the situation it was in. Unapologetically undermining the perfectibility of social man, he realized that war revealed not unethical politics and the follies of nationalism but the given nature of man. He discovered what one man could do to another—not the intelligent or exceptional man, but the average man. Golding's works are not just a powerful repudiation of the naïve optimism of Ballantyne and Wyss. His ideas are shaped by his own painful observations of the cult of the irrational, which sees the universe in "cosmic chaos" and the human species as fragmented. Man's progress into adulthood is seen as a regression into disgrace and guilt similar to Swift's image of the Yahoo's in *Gulliver's Travels.* Twentieth-century history, on the other hand, could be reimagined and imaged through the eyes of Gulliver as a "heap of conspiracies, rebellions, murders, massacres, revolutions and banishments, the very worst effects that avarice, faction, hypocrisy, perfidiousness, cruelty, rage, madness, hatred, envy, lust, malice, and ambition could produce" (98). Clearly, Golding is laying blame on man's egocentricity that is so riddled with inherent paradoxes that it renders him incapable of dealing with the terrible truth of modern civilization.

The most significant literary source for *Lord of the Flies* is R.M. Ballantyne's Victorian classic *The Coral Island* (1857). Published during the height of Britain's capitalist prosperity and colonial complacency, Ballantyne shipwrecks his three boys—Jack, Ralph, and Peterkin Gay—and relocates them on an uninhabited coral island. The narration centers on their idyllic existence and inherent goodness that is threatened by external sources in the form of savage natives and cruel pirates. In due time, the pirates are destroyed and the natives undergo an unsolicited conversion to Christianity. The dichotomy between nature and culture is sustained, and throughout the book the focus remains on the resourcefulness and grit of the boys, expediently hyped as British traits. Golding refutes Ballantyne's emulsified claim and negates the romantic notion of childhood innocence by crashing his boys on a deserted island in an orphaned and wretched twentieth century.

Lord of the Flies is the story of a group of adolescent boys aged between six and twelve who accidently find themselves on a tropical island as a result of supposedly civilized nations going to war. The abundance of food, water, sun, and sand is enough to enthuse their facile notions that have been ideologically constructed on traditional colonial narratives of exotic lands and conquered savages. The discovery of the conch by Ralph brings them together in harmony. As Ralph, Jack, and Simon explore the island, they are conscious of a "kind of glamour [that] was spread over them" (LoF 22). The island exerts an invisible pressure forcing the boys apart, and soon the presence of the "beast" challenges their idyllic world; the conch is destroyed, Piggy and Simon are killed and the island is set on fire. The smoke, however, attracts the attention of a naval cruiser and by sheer irony of circumstances the boys are rescued from each other and from total collapse for the time being. One might as well ask: what is wrong? What makes things break up on the island like they do? What results in transforming a tranquil paradise into a wasteland? Even more so, why do a group of minor boy scouts behave so shamefully? An attempt to address these issues can be achieved through a close examination of the psychic complexities and behavioral patterns of Ralph, Jack, Piggy, and Simon, and in doing so explore the heart of darkness and possibly suggest that the more civilized man has become, the more destructive his inclinations are.

"After all, we're not savages..."

Ralph and Jack are fundamentally opposed in their nature and attitudes—"two continents of experience and feeling unable to communicate" (LoF 57). Their two worlds are essentially incompatible: "the brilliant world of hunting, tactics, fierce exhilaration, skill and the world of longing and baffled commonsense" (57). Early descriptions of Ralph depict a carefree, cheerful boy, "with a mildness about his mouth that proclaimed no devil" (11). Jack, on the other hand, is introduced in a way that is distinctly threatening. With his freckles and unruly red hair, he is truly a force to be reckoned with. From a distance, he and his followers appear to Ralph as a dark creature winding its way to the platform from where he has blown his conch: "Within the diamond haze of the beach something dark was fumbling along. [...] [T]he creature was a party of boys [...] hidden by black cloaks [...]. The boy who controlled them was dressed in the same way [...]" (15).

The first note of antagonism between Ralph and Jack is struck on the question of priorities and, subsequently, on the issue of leadership. While Ralph says that the best thing for them is to get rescued, Jack retorts, "Rescue? Yes, of course! All the same I'd like to catch a pig first" (58). The possession of the conch makes Ralph the best candidate for leadership. In appearance, the conch, with its translucent, fragile white shell, reflects a civilized world of ceremony, ritual, and assemblage, to which they desperately need to cling. With his "opaque mad look," Jack, too, asserts his claims, but only by virtue of sheer brute power asserted through his position of authority as head boy of the chorister group, supported by his act of slamming a knife into a tree trunk. However, not having the conch deprives him of the authority to back his power. Right at the outset, he begins manifesting traits of Freud's "man of action" who will never give up the "external world on which he can try out his strength" (31). Aided by his sinister henchmen, Roger and Robert, his behavior consistently worsens during the course of the narrative.

Piggy is a fleshy, bespectacled, and asthmatic child. His obesity renders him the butt of many a joke along with ones being cut at the cost of his sloth, gluttony, and asthma, which Jack repeatedly mocks as "ass-mar." However, his role is significant, for it is at his behest that Ralph blows the conch to call an assembly in order to bring the boys together, and he continues to support Ralph until his dying breath. His incessant emphasis on the value of the assemblies as indicators of order and decorum are glimpses of what was once—and what could still be—a civilized state of affairs. Despite the perspicacity and rationalism he displays, he forgets that there are critical moments in life when reason fails. His inability to command respect and communicate his ideas to his peer group limits his leadership.

Mature beyond his years, Simon is Golding's saint-like figure. Like Piggy, he lacks communicative skills and relies, albeit a little too much, on intuition. Prone to epileptic fits, the children find him rather "batty" and reticent. He is far too engrossed in subtle communions with himself and with nature to really consider chiefdom. The polarities in their temperaments are illustrated in their first mountain expedition:

> Here they paused and examined the bushes round them curiously.
> Simon spoke first.
> "Like candles. Candle bushes. Candle buds."
> The bushes were dark evergreen and aromatic and the many buds were waxen green and folded up against the light. Jack slashed at one with a knife and scent spilled over them.
> "Candle buds."

"You couldn't light them," said Ralph. "They just look like candles."
"Green candles," said Jack contemptuously. "We can't eat them. Come on" [28–29].

The collapse of society can then clearly be structured around Ralph and Jack's varied opinions on everything—leadership, survival, fire, and shelter, among other things. If the conch is a totem of authority, power, order, and harmony for Ralph, then the next step for Jack is to reject it and aggressively pursue power that ultimately culminates in anarchy. Within Freudian terms, the conch would represent civilization and social conditioning, which would impose "restrictions on the liberty of the individual" and therefore always be an impediment for Jack (42). The four assemblies steadily record the appropriation of harmony by primitivism.

From the very first assembly, the priority of a smoke signal is established beyond doubt amongst all the boys except for Jack and his choir. While Ralph dons the mantle of a provider and desperately tries to build shelters and promote social bonding through establishing a community, Jack discovers in himself the primeval instincts of a hunter. Thus, on all fours like an animal, he learns to flare his nostrils and assess the air and the landscape around him. The forest becomes not only a place to hunt but also a place where one feels hunted:

> Only when Jack himself roused a gaudy bird from the primitive nest of sticks was the silence shattered and echoes set ringing by a harsh cry that seemed to come out of the abyss of ages. Jack himself shrank at this cry with a hiss of indrawn breath, and for a minute became less of a hunter than a furtive thing, ape-like among the tangle of trees [50].

Seeped in animalistic regression, Jack doggedly follows the fecal trail of the pigs until he finds what he wants: "The ground was turned over near the pig-run and there were droppings that steamed. Jack bent down to them as though he loved them" (50). In more ways than one, Jack has so regressed to a savage, animalistic existence that the idea of a rescue is hardly real for him anymore and pigs matter more than a ship that might restore them to civilization. Interestingly, all the children discard their clothes as a sign of liberation from cultural expectations, yet Jack and his hunters discard their clothes only to mask themselves behind face paint, providing them with an unbridled license to dissipate into savagery. Their newfound role makes them heady, and they feel no remorse when, due to their negligence, the smoke signal dies out and they lose a chance of being rescued. Instead, they recall with pride how they hunted, outwitted a living thing, imposed their will upon it, and took away its life:

> "We got in a circle—"
> "We crept up—"
> "The pig squealed—"

[…]
"We hit the pig—"
"—I fell on top—" [174].

Perhaps Jack's inability to resist perverse instincts and attraction in general towards things forbidden by culture would find an economic explanation within Freud's theories: "The feeling of happiness derived from the satisfaction of a wild instinctual impulse untamed by the ego is incomparably more intense than that derived from sating an instinct that has been tamed" (26). Having overcome their initial ethical-cultural restrains in taking a life through a "will to overpower" a weaker species, they will soon be seen appropriating a "littleun" instead.

The second assembly is summoned in order to alter the situation. Ralph's utilitarian program for better sanitation, keeping the fire going at all times, and only cooking on the mountain top is challenged, for at a deeper level he knows that things are breaking up due to Jack's rebellious behavior and the fact that the littleuns are frightened of the "beastie." Ralph's belief in solving the issue of the beast through logical democratic reasoning is ruptured due to Jack's violent behavior exhibited when he attacks Piggy. Herein emerges foulness, for mere irresponsibility has turned into viciousness, and a will previously imposed forcefully on an animal has now turned into destructive violence on a human being. In Jack's chant of "kill the pig, cut her throat, do her in," one can detect the firming up of a diminished sense of civilization. Ironically, the antagonism between the "demands of instinct" and the "restrictions of civilization" (Freud 18) becomes irremediable and Ralph can no longer convince the boys about the imperative need to be rescued. Soon, all becomes suspect in the face of imminent crisis.

The novel has been interpreted as a conflict on the societal level between "law breakers and law makers, between champions of order and forces of anarchy" (Subbarao 12). On a political level, these divergent behaviors represent a clash between utilitarian democracy—symbolized by Ralph and Piggy—and the authoritarian—represented by Jack and Roger. Whereas Ralph, with his slogan of signal fire and shelter, may be taken as representing the "enlightened self-interest of Bentham and Miller," the pig hunt is an expression of "lust for power" (Subbarao 12). Possibly, Ralph's inability to comprehend the burgeoning crisis manifests his position as a type of "befuddled everyman, a stray boy of democracy tossed about by forces he cannot cope with" (Oldsey 5). He becomes steadily disillusioned with the democratic process and willingly betrays its hollowness: "talk," said Ralph bitterly, "talk, talk, talk" (LoF 140). His socialist ideals never translate into successful praxis and blatantly manifest the mowing down of Socialism by totalitarian/communist ideologies during the war decades.

In his chapter on the analysis of the roots of Adolf Hitler's aggression,

Fromm speaks of the rational and irrational will. By rational will he refers to the "energetic effort" to reach a rationally desirable aim; it requires "realism, discipline, patience and the over-coming of self-indulgence" (428). The irrational will is formidable: "[I]t is like a river bursting a dam; it is powerful, but man is not the master of this will; he is driven by it, forced by it, its slave" (428). The binary is unmistakable. If Ralph represents the rational, then Jack is so obsessed with the pig-hunt that it subsumes his spirit and energy. He confesses to a feeling of being pursued, as if something is behind him all the time in the jungle. Since "never the twain shall meet," Jack blows the conch in the third assembly and blatantly challenges Ralph's leadership, and he splinters away to form his own military faction. Regression into belligerent behavior is objectified by the desire of the hunt, which becomes a correlative of exercising absolute control. An illustration of this would be the killing of the sow. Critics Kinkead-Weekes and Gregor designate the feverish act of chasing the sow in the oppressive afternoon heat as being "wedded to her in lust" as they "hurl themselves at her" (LoF 152). The violence has palpable sexual overtones in the "sow collapsing under them," they having fallen "heavy and fulfilled upon her," and Roger sticking a spear "[r]ight up her ass" (LoF 152).

Within a more customary existential casing, Ralph sustains his wholeness by virtue of choosing goodness over evil. He too wants to hunt and swim, but instead, he chooses to build shelters, to keep the signal fire going, and to construct a sense of *communitas* by bringing the boys together. He may have his flaws, but he does not despair in the idea of being rescued and restored to civilization. Maybe Simon understands Ralph's temperament much better than most, and predicts pertinently, "I think you'll get back alright" (124). Jack, on the other hand, abandons his spiritual center in abusing goodness and reason. Like Beelzebub, his metamorphosis into the league of fallen angels is the quickest. At the end, he stands punished into muteness like the abhorred legions of Milton's devils when he is unable to respond to the Naval officer's question of "Who's boss here?" (230).

By the time the fourth assembly is called, the breach is complete: the boys replicate the war stricken landscape of Europe on the island. It is transformed into a war zone replete with territorial demarcations and military buttressing, sieges and stratagem, assault and mortality. In this entropy, nothing can enter or exit. If something does arrive, it is death in the form of the dead helmeted parachutist who becomes a sinister motif of destruction caused by war. In this raging blaze, no one is spared, and, pessimist that he is, Golding gives Simon one flaw—the inability to communicate. Therefore, Simon is brutally killed on account of being mistaken for the "beast," and for Jack's tribe his death is simply another pig hunt. Unlike Ralph and Piggy who expiate their guilt by hiding, Jack and his tribe overcome it by projecting evil into the beast. Jack finally secures absolute authority when he captures Piggy's glasses, and the "vicious snarling," the hitting and biting are now deliberate and not accidental. The sound of the shell is heard for the last time. The final assembly is a desperate attempt by Ralph to bring back into the savages the consciousness of civilized values. In this meeting, Piggy is the one to be killed deliberately and ruthlessly, but not before he brings out the fundamental message in the encounter that has resulted in madness:

> "Which is better—to be a pack of painted niggers like you are, or to be sensible like Ralph is?"
> [....]
> "Which is better—to have rules and agree, or to hunt and kill?"
> [....]
> "Which is better, law and rescue, or hunting and breaking things up?" [205].

Samuel Hynes analyzes the psychological and political implications of the destruction of the "bearers of truth," and writes that "a demented but partly secure society" will resist and attempt to destroy anyone who offers to substitute reason and responsible individual action for the irresponsible, unreasoning, secure action of the masses" (99). Subsequently, the cloak that masks the pig hunt is thrown aside to reveal the bloodlust to destroy Ralph, and just as Ralph is about to be killed, a naval officer arrives on the island. Ironically, on being asked by the officer who is the leader, Jack remains silent and Ralph assents.

Remarkably, Jack's splinter tribe had much more cohesion than Ralph's parent tribe. His idea of the hunt was more popular than Ralph's thesis for rescue-fire, and his castle rock was almost impenetrable unlike Ralph's porous poolside. Unlike Ralph, Jack did not need to call an assembly, for he shot to power as a reaction to his public humiliation. His order was neither democratic nor utilitarian, but based on survival of the fittest and the "will to power." Amiya Dev suggests that the code set up by Jack to deal with the poolside was "absolutely amoral," and that "Jack and his company had the potentials of the Third Reich" (14). The relapse into barbarism turns out to be a mordant denunciation of the notion of European man's faith in the power of nation and culture to redeem him. No dialectic is sustained between civilization and savagery, reason and passion, ambition and stability. The moment of realization wherein Jack the chorister boy is transformed into a savage warlord concurs with the moment of wisdom when Ralph weeps for the "end of innocence, the darkness of man's heart" (230).

"We did everything adults would do. What went wrong?"

However, if such a traumatic experience is necessary for Ralph to recognize the demonic potential of man, there is only one boy in the text—

Simon—who right from the outset has an instinctive grasp of why things are breaking up, why evil is "no go." Evil, he intuits, is "no go" because it is "only us." In his encounter with the Lord of the Flies, Beelzebub—Prince of Devils, in the chapter "Gift for the Darkness," Simon falls into an epileptic fit. His physical disability bequeaths an alternate spiritual vision and arms him with the knowledge that evil is a product of man's mind and can turn against him. His recognition of the notion that neither rationalism (Piggy) nor utilitarianism (Ralph) nor Communism (Jack) can purge the "beast" in man is a telling revelation: "You knew, didn't you? The beast warns him. I'm part of you? Close, close, close! I'm the reason why it's no go? Why things are the way what they are?" (161–62).

In embracing the intuitive and mystical, Simon discovers the truth, which would remain undiscovered by many rational and scientific sensibilities. The realization that instincts are a more superior medium than *telos* to comprehend "the horror, the horror" of man's degenerate existence is a tight moral that Golding insists on establishing. At this juncture, Simon discovers that the beast on the mountaintop is the rotting carcass of a dead parachutist. The "poor, misguided child" releases the body and consequently goes to free the boys from their fear psychosis and is killed instead. His death can be taken to be yet another instance of the failure of the utopian quest for truth and goodness. Within Fromm's categorization of "benign" and "malignant" aggression, the violence displayed by the boys in relation to Simon and Piggy's death is clearly malignant as neither of the two threaten nor harm their basic existence. Killing them is not an instinctive animalistic act of self-defense and self-preservation. Instead, the boys' exhibition of motiveless "killing and cruelty" is harmful because it is socially disruptive (Fromm 187).

Conversely, Golding does not absolve the other boys for their shameful and hostile behavior. The violence exhibited may vary in degrees, but it is discernibly a part of their individual and collective consciousness. Ralph, Maurice, Piggy, and few of the littleuns display instances of "pseudo aggression" through acts of "playful aggression" that may cause harm but are not intended to do so (Fromm188). Simon is accurate in visualizing the nature of the brute, as a kind of darkness within, which is visible in the spontaneous and unconscious display of violence by the boys. Even Ralph is culpable, and Golding unhesitatingly writes that, much like Jack, Ralph, too, is surrounded by a "darkness, which seemed to flow around him like a tide" (LoF 132). He also gets excited by the power he can impose on a living thing and narcissistically "sunned himself" in the admiring glances of the boys on the beach.

Ralph and Piggy can be called victims only in relative comparison to Jack and Roger's cruelty. Yet, ignoring their complicity in Simon's death and slinking off into the bushes to hide demonstrates the dangers of a stunned and blinkered post-war generation keen on normalizing the "terrible beauty" of post war existence. In the fourth chapter, Roger and Maurice can be seen walking through the sand castles built by the littleuns and carelessly flicking sand into Percival's eyes (63). Furthermore, little Henry's unconscious aggression emerges in his attempts to control the motions of tiny, lucent sea creatures with a stick. While the boy is thrilled at finding himself exercising control over living things, granting him an "illusion of mastery," Roger, hidden behind a palm tree, is busy throwing stones at him, gloating in his power to be able to hurt him (66).

Incidentally, Ralph shows the first signs of sinister play on hearing Piggy's name, reacts playfully by mimicking a fighter plane, and tries to gun him down. He also divulges Piggy's nickname, Fatty, and therein begins a game of group teasing and a steady emotional withdrawal from him. A little later, Jack transforms show into praxis when he forcefully sticks his fist into Piggy's stomach and blinds him with pain. The fine line between reality and pretense is compromised again when Robert, in trying to relieve the tension between the boys, playfully mimes a pig being hunted and truly gets hurt. His frenzied struggles to free himself and the cries of pain produce thick excitement, which carries Ralph away too:

> "Kill him! Kill him!"
> [....]
> The desire to squeeze and hurt was over-mastering.
> [....]
> Jack's arm came down; the heaving circle cheered and made pig-dying noises. They lay quiet, panting, listening to Robert's frightened snivels [127, 128].

Such instances of childish play are minor expressions of the potential for destructiveness, and, in more ways than one, point towards the Hobbesian cliché of war as being the natural state of man.

The perception of cruelty and corruption being a part of the collective consciousness of the boys is reinforced with the naval officer's indifferent comment of "fun and games" followed by, "Nobody killed, I hope? Any dead bodies?" (229). It becomes a conscious reminder of Beelzebub's revelation to Simon about man's inability to recognize evil in him. The naval officer may ostensibly represent the disciplined adult world, but he is also an agent of war—the foulest and basest metaphor of man's pride, wrath, and desire to play God on earth. "The boys," writes David Spitz, "move not from one evil to another evil, but from one aspect or level to another of the same evil; they go from the Lord of the flies writ small to the Lord of the flies writ large" (28). Therefore, it is really no rescue at all, but rather a frightful pronouncement of their situation; an ironic fulfillment of Simon's prophesy: "You'll get back to where you came from" (LoF 122).

"What I mean is ... maybe it's only us."

In the Introduction to Darwin's *The Descent of Man* (1981), Bonner and May clarify that nineteenth- and twentieth-century social scientists saw human culture and civilization as being something so special and unlike anything in the animal world that "it can only be analyzed in its own terms and not in terms of the level below, i.e., biology" (xxi). However, Darwin keenly contends that civilized nations are formed when "the weak in body and mind are eliminated. Those that survive exhibit vigorous health" (168). His focus in *The Origin of Species* on the "preservation of favorable variations" and the "rejection of injurious variations" (94) as factoring into the process of natural selection and survival of the fittest finds validation in subsequent textual references. While the boys experience extreme physical deprivation in the form of dehydration and starvation, they also experience the mental and emotional strain that comes from being stranded on a desolate island. One can easily comprehend why several of them seem to experience psychological and physical breakdowns. The nausea, stomachaches, and diarrhea experienced by the littleuns seem to be psychosomatic symptoms of biological degeneration and, within nineteenth-century theories of *degenerescence*, preempt moral degeneration. If Simon's epilepsy can be taken to be symbolic of a neurological flaw, Piggy's obesity and acute myopia become metaphors of physiological limitations. From time to time, Piggy also complains of headaches.

In *The Origin of Species*, Darwin opines that in the process of natural selection and extinction of species, "less favored" forms of life will steadily decrease and "become rare" (269). One of the reasons for losing out in the race for survival of the fittest, he states, is the consistent disuse of physical and mental capacities on account of domestic habits. "Instincts," he proposes, are lost under "domestication" (269). Ralph's daily domestic roster of sanitation, hygiene, building shelters, toilets, tending the fire, and searching for food corrodes natural instincts of survival for himself and his followers. Simon and Piggy's demise and, subsequently, his own close shave with death find favorable explanations within this context.

Ralph's declining mental and physical health is evident in the form of weight loss and memory lapses. In chapter seven, Ralph notices that he has started biting his nails again: "They were bitten down to the quick though he could not remember when he had restarted this habit nor any time when he indulged it" (122). Ralph's nail chewing signifies a regression to habits that hitherto comforted him in times of insecurity when he was younger. Ralph remarks upon noticing his nails that he will "be sucking [his] thumb next" (109). Perhaps he resorts to these habits to filter the tremendous strain he feels. Still, he cannot remember when he actually chewed on his nails. Golding includes other details to suggest Ralph's memory loss in conversations with other boys, as when the boys prepare to visit Castle Rock. Ralph can barely recollect keeping the signal fire lit. When the other boys worriedly look at Ralph, he protests:

> "I hadn't," said Ralph loudly. "I knew it all the time. I hadn't forgotten."
> Piggy nodded propitiatingly.
> "You're chief, Ralph. You remember everything."
> "I hadn't forgotten" [197].

Although the other boys assure Ralph that he remembered, it is plain that they discern that Ralph's memory and control are slipping away: "The twins were examining Ralph curiously, as though they were seeing him for the first time" (LoF 197). Apparently, the emotional and physical strain of surviving on the island has impacted Ralph's mental health, resulting in memory loss and mental fatigue. Medical statistics state that one of the consequences of the war was a condition of perpetual exhaustion that Freud terms as neurasthenia. Within Hitler's racist program of Eugenics, these flaws would categorize Simon, Piggy, and most of the boys as biologically and intellectually unfit and thus, suitable for elimination. Appropriately then, Jack and his tribe survive all odds owing to their superior levels of physical fitness and mental tenacity.

Parenthetically, out of the three boys who are killed, two are referred to by nicknames—Piggy is called Fatty, and the boy who died in the first fire is clinically addressed as the "little 'un—him with the mark on his face" (LoF 48). Twentieth-century psychologists and behaviorists would interpret this tendency to substitute a clinical address for a personal one as part of the process of dehumanization, of depersonalizing the enemy, thus, expiating guilt after harming them. Furthermore, twentieth-century cultures are classic examples of persuading their people to believe that the enemy is not human. During the Vietnam War, the American marines referred to the Vietnamese soldiers as Gooks; for centuries, whites derogated the blacks as niggers or apes, and Asians as brownies. Through the First World War, the British called the Germans "Huns," and the Germans referred to the Japanese as "Japs," Jews as "vermin," and the Slavs as "yellow peril." The logic is to look at the enemy as a stranger, a nonperson, or, as Hitler called his political enemies, *untermenschen* or subhumans. In assigning the title of Fatty to Piggy, Jack and his comrades feel no remorse in exterminating his life like they did when they killed the pig. As Fromm says, "The other ceases to be experienced as human and becomes a thing—over there" (123). When a person ceases to be experienced as human, the act of cruelty assumes a sadistic quality. Indeed, both Piggy and Simon are killed through this sadistic expression of aggression.

"You'll get back to where you came from"

In the twenty-first century cultural context, the novel portends the unlikelihood of man achieving harmony either with himself or with his fellow men on account of his instinctive appetite for violence and power. Richard Pendergast observes, "Even if a new Adam and Eve were to start afresh on some distant planet like Earth, it seems virtually certain that the descendants would face essentially the same problems as we do" (162). At certain stages in the story, it does seem as though Golding deliberately makes us forget that these are only children. Their story embraces human conflicts and destabilizes markers of permanence whether in deciphering psychological or cultural realities. Through a de-realization of social and ideological conditioning on the isolated island, the text authenticates the notion that it is of little consequence whether the "beast" comes from the air, the sea, or the dark forest. Man creates his own hell and his own devils, and subsequently, his own nightmare reality. To a critic who suggested that good was equally an exclusive human concept, Golding replied, "Good can look after itself. Evil is the problem" (qtd. in Green 62). Contextualizing Golding's thesis within Freud's debate on individual and communal happiness, one can ask the crucial question for the human species: to what extent will an advance in their social and cultural consciousness succeed in "mastering the disturbance in their communal life by the human instinct of aggression and self-destruction"? (Freud 92). Freud is quick to assert, "Men have gained control over the forces of nature to such an extent that with their help they would have no difficulty in exterminating one another to the last man. They know this, and hence comes the last part of their current unrest, their unhappiness and their mood of anxiety" (92).

As Ralph self-reflexively sobs for the "end of innocence and the darkness of man's heart," he is apportioning blame on both mankind and modern civilization in general, and not on Jack and Roger in particular. Civilization, as historical facts have shown, has sublimated "individual liberty" and appropriated words such as "super-ego, conscience, sense of guilt, need for punishment and remorse" into sustaining a reified collective ideology (Freud 90). Thus, the schism in the psyche of the boys is evocative of what can be termed as "cultural frustration" that arises out of the irreconcilable conflict between "claims of the individual" and altruistic "cultural claims of the group" (Freud 43).

As a consequence, the degree of destructiveness has steadily increased with the progress of civilization. The boys and the ecosystem on the island do pay a price for this development, and as twenty-first century readers, we, too, uncomfortably recognize the tangible significance of Simon's dystopian learning. Adorno suggests that "the logic of history is as destructive as the people it brings to prominence: wherever its momentum carries it, it reproduces equivalents of past calamities" (53). Hence, in the conundrum of topical reality, the ghosts of the past have risen from their graves and are here to stay. Contemporary illustrations of mushrooming right-wing fundamentalism, war torn countries, ethnic polarities, mounting border security, émigré crisis, cybernetics, military upmanship, and severe ecological disorders will compel us to acknowledge the fact that "there are far worse things to fear than death" (Adorno 38). The cultural relevance of Golding's *Lord of the Flies* will endure because man is "just an ignorant, silly little boy" (LoF 161), a misguided victim of habit who will continue to stake claim to narcissistic liberty by creating worse chimeras than before.

NOTE

1. Subsequent references to the text *Lord of the Flies* will be cited as (LoF).

WORKS CITED

Adorno, Theodor. *Minima Moralia*. Trans. E.F.N Jephcott. London: Verso, 2005. Print.
Cassirer, Ernst, Paul Oskar Kristeller, and John Herman Randall, Jr., eds. *The Renaissance Philosophy of Man*. Chicago: University of Chicago Press, 1948. 223–25. Print.
Darwin, Charles. *Descent of Man and Selection in Relation to Sex*. Princeton: Princeton University Press, 1981. Print.
Darwin, Charles. *The Origin of Species*. Ed. Charles W. Eliot. New York: Collier, 1909. Print.
Dev, Amiya. "*Lord of the Flies*: Ironic or Dystopian?" Ed. Satyanarain Singh, Adapa Ramakrishna Rao, and Taqi Ali Mirza. *William Golding: An Indian Response*. New Delhi: Arnold-Heinemann, 1987. 9–20. Print.
Freud, Sigmund. *Civilization and Its Discontents*. Trans. and ed. James Strachey. New York: Norton, 1961. Print.
Fromm, Erich. *The Anatomy of Human Destructiveness*. New York: Holt, 1973. Print.
Golding, William. *The Hot Gates and Other Occasional Pieces*. London: Faber, 1974. Print.
_____. *Lord of the Flies*. 1954. London: Faber, 1999. Print.
_____. *A Moving Target*. London: Faber, 1982. Print.
Green, Peter. "The World of William Golding." *A Review of English Literature* 1.2 (April 1960): 62–72. Print.
Hynes. Samuel. *Moral Models: William Golding: Novels, 1954–67*. Ed. Norman Page. London: Macmillan, 1985. Print.
Kinkead-Weekes, Mark, and Ian Gregor. *William Golding: A Critical Study*. London: Faber, 1967. Print.
Oldsey, Brian, and Stanley Weintraub. "*Lord of the Flies*: Beelzebub Revisited." *College English* 25.2 (Nov. 1963): 90–99. Web. 25 April 2016. < http://www.jstor.org/stable/373397>
Pendergast, Richard. *Cosmos*. New York: Fordham University Press, 1973. Print.
Spitz, David. "Power and Authority: An Interpretation of Golding's 'Lord of the Flies.'" *Antioch Review* 30.1 (Spring 1970): 21–33. Print.
Subbarao, V.V. *William Golding: A Study*. New Delhi: Sterling Publishers, 1987. Print.
Swift, Jonathan. *Gulliver's Travels*. London: Wordsworth, 1997. Print.

Streets of Spectrality
Kevin Barry's *Dystopian* City of Bohane

Deirdre Flynn

The award-winning *City of Bohane* (2011) has captured the imagination of critics across the world. Set in a city in West Ireland in 2053, Kevin Barry's uncanny Bohane exudes spectrality as past and present merge in the dystopian future where technology is no longer a certainty. This brave new world imagined by Barry plays with postmodern notions of dystopia and utopia, as Irish and American cultural references mix with the old and the new. Time and space become postmodern in this strange, new, nostalgic, and urban dystopia, making it an eclectic mix of gothic, cyberpunk, steampunk and postmodern. Barry breaks down the traditional binary opposition of dystopia/utopia with his mix of Lyotardian eclecticism and uncanny depictions.

The liminal spaces in Barry's urban cityscape add to the ghostly feel, as the city slowly rises to its violent potential. Latham and Hicks claim in *The Cambridge Companion to The City in Literature* that over the past three decades "cyberpunk and steampunk have generated some of the most compelling and influential images of dystopia urban spaces" (173). Barry's Bohane is no different, offering the reader a unique version of the digital-free urban space of the future.

Postmodern

Through this style, Kevin Barry has created a postmodern city—an uncanny multiple space that mixes nostalgia with a gothic vision of a future devoid of technology. It is very much a Lyotardian space:

> Eclecticism is the degree zero of contemporary general culture: you listen to reggae; you watch a Western; you eat McDonald's at midday and local cuisine at night; you wear Paris perfume in Tokyo and dress retro in Hong Kong; knowledge is the stuff of TV game shows [8].

The Irish novel often engages with ideas of hybridity; it can be an eclectic mix of Anglo and Irish, colonial and postcolonial, rural and urban. These issues all come to play in the City of Bohane, most particularly in the blending of gothic and postmodern. The heterogeneity of the text has been noted before. The *New York Times* described Bohane as "an Icelandic saga welded to a ballad of the American West, although the location is in a place somewhere in Ireland, around the year 2053" (Hamill). Barry tells us that Bohane is in the West of Ireland, but the diverse cultural and references littered throughout the text make it impossible to locate it in a particular time or space.

Bohane is a fragmented and eclectic city all at the same time: the wealthy Beauvista, the vast Big Nothin' that lies outside the city, the dangerous Back Trace, the overpopulated and impoverished North Side Rises, the docks, the new town, the 98 steps, and the seedy Smoketown. Fragmented groups and factions roam the streets, making this a postmodern city space. Throughout the novel, the threat of violence is always there. As we are told, "it is a fond tradition in Bohane that families from the Northside Rises will butt heads against families from the Back Trace" (5). The inhabitants of Bohane are from all over the world, entering the city through the docks, and still these geographical categorizations are important. Barry is responding to and representing what Jolanta A. Drzewiecka and Thomas K. Nakayama in their article "City Sites: Postmodern Urban Space and the Communication of Identity" call the "tremendous changes in the international landscape," and this shows itself on the descriptions of the streetscape of Bohane—Barry is playing out this renegotiation between identities and locations:

> As multinational interactions and interconnections multiply and accelerate, it is no longer possible to maintain a modernist imagery of distinct cultural identities nested within a fixed configuration of culture, nation, and space. Cultures and ethnic identities are not isomorphic with particular spaces [20].

When Barry describes the streets of the city, they are a mishmash of everything, old and new, native and foreign, gothic and postmodern. Maebh Long describes this in one of the only articles about Bohane:

> A city of streetwalkers, a neo-noir urban hell of insomniacs and addicts who pound the pavement while the corrupt police hide in the shadows. Bohane's isolation renders it an aggressively independent frontier city, and its inhabitants treat those from Haiti and Tipperary as equally foreign. The rest of Ireland lies outside the insulating, isolating bogs of Big Nothin' [3].

De Valera Street is one such space where this mutli-layered, multi-ethnic, multi-cultural, multi-age city gathers together:

> There are soothsayers. There are purveyors of goat's blood cures for marital difficulties. There are dark caverns of record stores specialising in ancient calypso 78s—oh we have an old wiggle to the hip in Bohane, if you get us going at all. There are palmists. There are knackers selling combination socket wrench sets. Discount threads are flogged from suitcases mounted on bakers' pallets, there are cages of live poultry, and trinket stores devoted gaudily to the worship of the Sweet Baba Jay. There are herbalists, and veg stalls, and poolhalls. Such is the life of De Valera Street [32].

The references that Barry chooses to represent the fictional Bohane of 2053 are an uncanny, postmodern mix of the old and the new. He weaves images of a pseudo-dystopian future city with elements of a busy market town of a hundred years ago decentering and confusing the reader.

Dystopia and Utopia

Latham and Hicks describe the dystopic city that emerged as coinciding with and responding to an "outburst of utopia writing" in the second half of the nineteenth century. This "dystopia version" of the city they say depicted "baleful imaginary societies in which cities themselves feature as the main symbols of negative possibility, as spaces of oppression, blight and ruin" (163). They claim that these "grim ominous visions" now outnumber any "rosier alternatives." However, this machine-driven false utopia of Latham and Hicks is not one realized in *City of Bohane* (167) nor is it closer to the post World War II rural utopia. Bohane refuses to adhere to the rules and does not discuss environmental concerns or overpopulation, as seen in other utopic/dystopic urban representations. All Barry tells us is that the "lost time" is a time before 2053 as a result of something that happened in the last twenty years and now "juice" is at a premium and technology is nowhere to be seen.

Elements of Bohane's clash of the clans do tie in with Latham and Hicks' discussion of J.G. Ballard's *High Rise*, where the city, like the tower block, has "balkanised into clannish factions, enforced by vigilante violence [...] regressing to primal savagery" but that is where the similarity ends (170). This is not a discussion of class, and while the Beauvista, where Logan Hartnett lives, does suggest a classed city, that divide is not the cause of the violence or the "lost-time."

Barry also blends elements of cyberpunk and steampunk, while refusing to engage with the high-tech narratives of both. The city is filled with noir influences, from the detailed descriptions of how the characters dress to the "clandestine scenes and criminal subcultures" (172). The entire city of Bohane is located on the edge of the country, isolated from the "Nation Beyond"; it is a "marginal milieu inhabited by con men, grifters, loners, and freaks" engaging in the "traditional noir vices of gambling, drugs and sex." Steampunk's "retro-futuristic" notions can be seen especially in Girly Hartnett's movie nights; she would watch old movies "[a]s often as the hotel had juice enough to run a projector" on a pull down screen (64). But Barry refuses to allow Bohane to be categorized by any one genre.

The people of Bohane love their city, they have huge pride, and they do not want to live anywhere else. They look forward to the bubbling violence erupting, take pride in their spirit and strength, but worry about how the Nation Beyond will now react to their latest violent spree. Barry here is making reference to the past representations of Limerick, where he lived, which during its gangland days was referred to as "Stab City." (In fact, the Vintage publication features a knife on the front cover.) The national view of Limerick was often lambasted in the local media, as the citizens were keen to reinvent and regenerate the image of the city, just as the people of Bohane are keen to control the message they portray in the papers. The editor of the local paper tries to massage the headlines to keep the Bohane Authority on the right side of the Nation Beyond. He tells Logan Hartnett to keep the city calm until negotiations with the NB are complete:

> "[…] This place got a bad enough name as things stand, Logan."
> "You're saying that the Authority wishes for the Calm to persist, Dom, until such a time as the NB tit has been successfully massaged?"
> "That's very nicely put, Mr Hartnett" [40].

This mixing of the postmodern and the real adds to the layers of the novel and represents a self-conscious city that mirrors writers like Auster or Calvino. Nick Bentley, in his chapter "Postmodern Cities," describes this metropolis as "a labyrinthine enigma that metaphorically stands in for the dizzying plurality of contemporary urban living" while also engaging with postmodern "ambiguity" making the city "darkly exotic and alluring" (175). The inhabitants of Bohane mirror the genre of the book itself, rejecting categorization:

> Yes and here they came, all the big-armed women and all the low-sized butty fellas. Here came the sullen Polacks and the Back Trace crones. Here came the natty Africans and the big lunks of bog-spawn polis. Here came the pikey blow-ins and the washed-up Madagascars. Here came the women of the Rises down the 98 Steps to buy tabs and tights and mackerel—of such combinations was life in the flatblock circles sustained. Here came the Endeavour Avenue suits for a sconce at ruder life. The Smoketown tushies were between trick-cycles and had crossed the footbridge to take joe and cake in their gossiping covens. The Fancy-boy wannabes swanned about in their finery and tip-tapped a rhythm with their clicker'd heels [31].

Barry has created a plural city, and that plurality filters down through the topography and into the inhabitants. Their plurality is not just in their ethnicity but also in their fashion, dressed in a combination of styles as they "swanned about in their finery" through the hyperreal Bohane.

Gothic

This postmodern city is not just postmodern. There are elements of the gothic mixed in, and as I have mentioned before, this is often an Irish trope. The Gothic is a popular Irish genre, as it combines notions of invasion, fear, the "big house," and the unknown, which complement the Irish experience. Stoker, Le Fanu, Bowen, Banville—all gothic writers from Ireland—engaged with similar notions of rumor, secrets, violence, and identity as Barry does here in Bohane.

The postmodern and the gothic fit well together as they both share similar concerns. Siobhan Kilfeather in her work on Irish Gothic novels says it relates to the famine and the fragmentation of the bodies—the "morselisation" of bodies is both "ultra-realist as well as ultra-fantastic" (88). Long suggests that it is a fascination with melancholia that attracts the Irish writers to the gothic while Imhof proposes that it leads us to experimentation (173), and this is where contemporary gothic writers like Banville and Barry do well. They both turn to hybridity in their writing; it is often fragmented, gothic, and postmodern at the same time. As Derek Hand suggests, "the resulting instability is a reflection of how genres and forms from elsewhere must be molded and shaped to the peculiarities of the Irish experience" (18). To reflect the fragmented city of Bohane, Barry has to turn to a hybrid of gothic and postmodern. This is, after all, an Irish writer, writing about an Irish city, a pseudo-fictional city where tradition and nostalgia are seeping from the bog that surrounds it. The combination suits the "peculiarities" of the Irish experience—the Bohane experience.

Barry uses the postmodern and the gothic, creating a hybridity which works well with his fragmented text. The mixture of the unreal and the real, blending elements of Limerick and Cork with the Surreal, creates an uncanny city built on this relationship between its fragmented parts. The resulting novel is an Irish one that explores where postmodern and gothic meet. Maria Beville, in her book on Postmodern Gothic, explains this hybridity well: "[S]ome of the issues that are explored separately in Gothic and postmodernist fiction, are one and the same, namely: crises of identity, fragmentation of the self, the darkness of the human psyche, and the philosophy of being and knowing" (53).

The layers of the city are unknown and multiple, and this merging of postmodern and gothic is particularly obvious in the peat bogs that surround it. The city is powered by these bogs and they must excavate the peat. The citizens, so obsessed with the nostalgia that calls to them from the ground, are literally digging up the past. As Old Mannion notes on his walk through Big Nothin':

> These times, the city of Bohane was powered largely on its turf, and the bog had been cut away and reefed everywhere. Who knew what passages to its underworld had been disturbed? The bog's occult nature had been interfered with, its body left scarred, its wounds open, and might this also be a source of the Bohane taint? [116].

The scars are open and obvious and seem to be causing this taint; a curse left waiting to be fulfilled. It is exceptionally gothic that they dig up and fragment the bog and burn it, unearthing the physiological taint underneath, harking back to Siobhan Kilfeather's morselized bodies, to the Irish obsession with the past detailed in Hand.

Time Is Fluid

The postmodern hyperreality has fragmented the chronological flow of the narrative. In Bohane, the past infringes on the present, and the characters, like the narrative, can shift through time. Both Macu Harnett and the Gant Broderick easily slip back into their memories, into nostalgia for the past. This nostalgia haunts their present and clings to their futures.

What the Gant Broderick wants, what has drawn him back to Bohane, is an image of the city and the eighteen-year-old girl that he loved, Macu. Short for Immaculata, the daughter of a sailor from Portugal, she is now married to his uncanny doppelgänger, the leader of the Hartnett Fancy. The Gant in love is an image from his past, a simulacrum. Macu and the city become a Baudrillardian simulacrum, and he will never get back to the original image. When he sees her for the first time in twenty-five years, he realizes that this time is gone, that this image of his three-week relationship can never be reclaimed, only remembered:

> Every word that spilled from her spun him back to the lost-time. It was better if he didn't look at her—better to let the dream persist. [...] The dark girl he had known resurfaced, for an instant, in her glance but he knew now—he saw it with migraine intensity—that their time was gone. [...] The firelight traced out the lines of her aged skin. She was no longer what he needed or wanted. Reality infected him with its sourness and truth. (142–45).

Nostalgia, Barry tells us, "was a many-hooked lure" in Bohane and the Gant "had fallen victim to our native reminiscence" once he returned. As he walks to see Macu, we are told, "He could not settle. The level of drooling lust was unspeakable. Nostalgia was off the fucking charts" (129). The title of the chapter adds to the meta-layered textual nostalgia: "There Is a Light That Never Goes Out" references the title of what would be a sixty-year-old song from The Smiths. As Barry said in an interview, "the people are preoccupied with the past. It's a very Irish thing. The romance of Bohane is a romance with the lost-time" (Libran). For Barry, this is an Irish novel dealing with an Irish experience. The past is still a contested space as Ireland comes to terms with its colonial history. And in 2053 this preoccupation with the past, a history that emanates from the very site of this conflict—the land—continues.

This obsession with the past is an Irish concern as Derek Hand discusses in his study on another Irish postmodern writer, John Banville. The Irish postcolonial history has led to a sense that the past is always overshadowing the present, and, in Barry's case, the future streets and inhabitants of Bohane. Hand claims there is a sense that the Irish are "unable to move on, debilitated and held back. […] In Irish life and culture, this has led to a constant debate—battle even—concerning the past and its significance in the present" (25). The Gant Broderick is unable to escape his past. Despite leaving Ireland, he cannot escape the "lure" of the past that calls him back to Bohane. He becomes, as Hand describes the Irish, "debilitated" by his nostalgia, his need to revisit the past.

This battle plays out on the pages of *City of Bohane* as the sense of nostalgia seems to come from the streets. There is, in Bohane, "no way to escape the tingling of [the] past; it was ever-present, like tiny fires that burned beneath the skin" (214). In an interview, Kevin Barry has said this story could have as easily been set in 1853 as 2053. Time does not matter. What does matter are these "ever-present […] tiny fires" that connect these people to each other, to the urban geography of Bohane. Throughout the layers of time, history, and nostalgia are invisible threads tying these people to their city.

Like nostalgia, time is not tangible, but is, as Barry tells us in the text, fluid: "In the Bohane creation, time comes loose, there is a curious fluidity, the past seeps into the future, and the moment itself as it passes is the hardest to grasp" (60). This is also true of the structure of the novel, which offers us a fluid, fragmented chronology. Barry offers us glimpses into snippets of time. The novel is divided into sections October, December, and then finally April. We do not know what has happened between these sections, in the same way we are left in the dark regarding the digital apocalypse or what happened to create this new feature. Like the change, this is the lost time; it is unspoken, unknown, gone.

The residents of Bohane claim many things are gone with the lost time, and they often refer to traditions from the lost time. Like the Irish, mentioned by Barry and Hand, they are obsessed with the past. It is this obsession with time that brings Gant back to Bohane, to relive his past, to recreate his "lost time." Throughout the novel they rely on traditions that come from the lost time like the whistle that blows and marks the start of the feud:

> The whistle was a plain melody that rose once and then fell, that was melancholy, that was sourced from the lost-time in Bohane, that had a special power to it—a power that I cannot even begin to explain to those of you unfortunate enough not to come from this place [148].

The lost time has a power over them. The past still can call to them and influence them. It has a power over them that only residents of Bohane know. The use of the phrase "those of you unfortunate enough not to come from this place" is interesting, reminding us that they may be engaged in dystopic violence, but this city is their utopia.

A Digital Apocalypse

We do not know what happens that makes Bohane a futuristic city by 2053, why Girly Hartnett can only watch her movies when the hotel has "juice" for her projector, why they power the city solely from the bog, why "juice" is in high demand, or what the juice is. And neither does Barry as he told *The Paris Review*:

> With *City of Bohane* I tried to let loose. And in lots of different ways. I only realized as I was writing the first couple of chapters that it was set in the future. That was a very liberating thing—I realized I could do whatever the fuck I wanted.
>
> It's an invented place but its language is sprung directly from working class speech in the cities I grew up in, Limerick and Cork [qtd. in Lee].

As Barry points out, this is an imagined space rooted in real space—Cork and Limerick—using dialects and slang from these locations. The streets of Bohane carry with them the sounds and sense of these real cities, like a ghostly undertone. Consciously and subconsciously, physically and mentally, there is a spectrality to the city streets, to this fragmented space, something of which the characters themselves are aware. This is not just manifested in the physical cityscape, or even the bog, where nostalgia rises up from the peat, but it is even in the wind, which carries with it its own philosophy:

> When a wind blows in such ferocious gusts as the Big Nothin' hardwind, and when it blows forty-nine weeks out of the year, the effect is not physical only but [...] philosophical. It is difficult to keep a firm hold of one's consciousness in such a wind. The mind is walloped from its train of thought by the constant assaults of wind. The result is a skittish, temperamental people with a tendency towards odd turns of logic. Such were (and are) the people of the Northside Rises [25].

Again Barry calls on nostalgia, "such were (and are) the people." The people of Bohane cannot deny their location, their history, just as they cannot ignore the uncanny elements of other real working class dock cities. However, it is not just a physical uncanniness or spectrality—this city reflects its people as Drzewiecka and Nakayama tell us: "Fragmented urban space combines elements of time and place that people use to negotiate their multiple identities" (21). If the postmodern city is designed to mirror its inhabitants, the people who negotiate its streets, then the people of Bohane are also fragmented and diverse, exuding elements of nostalgia and spectrality.

Gant Broderick is one such layered person. Barry tells us that he is many versions of himself. He is a hyper-layered individual, he is "pikey," he is trace, he is bog, he is Bohane. Like the city, he is fragmented, created from tangible and intangible elements. And like the city, it is difficult to know who you will get. In the words of Girly Hartnett, you "can never quite get a fix on the fuckers" (64).

The Flaneur

Bohane's spectral overtone allows the many flaneurs to traverse the many realities in a location that is no longer distinctly Irish, but gothic, postmodern, utopian, and dystopian. Looking at what constitutes a postmodern city, we must move away from modernist tropes of dystopian and utopian locations, towards a much more hyperreal city, filled with simulacra, shifting perspectives and mutable representations. It is Lyotardian in its eclecticism, or urban space filled with Baudrillardian simulacra. The city of simulacra is best explained by Maria Beville as an urban space that can transport individual or multiple flaneurs through the hyperreal streets and spaces:

> Focusing on the city as a plural space, a complex of hidden and liminal sites, the city in postmodernist literature is effectively presented as a ghostly locus of the uncanny: decentred, fragmented and defined by the otherness encountered in the crowd and in the simulacra of signs that swarm our field of perception [14].

The signs that swarm around the city are familiar and strange, filled with nostalgia. As a result, there is a sense of the uncanny about this plural city. When Julian Wolfreys describes the idea of the uncanny city, he talks of how urban and uncanny are related, especially when we think of the urban location in terms such as dwelling, building, and home. Directly translated, Bohane means a little dwelling place; this city is homey, and for some residents its uncanny nature calls them home, and for others it becomes an unwelcoming metropolis. When we translate Freud's *uncanny* as "unhomely," a place that is strangely familiar, it becomes all the more relevant for Bohane. When Gant Broderick returns home to Bohane, it becomes something he cannot reach—like the image of Macu he cannot reach, that sense of Bohane he remembers.

His nostalgia clouds his current vision. The postmodern city has become this liminal space, containing a habitual topography of buildings, people and streets that remain unknown or uncannily familiar.

While Wolfreys used the film *Don't Look Now* to explain the idea of the uncanny city, its relevance to Bohane is similar. There is a sense as we follow the returned Gant Broderick through this city that nothing is the same for him, that he is clinging to the past in a city that seemingly radiates nostalgia from its very seams:

> [E]very alley leading on to another just like it, opens the city not as knowledgeable place but as abyss in which the iterability of the self-same only serves as a reminder that nothing is the same, and that each and every street is wholly other, in which one comes to find oneself adrift, without bearings, lost. [...] Nothing is to be found, nothing known, and anxiety twinned with obsession is exponentially generated in the face of the uncanny persistence of resistance to any epistemological mode that will comfort or make familiar [170].

Gant tries and fails to find this comfort in either the people or the streets. It is all vaguely familiar, but it is, as Wolfreys describes, "anxiety twinned with obsession." He has a vision of a utopia that is dystopic. Long describes the cityscape beautifully as a "claustrophobic labyrinth and an embodiment of melancholic space; a twisting, intestinal mapping of half-acknowledged yearnings and regrets" (3). She, like Barry, personifies the city. It is part of the people just as the people are part of it—it is a symbiotic relationship.

It is a city aware, alive, watching its inhabitants, complete with a gothic personification. The windows of the city are like "brilliant, unseeing eyes" (31) surrounded by an "evil air" (5), which has caused troubled lungs, the "sweet badness" from the river (3), a city that "reasserts" its shape (276). The voices of the dead and the living mingle through the topography of the city, "carried on the river's air," which "had in mysterious ways the quality of silence, for it blocked out all else; it mesmerised" (276). Even in death, you cannot leave Bohane. The dead become part of the city, leaving liminal messages for the current residents. The past is buried in the buildings, in the river, in the bog—it is inescapable. The city acts as a ghostly locale, a gothic big house that scars the landscape and reminds the residents that the secrets of the past could be uncovered at any time.

Nick Bentley, in his work on the postmodern city in literature, explains that it is "the postmodern flaneur or flanese who attempts to disentangle its multiplicity of texts" of the plural city (176). In Bohane, all the characters seem to act as a flaneur for us—another nostalgic harking back to urban and rural, the spectral undertones of Limerick, the layers of American noir culture, and the blending of the many traditional, clichéd, and modern Irish identities. Long calls these flaneurs "vicious," "urban," and "rural dreamers" who follow a route "tread of memory and regret" (4). As Ferdinand Lion says,

"Whoever sets foot in a city feels caught up as in a web of dreams, where the most remote past is linked to the events of today. One house allies with another, no matter what period they come from, and a street is born" (qtd. in Benjamin 435).

From the opening pages, Logan Hartnett guides us on our journey through this city that is both dystopia and utopia. This is his turf, he rules the clans and factions of the city, and he patrols the city like a flaneur, wandering through the streets to garner the atmosphere of its peoples. When the Gant returns to the city, he, too, secretly walks the streets, mirroring Logan Hartnett in an unnoticed twinning of the flaneury of both characters.

And finally the dystopia futuristic flaneur, the unnamed narrator of the story, acts as a flaneur of the past, of the nostalgia that Bohane clings to throughout the novel. He allows the citizens of Bohane to access this past through CCTV, bringing together Benjamin's mechanical reproduction and flaneur in one entity. He runs the Ancient and Historical Bohane Film Society frequented by men who want to "reach again for the whimsical days of their youth and for the city as it was back then" (178). There, the people of Bohane can watch old silent footage going back to the 30's of the streets of the city, while an old 78 plays on the turntable. As Long says, he is a collector of "memories and desires" he "assembles the past through his possessions" offering the people "a directly visual access to the past though his security tapes, and operates as an amalgamation of flaneur, who walks by and with the people of the crowd" (13). He allows them to virtually walk through the streets of old and encourages that "taint" of nostalgia so present in Bohane.

Doppelgänger

While the uncanny resemblances of Limerick, Cork, and Bohane cannot be denied, there are a number of other doppelgängers located throughout the text adding to the gothic plurality of the book. Most obviously are Logan Hartnett and Gant Broderick: "one broad and densely packed, the other tall and slender" (231). Other obvious connections are made between the young Jenni Chang, the silent incumbent leader of the fancy at the end of the novel, and Macu Hartnett, who are both tied to the male protagonists, although the dualism between young Jenni and the elderly Girly Hartnett cannot be denied either.

Both Gant and Logan mirror each other throughout the novel: their movements through the streets are similar, their relationships with Macu, their connection to the city. Despite their different appearances—Logan, whose clothes and style are important to him versus the unkempt nomadic Gant—they act as a reflection of each other as they finally meet on the eve of May at the Supper Room: "[They] both rested their forearms on the bar counter, and they both stared straight ahead, and they both rotated their glasses slowly with the tips of their fingers—each unconsciously mimicked the other" (231). Their mirrored movements echo the many similarities between these characters. The uncanny doubling of their gestures matches their similar relationships with Macu and Jenni, and duplication just further highlights the spectrality and fragmentation of Bohane.

The symbiotic relationship between henchmen Fucker Burke and Wolfie Stanners acts as another form of doppelgänger, but other more interesting relationships which play similar roles involve Jenni Chang and the interplay between her, Macu, and Girly Hartnett. Jenni, like Macu, connects Logan and the Gant, while Jenni's relationship with Girly is another important study. Representing three generations of Bohane, these women all play a central role in the power struggles of the city. Their relationships to the men of Bohane are compelling too.

Macu and Jenni's connection with both Logan and the Gant make them mirror images of each other, playing the men off each other for their own goals. While Jenni searches for power, Macu looks for self-contentment. Jenni engages in a casual sexual relationship with both men, but interestingly Macu, although married to Logan, sleeps with neither. Macu's teenage three-week relationship with the Gant was innocent, and her childless marriage to Logan seems to have soured. At the end, Jenni emerges victorious and Macu disappears. Ideas around age, power, sexuality, and fertility all abound in this uncanny interplay. Their strength is relative, as is their connection with both Gant and Logan; as one character gains strength or position, the other loses hers, more an antibiosis twinning than a symbiotic one.

Conclusion

City of Bohane is definitely an Irish novel that plays with its hybridity. Its fragmented and fluid use of postmodern, gothic, utopian, dystopian, retro, and futuristic references leaves us with an eclectic city of the future. Bohane is a physical cityscape that shapes and impacts its residents, that voyeuristically encourages violence in a post-digital age where Big Brother is still watching, and that somehow manages to encapsulate the difficulty of representing the Irish identity.

Barry also decenters the reader further by playing with style. He refuses to adhere to expectations of dystopia, gothic, or steampunk. Bohane is loved and hated in equal measure by its inhabitants. Technology is all but gone. Our references and expectations are unreliable. There are recognizable fragments throughout, but like the bog that surrounds Bohane it is unstable and seeping with nostalgia. Barry plays with the reader, and, as he told *The Paris Review*, he realized he could do "whatever the fuck" he wanted, and liberated himself from any rules (Lee 2013).

The streets of Bohane are steeped in spectrality because of the choices Barry makes. His decision to pinpoint a year while simultaneously using images from a range of timeframes confuses the reader. As a result, "time comes loose" for the reader also (60). It is another undependable sign, one more simulacrum. The multi-layered effect of mixing cultural references and an uncannily familiar cityscape creates a city of specters and half-seen signs of something vaguely familiar. Could this be Limerick? Just like the inhabitants, you can "never quite get a fix" on much in Bohane (64).

WORKS CITED

Barry, Kevin. *City of Bohane*. London: Vintage, 2012. Print.
Benjamin, Walter, et al. *The Arcades Project*. Ed. Rolf Tiedemann. 2nd ed. Cambridge: Harvard University Press, 1999. Print.
Bentley, Nick. "Postmodern Cities." *The Cambridge Companion to the City in Literature*. Ed. K.R. McNamara. Cambridge: Cambridge University Press, 2014. 175–87. Print.
Beville, Maria. *Gothic-Postmodernism: Voicing the Terrors of Postmodernity*. Amsterdam: Rodopi, 2009. Print.
_____. "Zones of Uncanny Spectrality: The City in Postmodern Literature." *English Studies* 94.5 (2013): 603–17. Web. 22 April 2017.
Drzewiecka, Jolanta A., and Thomas K. Nakayama. "City Sites: Postmodern Urban Space and the Communication of Identity." *Southern Communication Journal* 64.1 (1998): 20–31. Web. 22 April 2017.
Hamill, Pete. "'City of Bohane,' by Kevin Barry." 2016. Web. 17 June 2016.
Hand, Derek. *John Banville: Exploring Fictions*. Dublin, Ireland: The Liffey Press, 2002. Print.
Imhof, Rüdiger, ed. *Contemporary Irish Novelists*. Tübingen, Germany: Gunter Narr Verlag, 1990. Print.
Kilfeather, Siobhan. "The Gothic Novel." *The Cambridge Companion to the Irish Novel*. Ed. John Wilson Foster. Cambridge: Cambridge University Press, 2006. 79- 96. Print.
Latham, Rob, and Jeff Hicks. "Urban Dystopias." *The Cambridge Companion to the City in Literature*. Ed K.R. McNamara. Cambridge: Cambridge University Press, 2014. 163–74. Print.
Lee, Jonathan. *Jumping Off a Cliff: An Interview with Kevin Barry*. The Paris Review 12 Nov. 2013. Web. 17 June 2016.
libranwriter. "Kevin Barry in Pearse Street Library." Libran Writer (Lia Mills). 10 June 2013. Web. 17 June 2016.
Long, Maebh. "Black Bile in Bohane: Kevin Barry and Melancholia." *Textual Practice* 2 Nov. 2015. 1–18. Web. 17 June 2016.
Lyotard, Jean-François, et al. *The Postmodern Explained: Correspondence, 1982–1985*. 3rd ed. Minneapolis: University of Minnesota Press, 1992. Print.
McNamara, Kevin R., ed. *The Cambridge Companion to the City in Literature*. Cambridge: Cambridge University Press, 2014. Print.
Wolfreys, Julian. "The Urban Uncanny: The City, the Subject and Ghostly Modernity." *Uncanny Modernity: Cultural Theories, Modern Anxieties*. Ed. Jo Collins and John Jervis. London: Palgrave, 2008. 168–80. Print.

Interrogating Utopia
On Colin MacInnes' Absolute Beginners

ANDREW HAMMOND

Britain's recovery from the Second World War was so pronounced by the late 1940s that, as one historian describes it, "[t]here was much utopianism in the air" (Morgan 28). Only several months after the war ended, Clement Attlee's Labour Party swept to victory in a landslide election, promising that there would be no return to the injustices of the 1930s. Some twenty percent of the economy was nationalized, full employment became a government policy, and "cradle to grave security" was ensured by the Welfare State. Believing that they had found a "third way" between Soviet communism and U.S. capitalism, many in the Labour Party were euphoric. Hugh Dalton, the Chancellor of the Exchequer, was particularly upbeat. "That first sensation, tingling and triumphant, was of a new society to be built," he later wrote, "We felt exalted, dedicated, walking on air, walking with destiny" (qtd. in Shaw 19).

The benefits of state intervention were clear in the 1950s when, despite the defeat of Labour by the Conservatives in 1951, the tenets of Keynesian social democracy were retained and Britain entered a decade of relative affluence. Between 1951 and 1961, industry expanded, foreign trade improved, wages doubled, unemployment fell to a historic low, and consumer goods became widely available for the first time. With the extension of centralized planning from social reform to urban regeneration, initiating a flurry of industrial and residential building, the country's future seemed bright.[1] In the latter half of the decade, the Conservative Prime Minister was claiming that "most of our people have never had it so good," and even sections of the Labour Party were admitting that "[w]e stand on the threshold of mass abundance."[2] Yet the so-called "age of affluence" was not as secure as politicians claimed. As John Hill points out, the utopian declarations took no account of the persistence of economic hardship, and, as such, "affluence" was partly a political myth, one that aimed to "cover over the gaps between real inequalities and the promised utopia of equality-for-all" (10). It is this deconstruction of 1950s idealism that informs one of the most important anti-utopian texts of the period, Colin MacInnes' *Absolute Beginners* (1959).

By this stage in literary history, the genre of speculative writing was losing confidence in the human potential for improvement. In preceding centuries, the literary consideration of the state of perfection, initiated by Thomas More's *Utopia* (1516), had dominated textual visions of the future, expressing a belief in social progress even if perfection itself was deemed impossible. Such optimism was difficult to sustain in the twentieth century. The First World War, the Great Depression, the horrors of Stalinism and Nazism, and the carnage of the Second World War all put paid to the dream of advancement. By the early decades of the Cold War, when the world faced the prospect of nuclear obliteration, it was no surprise that "the positive utopia had been displaced in the system of literary genres available to novelists," as James W. Bittner has argued.[3] The skepticism was manifest not only in the decline in utopian fiction, but also in the wide-ranging opposition to utopian thought that now appeared in its dystopian opposite.

With social, economic, and military planners summoning up such abominations as the Third Reich and Mutually Assured Destruction, any idealistic blueprint for social change was viewed as a threat to humanity. "During the Cold War," Fredric Jameson comments, "Utopia had come to designate a program which [...] betrayed a will to uniformity and the ideal purity of a perfect system that had to be imposed by force on its imperfect and reluctant subjects."[4] The point is extended into the literary sphere by Derek Maus' work on dystopian fiction of the second half of the twentieth century. Focusing on Soviet-Russian and American literatures, Maus finds relevance in Gary Saul Morson's categorization of dystopianism as an "anti-genre" or "parodic genre": that is, as a form of writing that "establish[es] a *parodic* relation between the anti-generic work and the works and traditions of another genre, the target genre" (115; Morson's italics). After surveying the reductionist and conformist nature of Cold War idealism and the binaristic rhetoric that enforced it, Maus argues that "the prevalence of dystopian and anti-utopian sentiment in Russian and American fiction is a parodic-satirical response intended to subvert the utopianism rampant in both superpower cultures" (108). In this sense, the genre under attack may be a literary one, but may equally be the non-literary prescriptions found in state-sanctioned works of history, economics, and political science. Although critics occasionally distinguish between dystopian and anti-utopian writings, the counter-discursive strain is so prevalent in the former that the terms shade into one another, making the state of *dys-topos* (the "bad place") partly conditional on attempts at *eu-topos* (the "good place").[5]

The heightened anxieties of modern dystopian authors are also seen in their tendency to reduce textual reference to the future. Although typically defined as a genre that speculates on the consequences of contemporary historical trends, dystopianism came to view the ideological dangers of the twentieth century as so imminent and wide-ranging that many texts refused to distinguish between future possibilities and current realities. As Philip Stevick points out, the key task of the genre has always been to create "a sense of continuity with the historical situation of the author's present time," a task that requires allusion to that time to communicate "the writer's conviction that his [sic] imaginative vision is taking place" (234, 235). In an earlier era, this allusion could be largely symbolic. G.K. Chesterton's *The Napoleon of Notting Hill* (1904), Aldous Huxley's *Brave New World* (1932), and H.G. Wells' *The Time Machine* (1894–95) displace the events of the narratives by 80 years, 600 years, and 800,774 years, respectively, periods at such a temporal distance that their warnings can appear indirect or abstract. After 1945, the frequent reduction of the gap between present and future, or between the emergence of social degradation and its absolute fulfillment, was a clear indication of worsening conditions.

Indeed, a number of critics have argued that futurism is not a defining feature of the modern genre. For example, M. Keith Booker's critical studies of dystopianism, which he defines as "that literature which situates itself in direct opposition to utopian thought," suggests that the field of study can be broadened to include "[v]irtually any work that contains an element of social criticism" (3). The point is supported by literary production both in the western bloc, with its attacks on consumerism, media manipulation, and governmental propaganda, and in the eastern bloc, with its searing accounts of incarceration, displacement, and terror. For Erika Gottlieb, the social criticism found in eastern European writing was neither fantasy nor speculation but "an accurate reflection of the 'worst of all possible worlds' experienced as a historical reality" (17). In this way, the focus on the dystopian present can be viewed as the apex of anti-utopianism, targeting a contemporary structure of belief and practice "that complies in its essential features with [...] the hypothetical societies of the Western classics of dystopian fiction" and "refus[ing] to envisage a world worse than the existing world of reality" (17, 5).

The trend towards anti-utopianism is perfectly illustrated in British literature. It is here that some of the most important works of speculative fiction have been produced, from Thomas More's originary text to the early twentieth-century dystopias of H.G. Wells and Aldous Huxley which, along with such lesser-known novels as Katharine Burdekin's *Swastika Night* (1937), Rex Warner's *The Aerodrome* (1941), and C.S. Lewis' *That Hideous Strength* (1945), helped to shift dystopianism into a position of dominance. By the early years of the Cold War, dystopian writing had developed into a major outlet for literary reflections on national and international politics. From the 1940s to the 1980s, over fifty mainstream authors used the genre to express anxieties about contemporary trends, amongst them Doris Lessing, Angela Carter, Ian McEwan, Roald Dahl, Kingsley Amis, Alexander Cordell, L.P. Hartley, Alan Sillitoe, and Fay Weldon. It was not uncommon for their work to reveal the influence of George Orwell's *Nineteen Eighty-Four* (1949), a novel that shaped the British dystopian imagination for the rest of the Cold War. In the famous tale, Britain has been absorbed into a tyrannical U.S.-led power bloc whose authority rests on a single horrific principle: "'One does not establish a dictatorship in order to safeguard a revolution; one makes the revolution in order to establish the dictatorship,'" a party member explains, "'The object of persecution is persecution. The object of torture is torture. The object of power is power'" (227). The outcome may be "'the exact opposite of the stupid hedonistic Utopias that the old reformers imagined,'" as the party member continues, but the ideal of absolute power is no less utopian in the minds of its adherents (230).

The dystopian works published after *Nineteen Eighty-Four* continued to explore the ideological foundations, as much as the material outcomes, of centralized planning. These included Soviet communism in Kingsley Amis' *Russian Hide and Seek* (1980), socialism in Emma Tennant's *The Last of the Country House Murders* (1974), and nuclearism in Maggie Gee's *The Burning Book* (1983), as well as the key institutions of Cold War conflict, such as the secret services in Adrian Mitchell's *The Bodyguard* (1970) and propaganda agencies in Angela Carter's *The Infernal Desire Machines of Doctor Hoffman* (1972). Even the discourse of affluence that dominated British political life in the 1950s and 1960s was satirized in Anthony Burgess' *A Clockwork Orange* (1962), in which an implied period of economic plenty leads directly to anomie, violence and tyranny. In short, speculative writing in Britain had evolved into what Chris Ferns calls a "parodic counter-genre" that "satirizes both society as it exists [...] and the utopian aspiration to transform it" (xii, 109).

The implausibility of utopian faith is the central theme of MacInnes' *Absolute Beginners*. Set in London in the summer of 1958, the novel describes four months in the life of the unnamed first-person narrator, a working-class teenager whose picaresque journeys around the jazz clubs, drinking dens and coffee bars of inner London, and animated encounters with a thriving, leisured youth, seems to crystallize what Peter Hennessy terms the "'having-it-so-good' period" (245). Indeed, one of the few critical studies to consider the novel in detail views MacInnes' vision of the 1950s as the literary equivalent of official utopianism. Paula Derdiger draws links between the apparent idealism of *Absolute Beginners* and that of the architects, economists, town planners, and political policymakers tasked with redesigning and rebuilding urban space after 1945, particularly the advocates of New Brutalism. An instance of the post-war resurgence of architectural modernism, this was a British-led school of stark, geometrical concrete structures that utilized the new technologies of the 1950s and 1960s, not only in the construction of the buildings but also in their interior design and functionality, with a lavish range of built-in appliances offering "techno-utopian visions of the future."[6]

Compounding the utopianism was the overlap between New Brutalism and centralized civic planning. Most obviously, their shared commitment to "total environment," or to the zoning of cities into spaces of work, leisure, residence, and transportation, suggested an outlook more ethical than aesthetic, raising "questions about how people should live rather than questions about what their living spaces should look like" (Derdiger 55). It is this prescription on urban lifestyle that Derdiger finds so resonant. Judging MacInnes' message to be "the freedom to move and consume at will," Derdiger considers *Absolute Beginners* "irreverently optimistic" and "undeniably utopian" in its pursuit of a "future-orientated aesthetic derived from youth culture, transnational consumerism and popular culture" (54, 63, 60, 54). The present essay will take issue with this interpretation, arguing that the novel draws on official utopianism to test its limits, finding those limits in the multiple injustices and exclusions which shadowed post-war development.[7]

The novel's reputation for positivity tends to be evidenced by earlier sections of the narrative, where the focal character, at this point eighteen, describes his life in the districts of Notting Hill, Belgravia, Pimlico, and Soho. His journeys around London by taxi and scooter capture the freedom and mobility that many young people were enjoying, as does the spending power that he achieves through self-employment as a photographer. This inspires a crude philosophy of "gracious living," or "money power," the central precepts of which are "to work in your own time and not somebody else's" and to avoid association with "the great community of the mugs: the vast majority of squares who are exploited" (16, 43, 16). His individualism is enacted in the new spaces of youth consumption and displayed through what he calls "my full teenage drag": "the grey pointed alligator casuals, the pink neon pair of ankle crêpe nylon-stretch, my Cambridge blue glove-fit jeans, a vertical-striped happy shirt revealing my lucky neck-charm on its chain, and my Roman-cut short-arse jacket" (34). The commitment to material accumulation is introduced in the novel's opening scene, where the narrator and his friend Wizard, widely respected for being "the number one hustler of the capital," enter a high-rise department store and ascend "the white stair to the glass garden under the top roof":

I must explain the Wiz and I never came to this store to buy anything except, as today, a smoke-salmon sandwich and ice coffee. But in the first place, we have the opportunity to see the latest furnishings and fabrics, just like some married couple, and also to have the splendid outlook over London, the most miraculous I know in the whole city, and quite unknown to other nuisance-values of our age, in fact to everyone, it seems, except these elderly female Chelsea peasants who come up there for their elevenses [13, 9, 9].

The futuristic idealism of the passage ("glass garden," "circular plate glass," "glorious panorama") is linked to working-class access to privilege, as well as to the displacement of the traditional elite, relegated now to "Chelsea peasants" (9–10).

The narrator's symbolic and literal rise in status is even more resonant in the light of his family's past. This is a constant and traumatic reference point for his father, who laments the depression of the 1930s, which was not only a time of "'[p]overty, unemployment, fascism and disaster,'" but also one in which "'[n]obody would listen to you if you were less than thirty [...], nobody let you *live* like you kids can do today'" (37; MacInnes' italics). The narrator's refusal to associate himself with the working-class past is repeated in his rejection of the working-class present.[8] Although he rejoices in his neighborhood of Notting Hill ("however horrible the area is, you're *free* there"), he berates the slum districts of the city and their "horrible old anglo-saxon public-houses," much preferring "the big new high blocks of glass-built flats" and "clean new concrete cloud kissers" that reveal the architectural spread of New Brutalism (53, 87, 45, 10). The heartfelt commitment to social mobility appears in a conversation with his brother Vernon, whose accusation that he is "'a traitor to the working-class'" receives a blunt rejoinder: "'I am *not* a traitor to the working-class because I do *not* belong to the working-class, and therefore cannot be a traitor to it'" (41; MacInnes' italics).

The narrator's portrait of a metropolitan utopia continues in his accounts of the inhabitants of that utopia, the "teenagers," a term coined in the 1940s but that only gained currency in the 1950s with the emergence of a youth culture distinct from the mainstream. The novel is not only an important document of the new styles and social habits of the young—their clothing, speech patterns, leisure activities—but also a corrective to the alarmist accounts of working-class youth appearing in the middle-class media.[9] In the words of the sociologist Stanley Cohen, these tended to portray teenagers as "folk devils" (a mythologized other used to warn against deviance) and to encourage "moral panic" amongst readers (a response to "delinquency" out of all proportion to the actual threat).[10] In contrast, MacInnes treats his young characters without sensationalism, dramatizing the alternative social mores developing in the decade—drug usage in Dean Swift, pop culture in the Misery Kid, homosexuality in Big Jill and the Fabulous Hoplite—in a manner that insists on their right to exist. For example, homosexuality, still criminalized in the late 1950s, is treated as commonplace by the Fabulous Hoplite, who takes evident pleasure in the question: "'is there any other law in England that's broken every night by thousands of lucky individuals throughout the British Isles, without anything being *done* about it?'" (131; MacInnes' italics). The utopian potential of youth culture is shown not only in the absorption of marginalized groups but also in the achievement of equality between classes, sexes, sexualities, and ethnicities.

This is illustrated in the clubs frequented by modern jazz followers, a subcultural grouping that came to be known as the "modernists" or early Mods. As the narrator remarks,

> [T]he great thing about the jazz world, and all the kids that enter into it, is that no one, not a soul, cares what your class is, or what your race is, or what your income, or if you're boy, or girl, or bent, or versatile, or what you are—as long as you dig the scene and can behave yourself, and have left all that crap behind you, too, when you come in the jazz club door. The result of all this is that, in the jazz world, you meet all kinds of cats, on absolutely equal terms [...] [68–69].

The jazz club is a utopian space in which young people can resist the ideological failures of hegemonic culture, not least its hierarchies, prejudices and inequalities. That the author shared this idealism is evidenced in his "Pop Songs and Teenagers" (1958), an essay published a year before *Absolute Beginners*. Suggesting that "the 'two nations' of our society may perhaps no longer be those of the 'rich' and 'poor' [...] but those of the teenagers on the one hand and, on the other, all those who have assumed the burdens of adult responsibility," the author delights in the "great social revolution" that is allowing the former a measure of agency (56). The point is taken further by the narrator of *Absolute Beginners* who finds in youth culture a potential for insurgency. The massed ranks of liberated youth to be seen around the coffee bars and concert halls are so great in number that he is convinced that "the boys and girls [...] could rise up overnight and enslave the old tax-payers [...] even though they number millions and sit in the seats of strength," a change in the social order that he terms an "un-silent teenage revolution" (13, 74).

The significance of the narrative, however, lies in the divergence between author and focal character. While the two share a fascination with youth culture, MacInnes is aware that utopia, a term derived by More from the Greek *ou-topos* ("no place") as much as from *eu-topos*, is an unrealizable goal. Importantly, the author uses the first-person narrative to present the viewpoint of an eighteen-year-old adolescent while simultaneously questioning that viewpoint by revealing information that is unknown or unprocessed by the adolescent himself. The most obvious example is the text's insistence on the constructed or performative nature of teen identity, which, for all the narrator's investment in it, has little reality outside clothing, music, lifestyle and language.

Regarding the last of these, Allison James has shown that participation in the "shared symbolic resource" of language is central to identity and that "[s]peaking a language—knowing its subtle connotations, sharing in its nuances and irregularities and abiding by (or deliberately rejecting) the conventions of conversational form—is, in fact, a prerequisite for belonging."[11] In her study of the idioms of children and youth in the 1970s and 1980s, James found that three features—idiosyncrasy, vulgarity, and musicality—are especially important for announcing group membership and empowering that group against outsiders. The same features characterize the narrator's idiom in the novel. His usage of slang terms, abbreviations and nicknames, and his fondness for lyricism and rhythmicality, help to invent a speech community cut off from official culture. The pursuit of self-empowerment is best seen in his linguistic differentiation between age groups, an urgent necessity if his utopian vision of teenage distinction is to assume concrete form: so it is that one finds multiple neologisms for children ("kiddettes," "kidlets," "chicklets"), for adults ("oldsters," "venerables," "tax-payers") and for adolescents ("teens," "kiddies," "absolute beginners"). As with other examples of his vernacular, this is not the real language of 1950s youth but an emblem of that language, one taken to an aesthetic extreme to better communicate its purpose and impact. The departure from Standard English is an assault on traditional models of Britishness, even a libertarian attempt to emancipate youth from the discursive projections of outsiders through the act of self-representation. But the embellished, stylized, poetic language foregrounds the discursive nature of youth culture itself, indicating that generational division is merely a linguistic creation and raising further doubts about the narrator's credibility as an objective guide to the teenage scene.

The point problematizes the common critical interpretation of *Absolute Beginners* as a realist document of the 1950s; as Harriet Blodgett records, MacInnes was "accused by some reviewers of being merely a sociologist in the house of fiction" (107). The novel certainly contains features of conventional realism, such as a clear timeframe, everyday plotline and socially representative types, as well as constant allusions to the historical events and political figures of the decade. Yet its self-reflexive focus on language, combined with the use of an unreliable or limited narrator, is more suggestive of what Nick Bentley terms *experimentalism realism*, a style that in turn suggests the heightened subjectivity of modernism or the ontological skepticism of postmodernism.[12]

The sense of untrustworthiness is increased by other discursive weaknesses which, in the manner of an unreliable narrative, expose the flaws in the narrator's perspective without him being fully aware of them. The most obvious of these is his tendency to reinforce social division by separating sections of the population into essentialized and opposed categories. The demographics of his London are grounded in a range of binary opposites—adults and teens, squares and hipsters, mugs and non-mugs—which "split [...] humanity up into two sections absolutely," as he freely admits (16). Ironically, his tendency to manufacture division is exactly the shortcoming of the adult world he opposes, which marginalizes subaltern groups such as teenagers and migrants and, as we shall see, produces the conditions for social conflict. The stereotyping is even more ironic in the light of his own mixture of Jewish and non–Jewish heritage, as well as an ex-girlfriend's family background being "part Gibraltarian, partly Scottish and partly Jewish," indicating the typical plurality of cultural identities (16). Needless to say, the narrator is unable to sustain the categories he invents. Most importantly, the favored category of "absolute beginner" is riven by subcultural differences that he occasionally recognizes but always fails to accommodate. The egalitarianism found in the jazz clubs, for example, is not typical of youth culture as a whole, which is divided into such tribalistic groupings as the early Mods (with their "neat white Italian rounded-collared shirt, short Roman jacket [and] pointed-toe shoes"), the fans of skiffle ("white stiff-starched collar (rather grubby), striped shirt [and] tight trousers with wide stripe"), the Teddy Boys ("velvet-lined frock-coat [and] four-inch solid corridor-creepers") and the folk crowd ("scruffy and disapproving") (70–71, 70, 46, 145). As these sartorial types suggest, the various groups tend to homogenize both themselves and others, dramatizing Mary Jane Kehily's point that while "[y]outh subcultures frequently seek to define themselves as against the culture that exists around them [...], participation in subcultures also demands a considerable amount of conformity" (23). The suspicions and hostilities which exist between them, plus the hierarchies into which they are placed, indicate that the narrator's integrated teen utopia is based on highly unstable discursive foundations.

The narrator's primary weakness, however, is his failure to champion any features of youth identity that genuinely resist mainstream culture. The forms of youth culture that developed through the 1950s and 1960s gained their countercultural reputation not only through visible signs of difference, but also through active resistance to social and economic injustice. Yet as a dedicated individualist and materialist, the narrator eschews oppositional politics for a single-minded focus on group style, reminding us that even during its emergence in the 1950s, "the image of the 'teenager' was intimately bound up with the idea of the consumer society."[13] The failure to challenge capitalism is crystallized in his rejection of working-class identity, which he follows up with an equally staunch rejection of working-class politics. In a scene with Vernon, a Labour Party supporter, the narrator is lectured on how Attlee's social policies of the late 1940s "'emancipated the working-man, and gave the teenager their economic privileges,'" not least of them "'all these high paid jobs and leisure'" (40). His response is a churlish refusal to consider the matter, dismissing socialism as the "'parrot-cr[ies] of the Ernie Bevin club'" and labeling socialist politicians as "'pinko pals'" (40, 41). The denial of even the most basic form of political debate is seen throughout the earlier sections of the text, where he manages to avoid engagement with topics ranging from the major political parties to the British monarchy and the nuclear bomb (25–26, 27, 26). As this indicates, his utopia of emancipated teenagers can only be imagined by extracting those teenagers from history, although by doing so he invalidates them as agents of historical change.[14] The paradox of his position is that, when faced with an exponent of Marxism, he is in no doubt about the complacency and irresponsibility of utopian thought ("You're *in* history, yes, because you're budding here and now, but you're *outside* it, also, because you're living in the Marxist future. And so, when you look around, and see a hundred horrors [...], you're not responsible for them, because you're beyond them already, in the kingdom of K. Marx") (147; MacInnes' italics).

With his own retreat into a paradise of material accumulation, it is no surprise that the "un-silent teenage revolution" has no ideological aim other than replacing those in power with people of his own age. Indeed, in his career as a freelance photographer, the narrator proves himself no different to the "tax-payers" he rails against, pursuing quick money from the exploitative genres of pornography and advertising and seeking contacts amongst the financial elite, not only teenagers like Wizard, but also adults engaged in manufacturing and marketing. That other "teens" are just as money-orientated is seen in the narrator's extravagant account of their consumer habits:

> The disc shops with those lovely sleeves set in their windows [...] and kids inside them purchasing guitars, or spending fortunes on the songs of the Top Twenty. The shirt-stores and bra-stores with ciné-star photos in the window, selling all the exclusive teenage drag I've been describing. The hair-style saloons where they inflict the blow-wave torture on the kids for hours on end. The cosmetic shops—to make girls of seventeen, fifteen, even thirteen, look like pale rinsed-out sophisticates. Scooters and bubble-cars driven madly down the roads by kids who, a few years ago, were pushing toy ones on the pavement [74].

Here, the economic order is not being overturned but intensified, the young "sophisticates" exhibiting the kind of conditioned hedonism satirized in Huxley's *Brave New World*. The absurdity of their ambition is summed up in the narrator's arrogant declaration, "I want the whole dam city [...] and everything contained there" (149). At points like this, the satire is so overt that one struggles to find the "utopian social optimism" that Derdiger projects onto the novel (64).

Indeed, MacInnes' approach is closely aligned to that of the New Left commentators of the late 1950s and 1960s, including Richard Hoggart, Raymond Williams, and Stuart Hall, who were often scathing of the American films, fashions, and musical styles that were displacing older, "organic" forms of British working-class culture. Hoggart, for example, condemned British teenagers who, like "barbarians in wonderland," had submitted to "a world which is largely a phantasmagoria of passing shows and vicarious stimulations" (246). Stuart Hall, in a review of MacInnes' novel, found a measure of radical potential in his "Utopia with absolute beginnings," but little to admire in "the womb-world of mass entertainments" and the "wholly self-enclosed universe" of leisure pursuits (25, 21, 20). It is the vacuous nature of 1950s "affluence," an unstable mixture of "one-nation Toryism" and American-style consumerism that the narrator symbolizes, particularly through his self-declared devotion to "kicks and fantasy."[15]

The shortcomings of a depoliticized youth become clear when history finally intrudes upon the narrator's imagined world, which it does through the increasing visibility of (post-) colonial migration. Although immigration had been a feature of British life from the sixteenth century, the number of arrivants rose sharply after the British Nationality Act of 1948, when residents of the colonies were given full British citizenship and automatic right of entry, an outcome of the government's need for labor to service the post-war reconstruction drive. Between 1948 and 1958, some 125,000 West Indians and 55,000 Indians and Pakistanis came to Britain to take up jobs in factories, health and transport, or else to enroll in academic or training courses. As Gail Low and Onyekachi Wambu point out, the "Windrush Generation," named after one of the first ships, the *SS Empire Windrush*, to arrive from the Caribbean, contributed to "the making of a modern multicultural nation," its passengers "the harbingers of a social revolution" that "has steadily and radically transformed Britain."[16] Nevertheless, the migrants soon found themselves the target of racial hostility. An informal "colour bar" was established in many hotels, pubs, lodging houses and workplaces, and physical attacks took place in a number of towns and cities, including full-scale "race riots" in Nottingham and Notting Hill in 1958. The mood was worsened by the claims made in the right-wing media that the nation was under invasion and that national identity was being contaminated.

In an age of rapid imperial retreat, the same anxiety about territorial ownership was emerging amongst imperial elites in the colonies: as Wendy Webster argues, the process of decolonization saw a "convergence of the language of white settler communities [...] and white opponents of immigration in the metropolis, as both identified themselves as beleaguered, vulnerable, and embattled" (152). In *Absolute Beginners*, MacInnes' opposition to what he calls "race prejudice and all that crap" is seen in his references to a wide range of cultural groups from Africa, Asia, and the Caribbean, as well as from European countries such as Malta, Cyprus and Ireland, all of which are readily accepted into the textual/national narrative.[17] The resistance is mirrored in the attitudes of many of his young characters. Most obviously, the burgeoning jazz world is not only centered on black American music but also grounded in the principle "that no one, not a soul, cares [...] what your race is" (69). Yet the novel raises serious doubts about the ability of the younger generation to fight for justice. For all their apparent worldliness, the teenagers have no knowledge of the political organization needed to counter right-wing extremism and, in many instances, prove just as vulnerable to the discourse of racism as they are to the discourse of consumerism.

Although the earlier sections of the novel make little reference to racial tension, there are hints of the violence to come. These appear in the narrator's conversations with Mr. Cool, one of the tenants in his lodging house and another acquaintance for whom he has particular respect. Born to mixed-race parentage, Mr. Cool was "bred on this island" and is "as much a native London kid as any of the [...] pure pink numbers," having insight into the London scene that far exceeds that of the narrator (55, 62). Yet when Mr. Cool informs him that trouble is brewing for black communities, the narrator's frivolous reply—"'we English are too lazy, son, to be violent'"—merely repeats his earlier aversion to topics that require political engagement (62). The naiveté continues when he meets one of the local Teddy Boys—a subculture known for gang warfare and racist attacks—who asks the narrator to pressurize Mr. Cool into leaving the district, the first step in a racial "purification" of the neighborhood. The narrator struggles to acknowledge the horror of the request, even after being told by Mr. Cool that there are some four hundred racist youths in the neighborhood conducting a campaign of physical intimidation. Significantly, the way in which the narrator expresses his shock at the news—"I couldn't take all this nightmare"—is less a comment on racial prejudice than a response to the disintegration of his teenage utopia: with the prospect of youth pitted against youth, John McLeod writes, is it unsurprising that "[t]he 'nightmare' of racial violence punctures the narrator's dream-vision of London."[18]

So disturbing is the thought of teenage aggression that the narrator tries to find solace in adult institutions. "'They'd never allow it!'" he says to Mr. Cool. "'The adults! The men! The women! All the authorities! Law and order is the one great English thing!'" (157). The fact that this exchange does not affect the outlook of the narrator, who soon returns to self-absorbed hedonism, is hardly auspicious for the fight against racism. At the same time, the exchanges with Mr. Cool reveal one of the narrator's least appealing attributes. Despite a genuine antipathy to racial prejudice, his tendency to essentialize black identity and culture—not least via the attribution "cool"—reveals a sort of inverse racism, reminding us that this is an individual skilled at imagining social divisions, not at solving them. Nevertheless, he has one redeeming quality. Once the threat of violence becomes real, the knowledge that he will need to choose a side and that the choice will necessitate action, indicates an embryonic political stance.

The tensions come to a head in the final section of the novel when MacInnes turns his attention to the events that took place in Notting Hill in early September 1958. Significantly, the section starts with the revelation that *Absolute Beginners* has been a coming-of-age novel. With the narrator's announcement of his nineteenth birthday, he admits to reaching the end of youth and to entering an adult world in which teenage idealism must make way for more realistic views of the world. In this sense, it is appropriate that the episodic, non-developmental structure of earlier sections now passes to an event-driven narrative, as the necessarily static nature of utopia is replaced by the sequential patterns of public and private history. The accelerated pace of events—a veritable "nightmare" of thrown bottles, smashed windows, and pitched battles—is made even more nightmarish by the complicity of the government, police, and media, a merger of popular and official prejudice that denotes the "worst of all possible worlds" characteristic of dystopianism. The narrator reserves particular anger for the media. For example, he comes across one article on "mixed marriages" that encourages fears of miscegenation, and the "mongrel race, inferior physically and mentally," that it supposedly creates, in order to justify the "friction between the immigrants and the men of the stock so coveted, whose [...] sound and proper instinct was to protect their womenfolk from this contamination, even if this led to violence" (195).

In Notting Hill, this "sound and proper" violence is partly conducted by adults but mostly involves the youth, now referred to as "yobbos," "scruffos," "oafos" and "hooligans" (191, 192, 209, 222). The narrator's disillusionment with teenagers increases when he finds his friend Wizard, previously a model of teenage potential, involved in a rally of the White Protection League, and is compounded by the fact that the only members of the white community who take a proper stand against racism are two elderly members of the adult world. It is to the narrator's credit that he does choose a side, helping black residents out of the danger zone and taking a physical stand against a racist Ted, but this does not offset the lack of youth resistance: "You looked around to find the members of the other team—even just a few of them—and there weren't any. I mean, any of us" (205). His inadvertent use of "them" to designate the youth, despite being corrected to "us," shows how his social categories are collapsing, distinctions are fading and the simple binarisms of his invented metropolis are making way for a more complicated view of London.[19] In fact, he is soon forced to admit, in a conversation with Big Jill, that Britain is beyond his comprehension:

"I don't understand my own country any more," I said to her. [...] "Upstairs," I continued, "I've got a brand new passport. It says I'm a citizen of the UK and the Colonies. Nobody asked me to be, but there I am. Well. Most of these boys have got exactly the same passport as I have—and it was *we* who thought up the laws that gave it to them. But when they turn up in the dear old mother country, and show us the dam thing, we throw it back again in their faces!" [198; MacInnes' italics].

By the end of the novel, his disillusionment is so great that he decides to escape the site of his collapsed utopia and migrate to a less prejudiced country. Yet amid the pessimism about the future are glimmers of hope. First, he inherits the manuscript of a book that his deceased father has written, *History of Pimlico*, an expression of a lifelong attachment to working-class history and community that, it is suggested, may now be transferred to his son. Second, he determines to retain his dream of a more tolerant Britain. While waiting for a flight at the airport, reflecting on how the modern age has made "everything possible to mankind at last, and every horror too," he sees a group of African arrivals, and rather than establish himself abroad, he greets them and invites them to a party in Notting Hill (233–34). While the invitation is a small gesture of solidarity and while no return to utopianism is possible, the scene emphasizes collectivist acts of human kindness over the self-centered consumerism that has waylaid the young generation.

It may be the case that *Absolute Beginners* absorbs some of the racism of its times. Certainly, some of the racially charged language is unpalatable for a modern readership, and one wishes that MacInnes had allotted more space to migrant and diasporic characters. But this is one of the first literary attempts to create a more ethnically egalitarian view of post-war Britain and one of the few 1950s novels to take up the challenge of finding textual form for an increasingly multiethnic society. In doing so, the novel challenges the prevalent critical interpretation of 1950s British writing as a restrained, conservative affair that lacked political radicalism or stylistic experimentation.[20] The continuing importance of *Absolute Beginners* lies in its position at the intersection of the major literary currents of the decade: the aspirational narratives of the "angry young men," the social engagement of working-class fiction, and the internationalism of such diasporic authors as George Lamming, Sam Selvon and Andrew Salkey. The novel's importance also lies in its early treatment of youth culture, which was developed in such dystopian works as Burgess' *A Clockwork Orange*, Adrian Mitchell's *The Bodyguard* (1970), and Doris Lessing's "Report on the Threatened City" (1971).

In the context of twentieth-century speculative writing, MacInnes' cautionary tale is most notable for its accurate forecast of the social upheavals to come. By the late 1960s, the myth of an affluent, progressive Britain was collapsing in the face of steady industrial decline and rising social tension. The narrator's pessimism was fully justified by the Commonwealth Immigrants Act of 1962 which, partly encouraged by the events in Notting Hill and Nottingham, withdrew the right of residency from overseas citizens and limited immigration to a work permit system, a clear attempt to preserve the fantasy of an ethnically homogenous Britain. If we accept Darko Suvin's premise that "Utopia explicates what satire implicates, and vice versa," then MacInnes' critique of ethnocentrism perfectly captures the satirical or counter-discursive quality of dystopian fiction (54).

NOTES

1. See Dominic Sandbrook, *Never Had It So Good: A History of Britain from Suez to the Beatles* (London: Abacus, 2006), p. 109.

2. Harold Macmillan quoted in Dilwyn Porter, "'Never-Never Land': Britain Under the Conservatives 1951–1964" in Nick Tiratsoo, ed., *From Blitz to Blair: A New History of Britain Since 1939* (London: Phoenix, 1998), pp. 118–19; Anthony Crosland quoted in Morgan, *Britain Since 1945*, p. 157.

3. Bittner, "Chronosophy, Aesthetics, and Ethics in Le Guin's *The Dispossessed: An Ambiguous Utopia*," in Eric S. Rabkin, Martin H. Greenberg and Joseph D. Olander, eds., *No Place Else: Explorations in Utopian and Dystopian Fiction* (Carbondale and Edwardsville: Southern Illinois University Press, 1983), p. 244. See also Krishan Kumar, *Utopia and Anti-Utopia in Modern Times* (Oxford: Basil Blackwell, 1987), p. 380.

4. Jameson, *Archaeologies of the Future: The Desire Called Utopia and Other Science Fictions* (London and New York: Verso, 2005), p. xi. "To believe in utopia," Robert C. Elliott wrote in 1970, "one must have faith of a kind that our history has made nearly inaccessible" (Elliott, *The Shape of Utopia: Studies in a Literary Genre* (Chicago: University of Chicago Press, 970), p. 87).

5. For discussion of the relations between dystopian and anti-utopian writing, see Morson, *Boundaries of Genre*, pp. 115–16; Arthur O. Lewis, "The Anti-Utopian Novel: Preliminary Notes and Checklist," *Extrapolation*, Vol. 2 (1961), 27–32; and Alexandra Aldridge, *The Scientific World View in Dystopia* (Ann Arbor: UMI Research Press, 1984), pp. 1–18.

6. Ian Jeffrey, "The Cult of Creativity: Young British Architects," in David Alan Mellor and Laurent Gervereau, eds., *The Sixties: Britain and France, 1962–1973: The Utopian Years* (London: Philip Wilson Publishers, 1997), p. 126.

7. Derdiger is not alone in ascribing utopianism to *Absolute Beginners*. Although Alan Sinfield and Steven Connor both question the extent of the novel's optimism, they still emphasize its "utopian fusion of subcultural forms" and "outlandish visionary force" (Sinfield, *Literature, Politics and Culture in Postwar Britain* (Oxford: Basil Blackwell, 1989), p. 170; Connor, *The English Novel in History 1950–1995* (New York: Routledge, 1996), p. 91).

8. When the narrator disparages his father's recollections, referring sarcastically to "'those poor old 1930s of yours,'" he may be motived by his own experience of privation earlier in life, having been born in a "tube shelter" during the Second World War and bred in the working-class district of Kilburn (pp. 37, 185).

9. MacInnes was critical of how little British fiction of the 1950s had to say about youth culture. "As one skips through contemporary novels," he wrote, "it is amazing—it really is—how very little one can learn about life in England here and now" (MacInnes, *England, Half English: A Polyphoto of the Fifties*, new edition (1961; New York: Penguin, 1966), p. 206).

10. See Cohen, *Folk Devils and Moral Panics: The Creation of the Mods and Rockers*, new edn (1972; New York: Routledge, 2002), pp. 1–3. Writing on the 1960s, John Springhall defines a "moral panic" as "a periodic tendency towards the identification and scapegoating of 'folk devils' [...] whose activities were regarded by hegemonic groups as indicative of imminent social breakdown. Panics served as ideological safety valves whose effect was to

restore social equilibrium" (Springhall, *Youth Popular Culture and Moral Panics: Penny Gaffs to Gangsta-Rap, 1830–1996* (London: Macmillan, 1998, p. 5).

11. James, "Talking of Children and Youth: Language, Socialization and Culture," in Vered Amit-Talai and Helena Wulff, eds., *Youth Cultures: A Cross-Cultural Perspective* (New York: Routledge, 1995), p. 44.

12. See Bentley, "Writing 1950s London: Narrative Strategies in Colin MacInnes' *City of Spades* and *Absolute Beginners*," *Literary London: Interdisciplinary Studies in the Representation of London*, Vol. 1, No. 2 (2003), http://www.literarylondon.org/london-journal/september2003/bentley.html (accessed 22 February 2016); and Bentley, "Translating English: Youth, Race and Nation in Colin MacInnes' *City of Spades* and *Absolute Beginners*," *Connotations*, Vol. 13, Nos. 1–2 (2003–04), pp. 153–55.

13. Graham Murdock and Robin McCron, "Youth and Class: The Career of a Confusion," in Geoff Mungham and Geoff Pearson, eds., *Working Class Youth Culture* (New York: Routledge and Kegan Paul, 1976), p. 15.

14. As Jonathon Epstein argues, "Subcultural behaviour, style of dress, choice of music, and the further refinement of these cultural field elements should be understood not only as an attempt on the part of youth to set themselves apart from hegemonic, adult culture, but also as a way of completely denying their complicity in the events of current history" (Epstein, "Introduction: Generation X, Youth Culture, and Identity," in Epstein, ed., *Youth Culture: Identity in a Postmodern World* (Hoboken, NJ: Wiley-Blackwell, 1998), p. 16).

15. MacInnes, *Absolute Beginners*, p. 11. Despite railing against the commercialization of youth culture, the narrator is unaware of how vulnerable his beloved jazz music is to commercial exploitation, or of how his own identity is becoming Americanized, most obviously through his Cockney locutions ("dekko," "clobber," "on your Pat Malone") becoming mixed with Americanisms ("hobo," "daddy-o," "speakeasies") (MacInnes, *Absolute Beginners*, pp. 176, 110, 167, 110, 19, 69).

16. Low, "Streets, Rooms and Residents: The Urban Uncanny and the Poetics of Space in Harold Pinter, Sam Selvon, Colin MacInnes and George Lamming," in Glenn Hooper, ed., *Landscape and Empire, 1720–2000* (Aldershot and Burlington: Ashgate, 2005), p. 159; Wambu, "Introduction" to Wambu, ed., *Empire Windrush: Fifty Years of Writing About Black Britain*, new edition (1998; London: Phoenix, 1999), pp. 29, 20.

17. MacInnes, *Absolute Beginners*, p. 15. MacInnes tried to work against the racial prejudice, helping to set up the Stars' Campaign for Interracial Friendship and distributing anti-racist newssheets around Notting Hill (see Tony Gould, *Inside Outsider: The Life and Times of Colin MacInnes* (London: Faber & Faber, 1983), p. 137). For a bleaker view of his attitude to migrant communities, see Ed Vulliamy, "Absolute MacInnes," *Guardian*, 15 April 2007, http://theguardian.com/uk/2007/apr/15/britishidentity.fiction/print (accessed 20 February 2014).

18. MacInnes, *Absolute Beginners*, p. 157; McLeod, *Postcolonial London: Rewriting the Metropolis* (New York: Routledge, 2004), p. 54.

19. It was with some prescience that MacInnes wrote, in February 1958, that "it would be [...] possible to see, in the teenage neutralism and indifference to politics, and self-sufficiency, and instinct for enjoyment—in short, in their kind of happy mindlessness—the raw material for crypto-fascisms of the worst kind" (MacInnes, "Pop Songs," p. 61).

20. See Nick Bentley, *Radical Fictions: The English Novel in the 1950s* (Bern, Switzerland: Peter Lang, 2007), p. 15.

Works Cited

Aldridge, Alexandra. *The Scientific World View in Dystopia*. Ann Arbor, MI: UMI Research Press, 1984. Print.

Amis, Kingsley. *Russian Hide-and-Seek*. London: Hutchinson, 1980. Print.

Bentley, Nick. "'New Elizabethans': The Representation of Youth Subcultures in 1950s British Fiction." *Literature & History* 19.11 (2010): 16–33. Print.

_____. *Radical Fictions: The English Novel in the 1950s*. Bern, Switzerland: Peter Lang, 2007. Print.

_____. "Translating English: Youth, Race and Nation in Colin MacInnes' *City of Spades* and *Absolute Beginners*." *Connotations* 13.1–2 (2003–04): 149–69. Print.
_____. "Writing 1950s London: Narrative Strategies in Colin MacInnes' *City of Spades* and *Absolute Beginners*." *Literary London: Interdisciplinary Studies in the Representation of London* 1.2 (2003). Web. 22 Feb. 2016.
_____. "The Young Ones: A Reassessment of the British New Left's Representation of 1950s Youth Subcultures." *European Journal of Cultural Studies* 8.1 (2005): 65–83. Print.
Blodgett, Harriet. "City of Other Worlds: The London Novels of Colin MacInnes." *Critique* 18.1 (1976): 105–18.
Booker, M. Keith. *Dystopian Literature: A Theory and Research Guide*. London: Greenport Press, 1994. Print.
Burdekin, Katharine. *Swastika Night*. 1937. London: Lawrence and Wishart, 1985. Print.
Burgess, Anthony. *A Clockwork Orange*. 1962. New York: Penguin, 1972. Print.
Carter, Angela. *The Infernal Desire Machines of Doctor Hoffman*. 1972. New York: Penguin, 1982. Print.
Chesterton, G.K. *The Napoleon of Notting Hill*. 1904. London: House of Stratus, 2001. Print.
Cohen, Stanley. *Folk Devils and Moral Panics: The Creation of the Mods and Rockers*. 1972. New York: Routledge, 2002. Print.
Connor, Steven. *The English Novel in History: 1950–1995*. New York: Routledge, 1996. Print.
Cordell, Alexander. *If You Believe the Soldiers*. London: Hodder and Stoughton, 1973. Print.
Dahl, Roald. *Some Time Never: A Fable for Supermen*. New York: Charles Scribner's Sons, 1948. Print.
Derdiger, Paula. "To Drag out a Rough Poetry: Colin MacInnes and the New Brutalism in Postwar Britain." *Modern Fiction Studies* 62.1 (2016): 53–69. Print.
Elliott, Robert C. *The Shape of Utopia: Studies in a Literary Genre*. Chicago: University of Chicago Press, 1970. Print.
Epstein, Jonathon S., ed. *Youth Culture: Identity in a Postmodern World*. Hoboken, NJ: Wiley-Blackwell, 1998. Print.
Ferns, Chris. *Narrating Utopia: Ideology, Gender, Form in Utopian Literature*. Liverpool: Liverpool University Press, 1999. Print.
Gee, Maggie. *The Burning Book*. London: Faber & Faber, 1983. Print.
Gottlieb, Erika. *Dystopian Fiction East and West: Universe of Terror and Trial*. Montreal: McGill-Queen's University Press, 2001. Print.
Gould, Tony. *Inside Outsider: The Life and Times of Colin MacInnes*. London: Faber & Faber, 1983. Print.
Hall, Stuart. "Absolute Beginnings." *Universities & Left Review* 7 (1959): 17–25. Print.
Hartley, L.P. *Facial Justice*. London: Hamish Hamilton, 1960. Print.
Hennessy, Peter. *Having It So Good: Britain in the Fifties*. New York: Penguin, 2007. Print.
Hill, John. *Sex, Class and Realism: British Cinema 1956–1963*. London: BFI Publishing, 1986. Print.
Hoggart, Richard. *The Uses of Literacy: Aspects of Working-Class Life with Special Reference to Publications and Entertainments*. New York: Penguin, 1958. Print.
Huxley, Aldous. *Brave New World*. 1932. London: Triad Panther, 1977. Print.
James, Allison. "Talking of Children and Youth: Language, Socialization and Culture." *Youth Cultures: A Cross-Cultural Perspective*. Ed. Vered Amit-Talai and Helena Wulff. New York: Routledge, 1995). 43–62. Print.
Jameson, Fredric. *Archaeologies of the Future: The Desire Called Utopia and Other Science Fictions*. London: Verso, 2005. Print.
Kehily, Mary Jane, ed. *Understanding Youth: Perspectives, Identities and Practices*. Thousand Oaks, CA: SAGE, 2007. Print.
Kumar, Krishan. *Utopia and Anti-Utopia in Modern Times*. Oxford: Basil Blackwell, 1987. Print.
Lessing, Doris. *Documents Relating to the Sentimental Agents in the Volyen Empire*. 1983. London: Panther Books, 1985. Print.
_____. "Report on the Threatened City." *The Story of a Non-Marrying Man and Other Stories*. 1972. New York: Penguin, 1975. 133–66. Print.

Lewis, Arthur O. "The Anti-Utopian Novel: Preliminary Notes and Checklist." *Extrapolation* 2 (1961): 27–32. Print.
Lewis, C.S. *That Hideous Strength*. London: Bodley Head, 1945. Print.
Low, Gail. "Streets, Rooms and Residents: The Urban Uncanny and the Poetics of Space in Harold Pinter, Sam Selvon, Colin MacInnes and George Lamming." *Landscape and Empire, 1720–2000*. Ed. Glenn Hooper. Aldershot and Burlington: Ashgate, 2005. 159–76. Print.
MacInnes, Colin. *Absolute Beginners*. 1959. New York: Penguin, 1964. Print.
———. "Pop Songs and Teenagers." *England, Half English: A Polyphoto of the Fifties*. 1961. New York: Penguin, 1966. 48–61. Print.
———. "A Taste of Reality." *England, Half English: A Polyphoto of the Fifties*. New York: Penguin, 1966. 204–07. Print.
———. "Welcome, Beauty Walk." MacInnes, *England, Half English: A Polyphoto of the Fifties*. 1961. New York: Penguin, 1966: 82–114. Print.
Maus, Derek C. *Unvarnishing Reality: Subversive Russian and American Cold War Satire* Columbia: University of South Carolina Press, 2011. Print.
McEwan, Ian. *The Child in Time*. 1987. London: Vintage, 1997. Print.
McLeod, John. *Postcolonial London: Rewriting the Metropolis*. New York: Routledge, 2004. Print.
Mellor, David Alan, and Laurent Gervereau, eds. *The Sixties: Britain and France, 1962–1973: The Utopian Years*. London: Philip Wilson Publishers, 1997. Print.
Mitchell, Adrian. *The Bodyguard*. London: Jonathan Cape, 1970. Print.
More, Thomas. *Utopia*. 1516. Trans. Paul Turner. New York: Penguin, 1965. Print.
Morgan, Kenneth O. *Britain since 1945: The People's Peace*. 1990. Oxford: Oxford University Press, 2001. Print.
Morson, Gary Saul. *The Boundaries of Genre: Dostoevsky's* Diary of a Writer *and the Traditions of Literary Utopia*. Austin: University of Texas Press, 1981. Print.
Murdock, Graham, and Robin McCron. "Youth and Class: The Career of a Confusion." *Working Class Youth Culture*. Ed. Geoff Mungham and Geoff Pearson. New York: Routledge and Kegan Paul, 1976. 10–26. Print.
Orwell, George. *Nineteen Eighty-Four*. 1949. New York: Penguin, 1983. Print.
Porter, Dilwyn. "'Never-Never Land': Britain Under the Conservatives 1951–1964." Ed. Nick Tiratsoo. *From Blitz to Blair: A New History of Britain Since 1939*. London: Phoenix, 1998. 102–31. Print.
Rabkin, Eric S., Martin H. Greenberg, and Joseph D. Olander, eds. *No Place Else: Explorations in Utopian and Dystopian Fiction*. Carbondale: Southern Illinois University Press, 1983. Print.
Sandbrook, Dominic. *Never Had It So Good: A History of Britain from Suez to the Beatles*. London: Abacus, 2006. Print.
Shaw, Eric. *The Labour Party Since 1945: Old Labour, New Labour*. Hoboken, NJ: Wiley-Blackwell, 1996. Print.
Sillitoe, Alan. *Travels in Nihilon*. London: W.H. Allen, 1971. Print.
Sinfield, Alan. *Literature, Politics and Culture in Postwar Britain*. Oxford: Basil Blackwell, 1989. Print.
Springhall, John. *Youth Popular Culture and Moral Panics: Penny Gaffs to Gangsta-Rap, 1830–1996*. London: Palgrave Macmillan, 1998. Print.
Stevick, Philip. "The Limits of Anti-Utopia." *Criticism* 6.3 (1964): 233–45. Print.
Suvin, Darko. *Metamorphoses of Science Fiction: On the Poetics and History of a Literary Genre*. New Haven: Yale University Press, 1979. Print.
Tennant, Emma. *The Last of the Country House Murders*. 1974. London: Faber & Faber, 1986. Print.
Vulliamy, Ed. "Absolute MacInnes." *Guardian* 14 April 2007. Web. 20 Feb. 2014. <http://theguardian.com/uk/2007/apr/15/britishidentity.fiction/print>.
Wambu, Onyekachi, ed. *Empire Windrush: Fifty Years of Writing about Black Britain*. London: Phoenix, 1999. Print.
Warner, Rex. *The Aerodrome*. 1941. London: Bodley Head, 1966. Print.

Webster, Wendy. *Englishness and Empire 1939–1965*. Oxford: Oxford University Press, 2005. Print.
Weldon, Fay. *Darcy's Utopia*. 1990. London: Flamingo, 1991. Print.
Wells, H.G. "The Time Machine" (1894–95). *Selected Short Stories of H.G. Wells*. 1927. New York: Penguin, 1958. 7–83. Print.

"What if I said that he's a god?"
Messianism in Cormac McCarthy's The Road

WES YEARY

Cormac McCarthy's *The Road* invites a theological reading. With themes of the apocalypse, repeated references to God, and perseverance gesturing at hope for human survival, the text seems to encourage a search for the divine amongst its pages. Throughout *The Road*, the unnamed man imparts or reveals divinity present both in his relationship with the unnamed boy and in the boy himself. Echoes of baptismal rites surface when the man kills a cannibal intent on killing the boy, with the man declaring, "This is my child[....] I wash a dead man's brains out of his hair. This is my job" (74). The man tells the boy, "My job is to take care of you. I was appointed to do that by God" (77). Though they inhabit a world with "no godspoke men," the man says that, "If [the boy] is not the word of God God never spoke" (32, 5). The man thinks of the boy as a "Golden chalice, good to house a god" (75). While discussing the boy with Ely, a fellow road-traveler, the man asks, "What if I told you [the boy] was a god?" (172). Just before reaching the long-awaited coast, the man sees the boy "standing there in the road looking back at him from some unimaginable future, glowing in that waste like a tabernacle" (273). However, how literally should one read into these spiritual references given to the boy? Does divinity actually exist inside the boy? Or does the man, traumatized and grieving from the loss of the world, confer divinity onto the boy in an effort to give his life meaning? Throughout *The Road*, the divinity seemingly present in the boy appears as a result of the man's search for meaning and hope. If the boy stands as a messianic figure, a post-apocalyptic Adamic figure, then that understanding rests solely with the father.

Critics frequently reference the boy's standing as a post-apocalyptic messianic figure, arguing that the man and boy incorporate an ethical stance into their wanderings largely absent from many others on the road; the man and boy neither murder nor cannibalize the murdered, which serves as the principal difference between "good guys" and "bad guys" in the text. The vision of the boy as a messianic figure rests primarily upon this concept of good guys and bad guys; in a world "largely populated by men who would eat your children in front of your eyes," one who refuses such debased actions clearly stands apart (McCarthy 181). Ashley Kunsa notes the father and son's "status as good guys inheres in, if nothing else, their refusal to eat people or dogs. This is fact enough to separate them from the 'bad guys,'" describing the boy as "a messiah not unlike Christ himself" (59, 65). Manuel Broncano upholds Kunsa's reading, stating that the boy has come "to lead humankind to a second rebirth, to build a new world on the ashes of the biblical book that has finally been closed forever" (127). Broncano further argues that the man "sees himself as chosen by God to protect the new Jesus that his son is," and that the boy's judgment "is that which distinguishes between good and bad guys, between those willing to sacrifice themselves before sacrificing others and those willing to sacrifice others in order to survive themselves" (131, 127).

In like manner to Kunsa and Broncano, Lydia Cooper goes so far as to say that the boy "becomes the object that brings the essence of divinity back to a corrupted world," stating the text argues that humans "create God [...] in the sense that they create what there is of meaning and morality" and the man "[behaves] as if the child is indeed 'God'—the embodiment of all value and morality" (224, 229). Cooper links the boy's concern with others to mercy, stating, "[I]f, indeed, he is his father's and the world's grail, the symbol of hope for human survival, then that hope is nothing less than a radical commitment to mercy in a world where an act of mercy just may be a death sentence. What is at stake is nothing less than the divine in human nature" (232–33). D. Marcel DeCoste furthers the messianic contention by detailing the boy's immersion in his father's ethical teaching, arguing, "we see the son learn from and grow beyond the exemplary performance of the father" (73). According to DeCoste, the father displays "acts of tenderness which all but scream in McCarthy's savage setting [...] acts of mercy, acts of giving, and more profound acts of sacrifice" (73). While the text certainly lends support to these positions, some complicating factors remain. Are readers to take the man's position that the boy is literally a god? What does one do with the numerous arguments the man and boy have amongst themselves, arguments that involve the boy questioning whether they could or should help someone, arguments that imply that, from the boy's perspective, they cannot be good guys without helping others? How should readers understand the man and boy's arguing if the boy is, in fact, a god? The answer may lie in a reading which focuses more on what the boy desires his father to do, rather than on what the father actually does.

Reading the boy as a messianic figure potentially misses a significant component of the boy's life and the primary contention between father and son: the willingness to help another who urgently needs it. Throughout *The Road*, conflicts between the man and boy primarily rest not upon whether they will eat other people, though that is certainly a question the boy asks the man multiple times, but whether they will help other people. As DeCoste argues, "[T]he loving concern [the man] showers upon his boy is jealously kept for him alone"; the man repeatedly refuses to help others who desperately need it, giving rise to conflicts between the man and boy regarding what, exactly, constitutes good guys and bad guys (79). For the man, an unwillingness to murder, cannibalize, or give up serves as the primary distinction for a good guy. For the boy, one must help others when possible, even when helping others puts one's own survival at risk, a point Rune Grauland argues by stating that, for the boy, "base survival is not enough. The boy needs to invest life with meaning beyond the simple mechanics of continued survival" (73). The boy's understanding stands in direct contrast with his father, for whom "all other concerns are subsumed under the umbrella of survival" (73). The boy's liberality with others suggests his move beyond his father's concern strictly for the boy; the boy's actions, as DeCoste notes, constitute a "hopeful expansion of the human family" to potentially include all others he encounters (83). If the boy may be seen as a post-apocalyptic Christ-figure, it seems reasonable that that Christ-figure reinstitutes the primary teaching of Christ's life: that we love one another as we love ourselves, itself a reinstitution of a mandate from Genesis 4, that one is his brother's keeper.

In Genesis 4, two brothers, Cain and Abel, both present sacrifices to God. God accepts Abel's, rejects Cain's, and Cain becomes angry and murders Abel (*New American Standard*, Gen. 4: 4–8). God asks Cain about Abel's whereabouts, and Cain replies, "I do not know. Am I my brother's keeper?" (Gen. 4:9). In response to the murder, God places a curse on Cain, banning him from farming and forcing him to wander the Earth (Gen. 4:12). Cain argues that he will become a "vagrant and a wanderer on the earth, and whoever finds me will kill me"; therefore, God places a mark on Cain to protect him (Gen. 4: 14–15). If the boy sees himself as his brother's keeper, and that concept guides his interactions with others, the boy must also be seen as carrying over an ancient ethical or moral stance from well before the Earth's destruction, rather than instituting a new ethic. Consciously or not, the boy reestablishes the Old Testament concept of watching out for one another, a concept restated and rephrased by Christ in the New Testament as loving one's brother as oneself. Cain's wandering through the world seems echoed throughout *The Road*, wherein people wander through the ruined world, killing and being killed.

The roaming gangs of cannibals and road agents who wander the earth as Cain-like vagrants, straddling the border between human and animal, hunting and being hunted by other humans, embody Julia Kristeva's definition of the abject in *Powers of Horror*. Almost the entirety of *The Road* reads as "the recounting of suffering; fear, disgust, and abjection crying out [...] concatenated into a story" (Kristeva 145). Kristeva argues, "The abject confronts us [...] with those fragile states where man strays on the territories of animal" (12). In discussing Céline's *Journey to the End of the Night*, Kristeva describes the wartime text, which reads as a description of humans populating *The Road*:

> Human beings caught flush with their animality, wallowing in their vomit[....] Never perhaps [...] have human "nature" [...] or the divine been opened up with so much cruelty, and with so little satisfaction, illusion, or hope. This is the horror of hell without God; if no means of salvation, no optimism, not even a humanistic one, looms on the horizon, then the verdict is in, with no hope of pardon [147].

These road agents and cannibals are "death infecting life [...] the criminal with a good conscience," men who will "eat your children in front of your eyes" (Kristeva 2; McCarthy 181). This view of the world in which humans hunt others, absent of hope, optimism, and salvation, stands in opposition to the world inhabited by the man and boy; their quest for the coast, their merciful acts, and their obvious love for one another defy this hopeless perspective. The boy extends his father's love beyond their small family, demonstrating what being a brother's keeper entails in a destroyed world.

The text presents this ethical stance in stark terms after the man and boy escape a house with prisoners in the basement, being held by four cannibals. After the man and boy escape, the boy needs reassurance from his father that they will never resort to cannibalism, no matter the severity of hunger (127). The boy directly ties his and the man's refusal to cannibalize to their standing as good guys, but the boy questions whether they may remain good guys after abandoning the prisoners to their horrifying fate. The boy asks his father:

> We wouldnt ever eat anybody, would we?
> No. Of course not.
> Even if we were starving?
> [...]
> But we wouldnt.
> No. We wouldnt.
> No matter what.
> No. No matter what.

> Because we're the good guys.
> Yes [128–29].

The boy readily acknowledges that their status as good guys precludes cannibalism. However, his questions seem odd; if their status as good guys is so secure, why ask the questions in the first place? The man and boy neither murder nor consume the unfortunates in the basement, so if their refusal to murder and cannibalize cements their existence as good guys, why does the boy need such reassurance?

The boy's questions as to whether they remain good guys rest in the difference of perception between the man and boy, their distinct understandings of what constitutes a good guy, which appears numerous times throughout the text. The man, as DeCoste points out, schools the boy in "the theological virtues of Christian tradition," noting in particular the "powerful sacrificial love which obtains between father and son," and that "through that love the other virtues Augustine names become activated as humanizing forces" (68, 69). DeCoste further argues that God "is intimately bound to the hope for the future and the concern for others, and for right conduct toward them, that the father and son preserve" (70). The man's virtuous teachings, however, break down when sacrificial love, which the man bequeaths to his son with no reservations, retreats from view when others enter the picture. The boy notices the restrictions the man places on sacrificial love and actively resists them. After encountering a man who has been struck by lightning, the boy twice asks the man if they can help him (50). The man refuses; the next day, after the man discovers the boy still upset by their refusal to help, the man explains, "We cant share what we have or we'll die too" (52).

This same exchange occurs when the man and boy encounter Ely and a thief who steals their belongings. After sharing a meal with Ely, the man and boy give him a few cans of food (173). After separating, the man notices the boy's unhappiness, and says, "When we're out of food you'll have more time to think about it" (174). After eating some more, the boy responds, "I know. But I wont remember it the way you do" (174). That the boy will remember the incident differently than his father demonstrates their difference in perception: for the father, the food is only for him and his son; for the son, however, the food is available for any who may need it. The incident with the thief further reinforces the different perceptions between the boy and his father. The man concerns himself only with retribution when confronting the thief; the man retrieves his and the boy's belongings and leaves the thief devoid of all possessions (256–7). The boy, however, empathizing with the thief, perceives his father's actions as unnecessarily cruel; the boy views leaving the thief helpless in such a cruel world equal to murder. The boy begins to cry and says, "He was just hungry, Papa. He's going to die. [...] He's so scared, Papa" (259). The man responds that he, too, is scared, and tells the boy, "You're not the one who has to worry about everything" (259). The boy responds, "Yes I am. [...] I am the one," an answer which signals the boy's understanding of his position of leadership in the relationship and indicates his superior moral position over his father (259).

The boy expands his father's ethic of love and sacrifice, universalizing that love and sacrifice to all other people. This willingness to sacrifice for another person, a stranger who happens to be in one's presence, embodies Christ's command to love your neighbor as yourself (Mark 12:31). Christ's command, however, reinstates the notion from Genesis 4 of being one's brother's keeper. By extending the sense of family to all he encounters, expressing sympathy and empathy with those around him, arguing with his father over whether to help another on the road, and desiring to share what he does have, the boy fulfills the command to love his neighbors as himself. The man, however, seems unwilling or unable to do the same. DeCoste contends that the man cannot extend his love to others because he gives his whole heart to his son, thereby leaving no love to be given to others. DeCoste argues, "If the gift of his whole heart has kept the father from extending love and mercy to strangers, it has nonetheless safeguarded the son and taught him those theological virtues which allow him to become the best guy" (81). The man's statement that the boy is "the best guy" serves as his acknowledgment that the boy far exceeds his own ability to love; if the man is a good guy, the boy is the best guy, a title which Kunsa states "elevates the boy above simple 'good guy' status and sets him apart from his father and any other decent human beings" (65). However, how does the boy's status as the best guy correlate to his being a messiah?

The boy's messianic undertones appear universally through the eyes of his father, a grieving, traumatized man trying to find his place after he loses his entire world. The man seems to lose faith in God after the catastrophe, possibly evident when he enters "the charred ruins of a library," noticing the "blackened books" lying in water (187). Looking at the collected books, the man experiences "rage at the lies arranged in their thousands row on row" (187). The man looks through one book, arguably a Bible, and drops the book to the floor (187). The man expresses his loss of faith early in the text, when he asks, "Are you there? [...] Will I see you at the last? Have you a neck by which to throttle you? Have you a heart? Damn you eternally have you a soul?" (11–12). The man later asks himself, "Do you think that your fathers are watching? That they weigh you in their ledgerbook? Against what? There is no book and your fathers are dead in the ground" (196). The trauma the man suffers from both the world's and his wife's death appears even in the nature of the written text, which is disjointed, unconnected, with seemingly arbitrary narrations which indiscriminately jump time periods, recalling past events as if to move beyond them. The man's trauma manifests in the messianic qualities the man confers on his son, the last vestige of humanity in the man's life, the focalizing point around which to structure his life. In conferring these qualities on his son, the man follows his wife's advice: "A person who had no one would be well advised to cobble together some passable ghost. Breathe it into being and coax it along with words of love. Offer it each phantom crumb and shield it from harm with your body" (57). This embodies the salvational role the boy represents. In the man's loss of faith in God, in the loss of a world, in the loss of his wife, he constructs a god of his own flesh and blood, a totem to keep himself centered in a world with no center; he gives himself a reason, a meaning, to keep going, to not give up. If the boy serves a salvational role, if the boy operates as a messiah, his father alone receives that salvation.

Slavoj Žižek, in *The Sublime Object of Ideology*, points to the ability to create a substitute for the big Other in the symbolic world, a subject who operates in like manner to the big Other. Žižek argues that one may identify a subject with "some signifying feature [...] in the big Other, in the symbolic order" (104). According to Žižek, this feature "assumes concrete, recognizable shape in a name or in a mandate that the subject takes upon himself and/or that is bestowed upon him [...] to achieve self-identity, the subject must identify himself with the imaginary other, he must alienate himself—put his identity outside himself, so to speak, into the image of his double" (104). This move, instilling in a subject a signifying feature of the big Other, seems apparent in the man's projection of divinity on his son; the man's loss of faith in God, the ultimate big Other, manifests as faith in his son. The boy presents no obvious knowledge of his messianic standing with his father. The man bestows the title of "god" on the boy, but whether the boy accepts that title, and subsequently acts in a manner to attempt to make himself worthy of that title, seems unknowable, and ultimately beside the point. The man creates a god from his son, imbuing his son with the illusion of divinity, due primarily to the boy's relative innocence and, for lack of a better word, goodness, in a world gone mad. For his father, the boy serves as the *objet petit a*, masking the lack of the big Other. The man still symbolically identifies himself with his wife, evident in the extreme protection he provides his son predicated on her exhortation to breathe into being a reason for existence if one does not already exist. The man elevates the boy to messiah, a savior, and for the man, the boy serves that purpose, providing the man with a reason for existence, a goal, and a sense of hope. The text, however, for all its messianic insinuations, neglects to communicate that salvational role to others. Only the father comprehends his son as a god.

An important detail to remember when viewing the boy as a messiah is the position of the gaze from which the text presents the boy. During the lengthy discussion between the man and Ely, Ely betrays no evidence he perceives the boy as a messiah, or that he perceives the boy as anything but a boy. Ely does reference God in the discussion, but his comments are dismissive of faith. Ely states, "There is no God[....] There is no God and we are his prophets" (170). When Ely does discuss the boy, it is the father, not Ely, who introduces the divine into the boy's description. Ely says, "When I saw that boy, I thought that I had died" (172). The man asks, "You thought he was an angel?" (172). Ely responds, "I didnt know what he was" (172). The man presses him further, asking, "What if I said that he's a god?" (172). Ely's response is telling, particularly for what he does not say. Ely answers the man, saying, "I'm past all that now. Have been for years. Where men cant live gods fare no better ... to be on the road with the last god would be a terrible thing so I hope it's not true" (172). Ely's dismissal of faith in God seems peculiar if he were to know the post-apocalyptic messiah sleeps just a few feet away from him. Not until the next morning does Ely refer to the boy in religious terms, but even then he is dismissive of faith. Ely says to the man, "Maybe he believes in God" (174). When the man says he does not know what the boy believes in, Ely responds, "He'll get over it" (174). Once again, Ely's dismissive manner regarding faith in God underscores the fact that he sees nothing special about the boy, perhaps excepting the fact that a boy exists at all. However, this discussion also forces us to question the father's responses to Ely. Just how literally are readers to take the man's assertion that the boy is a god? If the text poses the possibility that the boy truly is a literal god, what sort of god is the boy, who the text also positions as a scared, weak, starving child? Once again, the text forces one to come to terms with the reality of the world the text depicts, a world "where men cant live," a postsecular world with a god of man's creation (172).

In *History, Literature, Critical Theory*, Dominick LaCapra describes a concept he refers to as "the postsecular" (136). LaCapra argues the postsecular lies "betwixt and between" the secular and religious or sacred, which "comes into its own in the attempt to re-enchant the world, even to evoke a sense of the uncanny, the epiphanous, the extraordinariness of the ordinary, indeed the miraculous or the endowed with grace, charisma, the gift of grace" (136). Recreating the boy as a post-apocalyptic god offers the man an opportunity to re-enchant the world, providing meaning and purpose to a life and world which, for all intents and purposes, ended with the cataclysm. The man achieves this re-enchantment through fantasy, through an attempt to re-engage his lost faith in God, with his son serving as a surrogate god, a substitution to fill the void opened with the man's loss of faith. Žižek argues, "fantasy functions as a construction, as an imaginary scenario filling out the void, *the opening of the desire of the Other*" (114). The man fills his son with both human and divine characteristics, but posits his son in place of God;

the faith, devotion, and loyalty the man once expressed toward God—the big Other—the man now expresses toward his son. Žižek states, "Fantasy appears, then, as an answer to the '*Che vuoi?*,' to the unbearable enigma of the desire of the Other, of the lack in the Other; but it is at the same time fantasy itself which [...] provides the co-ordinates of our desire—which constructs the frame enabling us to desire something" (118). The man's fantasy that his son exists as a god serves to make up for, or replace, the absence of God in the man's life. The man desires faith in God, but sees no possibility for the existence of that faith in the current destroyed world. In exchange for God, the man believes in his son. Žižek asks, "[H]ow does an empirical, positively given object become an object of desire[....] By entering the framework of fantasy, by being included in a fantasy-scene which gives consistency to the subject's desire" (119). While *The Road* offers no explanation as to exactly when the man begins believing his son exists as a god, by the time the text begins, the man already positions his son as the most important aspect of his life, occupying a symbolic role in which the boy fills in for the lack of the big Other.

The Road opens with the man waking from a dream, a dream in which he pictures his son in an almost supernatural light. The text states that, in the dream, "he had wandered in a cave where the child led him by the hand. Their light playing over the wet flowstone walls. Like pilgrims in a fable swallowed up and lost among the inward parts of some granitic beast" (3). At this moment, the man already positions the boy as ultimately being in control, as the boy leads the man in a reversal of traditional roles. The text indicates the unreality of the situation by comparing their wandering in the cave to "pilgrims in a fable," attempting to find their way out despite being lost (3). While the text acknowledges this as the man's dream, does it differ much from the man's waking world? While the text contradicts the man's dream to an extent, the boy does appear to lead the man to a large degree. The text presents the boy as almost perpetually scared. The boy does not want to go into the house his father grew up in, expressing his fear both before and after entering the house (25, 27). An earthquake frightens the boy, he suffers terrifying nightmares, he is scared to silence during the episode with the murderous cannibal, he fears being left alone, and he fears descending into the one relatively safe location he and his father locate: the underground shelter (28, 36, 66, 70, 137). But for the man, "the boy was all that stood between him and death" (29). In spite of the boy's constant fear, his hunger, his malnutrition, the boy is the man's god. The man does, as Cooper argues, "create God" in his son (224). The man, however, is not the boy's god, in spite of their being "each the other's world entire" (6). The boy incessantly pulls away from his father and develops his own ethical stance, one that empowers him to help whomever he can.

The boy's distancing himself from his father's ethics in the form of extending those ethics to potentially include everyone else on Earth signifies his move toward self-identity. The boy loses more of his identification with his father with each refused request to help another on the road, culminating with the man's disturbing treatment of the thief. This is not to say the boy does not love his father or feel close to him, but the boy recognizes his own autonomy and his ultimate living beyond his father's ethical position. The boy's declaration that he is the one "who has to worry about everything" indicates the boy's understanding of his relative position to his father (259). The boy self-identifies as de facto leader of the group for one rather glaring reason: the father is dying, and the boy knows it. Considering his father's terminal illness, the boy understands his imminent situation: he will soon be alone. He must be the one to worry because he will be the only one to continue. He will occupy some role in the ensuing days; does he occupy the role of post-apocalyptic messiah?

Many questions remain surrounding the characterization of the boy as a messiah, or even a brother's keeper. That the boy may be a messiah connotes some ability to serve a salvational role. Does neither murdering nor cannibalizing other people truly connote messianism, even in this dystopic world? Does loving one's neighbor as oneself inherently carry with it imprints of messianism? Is the boy's messianism strictly limited to the physical world, that he will possess the ability to father children to repopulate this world, operating as an "Adamic figure" as Kunsa argues, thereby saving the human populace? To what end? What does one do with a messiah who inhabits a dying world, whose death offers no hope for lasting generations? Are readers so hesitant to see the death of the world that we, like the father, hope in hopelessness? Does *The Road* even offer hope at the end of the text? What sort of hope can it be, beyond postponing the inevitable? The answers to these questions may hinge upon how literally one reads the father's statements that his son "[is] a god," or that the boy "[glows] in that waste like a tabernacle" (172, 273). Does the boy possess some special attribute, beyond his willingness to help others, which carries the promise of salvation? It appears that the boy does not. It seems the child endears himself to readers as "the best guy" in a depraved world, as the ultimate underdog we so desperately want to see succeed. But does the text really offer that as an option? Does hope survive at the end of *The Road*?

The controversial ending to *The Road*, with its images of hope against hope, the possibility of a future for humans in an inhospitable world, conflicts with the world the text proposes, which presents almost paradoxical notions of a messianic presence in a dying world. Thomas A. Carlson describes the setting as "an unnamed but devastated, dying, and deadly landscape where other people are few and those who do appear represent first and foremost the threat of torment and death" (54). Kunsa, however, argues, "The burned out landscape, strangely, is a new if unlikely Eden," a world "still in the stages of becoming, with regard to both form and content" (62, 64). Kunsa acknowledges, "[T]his world's very existence in the face of such unlikely odds is itself the hopeful suggestion of an alternative to stark existential nothingness" (64). Nevertheless, Kunsa notes the hopefulness and, for McCarthy, the optimism evident in the ending. Kunsa states, "McCarthy uncharacteristically writes possibility into the ending [...] by giving the child a fighting chance" (67). At the risk of being blunt, what is the point of placing a messianic figure in a world beyond salvation, in a dying world? Shelly L. Rambo argues that theology itself must be "re-thought on the other side of disaster. If the devastation of the world is totalizing, even the concept of redemption must be subjected to this devastation. The redemptive narrative shatters" (107). Salvation cannot exist in a completely destroyed world. The text provides no indication that the world is anything but destroyed; along with all life, the hope for salvation and redemption must be laid to rest. If life on Earth is destroyed, the hope that may come from those remaining living must follow suit.

Calling the boy a messiah elevates him from a brother's keeper—a good boy, someone who experiences and expresses empathy, sympathy, and love for other humans—to a spiritual position, a position the boy expresses no knowledge of holding, a position no character beyond his father recognizes. The focus on being a brother's keeper is significant because it humanizes a boy simultaneously dehumanized and elevated in a desire to find meaning in a ruined world devoid of any meaning beyond basic, day-to-day survival. Yes, there are spiritual qualities conferred upon the boy by his father. Yes, the text parallels Biblical stories in multiple ways. But what the text presents is not a superhuman, all-loving individual who offers salvation to a dead world. The text reveals a little boy, a scared, weak, starving boy who understands that eating another human being is an act in which he can never partake, a boy scared to lose his Papa, a boy doomed to die a horrifying death in a horrifying world at the hands of horrifying people.

Works Cited

Broncano, Manuel. "Grocery Shopping in the Commissary of Hell: *The Road*." *Religion in Cormac McCarthy's Fiction: Apocryphal Borderlands*. New York: Routledge, 2013. 125–39. Web. 29 Oct. 2015.
Carlson, Thomas A. "With the World at Heart: Reading Cormac McCarthy's *The Road* with Augustine and Heidegger." *Religion & Literature* 39.3 (2007): 47–71. Web. 13 Apr. 2014.
Cooper, Lydia. "Cormac McCarthy's *The Road* as Apocalyptic Grail Narrative." *Studies in the Novel* 43.2 (2011): 218–36. Web. 28 Apr. 2014.
DeCoste, D. Marcel. "'A Thing That Even Death Cannot Undo': The Operation of the Theological Virtues in Cormac McCarthy's *The Road*." *Religion & Literature* 44.2 (2012): 67–91. Web. 19 Apr. 2016.
Grauland, Rune. "Fulcrums and Borderlands: A Desert Reading of Cormac McCarthy's *The Road*." *Orbis Litterarum* 65.1 (2010): 57–78. Web. 19 Apr. 2016.

Kristeva, Julia. *Powers of Horror: An Essay on Objection.* Trans. Leon S. Roudiez. New York: Columbia University Press, 1982. Print.
Kunsa, Ashley. "'Maps of the World in Its Becoming': Post-Apocalyptic Naming in Cormac McCarthy's *The Road.*" *Journal of Modern Literature* 33.1 (2009): 57–74. Web. 13 Apr. 2014.
LaCapra, Dominick. *History, Literature, Critical Theory.* Ithaca, NY: Cornell University Press, 2013. Print.
McCarthy, Cormac. *The Road.* New York: Vintage, 2006. Print.
New American Standard: The New Inductive Study Bible. Eugene, OR: Harvest House Publishers, 2000. Print.
Rambo, Shelly L. "Beyond Redemption?: Reading Cormac McCarthy's *The Road* After the End of the World." *Studies in the Literary Imagination* 41.2 (2008): 99–120. Web. 20 Apr. 2016.
Žižek, Slavoj. *The Sublime Object of Ideology.* London: Verso, 2002. Print.

"Maps and mazes"
Mapping as Metaphor in Postsecular America

HAROLD K. BUSH

> "Once there were brook trout in the streams of the mountains. You could see them standing in the amber current where the white edges of their fins wimpled softly in the flow. They smelled of moss in your hand. Polished and muscular and torsional. On their backs were vermiculate patterns that were maps of the world in its becoming. Maps and mazes."
>
> —McCarthy 287

I begin with an ending: this long quotation, which is in fact the final passage of Cormac McCarthy's novel *The Road* (2006), leads me directly into a brief reading of the novel, now prominently regarded as perhaps the urtext in many of the most influential literary discussions of this new phenomenon in our field that has now become known as the "postsecular." First the narrator, who might be the spirit of the dead father but who might also be God, invokes the primeval codes on the trout as a significant guiding language for mankind's quest forward into the darkness. That seems to be the "default" understanding of those codes, pointing perhaps toward God. But on second thought, they might not be maps after all; they might be symbolic of the mazelike nature of our existence on this stained world, through the horrific landscape elaborated throughout the novel. Such a landscape is a prominent feature of almost all dystopian fiction, as is the questionable existence of any map that might aid those traveling through them.

I would like to suggest that this narrator's (or perhaps McCarthy's?) hesitation about the maps is especially significant. "Maps and mazes," the voice qualifies it. The fish, evidently now extinct within the world as depicted in the novel, are nevertheless recalled for some reason just as the story reaches its stirring conclusion. The narrator (and who is this voice?) hesitates, does the "postmodern shuffle"—meaning, he qualifies any appearance of a normative statement and admits to the hegemony of a multiculturalism that we all must take as default premise—and clarifies his position that any humans seeing those fish might have dramatically different interpretations of the beautiful, vermiculate patterns of those trout. The voice manages to save his politically incorrect misstep, the assertion of a definitive interpretation; rather, he admits that any interpretation reflects the widely divergent experiences humans have on this earth. Thus, this final paragraph perfectly encompasses some of the central premises of this thing we are calling the "postsecular." *The Road* ends with a decisive, well-wrought gesture toward postmodern epistemological confusion, illustrating with breathtaking aesthetic beauty and poignancy the willing acceptance of this default epistemological position for everyone, including even the godlike voice of the narrator.

So what are these "maps and mazes"? The voice tells us that they have something to do with the world in its "becoming": they are evidently able to guide us authoritatively (maps), but they might also take us deeper into confusion, even into a place of torment (mazes). Perhaps these "maps of our becoming" are clues to discovering what Charles Taylor has called "God's pedagogy" (*Secular* 302). Or perhaps, shockingly, they denote nothing at all. The "mystery" of it all ("mystery" being the final word of *The Road*), is that those patterns may lend themselves equally to the choosing of map or maze. Indeed, this numinous narrator seems to assure us that both may be acceptable interpretations.

Maps, it turns out, are a prominent motif in the novel itself—and beyond any consideration of dystopian fiction, I would argue, maps as metaphors have now become rather common in the theoretical meditations on the postsecular world, which we will examine in more detail later. Throughout the parable of *The Road*, the father consistently consults an old dilapidated map on the journey southward, so the map is also a reminder and a symbol of a long lost civilization. Illustrating hundreds of roads, his map, we are told, is from an old gas station and emblazoned with the name of a once-mighty petroleum company. It gestures toward America's glorious automobile past of freedom, luxury, transport, and sex. The title of this novel even echoes Jack Kerouac's classic parable of that romantic car culture, *On the Road*, but I think it's safe to say McCarthy ironizes that association. For instance, sex, a major theme in Kerouac's story, hardly makes an appearance in *The Road* at all. The relationship with roads is quite different as well. The father's map symbolizes his earnest desire to name his surroundings, to know which way to go, to discover guidance "from above" (the perspective of all maps), and to see some sort of pattern in all the darkness and incoherence of the world around him. This tattered map is symbolic of an old way of reading the world, and therefore a token of hope: a marker of the father's dwindling expectation that belief can shape an inarticulate future. The father's constant clinging to a map, in such a world as the one being traversed in *The Road*, betrays what Wendell Berry has called "difficult hope": "the hope of preserving qualities in one's own heart and spirit that would be destroyed by acquiescence" (62). It is a hope against hope, a hope against all rational odds for his beloved son—but also for himself, and it is symbolized by the map as much as by the fire that is most typically invoked by readers.

Sadly, the words on this old map—the towns, cities, parks, dams, rivers, highways, and so forth—are never once spoken in the novel. The map remains mute throughout. And yet, the final lines of the novel appeal to the "maps of the world in its becoming. Maps and mazes." True enough, the novel ends not with certainty, but uncertainty; qualification rather than declaration. But the allure of the "mappable" is clearly and powerfully evoked here, and most readers leave the tale with some level of hope. The ending also echoes the persistence of the map throughout the novel: it makes an appearance at least ten different times, with the predominant image being the father leaning over it, "studying" it (e.g., 36, 37, 78, 107, 153, 165, 168, 181). They "study" the map together (107, 165), and the son even memorizes the "names of towns and rivers by heart and he measured their progress daily" (181). The father's insistent desire is to be able to "map" the confusing, chaotic, smoky terrain of their current existence—and at the same time, to pass these skills on to his son as well. However, it is never clear how useful the map really is in the story.

On one level, this confusion and hesitation may be said to typify what we are now calling the "postsecular." Arguably, everyone wants a map—meaning, some set of useful directions, an overall and inclusive glimpse of the Real from above. The urge remains, though we have begun to doubt in earnest the very concept of normativity that a map seems to symbolize. Indeed, aren't all maps simply collective constructions, and are historical maps so different? How does a map misconstrue? For example, why is North America willy-nilly on the top of the globe? Such evasions; such skepticisms; such multiplied options for belief or unbelief, are by now a major feature of a world currently dominated by the results—fortunate or not—of what Charles Taylor has called the "nova effect" (*Secular* 299) of modern thought: a massive explosion of myriads of theories or explanations of how to see or read the world we all inhabit. Taylor describes this new landscape well:

> [W]e see ourselves adrift and cast into an anonymous, cold "universe": "Reality in all directions plunges its roots into the unknown and as yet unmappable. It is this sense which defines the grasp of the world as 'universe' and not 'cosmos'; and this is what I

mean when I say that the universe outlook was 'deep' in a way the cosmos picture was not ([*Secular,*] p. 326). And so we find ourselves now in the "dark abyss of time": "Humans are no longer charter members of the cosmos, but occupy merely a narrow band of recent time," for example ([*Secular,*] p. 327) [Smith 71].

I am particularly drawn to Taylor's sense that this new landscape is "unmappable"—or, at least, "as yet unmappable," leading to the possibility that perhaps if we do all put our heads together, a sufficiently practical map may be produced in the near or distant future.

We might then compare McCarthy's and Taylor's pregnant use of the map as metaphor with similar deployments from recent, influential theorists of the postsecular, none of which have been more influential for Americanists than John McClure's clearheaded overview, *Partial Faiths* (2007). In his trenchant introduction, McClure invokes the yearning for a map among today's postsecular "believers." On multiple occasions, throughout the book, he describes characters of conversion who all are nevertheless "still compelled to navigate without any reliable map of the cosmos or history, any full diagram of divine power" (6). Almost immediately after this statement, McClure promises to "sketch out a map of a broader postsecular movement," even though, a few pages later, he asserts that a postsecular religiosity "wants nothing to do with the comprehensive maps and scripts that are essential to sacred systems of domination" (7, 17). Thus, in his account we witness both a desire for better maps and a confession of their general implausibility in our secular age.

I do not wish to degrade in any way the accomplishment of McClure's excellent volume, for it has, perhaps more than any other study, led the way for many critics of American literature to begin "mapping" the postsecular, so to speak, even as it immediately qualified the viability of any such map. In this sense, *Partial Faiths* illustrates precisely the phenomenon it wishes to describe. Make no mistake about it: any theoretical paradigm is, to some extent, an attempt to map a certain terrain. As the influential religion scholar Robert Orsi has written,

> Whether contemporary Americans working to understand particular religious phenomena know it or not, they bring to their inquiries local histories of talk about religion in the United States over time both within and outside the academy. Built into the very tools of analysis are hidden normativities, implicit distinctions between "good" and "bad" religions, and these need to be unpacked [6].

The same is true for literary scholars and theorists, of course. Philosopher James K.A. Smith gets it precisely correct in his useful primer to the concepts of one influential branch of contemporary theology, which is tellingly titled, Introducing *Radical Orthodoxy: Mapping a Post-secular Theology* (2004). There, he states openly, "My goal in this book is to play the role of a cartographer—

mapping the coordinates of recent developments in contemporary theology. [...] I hope this book goes beyond a mere report from the front and can contribute to a constructive vision for how the church should orient itself in a postmodern, post-secular world" (25–26). Smith is convinced that such maps help show us a way forward, so we can speak of the eschatological nature of any map that can guide us along the path of "God's pedagogy."

In trying to work up a definition (or "map") of the postsecular, we should begin by noticing that the very plausibility of a map is enjoying a renaissance—for some people. A majority of our students today—millennials with their allergic reactions to any semblance of normative truth claims—are predisposed to regarding our current age as unmappable. They are precognitive victims of what Francois Lyotard called "delegitimation": a powerful consensus about the breakdown of authoritative explanations about almost anything. Incredulity on the ground, so to speak. At least in my experience, students (or anyone) now find any appeals to so-called authority extremely dubious. Students, in other words, are generally unequipped to imagine a map, let alone to discover one. They do not expect to discover truth in any traditional sense about God, humans, society, or anything else. Considering Christian Smith's analysis of adolescent epistemologies, students now typically reject older concepts of "truth" and choose not to choose. They are largely unwilling (and by now, largely unable) to think in those categories; for many of them, even the possibility of certainty about God or the universe is simply a nonstarter. They are embodiments of Lyotard's most famous phrase: "incredulity toward maps." And yet oddly, and despite their presuppositions, they are both deeply unsettled and intrigued in reading *The Road*, with its account of postsecular hope. There they find that those who are willing, in the words of William James, to go "at least halfway toward" the sublime objects of the sacred—such as the father—still might perceive a map, even in the most hostile environment imaginable.

But is the perception of a map, as Amy Hungerford argues, merely a "belief without belief," or a "belief in meaninglessness" (110)? Or are definitive or normative maps offering meaning and purpose even imaginable anymore? In truth, unless we can imagine a thing, it can never come into the Real. These seem to me to be among the primary questions to be posed in discussions of the "postsecular," however we might construe it. These kind of queries, it turns out, are also being asked by many of my millennial students, born and raised in the postmodern, post-9/11 world, with a smart phone in their hands for the past decade and a glazed look of irony in their eyes and the eyes of everyone around them. This earnest yet incredulous cohort of students finds expectation of a hopeful future quite difficult, if not absurd. But how they yearn for it! And it may sound melodramatic to say it, but many of them connect deeply with the father and son of *The Road*.

But expectation is the kernel of belief; expectation is the seed of hope. William James insisted in *Will to Believe*: "Here are, then, cases, where a fact cannot come at all unless a preliminary faith exists in its coming. And where faith in a fact can help create the fact, that would be an insane logic which should say that faith running ahead of scientific evidence is the 'lowest kind of immorality' into which a thinking being can fall" (qtd. in Taylor, *Varieties* 47). This is precisely the crucial meaning of James' "will to believe": an openness to various forms of evidence and experience. I would like to end with a pitch for expectation, for the possibility of hope in a world deeply suspicious of it, or for the plausibility of a map to find it. Where to begin? In my view, we must return to the rudimentary symbols of our faith, wherein hope resides. First and foremost, we begin by suggesting the possible existence of a map, with qualifications. As the cosmologist-turned-theologian John Polkinghorne asserts, any "credible eschatological hope must involve both continuity and discontinuity" (12). As Polkinghorne puts it, "[F]ailure to respect this balance can lead either to despair that anything will ever change for the better, or to violent imaginings of apocalyptic destruction in which the future can be attained only by the annihilation of the past" (29). The map in *The Road* speaks of a certain continuity, as do the symbols like "carrying the fire," but both appear in a context that is completely discontinuous from the world as we know it: a frightening place populated by degraded beings who are hardly more than moral zombies preying upon one another. The map is therefore a token of eschatological hope, even in a world that has gone off the deep end.

The modern critics have certainly mastered the first part of this equation, and so have our graduate programs of literary studies. Perhaps it is worth noting here that alongside the alleged emergence of the postsecular, a pushback against relentless critique has also arisen, led by the likes of Rita Felski. Felski's turn to the instrumental and pragmatic uses of literature has the ring of older forms of criticism before critique took over (1–22). In my own experience, a focus on beauty, in a profession that often labels beauty as hegemonic or oppressive, is deeply appreciated by students. Most importantly, foregrounding beauty begins the work of reimagining hope and expectation. Learning to see and embrace the beautiful is one roadmap toward the expectation of the beautiful and the attainment of even greater things. Thus does the father in *The Road* often instruct his son to notice the glimpses of beauty that they frequently encounter on their journey. The narrative voice is itself widely admired for its luminously wonderful depictions of various phenomena in the midst of this gray and foggy landscape. Even here, says the father and the narrative voice, there is beauty to be embraced.

Is there something beyond the beautiful? The theorist Paul Ricœur challenges us to ask that question: is interest in the object of the sacred even possible unless we "expect, from within understanding, this something to 'address' itself to [us]? Is not the expectation of being spoken to what motivates the concern for the object?" (30). Ricœur makes a telling admission regarding the search for this next stage of western interpretation: "It is this expectation, this confidence, this belief, that confers on the study of symbols its particular seriousness. To be truthful, I must say it is what animates all my research" (30).

Maybe Ricœur's emphasis on expectations of "being spoken to" is outlandish for many in the academy these days. It is similar to an idea expressed over a hundred years ago by William James, who insisted that "there are some domains in which truths will be hidden from us unless we go at least halfway toward them. [...] [An example] on the scale of the whole society is social trust; doubt it root and branch, and you will destroy it" (Taylor, *Varieties* 46). And again, here is James: "Here are, then, cases, where a fact cannot come at all unless a preliminary faith exists in its coming. And where faith in a fact can help create the fact, that would be an insane logic which should say that faith running ahead of scientific evidence is the 'lowest kind of immorality' into which a thinking being can fall" (Taylor, *Varieties* 47). James equates the complete dismissal of any kind of "faith running ahead of scientific evidence," such as a belief in even the possibility of map, with an "insane logic." It is an insanity, however, that seems to be more and more widespread.

What is an insane English teacher to do? One source that has rarely been mentioned by literary scholars in discussions of the postsecular is the rebirth of interest in the "spiritual" that coincides with what some scholars of religion, such as Harvey Cox, are calling the "Age of the Spirit": "Now we stand on the threshold of a new chapter in the Christian story. Despite dire forecasts of its decline, Christianity is growing faster than it ever has before, but mainly outside the West and in movements that accent spiritual experience, discipleship, and hope" (Cox 8). This explosive growth is commonly conceived to be at its most powerful in the global south, and generally Pentecostal or charismatic in nature, all well documented for many years now, largely thanks to the work of scholars like Phillip Jenkins. But the growth's influence is significant in North America as well. As Christopher Douglas argues in his recent volume, what he calls the "Christian resurgence" is always already part of the conversation when it comes to the handful of authors who are repeatedly invoked in accounts of the postsecular (a list that includes McCarthy, of course): it is "the unrecognized religious context for US literary production since the 1970s" (3). Clearly, growth in the institutional study of the postsecular, and more generally of religion and literature, is being provoked and shaped to some extent by the precocious spiritual proclivities of the culture at large—and of individuals within it. In James' terms, "truths will be hidden from us unless we go at least halfway toward them" (quoted in Taylor, *Varieties* 46). And flocks of seekers are taking that plunge, especially illustrated by how utterly fascinating it is to many of our students today, starved for some mystical enchantment in their lives.

Sadly, the widespread interest in and fascination with the spiritual that permeates American culture has been commonly overlooked, misunderstood, or completely dismissed by many current residents of English departments. Perhaps the real question to ask is why it took the literary scholars so long to figure this out. In her influential work *Postmodern Belief*, Amy Hungerford makes a brilliant observation about John Ames, the narrator of *Gilead* (2004), the widely acclaimed spiritual novel by Marilynne Robinson. Ames, says Hungerford, is "a character fully imagined to be living in Charles Taylor's secular age: he emerges in *Gilead* as a believer profoundly aware of the possibility—even the plausibility—of unbelief" (114). This is a striking claim, given the novel's setting in the early days after World War II, thus predating what is commonly considered the postmodern divide of our era, the 1960s. In that sense, the Rev. John Ames is prophetic in his ability to tap into the level of unbelief that is yet to fully emerge in America, and in his uncanny knack for "mapping out" the road ahead of him, one he would never live to experience himself. In her introduction, Hungerford describes as one of her prominent concerns the ways various writers like Robinson "imagine how intense religious belief can coexist with doctrinal diversity in the shared space of public life as well as in the private enclaves of religious community or the nuclear family" (xiv). Unfortunately, Hungerford never completely unpacks her sense of a character "fully imagined to be living in Charles Taylor's secular age," or how a person like John Ames, born in 1890, can in certain respects be somehow *more* attuned to this new age of belief than any of us are, as we enter 2018.

I would like to push back a bit here and notice how, in my view, John Ames is also a person profoundly aware of the possibility—even the plausibility—of *belief*. It is one thing he has in common with the nameless father of *The Road*. In addition, it is worth quoting Tracy Fessenden's uncanny remarks on Hungerford's study: she warns us of "the enduring hold of the secularization narrative" on our profession—including "the hold that secularization continues to have even on those who have supposedly rejected it" (154–55). And we have professors in major doctoral institutions in literary studies speaking forcefully of a desire to free their graduate students from the "stultifying misconceptions that plague our discipline [...] and so to enable them to unearth the strangeness and particularity of the acts of beliefs and disavowals of belief in the text" (Branch 9). Fessenden wryly notes that what Hungerford has written about contemporary novelists ("they want the fruits of religious power—or at least, they want to help us imagine compelling versions of religious power—without having to answer for the assumptions about the world, and about writing, upon which such visions are built") may ironically be true for the theorists of the postsecular as well (157–58). In my own mind, and riffing on some of Fessenden's concerns, I wonder at the supposed "discovery" by literary scholars of the weakened state of the notion of secularization at this late date, given the research of religious scholars such as those named above. In any case, why didn't the postmodern conceits of high theory, including the shibboleth of "incredulity," provoke the literary crowd against the metanarratives of secularization? Given all the evidence, what took so long?

Maybe it is because many within the fields of literary study have lost their first love, a love that previously included some level of enchantment, beauty, and the sacred. Hungerford gestures toward literature's ability to borrow from religion an "authority that can be mobilized at the level of feeling" (136). But I have met and conversed with many of the well-known professors of literature throughout the land, and it strikes me that feelings have received short shrift in the era of high theory. It is precisely this fact that animates the engaging work of Rita Felski. Instead, the widespread hermeneutic of suspicion has derided the simple pleasures of a text, producing a guild in which feelings, sentiment, or romance are to be cured rather than fostered. With so much media overload, and after a long and dreary presidential campaign, people are searching desperately for good feelings, and both religion and great literature have generally been pretty good at providing pleasant feelings.

To return to the novel and its profound ending, perhaps a reader's perception of a map of hope in *The Road* is in large part a mirror image of that reader's expectation of, or openness to, the voice of a God of hope, one that is always already in evidence in those "vermiculate patterns that were maps of the world in its becoming" (287). As with nature, the novel allows the reader to read those patterns in diversified ways: to find both "maps and mazes"—or to deny them both and assert nothing at all. Likewise, our students come to college equipped with almost no discernible expectation of finding a map—they have been well trained to see the mazes only. For many, if not most, of today's cohort of students, the default position may be to perceive the maze before even being able to imagine a map. Thus do millennials face a landscape without a map: a dystopian reality, indeed.

How might we turn the expectation of a "map" into a real possibility again? Or should we? Is it part of our job description? I vote yes, and here's why: some cognitive scientists are arguing that human imagination represents the culmination of our brains' capacities: according to Daniel Gilbert, the imagination may well constitute the "greatest achievement of the human brain" (5). Ironically, the human imagination has become almost "moribund in discussions of the arts and humanities," according to critic Alan Richardson (665). This conceit is ironic, given the newfound powers of the human imagination being uncovered by cognitive scientists—at just the time when some literary critics are interrogating this new concept of the postsecular. As Richardson suggests, perhaps it is the neuroscientists who will lead literary critics back to a "new romanticism" of human imagination (665). But he also provides a nifty critique of how science has ignored the long tradition of humanist thinking about imagination. In the end, Richardson calls for much further conversation between the poets and the brain scientists.

I would suggest adding to the mix a few English professors, theologians, and assorted other spiritual seekers as well. Perhaps together, we can rescue the human imagination from its premature burial. Lori Branch writes glowingly of "the possible goodness of *holding dear* love, beauty, creativity, art, or the hope for peaceful relation across difference. [...] I long for a discipline and a liberal arts in which we lead students with open eyes into the tall grasses of perhaps the aspect of human life most ignored" (28).

Branch's invocation of leading here is not unlike McCarthy's father, with his continual reference to an old, tattered map: both hint at some authoritative source, and perhaps even at hearing some sublime Voice at the end of our long and arduous journey. Such a voice does appear finally, out of the void, even in the hellhole that is the setting of *The Road*. Students are riveted when I propose to them the historical meanings of both *calling* (typically a Protestant term) and *vocation* (a Catholic term). Note how both terms invoke a speaker, and how expectation precedes hearing.

Can such a voice still speak to our millennial students today? Are there maps out there to lead us onward? I certainly hope so. In this sense, I am totally in agreement with Ricouer: "It is this expectation, this confidence, this belief, that confers on the study of symbols its particular seriousness. To be truthful, I must say it is what animates all my research" (30). My sincere prayer is that it animates my teaching as well.

Works Cited

Berry, Wendell. *What Are People For?* San Francisco: North Point Press, 1990. Print.
Branch, Lori. "The Rituals of Our Re-Secularization: Literature Between Faith and Knowledge." *Religion and Literature* 46.2-3 (Summer-Autumn 2014): 9–29. Print.
Cox, Harvey. *The Future of Faith*. San Francisco: HarperOne, 2009. Print.
Douglas, Christopher. *If God Meant to Interfere: American Literature and the Rise of the Christian Right*. Ithaca: Cornell University Press, 2016. Print.
Felski, Rita. *Uses of Literature*. New York: Wiley-Blackwell, 2008. Print.
Fessenden, Tracy. "The Problem of the Postsecular." *American Literary History* 26.1 (2014): 154–67. Print.
Gilbert, Daniel. *Stumbling on Happiness*. New York: Vintage, 2007. Print.
Hungerford, Amy. *Postmodern Belief: American Literature and Religion Since 1960*. Princeton: Princeton University Press, 2010. Print.
McCarthy, Cormac. *The Road*. New York: Vintage, 2006. Print.
McClure, John. *Partial Faiths: Postsecular Faith in the Age of Pynchon and Morrison*. Athens: University of Georgia Press, 2007. Print.

Orsi, Robert. *Between Heaven and Earth: The Religious Worlds People Make and the Scholars Who Study Them.* Princeton: Princeton University Press, 2005. Print.
Polkinghorne, John. *The God of Hope and the End of the World.* New Haven: Yale University Press, 2002. Print.
Richardson, Alan. "Defaulting to Fiction: Neuroscience Rediscovers the Romantic Imagination." *Poetics Today* 32.4 (Winter 2011): 663–92.
Ricœur, Paul. *Freud and Philosophy: An Essay on Interpretation.* New Haven: Yale University Press, 1965. Print.
Smith, James K. A. *Introducing Radical Orthodoxy: Mapping a Post-Secular Theology.* Grand Rapids, MI: Baker Academic, 2004. Print.
Taylor, Charles. *A Secular Age.* Cambridge: Harvard University Press, 2007. Print.
_____. *Varieties of Religious Belief Today: William James Revisited.* Cambridge: Harvard University Press, 2002. Print.

PART TWO: POPULAR DYSTOPIAN FICTION

Unmasking the Deception
The Hermeneutic of Suspicion in Lois Lowry's The Giver

C. CLARK TRIPLETT *and* JOHN J. HAN

Since the publication of Lois Lowry's novel *The Giver* in 1993, there have been a number of critical reviews of her work. Most of them tend to present a somewhat conventional reading of the text: the author portrays a seemingly utopian society that turns out to be dystopian. In her *New York Times* review, Karen Ray calls Lowry's work "a powerful and provocative novel" in which "sameness" is initially presented positively before "clues [...] suggest malevolence." By the end of the story, the main character, Jonas, makes a difficult decision to do something that no one in his community has done: "Set apart by his station, Jonas faces a lonely and desperate struggle with evil disguised as sameness, and ultimately, armed with knowledge of emotion as well as sensation, he makes a challenging choice" (Ray). An anonymous reviewer for *Publisher's Weekly* also sees *The Giver* as a novel about an ostensibly "ordered, pain-free society" that turns out to be perniciously deceitful: "[A]s his near-mystical training progresses, and he is weighed down and enriched with society's collective memories of a world as stimulating as it was flawed, Jonas grows increasingly aware of the hypocrisy that rules his world" ("The Giver"). Certainly, these two reviewers—and many others—rightly note the deceptiveness of what appears to be a superficially peaceful, pleasant, and comfortable society.

What is lacking in existing discussions of *The Giver* is an analysis of the recurring themes in this text that relate to the place of critical thinking and questioning which, in some cases, may be part of story itself or part of the story's implications for a broader society. Throughout Lowry's work, there is repetitive language dealing with hiding and concealing that seems to demand a deeper look beyond the obvious for another layer of meaning. In *The Giver*, language is used in an unusual way that leads to a suspicion that something is wrong or misleading. The story itself raises questions about the need for critical inquiry that may speak to something richer and deeper within the utopian community—something hidden that needs to be revealed. The invitation to look beyond and to unmask the cloudy language and behavior of the community for an alternative reading exists from the beginning of the story. Critique, in a sense, promises another narrative that turns out to be rich with new sensations and colors, but also full of pain and danger. Teasing out the multiple meanings and intentions of this story requires a methodology that is both rigorous and capable of opening up more imaginative ways of understanding and experiencing the life-world.

Indeed, although contemporary dystopian literature represents diverse settings and themes, there does seem to be an underlying thread of suspicion that permeates the narrative of these texts. Each story either patently or latently raises critical questions about the cultural, technological, or political solutions of both the text and world of the reader. This idea of a substratal critical direction of dystopian fiction may not find a very receptive audience in the current postcritical climate in literary studies. For many scholars, traditional critical methods are often viewed as static and repressive; they simply impose one literary convention on all others. Some methods may silence a multitude of voices for the sake of a stable and usually fixed perspective. Attitudes toward critique may vary depending on where scholars fall on a number of philosophical and ideological antitheses, including the modernism-postmodernism, structuralism-poststructuralism, close reading-distant reading, and/or explanatory-interpretive poles. Some scholars may understand critique from within a particular time and place while others may emphasize the importance of a broader epistemological framework. However, there are more "flexible" models that attempt to balance the need for philosophical and linguistic objectivity with the recognition that interpretation is always immersed in a particular time, place, and language. This model offers a useful tool for analyzing *The Giver* to garner helpful insight into its unique meaning(s).

Paul Ricœur's Hermeneutic of Suspicion

The hermeneutic of suspicion is a concept that was developed by French philosopher Paul Ricœur who wanted to "capture a common spirit that pervades the writings of Marx, Freud, and Nietzsche" (Felski, "Critique"). Although these fathers of contemporary theory represent varying disciplines and philosophies, they shared a common "suspicion" of the deceptions and illusions of modern thought. Ricœur particularly considers the work of Sigmund Freud in his classic work *Freud and Philosophy*. His interest in Freud's analytic method was linguistic and symbolic rather than psychological; in his words, "the psychoanalyst is a leading participant in any general discussion about language" (4). Freud's interpretive method, particularly related to dream analysis, emphasizes the importance of two levels of meaning. The first level of meaning is an obvious or manifest meaning (the dream account) that is fictive, disguising another meaning that reveals a wish or desire. For Freud, the manifest text (the dream) is presented in a distorted or disguised form, often condensed, displaced, or overdetermined, and the text means something other than what it says. Therefore, according to Ricœur, psychoanalysis attempts to discover the relationship between desire and language. In order to "reveal" the content of desire, however, another text must be substituted to understand the language of desire that underlies the disguised obvious meaning.

Extrapolating from Freud's psychoanalytic method, Ricœur develops a comprehensive theory of interpretation: "To mean something other than what is said—this is the symbolic function" (12). Starting with this idea, Ricœur subsequently builds a broad theory of interpretation that is based on Freud's "double-action" in the interpretation of dreams: "The world's expressiveness achieves language through symbol as double meaning" (15). Without getting lost in the details of Ricœur's complex philosophy of language and meaning, it is enough to say that, according to Ricœur, the process of interpretation always involves multiple steps to understand a text. There is a "showing-hiding" component within the text, and there is both an "unmasking" and "retrieving" function involved in interpretation: "Hermeneutics seems to me to be animated by this double motivation: willingness to suspect, willingness to listen; vow of rigor, vow of obedience" (27). The dual process includes both a critical and imaginative function—a look behind the text to unmask and explain and a look in front of the text to understand the possibilities of meaning. Like Freud, Ricœur believes that the subject and the message are never what they seem to be *prima facie*; language, culture, narcissism, desire, and illusion interfere with the search for meaning and truth: "Symbols give rise to thought, but they are also the birth of idols" (543). Interpretation requires both the shattering of idols and the retrieval of a new naiveté.

However, it is the second movement of Ricœur's hermeneutic that provides the bridge between critique and imagination that makes his theory pertinent to literary studies. The dual meaning of texts that both hide and reveal opens up the possibility for a rich and imaginative understanding of human experience. Criticism alone leads to a static description of reality that is trapped within a particular time and place. The ultimate purpose of critique, according to Ricœur, is to strip symbols of their particular cultural and linguistic shackles that limit the ability to understand the text from diverse angles. Meaning spreads beyond any particular horizon to a broader vista of possible experiences. Later, Ricœur will expand on this idea in his discussions about the fullness of language and the power of metaphor to explain reality. Biblical scholar Anthony Thistleton explains how his method reveals new options for understanding human life: "While cerebral concepts and factual reports *reflect already-perceived actualities*, metaphors and narratives *create possible ways of seeing and understanding* the world and human life" (351; original emphasis). The hermeneutic of retrieval, then, reveals creative new contexts and visions for redescribing the world. Ricœur uses the concept of metaphor to more clearly articulate the idea of double meaning. It is the primary means in narrative for revealing how giving something a name that belongs to something else expands understanding by analogy. It is interesting that metaphor becomes the primary heuristic tool for explaining the strange and bizarre worlds of quantum theory and the special theory of relativity.

The hermeneutic of suspicion and retrieval, unlike traditional critical models, proposes a double interpretive action that reaches beyond a mere static approach of critical description and reaches behind and beyond the surface meaning of a particular culture, time, and place toward expanded possibilities of narrative and experience. By thinking through restrictive categories of convention, language, and political ideologies, retrieval fleshes out creative new meanings in opposition to stodgy, reductionistic portrayals of reality. The hermeneutic of suspicion raises critical questions about the surface meaning of texts to uncover meanings that are often hidden behind special interests and the ideological hegemony of a particular culture. Suspicion questions the received version of meaning within a particular context and considers creative possibilities. Stephen Squibb explains how suspicion works against the obvious reading of any text: "[T]he suspicious critic is understood to be working against the articulated agency of the text in order to reveal what it conceals consciously or otherwise" (2). In turn, the hermeneutic of retrieval aligns and allies itself with the text and seeks an "overflowing" that reveals new possibilities.

Rita Felski, William R. Keenan Professor of English at the University of Virginia, reconsiders the place of critique in literature by re-examining Ricœur's hermeneutic of suspicion. She argues that the hermeneutic of suspicion has offered a "new vocabulary" for raising critical questions about literary texts that are particularly important in the context of postmodern and postcritical readings. Felski differentiates suspicion from broad traditional methods of critique: "It allows us to define critical and suspicious reading as one possible method among others rather than the manifest destiny and telos of literary studies" ("The Hermeneutics of Suspicion"). Interestingly, Felski argues that many of the current protests against the use of the critical method actually end up "doubling down" on their own form of critique in ways that indicate that they are still very part and parcel of the same world: "[C]ritique is to be replaced by critique squared" ("Critique"). Felski believes that Ricœur finds a path out of the usual maze of theories of reading by using the lens of philosophical hermeneutics. This form of analysis "has the singular advantage of allowing us to by-pass the exceptionalist tendencies of critique: its presumption that whatever is not critique can only be assigned to the ignominious state of the uncritical" ("Critique"). Ricœur's method provides a process of focus and distanciation while at the same time allowing for invention and strategy in understanding the meaning of the text. Critique is rather like a "muted affective state" or mood in which the reader spars with the text as a puzzle to be solved or a code to be broken to reveal what has often been concealed by the trappings of a particular culture or language. Felski thinks that the concept of suspicion is a "less prejudicial term [that] opens up a larger history of suspicious reading, including traditions of religious questioning and self-scrutiny that bear on current forms of interpretation, but that are occluded by the aggressively secular connotations of critique" ("Critique").

Although Felski makes a strong case for the place of suspicion in literary studies, the question is what this might look like in the analysis of a particular text or narrative. Perhaps even more importantly for this discussion, what are the broader implications of Ricœur's method on the thesis that dystopian fiction is implicitly a form of critique? How does the idea of suspicion shed light on the meaning and intent of dystopian works in general? This discussion specifically focuses on Lois Lowry's novel, *The Giver*, to demonstrate that critique or suspicion is an essential element of the story and how this attitude can be extrapolated to the broader culture at large.

Re-Examining The Giver *in Light of the Hermeneutic of Suspicion*

The Giver is set in a supposedly utopian world devoid of pain, hunger, and suffering. Twelve-year-old Jonas is selected as the Receiver of Memory, a unique and prestigious position, unlike all the others, that includes absorbing all the inherited memories of the community—both pleasant and unpleasant—that have been erased from the minds of the rest of the population. It is the responsibility of the current Giver to transmit these memories to Jonas through a gradual process. These memories are filled with diverse emotions as well as brilliant colors and experiences that are lacking in the utopian community where Jonas lives. As Jonas becomes familiar with the current Giver, he learns about the previous intern, the Giver's daughter, who was overwhelmed by these memories and asked to be released. When this happened, all the memories she had learned were dispersed throughout the community, creating pain and anxiety for everyone. After a period of intense experiences of learning the memories of the community and his growing awareness of the underlying intentions of the community leaders, he agrees with the Giver to escape to the world outside the community, called Elsewhere, which will automatically trigger a release to the whole community. The Giver promises Jonas that, when this happens, he will help the community come to terms with the past memories and painful emotions of humanity.

One of the consequences of gaining the memories of the community is that Jonas begins to discover things about the community that were not evident before. Jonas gradually realizes that the words and actions of the community may have a different purpose than what was apparent. One of the most appalling discoveries is that Gabriel, the infant that he has helped care for, is scheduled to be "released," which he realizes, to his astonishment, means that he is to be euthanized (*The Giver* 206). At that point, Jonas decides to take Gabriel and flee the community in search of Elsewhere. As he travels further into the depths of Elsewhere, the landscape begins to change and his feelings and awareness expand in both painful and joyful ways. In the final, somewhat controversial scene, Jonas and Gabriel brave a "bitterly cold" and "blinding" snowstorm, riding a sled down a snowy hill towards brightly colored twinkling lights and merry music (224–25).

In *The Giver*, Jonas is portrayed as someone who gradually begins to perceive things differently in his community. He begins to see beyond the obvious and raises questions about the apparent meaning of things. On the surface, the utopian community in the narrative seems to be an ideal society with practically no violence or serious crime. There is no war or fear of pain, and the community has the appearance of orderliness and peace. To maximize happiness for all, the community leaders do everything to create a context of "Sameness" (120). Babies are produced by "Birthmother[s]," and one boy and one girl are allowed for each married couple (26, 11). Every citizen is assigned an occupation, and important decisions are made by the Community of Elders. Peace is secured by keeping everything within a narrow range of behaviors and activities that are carefully monitored. In the words of Jonas, "We really have to protect people from wrong choices" (124). Conversations are tightly controlled to avoid the possibility of conflict or disruption. Intense emotions of any kind are discouraged, and the citizens of the community take medication to suppress feelings. Unfit babies, the elderly, and repeat offenders are released as a means of maintaining an even and peaceful climate throughout the community. Most importantly, with the exception of one person, individuals are devoid of past memories. This, of course, limits the choices and possibilities of citizens that might lead to wrong thinking or pathological behaviors. This ultimately means that existence is literally black-

and-white and predictable. In other words, the seemingly utopian community of *The Giver* is a tightly controlled totalitarian state.

The unique position of the Giver is that he lives separately from the rest of the community on the boundaries of "Elsewhere" (54). He alone retains the memories of the past, which are intensely vivid, filled with stunning colors and complex pleasant and painful emotions. These memories are hidden from the rest of the community because they are filled with the images and emotions that lead to violence and offense. Interestingly, the Giver is a highly respected member of the community who has the unique ability "to see beyond" (120). Despite every attempt to conceal these memories from the community, the Giver is called upon by the Community of Elders to impart wisdom when irresolvable problems emerge. Based on his gift to see beyond and to experience the emotional and stimulating memories of the past, he thus dispenses advice to solve the problems of the community.

A theme that runs throughout Lowry's novel is the place of concealment in the community. Words are used to hide unpleasant experiences, such as intense emotions, pain, and death. Instead of the words *kill* and *death*, indirect words such as *release* are used to disguise the harsh reality of pain and loss. Unpleasant things are hidden to curb intense reactions, and emotional conversations are discouraged. Subterfuge is a primary instrument for managing the community and manipulating the populace. As Jonas gains the memories of the community, he very quickly begins to notice the special use of words that demand another interpretation. For example, the use of the phrase "precision of speech" is a response of parents to children who use terms that express strong emotions (69). However, "precision of speech" is not a phrase that encourages authentic expression, but distracts from a clear and truthful response to what is actually occurring. The surface meaning of a special word or phrase is not to reveal or confess, but rather to make a threat against what is said. There is danger in the practice of honesty and openness. Precision of language in the utopia of *The Giver* is really a message about the need to conceal and hide. Other phrases, such as "I apologize" for possible offenses (4), seem to be empty of meaning and actually drain language of any depth or richness, thereby serving as a ritualistic incantation that magically takes away the force and significance of the offense.

Interestingly, from birth, citizens of this seeming utopia are taught never to lie. It is a prime rule of the community that one should not hold secrets or withhold anything, particularly from the Community of Elders. However, as Jonas soon discovers, "never l[ying]" does not necessarily mean telling the truth (89). Rather, it is a warning against using speech and language that contradicts the rules and expectations of the community; the precision of language in utopia is an opportunity for concealment and subterfuge. Instead of opening up and expanding discourse, language is used to dilute and tone down the extremes of life. Everything is described in flat, toneless, repetitive phrases that discourage revelation and discovery. The consequence of such bland and mundane interactions is the loss of music, color, and excitement. It also comes at the price of individual identity and freedom of choice.

As Jonas struggles through the process of absorbing the memories of the community, his world begins to change: the ability to see beyond initially opens up his experience in ways that are occasionally startling and frightening. Faded images begin to take on brilliant and stunning colors. The variety of polymorphous impressions that came from the collective memories of the community floods his consciousness and alters his understanding of reality. His first experience is when he observes a monochromatic apple that takes on a brilliant red hue. This is simply the beginning of a kaleidoscope of experiences that will irrevocably shift his perspective on the only community he has ever known. His capacity to see beyond, or see behind, the surface reality of his community eventually leads him outside the boundaries of his immediate experience into a world that is rich, complex, and dangerous. The ending of the text leaves the reader with questions about whether his expanded vision leads him to death or the promise of a new life as a flood of sensations fill his mind:

> Downward, downward, faster and faster. Suddenly he was aware with certainty and joy that below, ahead, they were waiting for him; and that they were waiting, too, for the baby [Gabriel]. For the first time, he heard something that he knew to be music. He heard people singing.
>
> Behind him, across vast distances of space and time, from the place he had left, he thought he heard music too. But perhaps it was only an echo [Lowry 225].

In an interview, Lowry offers her opinion that the ending of the novel is positive and that Jonas survives:

> I will say that I find it an optimistic ending. How could it not be an optimistic ending, a happy ending, when that house is there with its lights on and music is playing? So I'm always kind of surprised and disappointed when some people tell me that they think the boy and the baby just die. I don't think they die. What form their new life takes is something I like people to figure out for themselves. And each person will give it a different ending. I think they're out there somewhere and I think that their life has changed and their life is happy, and I would like to think that's true for the people they left behind as well ["In Her Own Words" 6].

Lowry's approach is not the only way to interpret the novel's ending. Indeed, in her introduction to the Houghton Mifflin Harcourt edition of the novel, Lowry allows for multiple ways of reading her work: "A book is such an individual and private thing. The reader brings his or her own history and beliefs and concerns, and reads in solitude, creating each scene from his own imagination as he does" ("Introduction" xi). The last sentence of the novel, "But perhaps [music] was only an echo," makes it possible to imagine that Jonas and Gabriel do not survive.

It is the elusiveness of both language and behavior in *The Giver* that leaves the novel susceptible to the hermeneutic of suspicion. The repeated use of particular words and phrases that cloud meaning raises questions about the meaning and intent of such misdirection. Only the Giver seems to have the capacity to unmask the hidden meanings of the community. The hiding-revealing nature of certain euphemisms and the strict insistence on corrective phrases such as the "precision of language" raises questions about the moral trajectory and strategic choices of the community. Both Jonas and the reader are compelled to look behind the given text for an alternate understanding of their experience. Do the messages of the community reveal sincere efforts to protect and save its citizens, or is it an effort to control the thoughts and choices of the community which might lead to dangerous ideas and decisions? As the story makes clear, the retrieval of memory does not necessarily guarantee a utopian experience, but it does bring an expanded scope of reality that makes life rich. Obviously, the vicissitudes of human freedom offer diverse experiences that can be risky and contingent. The cascading flood of images and visions that occur when the shackles of control and deception are thrown off also present the possibility of failure and tragedy. The possibility of understanding (*Verstehen*) in *The Giver* begins with critically questioning the obvious meanings of words and actions of the community. Interpretation starts with unmasking the confusing language and meanings of the received text. But the uncovering-revealing task of interpretation moves beyond mere description—it ultimately leads to a new wonder or naiveté that widens the parameters of experience and unfolds novel possibilities for understanding. Critique shatters the idols of convention, habit, and tradition and invites the reader to experience diverse alternatives for seeing the world.

As these examples show, critique is at the heart of *The Giver*. Paul Ricœur's hermeneutic of suspicion offers one way of examining the double-meaning implicit within the story of the novel. This is not to say, from an authorial perspective, that Lois Lowry was influenced by Ricœur in the creation of the text, but regardless of the author's intent, suspicion threads its way throughout the novel. In the 1993 Dell Laurel-Leaf edition of *The Giver*, a Readers' Guide raises a question about why the community uses words in a way that stresses the "precision of language" while at the same time "[building] upon language that is not precise but deliberately clouds meaning" (Schmidt 3). The interrogatory seems to imply that Jonas' concern for his community has implications for contemporary society and the need for critical reflection on cultural discourse that disguises and misleads rather than encourages truth-telling and intellectual openness.

Although this discussion has focused on a particular example of dystopian fiction, it is not difficult to see how the concept of suspicion and critique is integral to other classical dystopian works such as *1984*, *Fahrenheit*

451, and *The Children of Men*, to name a few. A recent work by *New York Times* bestselling author Thomas E. Ricks, *Churchill and Orwell: The Fight for Freedom*, argues cogently that both Churchill and Orwell had the foresight to raise questions at a critical point in history that challenged the totalitarian language and ideologies from the right and left that threatened the freedom of democratic societies. The clear critical message of both *Animal Farm* and *1984* provided a counter-narrative that alerted the public to the danger of such regimes. It is not difficult to see how dystopian novels such as *The Giver* offer narratives that elevate the value and importance of critique, particularly in the twenty-first century political climate in which the echo chambers of various splinter groups so easily influence the electorate with false narratives and misleading truths.

Conclusion

Although the series of essays in this volume argues for the implicit critical function of dystopian fiction, this discussion has focused on how critique is an essential component of the narrative in Lois Lowry's *The Giver*. The text was examined through the lens of Paul Ricœur's hermeneutic of suspicion, which offers a more flexible methodology that includes a double-movement that is both critical and interpretive. Although there is considerable controversy about the use of critique in literary studies, Ricœur's idea of suspicion seems better suited for literary studies because it emphasizes both the need for critical distance (looking behind the text) and the imaginative reception of the text (looking in front of the text) emphasized in reader-oriented approaches to interpretation. Rather than insisting on static traditional methodologies, the hermeneutic of suspicion simply raises questions that unmask the surface meaning of a particular narrative in order to consider alternative interpretations that both consider the novel and expand perspectives of human experience. Based on Rita Felski's interpretation of Ricœur's method, critique is understood as a "muted affective state" that spars with the text by employing "innovative strategies" that suggest alternate possibilities rather than a rigid structure imposed from the outside ("Critique").

The Giver is a particularly fruitful story for exploring the validity of the hermeneutical method in literary studies. The story of Jonas, the protagonist of the narrative, demonstrates the value of critique in a closed community that uses disguised and deceitful language to maintain control of the experience of its populace. Jonas' special ability as the chosen recipient of the community's past memories gives him the ability to see beyond the surface meanings of day-to-day communications to observe and hear a reality that becomes more apparent as he takes on the past experiences of humanity. The emphasis in the novel on the special use of language that hides meaning instead of revealing it begs Jonas and the reader to question the legitimacy of the obvious messages that guide the community in its efforts to provide a peaceful, safe society.

This analysis provides an example of how critical methods might be applied. The effort is not meant to propose an exclusive approach to literary critique, but one option among many. Ricœur's work seems to make it clear that the purpose of critical inquiry is not to discover settled truths, but rather to serve as a way of listening to many voices that offers an expanded and creative view of human experience. Ricœur's theory of double meaning provides an opportunity for rigorous questioning and imaginative and sometimes counter-intuitive answers.

Works Cited

Felski, Rita. "Critique and the Hermeneutic of Suspicion." *M/C Journal: A Journal of Media and Culture* 15.1 (2012). Web. 1 June 2017.
_____. "The Hermeneutics of Suspicion." *The 2014–2015 Report on the State of the Discipline of Comparative Literature.* 21 Feb. 2014. Web. 2 June 2017.
"The Giver." Rev. of *The Giver*, by Lois Lowry. *Publishers Weekly* Web. 5 May 2017
"In Her Own Words—A Conversation with Lois Lowry." *The Giver*, by Lois Lowry. New York: Dell Laurel-Leaf, 1993. 4–6. Print.
Lowry, Lois. *The Giver.* Boston: Houghton, 1993. Print.
_____. "Introduction: *The Giver*." Boston: Houghton, 1993. vii–xii. Print.
Ray, Karen. Rev. of *The Giver*, by Lois Lowry. *New York Times* 31 Oct. 1993. Web. 5 May 2017.
Ricks, Thomas E. *Churchill and Orwell: The Fight for Freedom.* New York: Penguin, 2017. Print.
Ricœur, Paul. *Freud and Philosophy: An Essay on Interpretation.* New Haven: Yale University Press, 1970. Print.
Schmidt, Gary D. "A Readers Guide: Questions for Discussion." *The Giver*, by Lois Lowry. New York: Dell Laurel-Leaf, 1993. 1–3. Print.
Squibb, Stephen. "From Suspicion to Solidarity?" *Arcade: Literature, Humanities, and the World* 16 March 2017. Web. 1 June 2017.
Thistleton, Anthony C. *New Horizons in Hermeneutics: The Theory and Practice of Transforming Biblical Reading.* Grand Rapids, MI: Zondervan, 1992. Print.

Ending Dystopia
The Feminist Critique of Culture in Suzanne Collins' Hunger Games *Trilogy*

JANE BEAL

In 1516, the publication of Thomas More's Latin *Utopia* originated a new genre for the critique of English society: utopian/dystopian fiction. More, a Catholic humanist, composed his satirical work with an eye to earlier Roman literary models (e.g., Plato's *Republic*) and an ear to Christian ethics.[1] His own narrative develops as a conversation between men, including one Captain Hythloday, who, while traveling in the New World, "discovered" the island of Utopia. The three key influences in More's Utopia—classical learning, a sense of justice informed by Judeo-Christian morality, and the discovery of a "new world"—shaped More's work and helped him to articulate his critique. More's purpose in *Utopia* was not, of course, to inform his highly educated, Latinate, mostly male readers about a "good place," a utopian country in the New World, but rather to critique a *dystopian* country in his own Old World: England.

Virtually all subsequent utopian/dystopian fiction in the western tradition is generically defined by elements found in More's *Utopia*, and feminist utopian writings and contemporary feminist dystopian fiction are no exceptions.[2] The later development of the genre branches out from its roots (Christian humanist satire), producing distinctly different fruit (literary works), because it hybridizes the tree (the genre). Whereas More's *Utopia*, like Platonic dialogues, is a conversation between men, feminist dystopias expand the conversation that critiques culture by

- internalizing it in their female protagonists, where its very interiority can give women power to resist male-dominated cultural forces of violence, deception, manipulation, corruption, and destruction in the dystopian environment;

- externalizing and articulating it between female as well as male characters;
- making part of it solely between women in their texts;
- focusing it on the human rights of women, especially the right to life, the right to freedom of the will, mind, heart, and body, and the right to self-determination in their relationships and roles in the world;
- and emphasizing the importance of *alliance* between women and children, women and men, women and women, women and the environment, and women and sources of cultural power in their world.

Authors of feminist dystopian fiction frequently take as a given that the world their female protagonists live in is being represented to those women as utopian, as a "good place" that is culturally and politically organized for their benefit, but they emphasize in no uncertain terms that the world is in fact dystopian. They show that the male-dominated cultural forces in their fictions consistently seek to exploit women's bodies, in violation of their will, at the expense of their minds and to the detriment of their emotional well-being. They do not hesitate to show how some female characters living in dystopia accept these forces while others actually become perpetuators of them, and they may also highlight how male characters are not only oppressors but may be oppressed by the mechanisms of injustice in dystopia. But in response to the "big lie" that women are living in utopia, when the actual conditions of their existence are mercilessly dystopian, authors send their female protagonists on a journey of personal and relational growth. The journey inevitably includes acquisition of new knowledge, new strength, and new, previously unknown, and virtually unimaginable freedom.

This trajectory is especially clear when reading the endings of feminist dystopian fictions. Because feminist dystopian fiction is very much in keeping not only with utopian satire but also with the fairy-tale tradition, it engages the human psychological realities of hope and fear, but often—quite purposefully—without the consolation of a traditional "happy ending." This raises a key question: since the endings are clearly not wish-fulfillment fantasies, intended for the temporary satisfaction of readers, what purposes are being accomplished by the endings of feminist dystopian fictions? To explore the question, this essay focuses on the ending of Suzanne Collins' *Hunger Games* trilogy (2008–2010).[3] As we shall see, her fiction makes new use of the generic elements of the utopian satirical tradition—classical learning, Christian ethics, and the discovery of a new world—in a "bad place" where the development of the psychological complexity of her female protagonist on her journey drives the critique of the real dystopia: the postmodern world inhabited by the author and her readers at the turn of the twenty-first century.

Hybridizing Genre

Like More's *Utopia*, Suzanne Collins' *Hunger Games* trilogy draws on classical learning, Christian ethics, and the discovery of a new world—discovered, that is, from the perspective of the protagonist, Katniss Everdeen, who is thrust from her home, District 12, into the larger world of Panem and its appalling Hunger Games. Collins creates dystopian fiction, an outbranching from both More and feminist utopian tradition. Specifically, Collins hybridizes the genre by incorporating generic elements from romance and fairy-tale to create quasi-realistic speculative fiction for young adults.

Collins draws on classical learning to create the world of Panem. The name of the world, *panem*, is Latin for "bread," and Collins draws it from a phrase of the Roman satirist Juvenal: *Duas tantum res anxius optat—panem et circenses* ("The [people] anxiously hope for only two things—bread and circuses") (*Satire* X.80). In so saying, Juvenal was drawing attention to the way that the failing Roman government of his day pacified the elite citizenry by distributing wheat and staging enormous spectacles in the Coliseum. This effectively satisfied the people's hunger for food and entertainment, but simultaneously prevented their political engagement with the real issues of the day. The phrase continues to be used in English to indicate when any government seeks to bolster its approval ratings, not through exemplary service or good policy, but through the appeasement and distraction of its population, with the result that bad government continues and citizens ignore their civic responsibilities. Collins is certainly using the idea behind the Latin word and the phrase it comes from in this way in her dystopia, where the Capitol is inhabited by wealthy citizens who eat remarkably well and, with obsessive fascination, watch the Hunger Games, a reality TV program in which children from the Districts must kill each other in a horrifying arena until one of them emerges as victor.

The Hunger Games and the arenas in which they occur are clearly extrapolations of Roman spectacles and the Coliseum. Collins has commented in an interview that she chose her genre, rather than a realist novel in which an actual war occurred, because

> there are sort of allegorical elements to it. The arena's very allegorical. It's the symbol—we're going to watch it transform. And I need to be able to create that, manipulate it, as I need it to work out. There's a basis for the war, historically, in the *Hunger Games*, which would be the third servile war, which was Spartacus' war, where you have a man who is a slave who is then turned into a gladiator who broke out of the gladiator school and led a rebellion and then became the face of the war. So there is a

historical precedent for that arc for a character. But I think I needed the freedom to create elements that I wasn't going to neatly find in history [Collins qtd. in Lawrence].

The idea that the arena is allegorical or symbolic is an intriguing one: within it, Katniss Everdeen becomes a young, female fictional gladiator, a version of the adult, male historical gladiator, Spartacus. She is trapped by a lottery system that, quite purposefully, looks remarkably like the ancient Cretan system, which demanded that Athens, once it had been conquered, send young men and women each year to be delivered to the Minotaur in the Labyrinth.[4] In Panem, the sacrifice of children from the Districts in the Hunger Games of the Capitol is justified as a means of punishment for the past rebellion of the Districts.

In Collins' web of classical allusion, President Snow might be compared to King Minos of Crete, but his first name, Coriolanus, aligns him with the Roman tyrant depicted in Shakespeare's *Coriolanus*. Indeed, the names of the citizens of the Capitol are typically Roman ones while the names of the disenfranchised residents of the Districts are associated with the natural world (Krule). Katniss, for example, is an edible plant of the genus *Sagittaria*, which is related to the Latin word *sagittarius*, meaning "archer" and referring also to the astronomical constellation and the ninth sign of the Zodiac, a mutable fire sign (Dictionarywww). Obviously both archery and fire feature significantly in Katniss, who uses bow and arrow to hunt and who is known by the moniker "the girl on fire," due to her stylist Cinna's decision to dress her in flammable clothing in honor of the coal-mining work which employs most families in District 12, including, at one time, her own before her father was killed in a mining accident.

Kathryn Strong Hansen sees in Katniss the influence of the Greek mythological figures of Artemis, the virgin goddess of the hunt who is associated with archery, and Philomela, a woman who was raped but found a way to tell her loyal sister her story through a tapestry before she was turned into a nightingale by the gods. Hansen argues that "the two figures provide Katniss with ways of navigating a dictatorial patriarchy, culminating in her ultimate rejection of both mythic characters to create a form of femininity that allows her to break free from her past and to change her society" (161). Others have compared Katniss to Perpetua.[5]

Vibia Perpetua (AD 181–203) was an early Christian martyr killed by the sword in the Roman Coliseum. A young breast-feeding mother, accompanied by her slave Felicitas in prison, she dreamed before her death of a bronze ladder reaching into heaven, with weapons such as swords and spikes attached to it, beneath which lay a huge dragon that sought to prevent climbers from ascending. She followed a fellow Christian, Saturus, in climbing the ladder, which brought her to a garden with a man dressed as a gray-haired shepherd in the midst of it. He was milking sheep and said, "I am pleased you have come, my child" (Perpetua, trans. I.A. Plant, 166). Then he gave her milk in her hands, which she drank. When she awoke, she knew she would die a martyr: a witness for Christ. Her dream suggests that she understood Jesus as a shepherd who nourished her with the milk of his encouraging word just as she breastfed her own infant son with the milk of loving-kindness: she saw herself as God's child just as her son was her child.

Later, Perpetua had a vision of herself led out of prison to the amphitheater by a deacon named Pomponius. Once there, she did not face beasts, as she expected, but an Egyptian gladiator; she herself was transformed into a man for the fight. A gladiator-trainer came forth and promised that if the Egyptian defeated her, he would kill her with the sword, but if she defeated him, she would win a green branch on which there were golden apples. In her vision, she did defeat the man and win the prize, as her supporters sang psalms around her, and the gladiator-trainer kissed her and said, "Peace be with you, my daughter" (167). Perpetua then realized, "I was going to fight against the devil, not wild animals, but I knew that I would be victorious" (168). From a Christian viewpoint, Perpetua was victorious, though she was killed the next day.

In many specific details, Perpetua and Katniss obviously differ, but they share some over-arching similarities:

- against their will, both are forced to participate in violent spectacles in the arena to entertain a wealthy, elite citizenry under the auspices of a tyrannical, imperial government (e.g., Rome and Panem);
- both are preoccupied with the well-being of children (e.g., Perpetua's son and Katniss' sister);
- both follow male role models to prepare to fight in the arena (e.g., the martyr Saturus, the deacon Pomponius, and Haymitch);
- both rely on internalized father-figures to strengthen their resolve (e.g., the gray-haired shepherd from Perpetua's dream, the gladiator-trainer from her vision, and Katniss' own father in memories and photographs);
- both take on characteristics traditionally associated with men in order to compete against their opponents in the arena (e.g., Perpetua is "smoothed off" and becomes a man (167) while Katniss attempts to fulfill her father's role as hunter and provider for her family);
- both have complex psychological responses to the crisis and trauma they face;
- and both rely on songs to uplift their hearts and those around them [e.g., the Psalms and the four-note signal echoed by the mockingjays as well as the song, "The Hanging Tree"].

While Perpetua dies, singing psalms full of faith and anticipating her heavenly home, Katniss lives, remains married to Peeta, and gives birth to two children in District 12 where she and Peeta re-establish a garden. Despite this difference, both women are represented as victorious in the narratives that tell their stories.

Like Perpetua, Joan of Arc and other female Christian martyrs and saints may provide interesting models for comparative study of Katniss Everdeen, but there are few, if any, direct references or allusions to Christianity in *The Hunger Games* trilogy. Yet as one blogger has commented in her book review, "While Suzanne Collins leaves out any mention of God, religion, or the supernatural in her story—almost intentionally it would seem—her story still touches these deeper, universal notes" (Liz Hansen). Indeed, the author's ethical critique of violence, violence specifically used to turn children into gladiators for entertainment and to economically exploit subjected districts to benefit only a few among the wealthy elite, is clearly not "Roman," but "Christian": Judeo-Christian ethics are what underlie, inform, and strengthen the moral objection to violence, murder, and the exploitation of the poor. The glorification of Katniss' self-sacrifice for her sister, motivated by selfless love to save her sister's life, is of course also the central theme of Christianity, realized in the person of Jesus, who gave up his own life on the Cross to save humanity and to show God's unfailing, covenantal love to everyone. In this sense, Katniss is Christ-like. The tendency to use Christian ethics to critique dystopia is, of course, a generic quality of utopian/dystopian fiction going all the way back to More (if not before).

Collins, like other writers of contemporary feminist dystopian fiction, hybridizes the genre, bringing in elements of romance (Broad 117) and fairy-tale as she writes speculative fiction for young adults. Her trilogy features a love-triangle in which the traumatized Katniss is adored by two young men, Gale her fellow hunter and Peeta the baker's boy, but for most of her story, Katniss is unable to decide between them. The process of relating to both in different situations spurs her personal growth. This feature of the *bildungsroman* is drawn from one of Collins lesser-recognized sources, Thomas Hardy's *Far from the Madding Crowd*. This nineteenth-century romance novel features a protagonist struggling to choose among suitors, a woman called Bathsheba Everdene: from her, Katniss gets her last name (Collins qtd. in Jordan).[6]

Humanizing Rights

While the romance elements help to perpetuate the plot and the "suitors" provide foils for Katniss who help her to grow, Collins' dystopian fiction can be characterized as feminist. It takes the conversation to critique culture, common in dystopian fiction, and internalizes it in Katniss, but it also externalizes and articulates it between other female as well as male characters, makes part of it solely between women, and focuses on the human rights of a young adult woman to life, freedom, and self-determination. In the person of Katniss Everdeen, Collins humanizes the need for those rights. The trajectory of the trilogy reveals the "big lie" of Panem's politics, originating in the Capitol and later corrupting District 13, namely that the establishment is organized for the good of everyone, even the tributes (or soldiers) selected from the districts to fight and die in the Hunger Games (or the fight against the Capitol). But as Katniss Everdeen suspects early on, and grows to comprehend from painful personal experience, this simply is not true. Instead, the wealthy elites in the Capitol exploit the working class in the districts, eating cake while common people—like Katniss and her family in the mining district—nearly starve.

The driving focus of Collins' feminist critique of culture is in Katniss' agonizing experience of psychological trauma and the way this highlights the radically unjust denial of the human rights of women, children, and the economic under-classes in Panem and the real world of her readers. Indeed, Katniss' life is repeatedly threatened, her will is continually being coerced by President Snow and the political forces of the Capitol (and then manipulated by President Coin and the political forces of District 13), and, significantly, she is never properly educated, either about the history of her country or her own unique value as a person, with anything like love or even basic concern for her well-being. This results in a variety of psychological dysfunctions in her character. Her defense mechanisms include "withdrawal, reaction formation, altruistic surrender, intellectualization, and suppression" (Rambert 2); her symptoms resemble nothing less than full-blown, untreated post-traumatic stress disorder (PTSD), complete with many episodes of fear and terror, nightmare and hallucination, over-reaction to cues and triggers, and a vicious startle reflex. In other words, Katniss is clearly being denied her human rights to life, freedom, and self-determination and is suffering the normal psychological reactions to such denial.

All of this is in the context of her lack of education, education that might have prepared her better mentally and emotionally for the systemic injustice she faces in her young life. As Collins has observed, Katniss' political education is particularly lacking:

> The interesting thing about Katniss is when the story begins, she doesn't have much political awareness. There are things she knows about her world to be true and untrue. But no one has ever educated her in that area. It is not in the Capitol's interest that she know anything about politics. And there's only the one TV channel, which is completely controlled by the Capitol. And so she is struggling to put things together as she goes through the series, and it's quite difficult, because no one seems

to think it's in their interest to educate her. So it's interesting, because even though hers is an extreme case, I think all of us have to work to figure out what's going on. It's hard to get the truth and then to put it in a larger perspective [Collins qtd. in Hudson].

Katniss goes to "the school of hard knocks," as it were, but she never actually goes to school or meets a healthy mentor-teacher or reads about the subjects that shape her life: history, politics, sociology, economics, or rhetoric, communications, and media (to say nothing of the hard sciences, the arts or the humanities or philosophy and theology). She is clearly intelligent, capable, and constantly learning, but there is no doubt that her formal education is completely neglected.

Yet through alliances with others, Katniss compensates for some of the deficits and makes progress in overcoming them. She makes alliances with other children, like Rue, and other boys and men, like Gale, Peeta, Haymitch, Cinna, and Finnick. Despite her frustrations with her own mother, she wins over Effie Trinket, her escort, and other female victors like Mags, Johanna, and Wiress, as well as film director Cressida and Commander Paylor. The alliances with adult women are problematized at many levels that make Katniss' relationship with young women and girls, like Primrose and Rue, look ideal, but of course the girls are from the districts while the women are associated with the Capitol (with the exception of Paylor).

Katniss even makes "alliances" with the flora and fauna of the natural world: from the kills she makes in the wild to feed her family to the poisoned berries she uses to coerce a win from the Capitol's Gamemaker for both herself and Peeta at the end of the first Hunger Games, from her singing dialogues with mockingjays to her rescue of Prim's hissing cat Buttercup, from her eventual mastery of the forces of nature in the clock arena of the Quarter Quell to her ability to escape the genetically altered human/wolf mutts (who resemble slain tributes) unleashed by the Capitol during District 13's invasion. As Megan McDonough and Katherine Wagner have noted, Katniss' "awakening is catalyzed by experiences in nature and [...] these experiences shape nature into a place ideal for claiming her agency" (157). In other words, the natural world is her ally, one empowering her to decide and to act. Katniss is not drowned in the flood of the clock-arena, and though she is eventually burned in a fire in the Capitol, she rises from the ashes, phoenix-like (though the phoenix is not mentioned by name): terribly scarred but healing. At the end of the trilogy, the answer to the Capitol's "bread and circuses" is the answer of her life: "bread and roses." Peeta, her husband and the father of her children, is literally a bread-maker and a planter of primroses in their garden in memory of her sister. With him, she makes her firmest alliance.

The contrast between the ideologies of *panem et circenses* and "bread and roses" is presented meaningfully at the end of *Mockingjay*. The imagery of bread and roses—not the white roses of death, fear, and intimidation that President Snow wears and litters about to trigger Katniss' fears, but rather the yellow-centered primroses of sisterhood, friendship, and alliance—repudiates "Roman" imperialism, tyranny, and exploitation of the under-classes. The imagery actually recalls a speech by Rose Schneiderman (1882–1972), a prominent female union leader in America who brought the Triangle Shirtwaist Factory of 1911 in New York to wider public attention, who famously said, "The worker must have bread, but she must have roses, too": fair, living wages and safe, dignified working conditions (Orleck). That Schneiderman's phrase was later turned to poetry by James Oppenheim (1911), then to music in songs by Mimi Farina (1974), John Denver (1976), Judy Collins (1976), Utah Phillips and Ani DiFranco (1999), and Joan Baez, among others, suggests that Collins was familiar with it and that it is a significant sub-text to her conclusion to *The Hunger Games* trilogy.[7]

Ending The Hunger Games

The end of the *Hunger Games* trilogy is worth closer attention. Indeed, the third volume of the trilogy, *Mockingjay,* ends surprisingly multiple times. It finishes with (1) the death of Katniss' younger sister Primrose, a healer, but also the near-death of Katniss, the hunter, in a terrible conflagration; (2) then with the death of male President Snow, who represents the cultural forces of violence, deception, manipulation, corruption, and destruction, but also with the death of female President Coin, who has been corrupted by those same male-dominated cultural forces; and (3) finally with the trial and exoneration of Katniss for the killing of President Coin, but also the return of Katniss and her beloved Peeta to District 12, where they re-establish a home, a garden, and, in due time, a family with young children. Significant details of these endings, as we shall see, comment directly on the real dystopia: the warfare of the Vietnam era, to which Suzanne Collins was a six-year-old witness, and the parallel situation of children witnessing multiple kinds of brutality and violence on-screen at the turn of the war-torn, twenty-first century.

Collins ends *The Hunger Games* in three distinct stages, which can be characterized as the stages of death, burial, and resurrection. In the first stage of the ending, death, Katniss Everdeen witnesses the death of her younger sister, Primrose, a healer, in a fire-bomb dropped as District 13 is invading the Capitol. Katniss herself is caught in a conflagration and nearly burns to death, thus ironically fulfilling the promise of the Capitol's nickname for her, "the girl on fire." The emotional agony of losing the sister whom she sacrificed her life to save is increased by the agony of her skin being burned away.

The imagery recalls the myth of the phoenix and the martyrdom of Joan of Arc, but more specifically, it brings to mind Phan Thị Kim Phúc, the nine-year-old Vietnamese girl captured in a photograph by Associate Press photographer Nick Ut as she ran naked down the road after being severely burned on her back by a napalm attack on June 8, 1972, in Trang Bang, Vietnam. After taking the photograph, Ut took the girl with other burned children to the hospital, where it was thought she would not survive. But she did, after many skin transplant surgeries, and she made her way from Vietnam to Cuba to Canada, where she took political asylum and became a citizen. On her journey, Phan Thị Kim Phúc converted to Christianity (1982), married (1992), and gave birth to two children. Because of her photograph, which was awarded a Pulitzer and the World Press Photo of the Year (1973) and which later became an iconic representation of the horrors of the Vietnam War, she became a public figure; because of her Christian faith, she became a public advocate of forgiveness (Chong, *The Girl in the Picture*).[8]

Suzanne Collins has indicated that the Vietnam War, her father's involvement in it, and her own six-year-old perception of what was occurring in it, mediated through television, influenced her critique of violence and media representations of it in *The Hunger Games*:

> My father was career Air Force and was also a Vietnam veteran. He was in Vietnam the year I was six. But beyond that, he was a doctor of political science, he was a military specialist, he was very well educated. And he talked about war with us from very early on. It was very important to him that we understood things, I think because of both what he did and what he had experienced. If you went to a battlefield with him you didn't just stand there. You would hear what led up to this war and to this particular battle, what transpired there, and what the fallout was. It wasn't like, there's a field. It would be, here's a story. [...] *The Hunger Games* is a reality television program. An extreme one, but that's what it is. And while I think some of those shows can succeed on different levels, there's also the voyeuristic thrill, watching people being humiliated or brought to tears or suffering physically. And that's what I find very disturbing. There's this potential for desensitizing the audience so that when they see real tragedy playing out on the news, it doesn't have the impact it should. It all just blurs into one program. And I think it's very important not just for young people, but for adults to make sure they're making the distinction. Because the young soldier's dying in the war in Iraq, it's not going to end at the commercial break. It's not something fabricated, it's not a game. It's your life [Collins qtd. in Hudson].

In this interview, Collins makes a key connection between her childhood experience of seeing Vietnam War violence shown on television and the desensitization of the twenty-first century audience who, "when they see real tragedy playing out on the news," fail to empathize and fail to act because what they are seeing does not make "the impact it should," but rather "blurs" together with the pornography of violence constantly available on screen. American viewers in particular are thus compared to the ancient elite of

Rome watching the Coliseum spectacles and the Capitol elite of Panem watching the Hunger Games. For these viewers, violence is entertainment, exploitation of the working under-class enables the cake and privilege they take for granted, and political awareness and responsibility evaporate in the heat of their *panem et circensis* mentality. The human rights of young women like Katniss—or Phan Thi Kim Phúc—are carelessly overlooked; only the body of the young woman, decked out in high style or completely naked, and her survival skills, put to spectacular effect, have any entertainment value.

In like manner, Collins makes a connection between the Vietnam War (1955–1975) and the Iraq War (2003–2011), between her own father fighting in Vietnam and the young soldier "dying in the war in Iraq." She points out, because it apparently needs pointing out, that "it's not going to end at the commercial break. It's not a game." Then she personalizes it: "It's your life." In her trilogy, Collins has written a story aimed to create empathy for the child traumatized by violence, to critique the American cultural obsession with warfare, oppression, and exploitation, and to create the opportunity for political education among young adults that could lead to change in the real dystopia: the present-day world. But that is only the first stage of ending dystopia.

In the second stage, burial, Collins portrays Katniss in the role of a soldier of District 13 called to a meeting with other soldiers and their commander in chief, President Alma Coin, in which Coin asks the remaining victors to vote on whether to re-institute the Hunger Games as a form of punishment for the rebellion of the Capitol. When Haymitch asks if this is Gamemaker Plutarch's idea, Coin replies, "It's mine. [...] We need to balance the need for vengeance with the least loss of life. You may cast your votes" (Collins 367). This is appalling on the face of it: President Coin, who has used a rhetoric of defense of innocent children of the districts during her time as leader of the resistance to the Capitol, is now shown to have no concern for the children of the Capitol—no real concern for human life, freedom, or self-determination. Of course, her name alone is an early warning that her rhetoric will become self-serving: her first name, "Alma," is Latin for "soul," and a Latin name in *The Hunger Games* associates her with Capitol values; her last name, "Coin," suggests her soul can be bought and sold for money, privilege, and power.

In response to Coin's call for a vote by the surviving victors (whom she could presumably blame in a future "propo" if her idea is not well received in Panem), some victors, like Peeta, vote against; others, like Johanna, are enthusiastic. Johanna even relishes the thought of President Snow's young granddaughter being a tribute in the new games. Katniss seems to be in favor, as she says, "for Prim" (368), but later on, clearly is not.

In this dystopian exchange between Coin and the surviving victors, the whole idea of voting looks shoddy given the "modest proposal" being debated, the horrifying motives of the one proposing it, and the voters themselves, who are neither elected officials nor citizens who know their rights or understand their responsibilities—so uneducated and emotionally traumatized are they. They are given no time to think, no opportunity to ask questions, no chance to consider alternative forms of justice—such as restorative rather than punitive ones. Beetee alone says, "It would set a bad precedent. We have to stop viewing each other as enemies. At this point, unity is essential for our survival. No" (368).

What Katniss was thinking when she voted in favor of new games—with Johanna and Enobaria but against Peeta, Annie, and Beetee—is unclear. Perhaps she was feeling vengeful; perhaps she was already formulating a plan to stop President Coin and leaned toward subterfuge in the vote, showing outward compliance with Coin's obvious wish rather than outright opposition. If the latter, then Katniss appears to be learning something about politics.

When the day comes for her to shoot the former president, now a convicted criminal, Cornelius Snow, with one of her arrows in a public execution, Katniss instead points at the watching president of the new regime and shoots Alma Coin—thus preventing the plan to re-institute the Hunger Games.[9] As a result of her action, the two presidents and the values they represent are "buried." So is Katniss—in a version of house arrest—while a trial of her actions is conducted in her absence.

In the world of Panem, Commander Paylor assumes the presidency, and Katniss Everdeen is, to put it in contemporary American legal terms, found not guilty by reason of mental defect. She returns home to District 12 under the eye of her mentor, Haymitch, where she has a difficult time eating or functioning until Peeta comes to plant primroses beneath her window. This turning point, a symbolic resurrection of Primrose and the values of life, love, and healing associated with her, brings about the third stage of ending dystopia, which is really a beginning: resurrection.

In her new life, Katniss devotes time to remembering rightly, creating a book of memories of those she loved who died. Her doctor from the Capitol, Aurelius, sends parchment sheets by train to her in District 12 so she can make the book. Peeta and Haymitch help her in the process:

> I got the idea from our family's plant book. The place where we recorded those things you cannot trust to memory. Each page begins with the person's picture. A photo if we can find it. If not, a sketch or a painting by Peeta. Then, in my most careful handwriting, come all the details it would be a crime to forget. Lady licking Prim's cheek. My father's laugh. Peter's father with the cookies. The color of Finnick's eyes. What Cinna could do with a length of silk. Boggs reprogramming the Holo. Rue poised on her toes, arms slightly extended, like a bird about to take flight. On and on.

> We seal the pages with salt water and promises to live well to make their deaths count. Haymitch finally joins us, contributing twenty-three years of tributes he was forced to mentor. Additions become smaller. An old memory that surfaces. A late primrose preserved between the pages. Strange bits of happiness, like the photo of Finnick and Annie's newborn son [Collins 384–85].

Katniss sets aside the relationship with Gale and chooses Peeta: "what I need is not Gale's fire, kindled with rage and hatred. I have plenty of fire in myself. What I need is the dandelion in the spring. The bright yellow that means rebirth instead of destruction" (Collins 386).

In the epilogue to *The Hunger Games*, Collins depicts Katniss Everdeen as a woman living with post-traumatic stress disorder, but nevertheless living: a wife and mother of two children, a boy and a girl, who sings to her children as she used to sing to her little sister, Primrose, about being safe and warm and loved. In her essay, Hansen has observed that

> while the epilogue could be read as a conservative reaffirmation of traditional femininity, the trilogy's oblique use of the figures of Philomela and Artemis suggests another possibility. The protagonist's transformations from Katniss to victor to Mockingjay are effected through key elements in the Philomela myth, such as clothing and silence, which keep her locked in a desire for revenge. Once Katniss rejects vengeance, she is able to accept the fact that aspects of conventionally feminine roles appeal to her [175–76].[10]

Despite this progress, Katniss wonders with Peeta how she will tell her children about the Hunger Games and how they came to an end. The point, of course, is that they did end—at least for Panem: "The arenas have been completely destroyed, the memorials built, there are no more Hunger Games. But they teach about them in school [...]" (387).

This conclusion to *The Hunger Games* trilogy clearly emphasizes the undeniable need in the twenty-first century for an end to our own hunger games and the need for effective education of young people about the history of violence in the real world. The atrocities of war that took place in Vietnam and Iraq—and are continuing to take place in the wars that plague our planet, exploit the under-classes, and traumatize children—are morally unjustifiable. The dystopian fiction of Suzanne Collins suggests that if Americans would awaken to their responsibilities as citizens—learning from the classical past, taking ethical action, and discovering that the real world around them does not exist solely for their self-gratification and entertainment—then that would be the beginning of ending the real dystopia.

NOTES

1. Fatima Vieira has remarked, "It is thus certain that although he invented the word *utopia*, More did not invent utopianism, which has at its core the desire for a better life, but he certainly changed the way this desire was to be expressed. In fact, More *made a connection between the classic and the Christian traditions*, and added to it a new conception of the role

individuals are to play during their lifetime" (my emphasis). See Fatima Vieira, "The Concept of Utopia," *The Cambridge Companion to Utopian Literature*, ed. Gregory Claeys (Cambridge: Cambridge University Press, 2010), 3–27. On utopian thought before More, see Janet Coleman, "The Continuity of Utopian Thought in the Middle Ages: A Reassessment," *Vivarium* 20 (1982), 1–23; Michael Uebele, "Locating Utopia: The Orient and the Cultural Imaginary of the Middle Ages" (University of Virginia Diss., 1997) and "Medieval Desert Utopia," *Exemplaria* 14 (2002), 1–46; Heiko Hartmann's entry on "utopias/utopian thought," *The Handbook of Medieval Studies*, ed. Albrecht Classen (Berlin: DeGrutyer, 2010); and Karma Lochrie, *Nowhere in the Middle Ages* (Philadelphia: University of Pennsylvania Press, 2016). For additional insight on the Greco-Roman sources of More's *Utopia*, especially Plato's *Republic*, see J.C. Davis, "Thomas More's *Utopia*: Sources, Legacy, and Interpretation," *The Cambridge Companion to Utopian Literature*, ed. Gregory Claeys (Cambridge: Cambridge University Press, 2010), 28–50.

2. For discussion of More's influence and feminist responses to it, see Alessa Johns, "Feminism and Utopianism," *The Cambridge Companion to Utopian Literature*, ed. Gregory Claeys (Cambridge: Cambridge University Press, 2010), 174–99. Johns notes that feminist utopias, in contrast to More's *Utopia*, stress the centrality of education, see human nature as social and adaptable, advocate gradual change and shared power, have a dynamic view of the environment, and are consistently pragmatic. She alludes to major texts in the feminist utopian tradition from Christine de Pizan's *City of Ladies* to Sandra Perkins Gilman's *Herland* to demonstrate these points. She observes,

Thomas More's *Utopia* (1516) epitomizes the traditional version: it is fully mapped, boasting uniform towns that are geometrically organized with a centrally located seat of power from which the sovereign can conduct surveillance. Infrastructure supports the discipline of inhabitants; architecture and institutions encourage certain behaviors and discourage others. Ancient books, repeated rituals, pervasive symbols and signs ground authority in the traditional utopia. Clothing is issued and regulated. Dissenters are expelled or incarcerated. Such traditional utopias have also been called "classical," "blueprint," or "end-state" utopias, and many critics have concurred that, even though inhabitants are provided for, such visions are distasteful. Despite readers' admiration for the wit and inventiveness of More's *Utopia*, few would want to live there. Women in particular have fared poorly in traditional blueprint utopias, where they have been forced to labor endlessly and bow to humorless patriarchs. Consequently feminist utopian authors and critics have generally sidestepped the blueprint form to privilege instead a "process" or "reproductive" or "critical" model. (174)

3. Other contemporary feminist dystopian fictions that follow a similar pattern include Joan D. Vinge's *Snow Queen* (1980), Margaret Atwood's *The Handmaid's Tale* (1985), and Veronica Roth's *Divergent* trilogy (2011–13), which like *The Hunger Games* trilogy, targets a young adult audience.

4. In the same interview with Francis Lawrence of *Time* in 2013, Suzanne Collins remarked on this myth as a source for her Hunger Games lottery. She has also noted Shirley Jackson's short story "The Lottery" (in which the female protagonist is selected by lottery in her village to be stoned to death), Jackson's 1962 novel *We Have Always Lived in a Castle* (which, I observe, features two mutually loyal sisters and the motif of poisoned berries), and the general dystopian literary tradition, naming *Lord of the Flies*, *1984*, and *Brave New World*, as inspirational. She also mentioned Betty Smith's 1943 novel *A Tree Grows in Brooklyn*, a *bildungsroman* that follows the young, tough, Irish-American Francie's pursuit of an education after her father's death, despite her mother's preference for her sibling and her disappointments and decisions in romantic love.

5. Megan Devore, associate professor of church history and early Christian history at Colorado Christian University, first observed this connection to me in 2012. At least three bloggers have made the comparison as well: Matt Gunter, "The Hunger Games: What Would Perpetua Do?" *Into the Expectation* (3.7.2012): http://intotheexpectation.blogspot.com/2012/03/hunger-games-what-would-perpetua-do.html; Allison Dilyard, "Into the Arena with *The Hunger Games* and the Saints," *Busted Halo: Sharing Faith Joyfully* (3.23.2012): http://bustedhalo.com/features/into-the-arena-with-the-hunger-games-and-saints; and Adam Ericksen, "The Fear of Death and the Hope for Life: Katniss and Perpetua," *The Raven Review*

(4.12.2012): https://www.ravenfoundation.org/the-hunger-games-part-6-the-fear-of-death-and-the-hope-for-life-katniss-and-perpetua/. See also a comment by Danielle on Liz Hansen, "The Hunger Games," *Ungrind* (2012): http://ungrind.org/2012/the-hunger-games/. Despite a search in the MLA and JSTOR databases, I have been unable to locate any academic articles analyzing the parallels between Vibia Perpetua and Katniss Everdeen, though I suspect that there must be one or more that pre-date my own, this chapter on "Ending Dystopia," written in February 2016.

    6. Collins has said of Bathsheba Everdene and Katniss Everdeen: "The two are very different, but they struggle with knowing their hearts" (Collins qtd. in Jordan). On a separate but related note, the slight change in spelling, from "Everdene" to "Everdeen," may be significant. "Deen," also rendered "din," is an English transliteration of an Arabic word meaning creed, religion or faith or even a complete (Islamic) way of life; in Arabic, it especially conveys the idea of the act of submission to God. In Hebrew, in contradistinction to the Arabic term, "din" means law, judgment or, broadly understood, governance. Thus, Katniss may be "ever-faithful" or ever a bringer of judgment against those who have violated a righteous standard.

    7. James Oppenheim's poem, "Bread and Roses" (1911), is as follows:

> As we go marching, marching, in the beauty of the day
> A million darkened kitchens, a thousand mill lofts gray
> Are touched with all the radiance that a sudden sun discloses
> For the people hear us singing, bread and roses, bread and roses.
>
> As we come marching, marching, we battle too, for men,
> For they are in the struggle and together we shall win.
> Our days shall not be sweated from birth until life closes,
> Hearts starve as well as bodies, give us bread, but give us roses.
>
> As we come marching, marching, un-numbered women dead
> Go crying through our singing their ancient call for bread,
> Small art and love and beauty their trudging spirits knew
> Yes, it is bread we fight for, but we fight for roses, too.
>
> As we go marching, marching, we're standing proud and tall.
> The rising of the women means the rising of us all.
> No more the drudge and idler, ten that toil where one reposes,
> But a sharing of life's glories, bread and roses, bread and roses.

    8. Kim Phúc has said, "Forgiveness made me free from hatred. I still have many scars on my body and severe pain most days but my heart is cleansed. Napalm is very powerful, but faith, forgiveness, and love are much more powerful. We would not have war at all if everyone could learn how to live with true love, hope, and forgiveness. If that little girl in the picture can do it, ask yourself: Can you?" ("The Long Road to Forgiveness," *National Public Radio*, June 30, 2008).

    9. Online reviews of *The Hunger Games* books and especially the films, which were released during the presidential campaign of Hilary Clinton (2012–16), speculated that Alma Coin was a type of Hilary Clinton and even wondered if Julianne Moore's portrayal of the character in the films could have been a factor in negative public perception of Clinton and her eventual loss of the presidential race. Others speculated, in a similar vein, that Cornelius Snow represented Barrack Obama, though Snow might just as well represent any of the sitting presidents who governed during the Vietnam and Iraq Wars, either individually or collectively.

    10. Hansen further observes of Katniss: "Her early belief that only traditionally male characteristics can aid in survival initially causes her to reject all conventional femininity. The trilogy's uses of the Philomela myth give Katniss an awareness of the power of some forms of femininity, but on their own, these silence-enforcing, textile-based elements cannot provide the transformation that she needs. Katniss therefore rejects the Philomelan form of femininity. Yet she also rejects the Artemisian insistence on remaining unmarried and childless, accepting neither that she is a superior and solitary goddess, nor that she is only fighting for herself, as if her own life were a never-ending Hunger Games. Consequently, in becoming a mother, Katniss demonstrates her faith that the world has changed enough to be a safe

place for children. Through Katniss' ultimate rejection of the Philomelan and Artemisian roles, Collins' trilogy indicates the importance of young women breaking with history to make their own personae, demonstrating that femininity need not simply replicate the forms that have previously existed" (175–76). To understand the epilogue of *Mockingjay* in the larger context of epilogues to children's fiction, see Mike Cadden, "All Is Well: The Epilogue in Children's Fantasy Fiction." *Narrative* 20.3 (2012): 343–56.

Works Cited

Broad, Katherine R. "'The Dandelion in the Spring': Utopia as Romance in Suzanne Collins' *The Hunger Games* Trilogy." *Contemporary Dystopian Fiction for Young Adults: Brave New Teenagers*. Ed. Balaka Basu, Katherine R. Broad, and Carrie Hintz. New York: Routledge, 2013. 117–30. Print.

Cadden, Mike. "All Is Well: The Epilogue in Children's Fantasy Fiction." *Narrative* 20.3 (2012): 343–56. Print.

Chong, Denise. *The Girl in the Picture: The Story of Kim Phuc, the Photo, and the Vietnam War*. 1999. New York: Penguin Books, 2001. Print.

Coleman, Janet. "The Continuity of Utopian Thought in the Middle Ages: A Reassessment." *Viviarium* 20 (1982): 1–23. Print.

Collins, Suzanne. *Catching Fire*. New York: Scholastic, 2009. Print.

———. *The Hunger Games*. New York: Scholastic, 2008. Print.

———. *Mockingjay*. New York: Scholastic, 2010. Print.

Danielle. "Comment." On Liz Hansen, "The Hunger Games," *Ungrind* (2012). Web. 20 February 2016.

Davis, J.C. "Thomas More's *Utopia*: Sources, Legacy, and Interpretation." *The Cambridge Companion to Utopian Literature*. Ed. Gregory Claeys. Cambridge: Cambridge University Press, 2010. 28–50. Print.

Dilyard, Allison. "Into the Arena with *The Hunger Games* and the Saints." *Busted Halo: Sharing Faith Joyfully*. 23 Mar. 2012. Web. 20 Feb. 2016.

Ericksen, Adam. "The Hunger Games Part 6: Fear of Death and the Hope for Life: Katniss and Perpetua." *The Raven Review* 12 April 2012. Web. 20 Feb. 2016.

Gunter, Matt. "The Hunger Games: What Would Perpetua Do?" *Into the Expectation*. 7 March 2012. Web. 20 Feb. 2016.

Hansen, Kathryn Strong. "The Metamorphosis of Katniss Everdeen: The Hunger Games, Myth, and Femininity." *Children's Literature Association Quarterly* 40 (2015): 161–78. Print.

Hartmann, Heiko. "Utopias/Utopian Thought." *The Handbook of Medieval Studies*. Ed. Albrecht Classen. Berlin: DeGrutyer, 2010. 1400–08. Print.

Hudson, Hannah Trierweiler. "Q&A with Hunger Games Author Suzanne Collins." Scholastic Website. n.d. Web. 20 Feb. 2016.

Johns, Alessa. "Feminism and Utopianism." *The Cambridge Companion to Utopian Literature*. Ed. Gregory Claeys. Cambridge: Cambridge University Press, 2010. 174–99. Print.

Jordan, Tina. "Suzanne Collins on the Books She Loves." *Entertainment Weekly* 12 Aug. 2010. Web. 20 Feb. 2016.

Juvenal. Satire X.80. Trans. A.S. Kline. Web. 20 Feb. 2016. <http://www.poetryintranslation.com/PITBR/Latin/JuvenalSatires10.htm>.

Krule, Mirriam. "The Hunger Names." *Slate* 21 Mar. 2012. Web. 20 Feb. 2016.

Lawrence, Francis. Interview with Suzanne Collins. *Time Entertainment* 20 Nov. 2013. Web. 20 Feb. 2016. <http://entertainment.time.com/2013/11/20/i-was-destined-to-write-a-gladiator-game-a-conversation-with-suzanne-collins-and-francis-lawrence/>.

Lochrie, Karma. *Nowhere in the Middle Ages*. Philadelphia: University of Pennsylvania Press, 2016. Print.

McDonough, Megan and Kathrine Wagner. "Rebellious Natures: The Role of Nature in Young Adult Dystopian Female Protagonists' Awakening and Agency." Eds. Amy Montz, et al. *Female Rebellion in Young Adult Dystopian Fiction*. Farnham, UK: Ashgate, 2014. Print.

More, Thomas. *Utopia*. New York: Penguin, 1992. Print.

Orleck, Annelise. "Rose Schneiderman, 1882–1972." *Jewish Women's Archive*. Web. 22 Feb. 2016. <https://jwa.org/encyclopedia/article/schneiderman-rose>.
Perpetua, Vibia. "The Martyrdom of Perpetua." *Women Writers of Ancient Greece and Rome: An Anthology*. Ed. and trans. I.M. Plant. Norman: University of Oklahoma Press, 2004. 164–68. Print.
Phuc, Kim. "The Long Road to Forgiveness." *NPR* 30 June 2008. Web. 22 Feb. 2016. <http://www.npr.org/templates/story/story.php?storyId=91964687>.
Ramberg, Malin. "What Makes Her Tick? Katniss Everdeen's Use of Defense Mechanisms in *The Hunger Games*." Thesis. Karlstads Universitet. 2012. PDF. 20 Feb. 2016.
"Saggitarius." *Dictionary.com*. Web. 20 Feb. 2016.
Uebele, Michael. "Locating Utopia: The Orient and the Cultural Imaginary of the Middle Ages." University of Virginia, Diss., 1997. Print.
_____. "Medieval Desert Utopia." *Exemplaria* 14 (2002). 1–46. Print.
Vieira, Fatima. "The Concept of Utopia." *The Cambridge Companion to Utopian Literature*. Ed. Gregory Claeys. Cambridge: Cambridge University, 2010. 3–27. Print.

Commodifying the Revolution
Dystopian Young Adult Literature and Cultural Critique

Jillian L. Canode

In recent years, young adult (YA) dystopian literature has become immensely popular among readers of all ages. Like its "grown-up" counterpart, dystopian YA fiction often features worlds that mirror our own but are different enough for us to feel an uncanny discomfort. In a time of excessive consumption and waste, YA dystopian literature offers readers a point of view that criticizes Western capitalism and its dehumanizing influences and instead praises empathy, critical awareness, and kindness. Throughout this essay, I will focus on M.T. Anderson's *Feed* (2002), Scott Westerfeld's *Uglies* (2005), Elaine Dimopoulos' *Material Girls* (2015), and Alexander London's *Proxy* (2013) to exemplify how YA dystopian literature both criticizes consumerism and undermines capitalism's commodification and appropriation of revolution. As a result of this examination, we will see dystopian YA fiction as an invaluable tool for teaching readers—especially younger readers—the value of empathy and hope in creating change.

Consumption, Memory and Imagination

Now more than ever, young people are subject to a nearly inescapable advertising onslaught: their social media feeds are cluttered with ads based on their web browsing, their public elementary and high schools are slowly being co-opted by corporations looking for captive markets, and their lives, much more digitally reliant than any generation before them, are structured around sound and video bytes that require viewing an advertisement before they can enjoy the twenty seconds of content they clicked on in the first place. Henry Giroux, in *The Violence of Organized Forgetting: Thinking Beyond America's Disimagination Machine*, comments on the reality of education and consumption in the United States today:

> When not being arrested for trivial rule violations, students are forced to look at walls, buses, and bathrooms that have become giant advertisements for consumer products, many of which are detrimental to the health of students and indeed might be contributing to the obesity crisis in America. Increasingly, even school curricula are organized to reflect the sound of the cash register, hawking products for students to buy and promoting the interests of corporations that celebrate fossil fuels as an energy source, sugar-filled drinks, and a Disney-like view of the world.

Children and teenagers have become a massive captive audience. In his novel *Feed*, M.T. Anderson carries the kind of corporate invasion of which Giroux speaks to its frightening conclusion. Instead of children learning how to solve problems and spell, we see *Feed*'s teenagers at School™, which is owned by a corporation and therefore trademarked, learning how to maximize their use of the feed in order to consume goods (109). Titus, the protagonist, explains that everyone is smarter than they used to be because they can just look online for whatever answers they need (Anderson 47), so no one wastes time in school trying to remember history, when learning how to make the most of the feed is more useful.

Learning to use the feed, which is hard-wired into the central nervous system, is, at its core, a way for the private corporations that control the feed to ensure that people continue to consume products. Consumption feeds demand, supply meets demand, and demand requires industrial growth. In Anderson's novel, trees are cut down to make room for oxygen factories (Anderson 125) because trees are far less profitable, and the sea is toxic (179). In the world of *Feed*, Marx's prediction that capitalism would continue expanding until it consumed the planet comes true (162).

Feed not only highlights the environmental dangers of privatization and rampant capitalism; it is also a warning against allowing ourselves to lose our collective cultural memory. The teenagers in the novel, with the exception of Violet, never question the status quo. They do not learn to. They are not taught to think; they are taught to buy. So, when some of the girls show up wearing the latest in the Kent State collection, Stonewall clogs, and Watts riot-inspired fashion, no one is critical, save for Violet. Here, Titus witnesses the exchange between Calista, Loga, Quendy, and Violet:

> "Yuh," said Loga. "It's Riot Gear. It's retro. It's beat up to look like one of the big twentieth-century riots. It's been big since earlier this week."
> "Hey!" said Loga to Quendy, pointing. "Kent State collection, right? Great skirt!" Quendy bowed her legs out. "It's not a skirt—it's culottes!"
> "Ohhh, cute!" Calista said, "That looks great on you!"

"Oh, and omigod!" said Calista. "Are those the Stonewall Clogs? They're so brag."
"Yeah," said Loga.
"Omigod. They look wholly comfy. Are they comfy?"
"They're pretty comfy." Loga picked up her foot and played with her flowery clog, and she was like, "I got a size seven, but it feels more like a man's size seven."
"This top is the Watts Riot top."
Violet said, "I can never keep any of the riots straight. Which one was the Watts riot?"
Calista and Loga stopped and looked at her. I could feel them flashing chat.
"Like, a riot," said Calista. "I don't know, Violet. Like, when people start breaking windows and beating each other up, and they have to call in the cops. A riot. You know" [159–63].

Violet's reaction to the clothing is sarcastic; she is the only character in the novel who understands the problems the world faces. Readers identify with her. Through Violet, we understand that there is something wrong with what the other young women are wearing. As disturbing as it is that these young women do not understand the historical significance of their clothing or even that riots are violent and frightening, more troublesome is that such products exist at all. To readers, this scene seems utterly fantastical, a perfect example of dystopian elements that would never exist in the real world. It is worth pointing out, however, that companies are willing to profit from trauma.

Urban Outfitters (UO) has taken to appropriating significant events of resistance. In 2014, UO stores featured a sweatshirt with the Kent State logo on it. It was a retro-style sweatshirt, reminiscent of styles from the 1970s. This sweatshirt, however, was covered with what unmistakably looked like blood spray or spatter. After enough public outcry, UO pulled the shirt and issued this apology via twitter:

> Urban Outfitters sincerely apologizes for any offense our Vintage Kent State Sweatshirt may have caused [....] It was never our intention to allude to the tragic events that took place at Kent State in 1970 and we are extremely saddened that this item was perceived as such. The one-of-a-kind item was purchased as part of our sun-faded vintage collection. There is no blood on this shirt nor has this item been altered in any way. The red stains are discoloration from the original shade of the shirt and the holes are from natural wear and fray. Again, we deeply regret that this item was perceived negatively and we have removed it immediately from our website to avoid further upset [Stump].

The Kent State shirt was neither UO's first nor last offense. In 2015, the retailer featured a shirt with a gold star and stripes very similar to what Jewish people were forced to wear in concentration camps during World War II. There are two possible explanations for why Urban Outfitters would have thought these items of clothing would be acceptable: the first is that their designers, staff, and anyone involved in the production of those pieces were wholly ignorant of the past; the second is that they wanted to use the attention the clothing would receive from being so shocking to make sales. The first explanation is as charitable as it is unlikely. The second seems more in line with current consumer culture.

Whatever discomfort readers feel from the fashion scene in the novel demonstrates the effectiveness with which *Feed* creates awareness of the more sinister aspects of what many do in the name of the free market. Through the teenagers' ignorance, *Feed* teaches readers the dangers of forgetting the past and the importance of resisting attempts from corporations to turn protests against war, violence, sexism, racism, and economic oppression into fashion.

Urban Outfitters' bizarre marketing choices help us understand why American capitalism has no conscience or memory. In *Society of the Spectacle*, Guy Debord writes a series of aphorisms declaring how the culture of capitalism permeates our lives so completely—mostly through images—that we no longer have any understanding of our identity or humanity. We see the spectacle in full force in *Feed*. The characters are subject to so many constant, streaming images that the individual images themselves lack all meaning. Titus and others like him rely on the spectacle for meaning, but the only meaning they come to understand is that consumption and production makes everything better. As Debord explains, "The first phase of the domination of the economy over social life is brought into the definition of all human realization the obvious degradation of being into *having*" (17). As subjects of the spectacle, the people in *Feed* feel most human when they are feeding their desire to acquire more stuff without realizing that this stuff has dark origins in economic exploitation.

While *Feed* presents the most obvious indictment of capitalism and consumerism out of the novels I analyze here, Elaine Dimopoulos' *Material Girls* also criticizes exploitation and consumerism. *Material Girls* focuses on two characters, Marla, who works in the fashion industry, and Ivy, a pop star. The first starts the story at the height of her career, while the second is already losing her hold on the limelight. These young women are teenagers, and they have peaked. They live in a world where children are assigned careers at the age of thirteen by way of a nationwide aptitude test called the TAP, and fashion trends will make or break a person's reputation.

Material Girls presents readers with a possible world where being trendy becomes so central to having a good life that spending large amounts of money to be able to wear the latest trends is common. Trendy clothing is very expensive, and, as is common in dystopian novels, there is a vast disparity in wealth among the classes. What is more, like the young women in *Feed*, there is not much reflection that goes on when it comes to what is popular, and Dimopoulos shows us what happens when unchecked consumerism dictates popularity—torture and war become trendy:

> Today she was modeling the Rudolfo label's armed-forces trend. She wore a tube dress in a fatigue pattern, combat boots, and a shiny necklace of dog tags attached end to end. A black leather bag with silver studs hung off her shoulder. [...] Aiko had on a sailor dress; Hilarie wore baggy Gestapo pants and a T-shirt with tell me your secrets printed across the front; Naia sported a bomber jacket and goggle headband [5–6].
>
> Instead of a skirt, she wore a bikini bottom made out of hair. Ivy itched just looking at it. She also wore metal garters, with chains wrapped around her legs and attached at the bottom to ankle cuffs. Her hands were tied together behind her back. And she marched in the shoes, those horrible shoes, though the spikes were metallic silver, not red. Instead of a gag, a bridle secured her jaw, its leather straps attaching behind her head [117–18].

Just like we saw in *Feed*, militarization, violence, and torture are removed from their normal contexts and robbed of their significance. Dimopoulos shows us that we forget why military clothing exists in the first place or why torture is so repulsive because we have been desensitized by Western capitalism. Violent acts are absorbed and reproduced as images that serve as buffers between fiction and reality. These moments in the novel, which are purposely absurd, force readers to reflect on their consumption.

While *Feed* ends on a note of hopeful, critical awakening, *Material Girls* leaves readers feeling a little defeated. Marla and Ivy, who staged a small, though important, culture and fashion uprising, were unable to undermine the hold the system of trends has. Marla starts her own clothing design company that operates as humanely and ethically as possible, but still conforms to many of the rules that were already in place and against which she wanted to revolt in the first place. Ivy is less fortunate, and as the novel ends, we see her taking pills to get her through her day while she wears clothing adorned with live butterflies whose legs have been torn off (Dimopoulos 315). Through Ivy, Dimopoulos illustrates how our desire to participate in the system makes us slaves to capital. Mark Fisher, in his book *Capitalist Realism*, refers to capital as "an insatiable vampire and zombie-maker" (15) because our pursuit of capital sucks the life out of us. By the book's end, Ivy is one of those zombies.

Anderson and Dimopoulos imagine frightening, capitalist, dystopian settings to show readers the dangers inherent in a system that unrelentingly promotes unconscious consumerism. In *Feed*, Titus does not have the imagination it takes to envision a world different from his own. This imaginative limit is one of the central conflicts he has with Violet. Titus is very much a product of a mindset Fisher calls "capitalist realism," which is the idea that we could more easily imagine the world ending than we could capitalism dying out (1). And in *Material Girls*, Marla does not try to transcend the system, but rather attempts to subvert it by creating her own trendless clothing line. Ultimately, she has not subverted anything; she has merely bought into "[t]he fantasy [...] that western consumerism, far from being intrinsically implicated in systemic global inequalities, could itself solve them. All we have to do is buy the right products" (Fisher 15). This is not to say that what Marla does is pointless; resistance is a crucial first step. What we should learn from Titus and Marla is that we have to begin resistance by way of imagination.

Imagination is the wheelhouse of young adult dystopias. Through these stories, authors can help younger readers understand that while the world may seem overwhelming, they can imagine something better, and not only can they imagine something better, they can help create that better world: "In the context of challenges such as these, dystopian fiction for young adults describes protagonists who reach a realization about their role in the larger society: they come to see themselves as agents, individuals with a will (often in sharp contrast to the will of the society) and with the capacity to not only disagree with prevailing opinions but to act out against them" (Scholes and Ostenson 5). The critiques of capitalism present in YA dystopias like the ones I am presenting here prove themselves to be valuable teaching tools when set beside broader theories about how young adults learn and to what they are attracted as readers.

The target reader of the YA dystopia is between childhood and adulthood, has begun to establish an identity independent of her/his parents, feels no nostalgia for childhood, looks forward to adulthood, and has begun to understand that the world might not be so great all the time. This is the reader who is not only a target for YA dystopian writers; she/he is also the reader with the most potential to do something about the chaos of the world in which she/he lives. As Scholes and Ostenson explain,

> Dystopian fiction features protagonists who are likewise questioning the underlying values of a flawed society and their identity within it [....] Every choice the characters make can carry enormous consequences, often to the point of significantly altering the world they've always known. Teenagers connect with these protagonists as they feel a similar weight on their shoulders [4].

Dystopias invite readers to see their world through a new lens and then imagine how to make that world better.

Consumption and Bodies

A central tenet of both *Feed* and *Material Girls* is that we should not be fooled into thinking consumption will bring us happiness. The consumption in these books is primarily goods-based, and there is an obvious distinction between those who can afford to buy whatever they want and those who cannot. Scott Westerfeld's *Uglies* and Alexander London's *Proxy* also focus on consumption, but in these dystopias, readers see how capitalism promotes the consumption of bodies.

In *Uglies*, people spend the first fifteen years of their lives being ugly—their ugliness seems akin to being what we would think of as the normal variations in looks we see among human beings. They eagerly await their sixteenth birthday when they have massive, full body surgeries and become pretty. The novel focuses on two young women, Shay and Tally, who start the novel very near their sixteenth birthdays. Tally is very excited about her operation, but Shay plans to run away to find the group of people who have resisted becoming pretty. There is a moment in the novel where Shay tries to get Tally to realize they have been conditioned to think that being pretty is normal, but Tally is not receptive:

> "But it's a trick, Tally. You've only seen pretty faces your whole life. Your parents, your teachers, everyone over sixteen. But you weren't born expecting that kind of beauty in everyone, all the time. You just got programmed into thinking anything else is ugly."
>
> "It's not programming, it's just a natural reaction. And more important than that, it's fair. In the old days it was all random—some people kind of pretty, most people ugly all their lives. Now everyone's ugly [...] until they're pretty. No losers" [79].

Readers identify with both characters in the novel; we have been both Shay and Tally. The pretty to which people aspire in the novel is a very specific type of pretty, and there is a software designed to help them choose what they will look like after the operation. In the default setting, the software will create an image of the standard pretty person: large eyes, a small nose, high cheekbones, full lips, and flawless, clear skin (Westerfeld 41). Included in the pretty package is a standardization of body size as well; if a person is too thin, they will be bulked up; if they are too fat, they will be slimmed down (42). The standards of beauty in *Uglies* are not arbitrary, just as standards of beauty in the West are not. Someone sets those standards, and we conform to them. Because of these standards, people develop eating disorders, spend thousands of dollars on beauty products, or alter their bodies in attempts to meet those standards. We consume ourselves in order to conform to an ideal that we can never meet, and there is always someone who profits from our struggles. *Uglies* engenders an understanding in readers that our insecurities make us susceptible to control.

Once a person is pretty, she/he moves to New Pretty Town, where life is a constant party. We learn that when someone becomes pretty, that person also becomes somewhat airheaded and distracted—very different from who he or she was before the surgery. Their problems seem to drift away, and they are placid. Later in the *Uglies* series, we discover that the doctors performing the pretty operation also change the patients' brains to ensure docility and control. Eventually, Shay is made pretty, and Tally, who avoided the surgery, tries unsuccessfully to lift the fog from Shay's brain: "Shay was silent for a moment, only the roar of white water and the rushing wind around them. Finally, she leaned closer, her voice thoughtful in Tally's ear. 'Yeah, I know what you mean. But that was all ugly stuff. Crazy love and jealousy and needing to rebel against the city. Every kid's like that. But you grow up, you know?'" (376). In this moment, readers come to understand that on one level, *Uglies* is about encouraging them to define "pretty" for themselves and to be comfortable in their own skin, but it also sends the message that what one does with his/her own body is a decision that should not be imposed from without. On a deeper level, *Uglies* serves as a warning to readers about the perils of conformity, unquestioning devotion to ideology, and submission to authority.

Control over people is a necessary factor for capitalism—not only to prevent resistance, but also to maintain the economic system itself. Without bodies to use, there can be no production of capital. The bodies that are used to create many of the goods, for the most part, belong to people of color from non–Western, poor countries. Alexander London, in *Proxy*, addresses this consumption of other bodies, especially the bodies of the poor, and the way in which a system such as capitalism encourages dehumanization.

Syd is a teenager who lives in impoverished conditions: "The Valve was at the lowest point in the Mountain City, where the wet heat lingered, unmoved by the breezes that kept the peaks of the Upper City comfortable. Breezes were for people who could afford them. All the Lower City kids got was the heat of nature's indifference" (London 10). In Syd's world, there are the rich, and there are those who have massive amounts of debt. Syd is in debt merely for existing, so to pay off his debt faster, he serves as a punishment proxy for a rich teenager named Knox. When Knox commits a crime, Syd takes the punishment. By taking the punishment, Syd's debt decreases slightly. This relationship between proxy and owner exemplifies the harsh reality of how so many are ignorant of the consequences of their choices. In Syd's case, Knox turns a blind eye to how his behavior affects others; in the real world, we turn a blind eye to what our consumption of goods does to the bodies that produce those goods for us.

One way Western capitalism justifies its existence is by placing the blame for living in impoverished conditions on the backs of those who live in them. Capitalism is meritocratic, so the simple idea is that if you work hard enough, you will succeed; if you do not work hard, you will starve, and it will be your own fault. Ideas of meritocratic success are a means by which to distract people from the real issues of exploitation of the poor by the rich; one of the most effective ways for those in power to stay in power is to pit lower classes against each other. London exemplifies this idea for us by way of Syd's reflection: "Using the poor to control the poor kept everyone in the Valve at one another's throats and kept them from looking too far up in the direction of the skyscrapers and the private communities. The Guardians [state security] rarely showed up to haul anyone off. The market preferred to keep its enforcers more invisible than that" (70). Because there are scarce resources in the Valve, the poor fight amongst themselves in the name of survival. As the less fortunate have to resort to violence and crime to survive, it is easy for the rich to justify segregation, discrimination, and poverty, and the Guardians make sure everyone knows, and stays in, their place.

The Guardians—guards of the system—are not merely state security; they enforce the proxy system as well. The cruelty the Guardians inflict on the proxies in the name of paying debt is substantial: "Knox had seen his proxy punished in all sorts of ways over the years: zapped with the EMD sticks, forced to work under the blazing sun out on the dam construction above the river, even just held alone in the dark for days" (London 58). Through Knox and his proxy, London shows us that our habits of consumption offer us our own proxies: we buy clothing made in factories thousands of miles away where the people working make pennies for each garment, or we clamor for cell phones produced in factories with conditions so brutal, the people assembling the phones jump off roofs (Johnson).

What is more disturbing is that when we hear of these deplorable working conditions, we too often respond by saying those people would not make as much money doing some other job, so they should be grateful. What *Proxy* offers readers, in ways that the other dystopias I have examined here do not, is an understanding that through capitalism, we become incapable of empathy. Empathy is dangerous for capitalism, because as an economic system that demands higher and higher profit margins, there is necessarily higher and higher poverty. Knox realizes, throughout the course of *Proxy*, that he has been complicit in a system that endorses torture. Through his realization, he befriends Syd, and they begin to destroy the debt system.

Final Thoughts: YA, Empathy and Hope

Human connection and empathy are things young adult literature is especially good at engendering in readers. While not every reader of YA literature is a young adult, the majority are, and studies have shown that younger readers respond differently to literature than adult readers do. This may not be surprising information. If we think back to our favorite books, chances are they are books we read in our youth. In "Young Adult Literature: Growing Up, In Theory," Karen Coats offers anecdotal evidence about how young adult literature affected her development as a young person and later on as an adult. She says, "I learned what was going on in the world outside my sheltered community. I got some insight into the people who sat across from me at the lunch table. It wasn't until I went back to those books as an adult that I realized how much of my own everyday speech, expressions, thought patterns, and values had been influenced by their words and ideologies" (315). Because the effect a book can have on a young reader is even more profound, generally speaking, than the effect the same book can have on an older reader, YA writers will often pay closer attention to the particular emotional and physical stresses of being a teenager. Coats explains that because there is so much growth that occurs in those middle years, teens will latch onto books that feature characters with whom they most identify. This is why YA books are powerful tools for promoting global engagement, social awareness, and critical thought.

YA literature's ability to connect with audiences in a way other genres cannot stem in part from the emotion and reflection with which the stories are told. If a writer wants her/his audience to internalize the message, especially the more revolutionary messages in YA dystopian works, that writer must appeal directly to the hearts of her/his readers. To get readers to feel a certain emotion, writers must make them feel that emotion; the characters must seem worth caring for. Or, as Maria Nikolajeva puts it, "a reader must be able to get empathically engaged with a character without sharing his or her literal or transferred point of view; to be curious about a character who is unpleasant, ugly, sick, criminal, mentally retarded, morally depraved or even inhuman" (98). Readers identify with Titus, Violet, Marla, Ivy, Shay, Tally, Syd, and Knox because those characters were designed to help readers find people similar to themselves within the pages. These are characters who have common experiences as teenagers but who also face adult responsibilities and worlds that need fixing. Through these characters who try to make their worlds fairer, kinder, and more human, readers find hope for their own futures.

Dystopian novels like the ones I have discussed throughout this essay show readers the dehumanizing influence of greed and consumerism engendered by Western capitalism. What is so important about the ability of YA novels—especially dystopian novels—to perform these kinds of social critiques is how they can help members of future generations become the kinds of people we talk about wanting to be. Children are vulnerable to their environmental influences, but we often forget that teenagers are vulnerable in ways small children are not. Or, "[i]n other words, we might say that adolescents are at a threshold of emotionally engaged understanding that makes them particularly susceptible to the development of a generative identity, especially if that kind of identity support is found in their cultural and artistic artifacts" (Coats 327). The stories that hit closest to home for teenagers are the ones to leave lasting impressions, so the types of stories to which they are exposed matter. This kind of impressionability is linked to YA literature's ability to stimulate in younger readers an understanding of what it means to be a compassionate global citizen.

Though YA dystopias are most influential on young readers, it is important that we do not assume this kind of literature is only effective for young readers; it can also help older readers find hope that is not always present in dystopian literature intended for more mature audiences. *Feed*, *Uglies*, *Proxy*, and *Material Girls* portray the grim reality of worlds dominated by consumerism, but they also remind readers that there are ways to resist these dystopias becoming a reality. The popularity of YA dystopian books attests to a longing for social change, and these books, more than their adult counterparts, offer readers the idea that fixing a broken economic system is possible.

Works Cited

Anderson, M.T. *Feed*. Somerville: Candlewick Press, 2002. Kindle AZW file.
Coats, Karen. "Growing Up, in Theory." *Handbook of Research on Children's and Young Adult Literature*. Eds. Shelby Wolf, Karen Coats, Patricia Enciso, and Christine A. Jenkins. New York: Routledge, 2010. 315–29. Print.
Debord, Guy. *Society of the Spectacle*. Detroit: Black and Red, 1983. Print.
Dimopoulos, Elaine. *Material Girls*. Boston: Houghton Mifflin Harcourt, 2015. Kindle AZW file.
Fisher, Mark. *Capitalist Realism: Is There No Alternative?* Ropley: Zero Books, 2009. Kindle AZW file.
Giroux, Henry. *The Violence of Organized Forgetting: Thinking Beyond America's Disimagination Machine*. San Francisco: City Lights Books, 2014. Kindle AZW file.
Johnson, Joel. "1 Million Workers. 90 Million IPhones. 17 Suicides. Who's to Blame?" *Wired*. Condé Nast, 28 Feb. 2011. Web. 16 May 2016.
London, Alexander. *Proxy*. New York: Philomel Books, 2013. Kindle AZW file.
Marx, Karl, and Friedrich Engels. "The Communist Manifesto." *Selected Writings*. Ed. Lawrence H. Simon. Indianapolis: Hackett, 1994. 157–86. Print.
Nikolajeva, Maria. "Memory of the Present: Empathy and Identity in Young Adult Fiction." *Narrative Works: Issues, Investigations & Interventions* 4.2 (2014): 86–107. Web. 20 May 2016.
Scholes, Justin, and Jon Ostenson. "Understanding the Appeal of Dystopian Young Adult Fiction." *The Alan Review* 40.2 (2013): 11–20. Web. 8 Apr. 2016.
Stump, Scott. "Urban Outfitters Apologizes for Shirt Appearing to Reference Kent State Shooting." *Today Style*. NBC News, 15 Sept. 2014. Web. 3 Mar. 2016.
Westerfeld, Scott. *Uglies*. New York: Simon & Schuster, 2005. Kindle AZW file.

Dystopia, Competition and Reality Television Tropes in *The Bachman Books*
"The Long Walk" and "The Running Man"

ALISSA BURGER

Stephen King's fiction has provided readers with a wide range of nightmares. From the reality-based horror of works like *Cujo* (1981), *Misery* (1987), and *Dolores Claiborne* (1993) to the supernatural monsters of *'Salem's Lot* (1975) and *IT* (1986), King explores a world where things have gone wrong and are about to get a whole lot worse. Among these myriad terrors, King also turns his attention beyond the present, imagining a dystopian day in the not so distant future where the fight for survival is just one more fact of life, whether that struggle is against the superflu and the post-apocalyptic struggle for dominance in *The Stand* (1978; 1990) or the zombie-like cell phone crazies of *Cell* (2006). However, King wrote some of his most haunting dystopian fiction early in his career under the pseudonym of Richard Bachman. These early novellas were published as *The Bachman Books* in 1985.[1] Two of the novellas included in that collection, "The Long Walk" and "The Running Man," introduce readers to dystopian futures shaped by brutal competition, reality TV-style surveillance, and the dehumanization of both the competitors and the viewers, who are themselves invested in the lives and—more potently—the deaths of those who compete for their own survival and the audience's entertainment.

Both "The Long Walk" and "The Running Man" are based in the near future, each with its foundation set in easily recognizable realities, showcasing the future while overtly critiquing the present—a central premise of the dystopian tradition. As M. Keith Booker argues, "To be dystopian, a work needs to foreground the oppressive society in which it is set, using that setting as an opportunity to comment in a critical way on some other society, typically that of the author or audience[...]. [T]he bleak dystopian world should encourage the reader or viewer to think critically about it, then transfer this critical thinking to his or her own world" (5). One of these cultural touchstones in "The Long Walk" and "The Running Man" is the reality television tradition, with its familiar tropes showcased in the games at the center of each novella. Though *The Bachman Books* are among King's earliest works, they continue to resonate with a contemporary audience, as reality television has pervaded popular culture in the decades since. This trope is well-established in both real life competitions from *Survivor* (2000–present) to *American Idol* (2002–2016), as well as in film and fiction, including in the dystopian competition featured in Suzanne Collins' enormously popular *Hunger Games* series and its quartet of blockbuster film adaptations.

Reality television positions "the viewer as voyeur" (Andrejevic 321), encouraging the viewer to take a titillating look into the lives of others, often as those being watched engage in heated competition to be declared the winner, whether that victory is based on talent and skill or through taking down their fellow contestants by any means necessary. Reality television occupies a liminal space between the real and the performed, packaging "unscripted" programming to follow a narrative trajectory that will attract and keep the attention of its viewers. As Annette Hill explains in *Reality TV: Audiences and Popular Factual Television*, "[R]eality TV is located in border territories, between information and entertainment, documentary and drama" (2). While the viewer is undeniably a voyeur, the competitors themselves are also acutely aware of the ways in which they are being watched, positioning themselves self-reflexively within that realm of surveillance and overtly performing— playing to the ever-present camera and the unseen audience it represents, making it necessary to critique the "reality" of reality television from several different perspectives. While reality programming is at times positioned as educational or instructive, competition shows instead deal in sensationalism and scandal, pitting contestants against one another for the greatest possible conflict and, hopefully, ratings—an approach which has contributed to the genre's reputation as being "voyeuristic, cheap, sensational television" (Hill 7). Turning to the personalities and contestants that fill the small screens of reality television, the genre is also often charged with being exploitative, a site of potential mistreatment and abuse for those who participate. As Wendy N. Wyatt argues in "Exploitation: When Reality TV Becomes Degradation TV," drawing on the work of Ruth Sample,[2] exploitation is a feature of interactions—of transactions or of relationships—where there is a lack of respect. That lack of respect falls generally into three broad divisions: (i) that which results from neglecting what is necessary for a person's well-being or flourishing; (ii) that which results from taking advantage of an injustice done to a person; and (iii) that which results from commodifying, or treating as a fungible object of market exchange, an aspect of that person's being that ought not to be commodified [Wyatt 163].

The danger of this exploitation and its dehumanizing and potentially fatal effects are taken to the extreme when these unethical practices are positioned within a dystopian future, where there is often a more oppressive system of control, a greater threat of violence, and fewer means of redress when the individual is exploited.

In King's "The Long Walk" and "The Running Man," reality television becomes the foundation for each novella's horror, positioned within the larger dystopian culture which surrounds it, in which the disenfranchised are watched and cheered on as they struggle, suffer, and in many cases, die. Their lives are commodified, packaged, and destroyed by the culture which surrounds them as the protagonists become objectified and exploited. This dehumanization expands well beyond the contestants themselves, as the viewers *en masse* prove eager to watch and even actively contribute to others' suffering, complicit with the totalitarian control that defines these images, reinforcing the stereotypes and structural inequities that shape each of these worlds, with reality television tropes mobilized to reinforce the values of the dystopian society.

"The Long Walk"

In the world of "The Long Walk," thousands of spectators watch the eponymous walk, especially as it nears its final miles, whether crowding the sides of the roads where the contestants trek or from a distance in the comfort of their own homes through the television broadcast coverage of the competition. In the Long Walk, one hundred boys compete against one another, the elements, and their own physical limitations to try to be the last one standing. As Douglas E. Winter contextualizes this dark future, it is "a bleak, science-fictional mirror of contemporary America in which World War II extended into the 1950s and the government has passed into the hands of the military. The Long Walk has become this brave new world's premier sporting event; held annually for a worldwide television audience, it draws an ever-eager host of contestants and billions of dollars in wagers" (180). The Walk is brutal in its simplicity: starting at the Maine/Canada border, one hundred boys begin walking south, required to maintain a steady pace of no less than four miles per hour. There are no breaks and no rest; anything the boys must do, from eating and drinking to relieving themselves, must be done within the larger demands of the Walk itself. Any boy who drops below the four mile per hour dictate gets a warning, and after three warnings he is publicly and summarily executed, shot in the road by one of the rotating cast of soldiers who follow the Walkers on nearby vehicles. Young men don't need to be drafted or conscripted into the Walk; they apply and volunteer. One hundred Walkers and one hundred alternates are selected by lottery from thousands of volunteers eager to be chosen; the one hundred selected even have the opportunity to change their minds and opt out, but very few choose to do so, swept along in the fanfare and notoriety of being selected. These unlucky few are but a small selection of the boys vying to compete.

The boys walk for different reasons, though most of their explanations ring hollow, a thin veneer on the self-destructive and suicidal impulses that drive them on. The winner receives any prize he desires, but the Walkers' motivation is more complex than this promise of riches. Winter explains that the protagonist, Ray Garraty, "like most of his companions, has joined the Walk impulsively, drawn by a sense of glory and the vague expectation of adventure" (180). A Walker named Abraham applied for the Walk on a whim, telling the others, "I took the exam completely on the spur of the moment. I was on my way to the movies and I just happened past the gym where they were having the test" (284). For others, the allure is darker. As one of the Walkers argues as the boys mull over this very question, "you didn't get into this thinking of winning out and getting the Prize. Most of these guys don't know why they got into it. Look at Barkovitch. He ain't in it to get no Prize. He's just walkin' to see other people die. He lives on it. When someone gets a ticket, he gets a little more go-power" (211). Each boy walks on and while they are undeniably aware that the odds are stacked against them, like most teenagers they also wholeheartedly believe in their own invincibility, that death is something that happens to other people, even as they see their fellow Walkers fall and die beside them. When Garraty asks Stebbins, a taciturn and enigmatic fellow Walker, why he did it, he gives Garraty a haunting response, telling Garraty that he's walking, "For the same reason we're all doing it. [...] We want to die, that's why we're doing it. Why else, Garraty? Why else?" (222). The Walkers bear witness to the destruction of themselves and the boys around them, all while being witnessed themselves, serving as a spectacle for the eager audience both in person and at home.

King heads most of the chapters of "The Long Walk" with game show quotations from Dick Clark, Bob Barker, Art Fleming, and others, repeatedly underscoring this larger context of spectatorship and competition. At the start of the Walk the boys are largely alone, but as the miles pile up and the bodies start to fall, viewers line the roads with their lawn chairs and picnic lunches while the camera crews show up to watch, record, and transmit a shared ritualistic experience of suffering and death as entertainment to millions of television sets across the country and throughout the world. The boys are assigned numbers and turned into products, dehumanized as commodities that can be cheered for, bet on, but not empathized with in their suffering or mourned in their deaths. Mark Thomas argues, "The first step in accepting cruelty and barbarism is the dehumanisation of the victim, inscribing them as *les étrangers*. So constructed, they are denied the respect given to insiders, so as to permit a delight in their harm" (381). The people who watch are not just complicit in this spectacle of cruelty and murder, but actively cheer the Walkers on as they succeed and as they fail, eager for their chance to see these boys die. Once the Walk begins, the Walkers are no longer seen as someone's son, brother, or friend, but instead as no more than a piece in the larger game: expendable and disposable.

Once on the road, the Walkers themselves find that they can no longer share the spectators' distance. While they may have gotten into the Long Walk seeing the other ninety-nine boys as faceless numbers, nameless competitors that must be walked down on the way to victory, in the agonizing hours and days they spend walking alongside one another, they come to know and care for their fellow Walkers, echoing a larger reality TV trope that frames "the contestants as a kind of community" (Cavendar 159) albeit in this case a grim one. Garraty forms an intense friendship with another Walker, Peter McVries, and the two boys save each other's lives on more than one occasion. However, with the Walk whittled down to just over twenty remaining, the Walkers come to an agreement: "No help for anybody. Do it on your own or you don't do it" ("The Long Walk" 304). Thomas argues, "The ultimate mode of dehumanisation lies in the co-operation of the oppressed in the mode of their oppression" (381) and as Garraty and the other Long Walkers assent to this proposal, the last bits of humanity that they have managed to hang on to in themselves and in their connections with one another begin to slip away.

Turning to Wyatt's three components of exploitation and their application to reality television, all are on display throughout "The Long Walk" in the spectacle made of the Walk itself and viewers' responses to it. The first of these is the willful "neglecting of a person's well-being" (163). The boys' well-being is anathema to the Long Walk, since they can only be eliminated from competition through their deaths, the winner earning his victory through the deaths of the other ninety-nine. The Walkers are well supplied with water and receive a ration of food supplements each morning, designed to meet their most basic physical needs, but they cannot rest, sleep, stop walking, or even slow their pace too much for too long without facing a gruesome death. It is this suffering, rather than the boys' survival, that the crowds come out or tune in to see; they revel in the starvation, exhaustion, and pain on display before them, the dehumanization and destruction of the Walkers, one after another and year after year. Wyatt's second component addresses instances in which "[reality] shows not only take advantage of an injustice but facilitate or even create that injustice" (164). The competitors all volunteered for the Long Walk, can even be said to have competed for the privilege, and entered the contest of their own free will and a clear—or at least academic—understanding of its barbaric rules and realities. The injustice highlighted and simultaneously elided in the Long Walk is that of the surrounding society itself, the totalitarian regime headed by The Major, this dark future's militaristic leader. In the larger dystopian tradition, as Erika Gottlieb explains,

> [I]nstead of the rule of civilized law and justice, dystopian society functions as a primitive state religion that practices the ritual of human sacrifice. It is here that the reasoning that motivates the dystopian state's dualities of law and lawlessness, propaganda and truth, advanced technology and regression to barbarism is revealed to us, and this revelation further contributes to the nightmare atmosphere of the dystopian novel [11].

The injustice against these boys is part and parcel of the larger society that sanctions the Long Walk as the nation "exploit[s] them for the purposes of entertainment" (Strengell 198), echoing an immutable reality of the daily life which has informed these young men's understanding of the world and driven them to this fatalistic contest. The individual injustices within the Long Walk itself—such as the Walker who receives his requisite warnings and is executed for not walking after his legs have been run over by one of the accompanying military vehicles ("The Long Walk" 231)—are microcosmic reflections of the larger control and injustice that characterize life in this dark future, and therefore garners little notice and no outrage from the watching masses. Finally, Wyatt's third component of exploitation is in reality television's showcasing of "interactions that commodify people" (165). The Walkers are dehumanized, pieces in a game, a line upon which to bet. They are assigned a number at the start of the Walk and from that moment on, within the confines and consumption of the spectacle, they are no longer individuals, no longer human. They are marketed, packaged, and sold to viewers as not just entertainment, but as a reminder of control of The Major's totalitarian regime, its omnipresence and its power, both externally enforced and internalized by the Walkers themselves, and what happens to citizens who dare to step out of line.

Their government has dehumanized the Long Walkers, as have the crowds, and even as they fight to survive, the Walkers legitimize the systems that started them down the road. As Tony Magistrale explains, "In their decision to participate in the Long Walk, these boy-men have unwittingly capitulated to their government's sadistic system of control" ("Evaluating the

156 Part Two: Popular Dystopian Fiction

Bachman Books" 56). The Walkers have grown up in a world that is strictly controlled, built around a core of surveillance. Those who refuse are harshly punished—Garraty's own father was arrested and taken away, or "Squaded," for speaking out against the barbarity of the Long Walk ("The Long Walk" 219)—which leaves little choice for citizens but to remain complacent, whether through their silence or their cheers. Exploring another explanation for why the boys choose to walk, Magistrale argues that "involvement in the Long Walk is motivated by such pessimism about the future—financial, personal, political—that the race represents the one chance for the Walkers to escape the death-in-life circumstances of mature citizenship" ("Evaluating the Bachman Books" 56). The dystopian world in which they live has dehumanized these young men, commodifying their lives and deaths, and in the televised annual spectacle of their living and dying, they reiterate and reinscribe that dehumanization for the generation to follow, which will provide the next year's Long Walkers. Garraty is the sole survivor of the Long Walk, though "his victory proves hollow, because he is now completely absorbed by the machinery of the state and lacks a will of his own" (Strengell 199). The last man standing—or walking, rather—he finds himself unable to stop, running madly on as he tries to catch up with an ephemeral dark figure before him, a personified death that encompasses his murdered friends, his sanity, and his own lost humanity.

"The Running Man"

Like "The Long Walk," "The Running Man"[3] is set in a dystopian future characterized by deprivation, desperation, and constant surveillance, "where most of the population—unemployed, impoverished, and ravaged with the diseases of environmental neglect—sit dull-eyed in the wash of Free-Vee, a blackly comic exaggeration of contemporary television" (Winter 184). However, "The Running Man" is much more overtly structured around reality television tropes than "The Long Walk," where the televisual spectacle is a small part of the larger competition. In "The Running Man," the game show format is the central narrative structure and part of a larger trend, as "The Running Man" is but one of many series on the Network, all of which demand that contestants put their literal lives on the line. While these competitions are inhumane and life threatening, much like the boys who queue up for their chance to be contestants in "The Long Walk," the Network never has a shortage of willing participants.

Ben Richards, the novella's protagonist, submits himself to the testing and assessment of the game makers in a desperate bid to save his young daughter's life; unemployed and with his wife resorting to prostitution to buy groceries as their child's fever spikes to one hundred and four degrees, he finds himself left with no other options ("The Running Man" 533). As Winter sums up the premise of "The Running Man" competition, "Its rules are simple: to win its prize of one billion dollars, the contestant must survive for thirty days, eluding a team of trained killers whose hunt, aired nightly on Free-Vee, is aided and abetted by citizens eager for cash rewards. This high-tech version of 'The Most Dangerous Game' has never been won; indeed, the longest life span of a running man is eight days" (Winter 184). Richards effectively has no chance of survival and acquiesces to this fact as he agrees to compete. The only chance he has been given to provide for his family and save himself is really no chance at all, but for the sake of the money that will be sent to his family and the life-saving medicine it will afford his child, he accepts it, along with his own inevitable death.

In appealing to its viewers to participate in the death of Richards and the other running men who have come before him, the Network manipulates the images of its contestants, turning them into high-profile public enemies with a charged rhetoric designed to put fear in the hearts of the viewers at home. When the host of *The Running Man* introduces Richards to his not-so-adoring public, Richards' image is one of threat, mayhem, and potential destruction, turning this man into a dangerous monster that the public can feel righteous about helping take down. As Richards considers the picture they project when he is introduced,

> It had been retouched [...] to make his eyes deeper, his forehead a little lower, his cheeks more shadowed. His mouth had been given a jeering, curled expression by some technico's airbrush. All in all, the Richards on the monitor was terrifying—the angel of urban death, brutal, not very bright, but possessed of a certain primitive animal cunning. The uptown apartment dweller's worst nightmare [567].

His wife's image receives the same treatment, turning her "sweet, not-so-good looking face [...] into that of a vapid slattern" (567). The system dehumanizes Richards not just through the manipulation of his own image but through the suggestion that his family and relationships are indecent and depraved, isolating him from the larger scope of humanity, depriving him of his place within it and any empathy or identification those connections might have inspired in the audience.

This echoes the rhetoric of reality television designed to inspire fear and encourage viewer participation in combatting crime, like the long running and popular series *Unsolved Mysteries* (1987–2010) and *America's Most Wanted* (1988–2012). As Gray Cavendar explains, "[P]rogramming which taps into the fear of and anger at crime (or other anxieties)—relates to the matter of community. [...] Real-crime programming presents the community as under attack (by crime) and appeals to the community to aid in the fight against crime" (157). In coming together, the viewers play an integral part in keeping a watchful eye on their neighborhoods, helping apprehend criminals and working "to re-establish a sense of community" (Cavendar 158) threatened by these fugitives' deviance and the threat of violence. In series like *America's Most Wanted*, a dichotomy of "good versus evil" and "us versus them" is visually and narratively established in the opening segments, as "[j]uxtaposed with community members are the criminals. If victims are attractive and worthwhile, criminals are 'ugly' and worthless outsiders" (Cavendar 161), a contrast that is also employed in King's novella.

The Running Man is a battle to the death, a matter of kill or be killed. After a confrontation with his hunters in which five policemen die, Richards is portrayed and broadcast as a monster rather than a man struggling to survive. The Games Commission edits Richards' message to the viewers—an attempt to inform them about the government's role in the crippling pollution and its impact on the nation's citizens, including the disproportionate suffering of its poorest people—to an angry, curse-filled diatribe of hatred and murder. As the show's host exhorts the viewing audience, "Behold the man. [...] The man who would kill. The man who would mobilize an army of malcontents like himself to run riot through your streets, raping and burning and overturning. The man would lie, cheat, kill. He has done all these things" (600). In addition to the dehumanization inherent in repeatedly referring to Richards as "the man," denying him his name and the humanity such individualization implies, Richards is also contrasted starkly against images of each of the dead policemen, fallen heroes whose images are featured looking "fresh, full of sap and hope, heart-breakingly vulnerable" (601), followed by pictures of their wives and children, now in mourning. In this control of the narrative and the manipulation of viewers' perspectives, Richards is irredeemably monstrous, the bogeyman that must be destroyed to make the world safe—or at least safer—for the civilized; he is cast out from the larger brotherhood of man, becoming inhuman, able to be destroyed violently, even gleefully, and without compunction.

Wyatt's three characteristics of exploitation television—the neglect of the individual's well-being, capitalization on injustice, and the dehumanization and resultant commodification of its contestants (163)—are also on display in *The Running Man*. All of the shows on the Network put their contestants' health, safety, and very lives at risk. For example, on one of the Network's lesser shows, *Treadmill to Bucks*, the competitors are "chronic heart, liver, or lung patients" forced to run on a treadmill while answering trivia questions, with the treadmill getting faster and their winnings dropping lower with each incorrect response (533). These risks are accepted by the desperate competitors as a matter of course and with names like *How Hot Can You Take It, Run For Your Guns,* and *Swim the Crocodiles* (554), maiming and mutilation seem almost inevitable, all played for the entertainment of the Free-Vee viewing audience at home. *The Running Man* is even more disastrous to the "well-being" (Wyatt 163) of its contestants. As one of his fellow competitors sardonically says to Richards as they wait to find out where they're being sent, "I think we're getting the big-money assignments. The ones where they do more than just land you in the hospital with a stroke or put out an eye or cut off an arm or two. The ones where they kill you. Prime time, baby" ("The Running Man" 555). These lesser assaults and abuses pale in comparison to impending death—and the prestige and payouts that presumably come with it.

In the Network's development of these shows and the audience's viewing (in the case of *The Running Man*, enthusiastic participation), they deal in injustice. Even more overtly than in "The Long Walk," the initial injustice is created and maintained by the society itself (Wyatt 164). The Free-Vee programming's "various technologies serve to divert the collective attention of an oppressed populace away from the state's daily acts of ethical misconduct and toward the grisly illustrations of what occurs to 'criminals' who exist outside the mainstream" (Magistrale, *Hollywood's Stephen King* 158). The contestants are driven to compete out of the desperation created by poverty and pollution, two pronounced disparities that the government and Free-Vee Network do nothing to alleviate. Instead, they lull the citizens into complacency with mindless entertainment, with the punishment of their peers also serving as a constant reminder that resisting is futile and perhaps even deadly. Finally, Richards is dehumanized and literally turned into a bankable commodity, as the viewers at home can win cash prizes by calling in with their tips and sightings. Richards is packaged and projected by the Network, which reaps the benefits of the high ratings and manipulates the narrative to make his exploitation as profitable as possible, while the viewers at home have their own chance to make some money by informing on Richards, their poverty and desperation coupling with Richards' public dehumanization, filling their pockets while fulfilling their civic duty, doing their part to end a man's life.

Like the world of *The Long Walk*, *The Running Man* and Richards' competition within it are indicative of a much larger social dysfunction, in the creation of a world that would willingly sacrifice its own citizens in such barbaric and inhumane ways. The America of *The Running Man* in 2025 is recognizable but nightmarish, as pollution has made the air unbreathable. Additionally, as Magistrale argues, "*The Running Man* is a terrifying examination of the importance of class position and wealth as determinants of survival" ("Evaluating the Bachman Books" 59–60). With enormous class disparity, the wealthy are able to buy breathing filters and live their lives in health and comfort while the poor are left to sicken and die from a variety of devastating illnesses, with little outrage at or alleviation of their suffering. While the boys of "The Long Walk" remain largely complacent to the inequities and abuses of their larger society, Richards refuses to do so. He finds similarly down-trodden allies along his path, with whom "his bond is solidified in a common hatred for the Network; more importantly, these characters come to recognize the need for revolutionary change and willingly sacrifice themselves to this cause" (Magistrale, "Evaluating The Bachman Books" 60) as Richards' struggle becomes not just about one man's fight for survival, but a larger portent of uprising and revolution to come. After besting the Games Commission and making small steps toward shedding light on the inequalities that are shaping and breaking the world around him, the Games Commission offers Richards the opportunity to join them, not only to live but to do so comfortably, as one of the rich whose "bogeyman" he had so recently been forced to play. This is an offer Richards refuses, instead unleashing the fury that the viewers have been trained to fear, commandeering a plane, killing almost everyone else onboard, and crashing it into the Games Building, "His face smeared with blood, his black eyes burning like the eyes of a demon" ("The Running Man" 691). As Magistrale argues, Richards' "suicide is an act of political terrorism as much as it is an expression of personal despair" (*Hollywood's Stephen King* 159–60). Instead of taking his place as one piece within the larger machinery, as Garraty does at the end of "The Long Walk," Richards attempts to destroy the machine itself, and while his sacrifice will likely fall short of dismantling the structural inequalities that shape the lives of the poor in devastating ways, it may set a spark to their simmering rage, creating a possible world in which they can fight, even if they may not be able to win.[4]

Conclusion

In "The Long Walk" and "The Running Man," King's protagonists struggle in dark worlds from which there is no escape. As Magistrale explains, "There are no golden futures in King's dystopian portrayal of contemporary technologies" (*Hollywood's Stephen King* 171). Ray Garraty and Ben Richards both live the most painful moments of their lives under scrutiny for the entertainment of the watching masses as they are abused, exploited, and destroyed. Each enters into the competition as an act of desperation, hoping for some alleviation of poverty and a struggling existence, in the full knowledge that they stand little to no chance of making it out alive. However, these contests are but a reflection of the larger dystopian society which surrounds and condones them, a twenty-first-century America which dehumanizes and commodifies its own citizens as a means of entertainment and control. There is no way out for Garraty or Richards, or for any of the Long Walkers or Running Men who have taken their places beside them or before them.

NOTES

1. The *Bachman Books* collection includes four of King's early novellas: "Rage," "The Long Walk," "The Running Man," and "Roadwork." King included an introduction to this collection in which he considered the question "Why I Was Bachman." King pulled *The Bachman Books* from publication after copies of "Rage" were connected to school shootings; see King's ebook *Guns* for more on this decision. King also published the novels *Thinner* (1984), *The Regulators* (1996), and *Blaze* (2007) under the Bachman pseudonym, after the King/Bachman connection was well-known.

2. Sample's argument is more broadly and philosophically based, explored in her book *Exploitation: What It Is and Why It's Wrong* (2003), a theoretical framework that Wyatt applies to the tropes and traditions of, and audience responses to, reality television.

3. "The Running Man" refers to King's novella, while *The Running Man* refers to the reality competition within the novella.

4. While King's stories and novels have been prolifically adapted for film and television, those he published as Bachman have been less attractive to Hollywood, with the exceptions of *Thinner* (1996) and Paul Michael Glaser's 1987 adaptation of *The Running Man*, in which Arnold Schwarzenegger plays Ben Richards, who is hunted by "Stalkers" played by action-adventure legends including Jim Brown and Jesse Ventura, with iconic game show host Richard Dawson in the role of Damon Killian, host of *The Running Man*. The conclusion of the film version is much more optimistic than that of King's novella, as Richards "defeats the superior weaponry of The Stalkers and demonstrates that one man is capable of facing down an entire evil corporate monolith. [...] The film version of *The Running Man* is thus a paean to the power of the individual—his self-reliance triumphs over all obstacles, political as well as personal" (*Hollywood's Stephen King* 160).

WORKS CITED

Andrejevic, Mark. "Visceral Literacy: Reality TV, Savvy Viewers, and Auto-Spies." *Reality TV: Remaking Television Culture*. Ed. Susan Murray and Laurie Ouelette. New York: New York University Press, 2009: 321–42. Print.
Booker M. Keith. "On Dystopia." *Dystopia: Critical Insights*. Ed. M. Keith Booker. Ipswich, MA: Salem Press, 2013: 1–15. Print.
Cavender, Gray. "In Search of Community on Reality TV: *American's Most Wanted* and *Survivor*." *Understanding Reality Television*. Ed. Su Holmes and Deborah Jermyn. New York: Routledge, 2004: 154–72. Print.
Gottlieb, Erika. *Dystopian Fiction East and West: Universe of Terror and Trial*. Montreal: McGill-Queen's UP, 2001. Print.
Hill, Annette. *Reality TV: Audiences and Popular Factual Television*. New York: Routledge, 2005. Print.
King, Stephen. *Guns*. Bangor, ME: Philtrum, 2013. Ebook.
_____. (as Richard Bachman). *The Long Walk*. *The Bachman Books: Four Early Novels by Stephen King*. New York: New American Library, 1985: 133–322. Print.
_____. (as Richard Bachman). *The Running Man*. *The Bachman Books: Four Early Novels by Stephen King*. New York: New American Library, 1985: 531–692. Print.
Magistrale, Tony. "Evaluating the Bachman Books: *Rage, The Long Walk, Roadwork, The Running Man, Thinner, The Dark Half*." *Stephen King: The Second Decade, Danse Macabre to The Dark Half*. New York: Twayne, 1992: 47–66. Print.
_____. *Hollywood's Stephen King*. New York: Palgrave Macmillan, 2003. Print.
Strengell, Heidi. *Dissecting Stephen King: From the Gothic to Literary Naturalism*. Madison: University of Wisconsin Press, 2005. Print.
Thomas, Mark. "*Survivor* on Steroids: Law, Law and Power in *The Hunger Games*." *Griffith Law Review* 22.2 (2013): 361–402. Academic Search Complete. Web. 10 May 2016.

Winter, Douglas E. *Stephen King: The Art of Darkness*. New York: New American Library, 1986. Print.
Wyatt, Wendy N. "Exploitation: When Reality TV Becomes Degradation TV." *The Ethics of Reality TV: A Philosophical Examination*. Ed. Wendy N. Wyatt and Kristie Bunton. New York: Continuum, 2012: 159–74. Print.

Stranger Than Fiction
Locating the Digital Dystopia in Contemporary Fiction

ROBYN N. ROWLEY

Literature has long reflected and examined cultural patterns, social norms, and major changes in thought and convention. Genre novels like the dystopian works considered in this volume of essays seem particularly attuned to social moments as they grapple with the structural mechanisms of culture. As Margaret Anne Doody's history of the novel suggests, these novels and their authors do not accidentally encode their works with historical and social milieu unique to their moment. Doody notes, "Not only the era and the language but also the genre speaks through the Novelist" (306). The dystopian genre is a keen exemplar of this tendency, engaging issues of technology, science, environmental changes, governance, and economics while providing insights about the nature of certain paranoias and anxieties.

A salient theme across the dystopian genre is a fixation on technology's interventions in contemporary life. Emerging amid increasing automation, the arrival of the first computers, and a dearth of new gadgets in the Atomic age, dystopian novels of the 1950s through the 1980s frequently depicted surveillance states populated with sentient robots, trans-human cyborgs, and supercomputers capable of outwitting and eliminating human intelligence. These narratives thrust readers into distant future settings. In contemporary fiction, however, the genre has been marked by a departure from distant future settings of science fiction to contemporary settings that draw heavily on extant technology. Such works are time-specific rather than transcendent, with "hyper-present," settings that immerse the reader in an alternate view of the current world, using satire to exaggerate and parody the contemporary world. Yet beneath the cloak of satire, more serious nihilism and anomie about society's future exist, along with an invitation for dialogue and reader response to its own burlesque.

This reworking situates digital technology as a powerful, nuanced force shaping culture and society. A growing subset of contemporary dystopias considers the transformations already underway in regard to culture and human consciousness as a result of contemporary culture's shift to digitality and digital mobility. Given their characteristic saturation by and fixation on elements of digital technology, the term "digital dystopia" is an apt description. The hyper-presence of digital dystopian novels offers a powerful reading of modern capitalism, corporate greed, and contemporary consumerism. Because such works emerge as products of a cultural moment, and at a time when wealth in capitalist America has been redistributed, the focus on corporate capitalism is a relevant and urgent facet of their critiques.

Authors of digital dystopian novels probe ethical issues surrounding digital labor, demonstrate the erosion of privacy in the digital era, consider digital technology's disintegrating effect on language and communication, and explore the tension between Luddism and technophilia. These themes reflect the growing unease concerning life in an increasingly digitally immersed society. Such novels lend themselves to critical digital studies and theories, and parallel the impulse by theorists and writers to understand contemporary life. A survey of contemporary dystopias reveals a growing list of novels that fit these themes, many of them making unique stylistic interventions that engage the notion of digital mediation through form as well as content.

To elaborate the digital dystopia as a subset of the broader dystopian genre in contemporary fiction, I will examine a sample of three texts: Alena Graedon's *The Word Exchange* (2014), Dave Eggers' *The Circle* (2013), and M.T. Anderson's *Feed* (2002). Each of these texts is heavily marked by themes of the digital dystopia, critiquing capitalist structures of contemporary culture, examining consumer-producer relationships, language and communication, privacy, and Luddism and technophilia. These novels explore contemporary tensions between analog and digital technologies, generational divides, and society's vacillation between anxiety and hope for the future of humankind.

Daniel Chandler notes that each new work in a genre has the ability to influence changes within the genre or stimulate the emergence of new subgenres, which may, he writes, "later blossom into fully-fledged genres" (3). Other critics have noted that the distinctions between genres have become less defined and more permeable in recent years, allowing for more latitude between genres. Whether the type of dystopia this paper has thus far sought to delineate will in fact emerge as its own subgenre will be decided by novels that have yet to be published or imagined. However, as more new novels in this mode appear, the contours of the digital dystopia are becoming increasingly well-defined, pointing toward an emergence of a new style of dystopia that is distinct from the genre at large, and is indicative of the permeability of genre boundaries. The stakes of recognizing the distinct characteristics of digital dystopias lies in their astute portrait of modern society and the engagement of themes that reveal the novel's coadjuvant relationship with culture. Recognizing the digital dystopia as a prescient critique of contemporary culture is consistent with the notion that fiction writing of all types can act as a mirror for self-reflection and a medium for critical discourse.

The digital dystopian novel's arrival in contemporary fiction parallels the emergence of Web 2.0, a term used to signify the switch to mobile internet and the digital explosion facilitated by wireless networks and connectivity. The term *Web 2.0* was coined by Darcy DiNucci in 1999 to describe the then-nascent phenomenon. The first hints of Web 2.0 were just beginning to appear when DiNucci wrote about imagined possibilities for the near future, "The Web we know now [...] is only an embryo of the Web to come." She continued, "The Web will be understood not as screenfuls of text and graphics but as a transport mechanism, the ether through which interactivity happens" (38). As DiNucci predicted, with the shift to mobility and the explosion of smartphones and devices like tablets and netbooks, connectivity has become a part of life outside of the home, on an individual level rather than as a group accessing of networks.

These major shifts in technology and the heralding of the digital era by Web 2.0 have transformed daily life, making content creation and information sharing an interactive, participatory and constant experience. The ability of individuals to communicate in real-time via audio, visual, and text interfaces, the automation of daily tasks through location based services and GPS, and the popularization of social media—to mention only a few aspects of this technology—have had far-reaching effects. But the rapidity and scope of these changes have also resulted in latent anxiety, anomie, and distrust. It is these sensibilities that are encoded in digital dystopian novels and which likewise are felt by real world consumers. The hyper-present, time-period specific nature of the digital dystopia defines these as post–1999 novels with characteristic reflexivity and contemplation of the cultures and societies they both depict and are produced in. The growing number of digital dystopias and their coadjuvant relationship with culture is captured by David Buckingham's comment that the genre "is in a constant process of negotiation and change" (137).

Consumer, Producer and Labor

Authors of digital dystopian novels consider not only the potential for technology to go awry, as in the trope of the sentient-robot-gone-bad like in

Vonnegut's *Player Piano* (1952) or Clarke's *2001: A Space Odyssey* (1968), but they further contemplate the ways that consumers willingly engage with and seek out seemingly benign forms of digital technology. In such cases, this new technology does not resemble a nefarious entity; in fact, it isn't always clear that the technology is part of an "entity" at all. Rather, digital technologies are tools used by consumers who—at least initially—enjoy the impacts of technology in their lives. Among the technologies considered are the constant connectivity of digital telecommunications; global positioning systems used to track, guide, connect, and locate users via various applications; ecommerce; creation of new visual and textual content at will; and the ability to store content in intangible banks of data that can be accessed anywhere.

Producers of digital technology are driven by capitalism to constantly devise new products and platforms available for use by consumers, ostensibly making modern life more streamlined and convenient. But as consumers' lives become increasingly saturated with devices and digital products, the overwhelming number of platforms any one person may use seems to create more demands on their time and attention. To that end, digital dystopias consider the relationship between a consumer's embrace or distrust of technology.

As Erika Gottlieb argues, a defining characteristic of the dystopian genre at large is the oscillation between what Béla Hamvas called "Messianism" and tyrannical dictatorships. Gottlieb suggests that this tension is played out in dystopias when the reader (or audience) realizes that the messiah and the tyrant in the mask are one in the same (5). Rather than solving problems, these perceived saviors actually cause more societal ills, revealing themselves as tyrants in messianic masks. Digital dystopian novels exhibit the same phenomena and follow a similar trajectory. Graedon's, Eggers', and Anderson's narratives posit that the masked messiah is the corporate producers of digital technology. In *The Word Exchange, The Circle,* and *Feed,* digital technology corporations begin as messiahs, but as tension builds, they are revealed as tyrants. Similarly, the character's view of digital technology shifts from naiveté and eagerness to suspicion and distrust.

Displaying the messianic phase of the dystopian narrative, consumer use of technology is at first celebrated and encouraged in digital dystopias. In *The Circle,* the protagonist Mae lands a dream job at Circle Technologies, a next generation social network company which provides products that do everything: tracking children via microchip implants, uncovering the secrets of a person's genetic past, and centrally managing all of a person's networking and internet connectivity. The consumers of this technology in Eggers' novel are called "Circlers" and eagerly embrace each new product. In a parody of real life consumerism and its eager embrace of new platforms and technologies, *The Circle* also satirizes the culture industry's role in determining user tastes, purchases, and choices. Like the consumers Eggers satirizes, Mae is an obedient and predictable user of each new product developed by The Circle. But with each new device or product, the company encroaches more and more into Mae's life, and the reader is left to ponder the creeping influence of digitality. Mae's lack of reflexivity creates a jarring effect for readers who identify their own consumer habits in Eggers' narrative.

In Graedon's *The Word Exchange*, a powerful corporation known as Synchronic develops sophisticated smartphones and applications with invasive effects on user consciousness. A device known as a meme syncs with users' thoughts and movements, anticipating their actions and communications. Though the meme device ostensibly functions to streamline work and pleasure in daily life by reducing time and effort spent on mundane tasks, it also nefariously dismantles privacy. Readers—who recognize the meme and Synchronic as dictatorial and tyrannical well before the main character does—also eventually perceive its more nefarious effect: meme users unknowingly become almost entirely dependent on their devices to function. Satirizing smartphone use, Graedon invites readers to insert themselves in the narrative and question their own consumerism.

Digital dystopian novels often consider the implications of consumer digital labor, exposing latent or unrealized labor as a method of consumer exploitation and alienation. Though consumer labor is often a latent aspect of their usage of digital technologies, consumers provide useful data that can be gleaned by corporate producers, leaving these consumer laborers unpaid for their work. Similarly, data about consumer interaction with online advertisements, search engines, and internet browsing are collected and recorded. This data can be refined to allow the program to make better and more accurate recommendations—ostensibly benefitting the laborer-user—but on a mass scale, this unpaid labor becomes exploitative. Trebor Scholz comments, "The internet has become a simple-to-join, anyone-can-play system where the sites and practices of work and play increasingly wield people as a resource for economic amelioration by a handful of oligarchic owners" (1). The technology taken up in digital dystopias tends to lend itself to examination of labor practices as work and play converge.

In *The Word Exchange*, characters engage with a smartphone game application called "Meaning Master" that relies on consumer-created content. The more users play the game, the stronger the game—and Synchronic, the corporation behind it—becomes. In a narrative turn, the massive bank of user-created content is then sold back to consumers. Graedon positions the user of seemingly benign digital technologies at the center of a Marxist nightmare wherein the rich profit exponentially off the labor of unwitting users.

Anderson too takes up this issue in *Feed*. The teenage Titus and his friends have chip-like devices implanted in their brains, which allow them to view and use an internet feed without an external device. Though the technology of the feed may at first appear too fantastical to belong to the digital dystopian, like the other novels in this paper, *Feed* is inspired by extant technology: the first microchips implanted for human use appeared in 1998, just prior to the digital explosion that followed the advent of Web 2.0. Cybernetics scientists such as Mark Gasson have used the chips to store data securely, active devices, send payments, and study the boundaries of the human body and bio-technologies (Warwick). In *Feed*, Anderson extrapolates from this technology to imagine its yet untapped capabilities in a hyper-present world where digital technology has run amok.

Feed considers the exploitative nature of consumer digital labor and portrays the corporation FeedTech as a greedy, profit-driven capitalist entity. The feed device technology is primarily used for communication, entertainment, and ecommerce, with data about such use gathered by FeedTech and used to create an accurate consumer profile for marketing purposes. The problems of data mining and digital labor are explored by Anderson through Titus' girlfriend Violet, who attempts to resist the feed by preventing FeedTech from generating an accurate consumer profile of her by purposefully providing erratic data. Violet and Titus visit the mall, where they browse a wide variety of unrelated products. Violet shops for a searchlight, a rug, an obscure "Bleakazoid" action figure, and a "slinky, silky" dress for her boyfriend. Violet's antics do prevent FeedTech from creating a profile for her, but this is an action she is later punished for, a consequence that portrays digital technology corporations as nefarious tyrants driven by greed and profit.

The digital dystopia conflates digital technologies with corporate greed and excess, but it is clear that the masked dictator is not the technology itself; the corporate entities produce it. FeedTech, Synchronic, and The Circle eerily evoke modern-day media conglomerates that gather valuable data about a consumer's use of their product, ostensibly without the consumer's realization. By critiquing the capitalist structures and corporations behind digital technology, Eggers', Graedon's, and Anderson's novels each suggest that corporate profits and consumer digital labor are at odds with the claim that such products are developed with a level of altruism, instead declaring that reliance on digital technology has unseen ill effects and that messianic figures of digital dystopian novels are masked tyrants.

Linguistic Disintegration

Linguistic disintegration and the breakdown of communication is another characteristic element distinguishing digital dystopian novels from the wider genre. *Feed* begins with a group of teenagers casually conversing together in nonsensical slang phrases. But this vernacular is not a register of teenage slang—throughout *Feed* it's also used by adults and appears in advertisements, songs, and feed broadcasts. The constant interiority of the feed devices has a seemingly disintegrating effect on language as the characters repeat meaningless phrases like "She was now completely younch" (24) and "like, meg hard" (4).

Digital technology and its effects on human consciousness are satirized when Titus unexpectedly loses access to his digital device after being infected by a virus. When the feed stops, the sudden silence awakens Titus, who comments, "Everything in my head was quiet. It was fucked" (44). In contrast with the incessant bombardment of the feed, Titus' discomfort at his own silent thoughts demonstrates the impact of digital immersion on linguistics and communication. The vocabulary of the feed content and the character's dialogue demonstrate technology's ability to dismantle language.

The simplistic, colloquial speech of Titus and others in the novel is contrasted with Violet and her father, whose feeds were installed later in life, rather than at birth. Violet and her father both use markedly less slang and colloquial language, and they frequently use complex, obscure words that others don't understand. At a party, she tells Titus via the feed, "*I made the mistake of saying that we were back to the picayune grind. Now she keeps going, '"Picayune"?!? "Picayune"?!?' and pretending I'm French. I wish I hadn't said anything*" (83; italics in original). When Titus first meets Violet's father, he greets him by saying, "I am filled with astonishment at the regularity of your features and the handsome generosity you have shown my daughter. The two of you are close, which gladdens the heart, as close as twin wings torn off the same butterfly" (136). Titus remarks that he has not understood anything her father has said, and Violet explains, "He says the language is dying. He thinks words are being debased. So he tries to speak entirely in weird words and irony, so no one can simplify anything he says" (137). Though her father uses the feed, it is an older analog version, which, along with his attempts to preserve language and his suspicion of technology, marks him as a Luddite.

Anderson uses the feed devices to demonstrate that the feed's technology, which can convert thoughts to readable text or audio, is used for communication, to advertise to users, for e-commerce, and to play various types of media. But its constant interiority also lends it the insidious powers to dictate thoughts, influence feelings, and to entertain and cater to a user's needs in such a way that supplants independent thought and activity, signified when, after the feed malfunctions, Titus and the others simply stare at the walls of the hospital for hours as they find verbal communication difficult. Titus compares talking aloud to "trying to perform brain surgery with old, rusted skewers and things" (54). This scenario parodies the way that text communication differs from verbal communication and hints at the generational divide theorized by Marc Prensky who distinguishes between digital natives born into the digital era who did not experience life prior to the advent of the mobile digital web, and digital immigrants who learned to use this technology later in life, and thus relate to it differently (1–2). Titus and Violet are digital natives who are unaccustomed to life without digital technology. For them, text communication is a primary means of speaking to another person.

Digital dystopian novels imply that use of these technologies may also have a disintegrating effect upon meaningful interpersonal communication. In a generational sense, digital natives are the group most at risk for these harms because of their inability to view the technology objectively, or to imagine life without it. In each novel, a parent figure represents a digital immigrant with greater doubts, suspicion, and less interest in technology and its advance.

Similarly, in *The Word Exchange*, digital technologies have a disintegrating effect on language. As a result of random code mashups in cyberspace, a digitally-borne virus transfers to human organisms resulting in an illness called "word flu." Once infected, an ill person gradually loses communicative ability. Meanwhile, users of the Synchronic app game "Meaning Master" unwittingly create nonsensical content that supplants English words. These new words become part of a digital lexicon which can only be accessed on a pay-per-word basis. This entanglement of consumer's language loss and the profitability of words for pay via Synchronic's lexicon, "The Word Exchange," strengthen the novel's critique of capitalism.

The Word Exchange suggests that the digital can both dismantle and supplant language. As word flu spreads, Ana, Bart, Max, and other characters find their basic linguistic ability to form intelligible words is weakening. Through a novelistic conceit, Graedon demonstrates the linguistic breakdown through dialogue that creates a disorienting effect for the reader. Bart, who has been infected, wonders what is happening: "[T]his sickness, or whatever it is, scares the pask out of me. I'm not just feeling queasy and sweaty and weak, I'm also jwayvo slightly divided from my psyche. [...] I keep coming back to those words with the made-up meanings Max wants me to jurate [...]" (163). As word flu illness becomes more advanced, speech becomes increasingly garbled and unintelligible, and the victim may eventually become mute, or even die.

The breakdown of communications technologies in digital dystopias leads characters to revert to analog methods of communication. Titus' and Violet's defunct feeds mean that they cannot use them to communicate and must develop their verbal communication skills to connect with one another. For Ana, most modes of communication are corrupt, and she must rely on analog cellphones, underground tubes which can send hard copies of messages, or face-to-face meetings. The breakdown of communication technologies in digital dystopian novels represents a potential danger in reliance on digital tools and devices which contributes to the feelings of chaos and disorder typical across the dystopian genre.

These assumptions point back to the digital dystopian novel's hyperpresence. Linguistic disintegration—or at least major shifts—can be identified in the linguistic registers of internet communities—the prevalence of emojis[1] as a form of communication, meme phenomena, and the instant gratification of low-stakes interactions on social networking sites—that reduce the amount of in-person communication taking place in society. In *Feed*, Violet concludes as much, stating, "Because of the feed, we're raising a nation of idiots. Ignorant, self-centered idiots" (Anderson 113). In an argument, Mercer, Mae's ex-boyfriend in *The Circle*, insinuates that Mae's immersion in digital technology has had a similar effect on her: "[...] You're not very interesting anymore. You sit at a desk for twelve hours a day and you have nothing to show for it except for some numbers that won't exist or be remembered in a week. [...] Mae, do you realize how incredibly boring you've become?" (Eggers 263).

Privacy

Digital dystopian novels typically exhibit a characteristic rumination on privacy, the erosion of which is a result of the creeping influence of digital technology in daily life. This phenomenon is depicted as a major threat to society. In the world of *The Circle*, consumers are obligated to share everything about their lives via their circle accounts. This ethic of compulsory sharing interpellates consumers as subjects of The Circle, in an Althusserian sense. Like FeedTech in Anderson's novel, and Synchronic in Graedon's, The Circle acts as a powerful masked messiah figure that by the novel's conclusion is revealed to be a depraved and tyrannical despot. Eggers deploys Mae as a loyal subject of The Circle, who is reliant on the digital technology that dismantles her privacy and sense of interiority. Parodying contemporary consumers' relation to technology, Mae dutifully observes the rules of The Circle: Presence, Participation, and Transparency.

In keeping with the dystopian trope of satire, Eggers presents a series of ever more absurd privacy violations, using Mae and the other circlers to criticize consumerism-induced apathy. When The Circle launches its new program SeeChange, a network of tiny, easily placed wireless cameras that can stream footage from any place at any time, the audience immediately cheers, even when the program creator ominously announces, "All that happens must be known." Believing that surveillance will create accountability, reduce crime, and keep people safe, Mae and the other audience members greet SeeChange with enthusiasm. The growing power of The Circle and the possibility of a surveillance state are foreshadowed in Bailey's Orwellian statement that "[w]e will become all-seeing, all-knowing" (68–71).

At these increasingly dictatorial statements, readers recognize the first hints that the individuals helming The Circle are tyrannical despots rather than humanitarian innovators. The novel's criticisms are more pronounced when contrasted with Mae, who is unable to recognize The Circle's darker side or perceive the greed of the corporation she works for. Even when Mae experiences several personal privacy violations in regard to her health and personal history, she displays willful ignorance about The Circle's true nature.

In *Feed*, privacy is also taken up as a primary issue. Though Violet attempts to resist the feed, she later discovers that her private information is being accessed through her dreams. This scenario demonstrates the potential for digital technologies to turn upon users, surveilling even the most private of data, as in Violet's dreams. Anderson's novel suggests through this turn of events that privacy is illusory when consumers use digital technologies to such an extent, warning against the encroachment of trans-human technology such as microchip implants.

For Eggers, meanwhile, reduced privacy can come when consumers like Mae are interpellated as subjects of ideological state apparatuses like The Circle. After being caught on a SeeChange camera committing a petty crime, Mae responds with sincere self-reproach, ultimately helping to craft The Circle's penultimate new mantra, which guides the corporation's invasive and tyrannical policies throughout the remainder of the story: "SECRETS ARE LIES. SHARING IS CARING. PRIVACY IS THEFT." In order to prove her allegiance to The Circle, Mae decides to "go transparent," and become "the face of The Circle." She wears a tiny camera on a necklace that captures and live broadcasts everything she does. But on camera, Mae's interactions with others become forced and scripted. These interactions point to the disintegration of interpersonal communication and human relationships when they are mediated by digital technology. The camera's intrusion into Mae's friendship with Annie stimulates a performative element in their interactions, rendering the communications inauthentic and hollow.

Ruminations on privacy within the digital dystopian novel ultimately seem to posit the question of whether privacy can be fully dismantled, inviting readers to consider the implications of the total loss of private ways of being and communicating. The true mission of The Circle is to eliminate privacy, incorporating all of society into the social media platform of The Circle and achieving a surveillance state where no members of society can hide. This, Bailey explains to Mae, is the mission to "close the circle." While the Circle's founders, known as "The Wise Men," envision this as perfect utopia, readers perceive this parody as a dystopian totalitarian state where all of society's freedoms would evaporate. This situation presents a chilling warning from

Eggers as the reader contemplates the real-world parallels with increasing connectivity, surveillance, and obligatory disclosure.

Luddism and Technophilia in the Digital Age

The digital dystopian novel questions the potential harms of technology and the creeping abuses of capitalism via tension between characters who alternately embrace or reject digital technology. In contrast to the technophiliac, the Luddite is a mouthpiece for the expression of doubt and paranoia about technology, and thus serves as a foil to the main characters who embrace it. In Graedon's, Eggers', and Anderson's novels, Ana, Titus, and Mae first embrace the new technologies with zeal, but then must attempt to reorder their lives without the technology. This reordering draws on the wisdom and knowledge of the Luddite. In each case, characters seek to regain order after the symbolic unmasking of the Messianic figure. Revealing the latent harms of technology precipitates reorder and a reversion to former modes of communication. Graedon's novel situates groups of technophiliacs and Luddites as two organizations, the corporation "Synchronic," meaning contemporary, and "The Diachronic Society" referring to the past or to a reversion to former ways.

Luddism is represented in *The Word Exchange* by Doug, Ana's father. A lexicographer at The Dictionary, where Ana and Bart also work, Doug is a devotee of older forms of technology and a collector of print artifacts. Doug warns Ana against using the meme, occasionally using a less trackable device called an Aleph, a name Graedon borrows from a Borges tale. When Doug is targeted by the Synchronic Corporation for his refusal to sell the North American Dictionary of the English Language, or NADEL, he flees the country with the help of other Luddites from the Diachronic Society. Because of his refusal to use a meme, Doug is able to escape undetected. Before his departure, he leaves Ana a series of clues—a literal paper trail—that allow his daughter to locate him. When contrasted with the fate of technophiliac Max, Doug and Ana's survival suggests the possibility of being harmed or endangered by digital technology, particularly the products of powerful corporations like Synchronic. Only by disconnecting her meme and seeking her Luddite father's assistance does Ana escape being captured by Synchronic's henchmen.

Similarly, in *Feed*, Anderson contrasts technophiliacs and Luddites to critique corporate greed and capitalism. Violet's father is suspicious of the disintegration of language due to the feed's digital technology. Though their family can't actually afford feed devices, they also feel that they are better off without them. But when the feed devices become ubiquitous in society, he eventually realizes that lacking technology disadvantages his family.

> Then one day, when her mother had left, and I needed work, I was at a job interview. I was an excellent candidate. Two men were interviewing me. Talking about this and that. Then they were silent, just looking at me. I grew uncomfortable. Then they began looking at each other, and doing what I might call *smirking*.
> I realized that they had chatted me, and that I had not responded. They found this funny. Risible. That a man would not have a feed. So they were chatting about me in my presence [...]
> I did not get the job.
> It was thus that I realized that my daughter would need the feed. She had to live in the world [288].

Because Violet's illness is a side effect of her feed installation, her father blames himself. Since Violet is identified as an unreliable consumer, FeedTech refuses to offer medical-technical support to fix her malfunctioning feed device. This scenario probes issues of class and economics as they relate to the digital divide separating those who cannot afford the technology necessary to fully participate in society. Moreover, Violet's situation critiques the power of corporations who view their consumers in terms of profit margins: FeedTech determines that Violet's value as a consumer is in her marketability and profitability. Because she offers none, she is expendable.

These novels may also suggest the susceptibility of Luddites to victimization by a society that doesn't accept or understand their reticence. Mercer, as contrasted with the technophilia of Mae and the other circlers, is a victim of technology. Mercer's disgust with The Circle and Mae's participation in it leads him to go off the grid. Through a mailed letter, Mercer critiques the Circle's invasion into people's private lives and its growing power, predicting that others like him will try to leave society and live underground. Mae laughs at this proposition and comforts herself by ridiculing Mercer and entrenching herself deeper into The Circle. When she reads Mercer's letters on camera after going "transparent," Mae's followers stalk any remaining trace of Mercer's online presence, demonstrating society's collective rejection of privacy and hinting at the rise of cyber bullies.

The attacks on Mercer culminate in a SoulSearch demonstration given by Mae at the Circle campus. The Circle claims that its massive network of SoulSearch cameras has the ability to track any person to any place in the world. Touting the program as a tool to help capture fugitives from justice, Mae shows a photo of an accused child killer known as Fiona Highbridge to a live broadcast. In only 10 minutes and 26 seconds, the Circle's 1.1 billion viewers track Fiona to the small town of Carmathen in Wales. In a dramatic, live-broadcasted scene, circlers in Wales stalk Fiona to a back room in a laundry facility, trapping her against a wall. Under the auspices of justice and public safety, Fiona is located and placed in police custody.

But Eggers' depiction of a type of vigilante justice is worrying. Without ever having been convicted in a formal trial, Mae declares Fiona's guilt to over a billion live viewers. After Fiona is taken into custody and Mae cuts the video feed, the crowd demands another SoulSearch demo. It is Mae's idea to use the technology to locate Mercer. She announces, "Our second target today is not a fugitive from justice, but you might say he's a fugitive from, well, friendship" (457). The Circle's mantra that "Privacy Is Theft" underscores the comparison of Mercer to Fiona, implying that Mercer's retreat from public life is a criminal act. Mae's deteriorating relationships with Annie and her parents along with her invasive actions against Mercer suggest that an individual's immersion in technology leads to alienation rather than connection and that society's saturation with digital technology has a disintegrating, harmful effect.

Mercer is quickly tracked to a remote cabin in Jasper, Oregon. Mercer's property is invaded and he flees in his truck, but a participant places a SeeChange camera on the dash, allowing a live audience of millions to view Mercer driving recklessly through the woods, "his mouth a terrible slash of anger" (461). Mae, meanwhile, gleefully shouts, "Release the drones!" (462). A swarm of privately owned local drones take to the air, and the crowd tracks Mercer's truck high up a mountain road. Mae and the other circlers scream taunts from the speakers on the drones while viewers online cheer and comment on "the greatest viewing experience of their lives" (465). Then suddenly, Mae notices a "determination, something like serenity" come over Mercer's face, as he jerks the wheel, intentionally careening his truck over the edge of a bridge guardrail and into the gorge below.

Through Mercer's death, *The Circle* suggests that digital technology can have dehumanizing effects on consumers. In the aftermath of Mercer's death, Mae seems increasingly robotic and suggests that she feels no guilt over her invasion of Mercer's privacy. In addition, Mae expresses little regret over her estrangement from her parents, who have also gone off the grid, even though her father is very ill. Mercer is dehumanized because his value as a person is determined by his willingness to embrace digital technology. These novels suggest an inherent danger in valuing people according to their digital connectivity and raise questions about those who deliberately choose not to gain access.

Conclusion: The Digital Dystopia as Contemporary Reality

In *The Word Exchange,* Ana and others realize that they can be harmed by their memes and limit their use of them. Yet for many readers of this novel, Ana's story is being read on a digital screen not unlike a meme. Ana's narrative probes the changes wrought to the publishing world by the advent of the digital, wherein writers like Graedon grapple with a host of new issues connected to publication, including dwindling shelf space as retailers move online and competition with digital publishing formats. In Joshua Cohen's 2015 digital dystopia, *Book of Numbers,* the narrator begins by stating, "If you're reading this on a screen, then fuck off" (1). Through metafictional gestures such as these, the digital dystopia acknowledges itself as a mode of writing that can never be free of the digital.

Eggers', Anderson's, and Graedon's novels help tease out latent concerns regarding the implementation of these technologies by encouraging readers to think more deeply about real-world implications of extant technologies that inspire the digital dystopia. Additionally, the ability to glean important insights from this literature when it is placed alongside the discourse of critical digital studies supports the notion that genre writing should not merely be viewed as a mode of writing that seeks to entertain, but as literature that can offer valuable critical insights.

In addition to the texts considered in this analysis, other novels that could be examined for digital dystopian themes include Tao Lin's *Tai Pei* (2013), Hari Kunzru's *Transmission* (2005), Gary Shteyngart's *Super Sad True Love Story* (2010), David Shafer's *Whiskey Tango Foxtrot* (2014), and Cohen's 2015 novel *Book of Numbers.* Though not all of these novels may fit neatly with the themes examined in *Feed, The Circle,* and *The Word Exchange,* they offer narratives that examine the transformative effects of digital technology on contemporary culture and maintain the hyper-present settings that allow readers to easily draw strong parallels and consider such issues in their own lives while considering other issues this analysis has undoubtedly left unexamined.

The immersive worlds of digital dystopian novels invite readers to pause and reflect critically on how "the feed" of digitality shapes our lifestyle, impacts our relationships, and alters our consciousness. Anderson's novel ends with a compelling scene as Titus sits at a dying Violet's bedside. He says, "I sat in her room, by her side, and she stared at the ceiling. I held her hand. On a screen, her heart was barely beating. I could see my face, crying, in her blank eye" (298). In the background of his thoughts, an advertisement for blue jeans asks Titus, "*Feeling blue? Then dress blue! […] [P]rices so low you won't believe your feed! Everything must go!*" (299; italics in original).

Like Titus, who must grapple with the meaning of Violet's death amid a background of digital chatter, readers of Anderson's novel are invited to consider how to "resist the feed." Through the lens of dystopia, these works of contemporary fiction provide satiric and astute observations on a tenuous contemporary moment. In the words of Margaret Doody, the digital dystopia, like other genre novels, exhibits how "the era and the language [speak] through the novelist" (306). These novels initiate reflection and contemplation through their critiques amid the incessant and often meaningless digital noise of contemporary society.

Note

1. Mike Ayers of *The Wall Street Journal* reports that emojis have now grown into an institutionally recognized linguistic form: The Oxford Dictionaries selected its Word of the Year for 2015: An emoji depicting the "face with tears of joy." Oxford Dictionaries cited an explosion in "emoji culture" over the last year as one of the reasons "face with tears of joy" was selected. November 16, 2015.

Works Cited

Anderson, M.T. *Feed*. Berryville: Candlewick Press, 2001. Print.
Ayers, Mike. "Oxford Dictionaries Selects an Emoji as Word of the Year." *The Wall Street Journal*. 16 Nov. 2015. Web. 29 Nov. 2015.
Baym, Nancy K. *Personal Connections in the Digital Age*. Cambridge, UK: Polity, 2010. Print.
Buckingham, David. *Children Talking Television: The Making of Television Literacy*. Washington, D.C.: Falmer Press, 1993. ProQuest. Web. 29 Nov. 2015.
Chandler, Daniel. "An Introduction to Genre Theory." 1997. Web. 14 May 2017. http://www.aber.ac.uk/media/Documents/intgenre/chandler_genre_theory.pdf.
Clarke, Arthur C. *2001: A Space Odyssey*. English Language edition. New York: Roc, 2000. Print.
Cohen, Joshua. *Book of Numbers: A Novel*. Reprint edition. New York: Random House Trade Paperbacks, 2016. Print.
Dick, Philip K., and Roger Zelazny. *Do Androids Dream of Electric Sheep?* New York: Del Rey, 1996. Print.
DiNucci, Darcy. "Fragmented Future." *Print Magazine* April 1999: 38, 221–22. Print.
Doody, Margaret Anne. *The True Story of the Novel*. New Brunswick: Rutgers University Press, 1997. Print.
Eggers, Dave. *The Circle*. New York: Vintage Books, 2014. Print.
Gottlieb, Erika. *Dystopian Fiction East and West: Universe of Trial and Terror*. Montreal: McGill-Queen's University Press, 2001.
Graedon, Alena. *The Word Exchange*. New York: Anchor Books, 2014. Print.
Kunzru, Hari. *Transmission*. Reprint edition. New York: Plume, 2005. Print.
Lin, Tao. *Taipei*. New York: Vintage, 2013. Print.
Masamune, Shirow. *The Ghost in the Shell Volume 1*. New York: Kodansha Comics, 2009. Print.
Pickert, Kate. "Inside Reddit's Hunt for the Boston Bombers." *Time* 23 April 2013. Web. 5 Dec. 2015.
Prensky, Marc. "Digital Natives, Digital Immigrants." *On The Horizon* 9.5 (2001). Web. 12 Feb. 2016.
Scholz, Trebor. *Digital Labor: The Internet as Playground and Factory*. New York: Routledge, 2013. Print.
Shafer, David. *Whiskey Tango Foxtrot*. Reprint edition. New York: Mulholland Books, 2015. Print.
Shteyngart, Gary. *Super Sad True Love Story: A Novel*. New York: Random House Trade Paperbacks, 2011. Print.
Vonnegut, Kurt. *Player Piano: A Novel*. New York: Dial Press, 1999. Print.
Warwick, Kevin, et al. "The Application of Implant Technology for Cybernetic Systems." *Archives of Neurology* 60.10 (2003): 1369–73. Web. 14 May 2017.

Disembodied Heads and Headless Philosophies
C.S. Lewis' Aesthetic Rejoinder to Dystopian *Utility in* That Hideous Strength

MATTHEW BARDOWELL

C.S. Lewis' 1945 novel *That Hideous Strength* can be counted among a small group of his works of fiction that deal with dystopian themes. One might attribute this dark focus to Lewis' first-hand encounter with the grim realities of war. As a young man, Lewis fought in the First World War and was wounded at Mount Bernenchon during the Battle of Arras in 1918 (Lancelyn Green and Hooper 54–55). Because of this experience, Tom Shippey includes Lewis among a group of twentieth-century writers whom he calls "traumatized authors" (xvii). Also named among Shippey's group of "traumatized authors" are George Orwell, William Golding, and Kurt Vonnegut, Jr. (xvii). Shippey observes that these writers employ the fantasy genre to explore "the most pressing and most immediately relevant issues of the whole monstrous twentieth century" (xvii).

It should not be surprising, then, that many of these same authors blend fantasy and dystopian themes to consider the moral questions raised by an increasingly industrialized and technocratic society. The political climate of the 1940s may also have played a role in the central conflict of *That Hideous Strength*. Writing specifically about the dystopic elements of the novel, Marina MacKay argues that Parliamentary legislation that granted the British government emergency control over the private property of its citizens induced novelists writing in the 1940s to criticize this totalitarian impulse through their fiction (27). MacKay cites Lewis' political and religious conservatism as motivation for his critique (36–7), but his particular response to the pragmatic and totalitarian regime in his novel has affinities with other novelists active in that period whose opinions differed radically from his own. In comparing Lewis to George Orwell, for instance, Peter J. Schakel observes that while both men differ in their politics—Orwell was, in Schakel's words, "a socialist and revolutionary" (36)—their respective condemnations of oppressive governments took on a similar shape. Lewis' *That Hideous Strength* and Orwell's *1984*, for instance, both depict organizations that aim to "eliminate myth" in order to more easily shape and subjugate a populace (Schakel 38).

The strategy Schakel mentions has a distinctly aesthetic character, and this essay argues that, for Lewis, excluding aesthetic judgments from knowledge formation creates a crisis of meaning that makes individuals vulnerable to totalitarian philosophies. Thus, the dystopic elements of *That Hideous Strength* arise from a particular kind of education. In his preface to *That Hideous Strength*, Lewis remarks, "This is a 'tall story' about devilry, though it has behind it a serious 'point' which I have tried to make in my *Abolition of Man*" (7). Lewis' *The Abolition of Man* (1943), alternatively entitled *Reflections on Education with Special Reference to the Teaching of English in the Upper Forms of Schools*, treats the dangers of an educational model that neglects judgments of value. Lewis' attack on such educational models is withering, and implicit to his argument is the notion that aesthetic judgments foster proper relationships between individuals and the people and objects that surround them in the world. I aim to show that a similar philosophical commentary concerning aesthetic value runs through the warring groups in *That Hideous Strength*. The community at St. Anne's, led by Dr. Elwin Ransom, permits aesthetic value into their experience of the world and thus may properly order themselves within it and with respect to one another. Conversely, the National Institute for Coordinated Experiments (N.I.C.E.) reject any such supervening philosophy. The pragmatism of the N.I.C.E. depends on stripping aesthetic judgments of their meaning and import. Without the benefit of aesthetic value, the aims of the N.I.C.E. become disordered and vicious. First, I will present the aesthetic argument I observe within Lewis' *The Abolition of Man*. I will then focus on the aesthetic encounters depicted in the novel to demonstrate how the N.I.C.E. seeks to sever the link between one's perceptions and the form of the thing perceived. Finally, I will consider aesthetic uselessness and the idea of justice in Elaine Scarry's *On Beauty and Being Just* to demonstrate how aesthetic value promotes just relationships—a notion that offers a rejoinder to the dystopic philosophy of the N.I.C.E.

An Aesthetic Reading *of* The Abolition of Man

The Abolition of Man is most often framed as an argument for objective truth, but this thesis is sometimes emphasized to the detriment of other facets of Lewis' complex argument. Schakel, for instance, observes that the novel is a "call to all readers to align themselves with the Good—to accept the objective values of traditional morality (what Lewis in *The Abolition of Man* called the *Tao*)" (38). That Lewis in both books is a proponent of objective truth and conventional morality is not controversial, but this characterization overlooks a significant element of Lewis' argument, which centers on the rootedness of one within the other—of a conventional morality that stems from the reality encoded within all objects in the world. Stanley Monick calls the value Lewis defends in *The Abolition of Man* "poetic truth," and he goes on to remark that the loss of poetic truth is what inevitably leads to "a society which will be controlled totally by a small minority" (62). Thus, for Lewis, valuing objects justly links to moral behavior, and the anecdotes he uses to develop this point employ two aesthetic arguments: first, that subjective perception can be rooted in objective form, and second, that aesthetic judgments can attain to justice.

On the first point, that perception can be rooted in the form of an object, the story of Coleridge at the waterfall proves instructive. Lewis summarizes the story as follows: "You remember that there were two tourists present: that one called [the waterfall] 'sublime' and the other 'pretty': and that Coleridge mentally endorsed the first judgment and rejected the second with disgust" (*Abolition of Man* 14). Lewis presents this story as it is discussed by the pseudonymous authors Gaius and Titius who have written the textbook Lewis calls *The Green Book*. Their analysis of Coleridge's waterfall story gives Lewis his point of departure in his own text: "Gaius and Titius comment as follows: 'When the man said *That is sublime*, he appeared to be making a remark about the waterfall. [...] Actually [...] he was not making a remark about the waterfall, but a remark about his own feelings. What he was saying was really *I have feelings associated in my mind with the word "Sublime,"* or shortly, *I have sublime feelings*'" (14; italics in original). Lewis calls this lesson and others like it an exercise in "debunking"—in this case, what they debunk here is the notion that "predicates of value" arise from qualities inherent to the objects about which we speak. Instead, Gaius and Titius teach the lesson that all predicates of value are to be mistrusted as merely statements about oneself. In other words, Gaius and Titius aim to sever the link between object and perception in order to locate judgments of value entirely within oneself. Lewis' disagreement with Gaius and Titius' interpretation of the Coleridge anecdote lays the foundation for his defense of objective truth, but it also serves to place that argument within an aesthetic register, and I will consider how the link between perception and the form of the perceived objects is an aesthetic concern later in this section.

The second facet of the waterfall anecdote that attains to an aesthetic reading is that to ascribe sublimity to the waterfall was more fitting than to ascribe to it prettiness. Lewis explains, "The reason why Coleridge agreed with the tourist who called the cataract sublime and disagreed with the one who called it pretty was of course that he believed inanimate nature to be such that certain responses could be more 'just' or 'ordinate' or 'appropriate' to it than others" (25). The adjectives Lewis uses here are instructive, especially when we consider them as synonyms of each other. In arguing that certain descriptors can be more fittingly applied to objects, Lewis suggests that some judgments agree with the form of an object while others do not. Furthermore, to render a judgment that agrees with an object's form is to render a just judgment—one that is more appropriate to it than other judgments. Even to call a response "ordinate" as Lewis does is to envision judgments that are properly oriented and directed toward some external standard. Earlier in *The Abolition of Man*, Lewis relates his notion ordinate responses to St. Augustine's notion of *ordo amoris* (the order of loves) (26). For Augustine, cultivating virtue lies not simply in loving, but in loving things in their proper order, as creatures of the highest good, which is God (*The City of God* XV. 22).[1] For Lewis, it is crucial to the notion of value that it, in some way, be a property of the object as well as a judgment rendered by a subject. Moreover, our ability to render just judgments relates to our ability to treat the objects in the world with justice.

This idea surfaces again through another example of debunking, this time having to do with the description of a horse. In another text, the author, who Lewis refers to as Oribilius, criticizes a bit of prose in which horses are called "'willing servants' of the early colonists in Australia" (20–21). Lewis admits that this is a bad description and argues that it would be better to teach students to distinguish between meritorious descriptions of value and poor ones. As Oribilius proceeds to debunk this admittedly inapt description of horses, Lewis complains that "why the composition is bad, when others that lie open to the same charge are good, [the pupils] do not hear" (21). The unwitting consequence of this type of neglectful instruction will be for some students that "pleasure in their own ponies and dogs they will have lost: some incentive to cruelty or neglect they will have received: some pleasure in their own knowingness will have entered their minds" (22). What makes this technique of debunking objective value lead not only to the loss of pleasure in the care of animals but an "incentive to cruelty and neglect"? Lewis does not offer a straightforward answer, but he does appear to acknowledge that aesthetic judgments can makes people more or less likely to behave morally toward the objects they judge. The incentive to cruelty and neglect the pupils feel at having value divorced from their ideas about horses goes hand in hand with the break in objective value. If, Lewis seems to suggest, people have no capacity for appreciating the dignity of horses, their diminished view of the object will inexorably lead toward abusing that object.

Later in the text, Lewis offers a more focused explanation of how impoverished aesthetic judgments may induce people to harm those objects. He goes on to argue that separating form and perception leads to an explicitly utilitarian approach to the world. Such a view causes us to see the world solely in terms of how we may shape, process, and use it. A failure in aesthetic judgment results in an objectified and mechanized world. Within such a philosophy, ends find no root in anything but the person who holds them. Waterfalls demand no response in particular. Only false anthropomorphism can explain the dignity some find in horses. According to Lewis, such philosophies produce "men without chests"—the organ responsible for "magnanimity" and "sentiment," "the indispensable liaison officers between cerebral man and visceral man"—bodiless heads that adhere to headless philosophies (34). For Lewis, accurate aesthetic appraisals lead to just treatment of those objects, and a brief look at aesthetic theory helps to explain why this would be the case.

Immanuel Kant's aesthetic theory sets forth two ideas that show how Lewis' argument in *The Abolition of Man* can be read aesthetically: first, the concept of reflective judgment, and second, the concept of disinterest. The first of these notions, reflective judgment, shows that the objective value for which Lewis argues arises from an aesthetic process. The second, disinterest, pertains to the question of justice Lewis hints at in his discussion of debunking.

One sees glimpses of the sort of rootedness Lewis describes in the waterfall anecdote in Kant's discussion of reflecting judgment early in his Third Critique.[2] There are three premises upon which Kant's reflecting judgment proceeds. First, appearances—that is, the things humans encounter as they move around in the world—are cognizable based on laws. Second, those laws can sometimes be known. Third, at other times those laws, those larger categories into which our minds organize and sort the particulars of experience, must be inferred from those particulars on the basis of their form. As Kant introduces his Third Critique, he presents the process whereby those larger categories can be inferred by particulars, a process that he calls *reflecting judgment*. Perhaps the best way to understand reflecting judgment is to contrast it with determining judgment. Kant offers this elaboration: "The power of judgment can be regarded as a mere faculty for reflecting on a given representation, in accordance with a certain principle, for the sake of a concept that is thereby made possible, or as a faculty for determining an underlying concept through a given empirical representation" (Kant 15). Here Kant divides the power of judgment into two kinds: reflecting and determining. Both powers have as their goal to aid the mind in cognizing the things it perceives.

As an example, let us take Coleridge's waterfall. The waterfall itself is what Kant would term the "appearance" or the "empirical representation," and the tourist is employing the faculty of judgment in voicing through his value statement the way he has categorized, or cognized, the object. In Kant's determining judgment, one begins with a concept and then uses that knowledge of the concept to discern a particular that fits the larger concept. Kant scholar Lucas Thorpe offers this example: "one may already possess the concept 'cat' and when one sees a particular cat one may judge: 'this is a cat'" (Thorpe 175). Reflecting judgment, however, is a reverse operation, and it is made possible through an aesthetic process. In reflecting judgment, one starts with a particular and then, because Kant believes that the world is ordered in such a way as to obey laws even when individual minds do not know what those laws are, a general, universal concept is sought. The waterfall, then, is the particular the tourist encounters. The judgment "sublime" is an attempt to find the larger category into which the appearance of the waterfall may be subsumed. Lewis' insistence that the judgment "sublime" must really attain to an apt judgment of the value in the object therefore follows a Kantian process whereby knowledge of the world can be formed through aesthetic reflection.

Indeed, Kant sounds rather Lewisian when he states that without the reasonable expectation that the objects of nature conform to laws within nature that are knowable to us, "all reflection would become arbitrary and blind, and hence would be undertaken without any well-grounded expectation of its agreement with nature" (15–16). It is this blindness and this arbitrariness that Lewis sees as a threat to all predicates of value and as a threat to the necessity of a rooted sense of value to preserve our humanity, and further into his lectures he begins to suggest why observing this link between form and content is imperative to humane and just behavior.

First, the judgment each person viewing the waterfall renders is described in terms of an aesthetic response. On that ground, "pretty" would be as apt an aesthetic judgment as "sublime," but later in the text Lewis explains his interpretation of the Coleridge episode: "The reason why Coleridge agreed with the tourist who called the cataract sublime and disagreed with the one who called it pretty was of course that he believed inanimate nature to be such that certain responses could be more 'just' or 'ordinate' or 'appropriate' to it than others" (25). Two elements of Lewis' explanation suggest the aesthetic dimension of his argument for objective truth. First, that in observing the world, it is possible that our perceptions of the objects can be rooted in their concrete qualities. In other words, Lewis' theory of objective truth depends upon a perceptible link between form and perception. Lewis rejects the notion that the tourist who called the waterfall "sublime" was only making a claim about his own feelings. Rather, through an aesthetic encounter with the object, the tourist renders a judgment in which form and perception are appropriately described by the quality of sublimity. Lewis' claim that Coleridge "believed inanimate nature to be such that certain responses could be more 'just' or 'ordinate' or 'appropriate' to it than others" is a claim that value can be reliably induced through a process of aesthetic reflection whereby an object's appearance and a subject's imagination interact to produce an aesthetic experience.

One way in which Kant's aesthetic theory aims to free itself from moral complications is to free aesthetic judgment from questions of use. In another section of the Third Critique, the *Analytic of the Beautiful*, Kant argues for the centrality of disinterest to aesthetic judgments. On this matter he instructs, "But if the question is whether something is beautiful, one does not want to know whether there is anything that is or that could be at stake, for us or for someone else, in the existence of the thing, but rather how we judge it in mere contemplation" (90). One such interest is the possibility of my using an object for my own purposes. Kant elaborates further, "Concerning the interest of inclination in the case of the agreeable, everyone says that hunger is the best cook, and people with a healthy appetite relish everything that is edible at all; thus such a satisfaction demonstrates no choice in accordance with taste. Only when the need is satisfied can one distinguish who among the many has taste or does not" (95–96). Here Kant argues that in consuming a meal, purely aesthetic judgment is impossible so long as those who sit down to it use it to satisfy a need, in this case hunger. It is only after hunger has been satisfied that an aesthetic judgment can take place. As I aim to show in the following section, Lewis' *That Hideous Strength* develops the dystopian character of the N.I.C.E. within a similar aesthetic framework. The N.I.C.E. refute the rooted nature of value judgments, and as a result they reduce the objects and the people they encounter to mechanisms for the satisfaction of their various goals.

Lewis frames the consequences of abandoning the rootedness of value judgments in terms of use and interest. If those educated by Gaius and Titius take their lesson to its logical conclusion, the future will be populated by "men who have sacrificed their own share in humanity in order to devote themselves to the task of deciding what 'Humanity' shall henceforth mean" (Lewis, *Abolition* 76). Lewis describes people who have ceased to see themselves as participants within humanity and now look upon themselves as shapers of humanity. To perceive a thing solely in terms of use and our own interest is to banish all aesthetic associations that inculcate ideas antithetical to that use. As Lewis remarks, "we do not look at trees as either Dryads or as beautiful objects while we cut them to beams" (82). In debunking aesthetic valuations, the world is diminished: "We reduce things to mere Nature *in order that* we may 'conquer' them" (82–83). For Lewis, when we sever the roots linking form to perception, we cannot but sever our own heads. Lewis calls this condition in Gaius and Titius' pupils "Men without Chests" (34). The parts of the body necessary for normal human functioning have been disconnected, and in a final, self-destructive irony, we reduce even ourselves to raw materials, pliant toward ends over which we have lost all control. Lewis makes this point explicitly when he writes, "It is in Man's power to treat himself as a mere 'natural object' and his own judgments of value as raw material for scientific manipulation to alter at will" (84). Lewis sets forth these themes in *That Hideous Strength*, and aesthetic notions figure into his fiction on this topic as significantly as they do in his essays. A major source of conflict for Mark Studdock, one of the novel's protagonists, is precisely his discomfort in dismissing the aesthetic dimension from his work at the N.I.C.E. The other members of the Institute, however, have effectively severed their ability to connect their work with the larger goals of the Institute, which enables them to treat all objects merely as tools to be used to bring about the N.I.C.E.'s vague agenda. It is only through Mark's ability to render aesthetic judgments that he resists the reductive philosophy of utility that all his colleagues have accepted.

Aesthetic Value and Dystopian Resistance

Aesthetic value, according to Kant, observes that aesthetic judgments are grounded in the form of the objects we judge, and this link between form and perception can promote just appraisals and even just behavior. Lewis develops these ideas in *That Hideous Strength* as Mark Studdock begins to learn about the N.I.C.E. and gradually becomes swept up into its core group of adherents. The portrait Lewis paints of N.I.C.E.'s involvement is one in which many of the organization's members work fervently to entrench the Institute's influence in the country while remaining ignorant of the group's ultimate goals. The work of the N.I.C.E. deliberately severs actions from the ends they serve, and this directionless activity arises from a philosophy of utility that precludes the possibility of aesthetic judgment that is, by its very nature, rendered without respect for an object's usefulness. David C. Downing observes that the antagonists of Lewis' Ransom Trilogy often exchange morality for utility (Downing 84). In the novel, the rootedness between judgment and object promotes a kind of just response that makes those who render that judgment more attuned to just relations, whereas severing the connection between judgment and object promotes a blind pragmatism in which one may only consider objects and people insofar as they are useful to one's immediate purposes.

In the present section, I will focus on significant moments within Mark Studdock's initiation into the N.I.C.E. to show that the dystopia Lewis creates depends on excising the development of aesthetic values by severing the connection between object and subject that leads those within the organization to approach the world in an exclusively pragmatic and unjust way. Early in the novel, Lewis characterizes Mark as a man who desires to enter the inner circle of the various groups with which he is affiliated (Brew 11). When the novel begins, Mark is a sociology fellow at Bracton College in Edgestow, where he seeks inclusion among what he calls the "Progressive Element" within the College (Lewis, *That Hideous Strength* 15). His associations mark his progress as he moves more deeply into the confidences of the leaders within the Progressive Element. Mark first associates with men of middling importance to this group at Bracton—Curry, the sub-warden, and James Busby, the Bursar. However, later he makes the acquaintance of Lord Feverstone, who is yet more central to the Progressive Element at Bracton but who also recruits Mark to join the N.I.C.E. After the dinner with the sub-warden, Feverstone brings Mark into his confidence by sharing his estimation of Curry and Busby. As Feverstone confides in Mark about the future of the Progressive Element, he remarks, "[O]ur two poor friends, though they can be persuaded to take the right train, or even to drive it, haven't a ghost of a notion where it's going to, or why. They'll sweat blood to bring the N.I.C.E. to Edgestow: that's why they're indispensable. But what the point of the N.I.C.E. is, what the point of anything is—ask them another" (38). In this passage, Lewis begins to develop some of the principles under which the N.I.C.E. operate. First, the ends of the organization are often obscured from many of the individuals responsible for its advance. Curry and Busby have chosen the right side, according to Feverstone, and they may even be called upon to direct and move the organization nearer to its objective, but they are both ignorant about precisely what that objective is. In this description, one observes Lewis' distaste for progressivism, which critics often remark upon (MacKay 36–38), but here progressivism is figured not as a political agenda guided by principles and values, but as forward motion disconnected from larger ideas. Progress without values is, for Lewis, objectless forward motion, and this is the very philosophy he warns of in *The Abolition of Man*.

Concomitant with this objectless movement is a rigid and reductive adherence to immediate goals, even when those who labor toward these short-range goals do not know where they lead. Partly responsible for this mindset is a gradual blindness to aesthetic judgment already present in Mark from his first introduction: "Mark [...] was walking down Bracton College, and thinking of a very different matter. He did not notice at all the morning beauty of the little street that led him from the sandy hillside suburb where he and Jane lived down into the central and academic part of Edgestow" (14). From the first, Mark's attention to practical and pragmatic matters leaves no room for aesthetic appreciation. Instead, his mind is full of all the things pertaining to the meeting he is about to attend and the slightly larger personal objective of his own career advancement within the Progressive Element at Edgestow. This theme of use and inattention to one's surroundings develops as Mark is inducted into the higher rungs of the N.I.C.E.'s hierarchy.

When Mark first arrives at Belbury, the location of the N.I.C.E.'s main headquarters, he finds that he is similarly ignorant about the Institute's objectives and even to the sort of work the Deputy Director, John Wither, has asked him to carry out. He repeatedly questions Wither with varying degrees of directness. He is pleased to be brought into the next stratum of the organization and fears spoiling his chances of making it fully into the organization and thus being "exclude[d] [...] from the warm and almost drugged atmosphere of vague, yet heavily important, confidence in which his was gradually being enfolded" (52). He is at last connected with the sociology department within the N.I.C.E. and tasked with the "liquidation of anachronisms" (72) at a village called Cure Hardy, where they intend to divert the river Wynd as the organization continues to excavate Bragdon Wood (82). "Liquidation" is the same terminology used to describe the elimination of what Lord Feverstone calls "backward races" and is later used to describe the murder of William Hingest—a N.I.C.E. member with the temerity to defect (40, 252). 'Liquidation' is a euphemism for 'destruction,' and this is what the N.I.C.E. does with people and things they cannot use, incorporate, or repurpose.

The liquidation of Cure Hardy demonstrates the reductive utility of the N.I.C.E. as well as how aesthetic judgments can serve to undermine the group's limited engagement with the world. When Cosser, one of Mark's colleagues in the sociology department at the N.I.C.E., informs him that their latest job will be to divert the Wynd away from Edgestow and through Cure Hardy, Mark replies, "[T]here'll be a devil of a stink about this. Cure Hardy is famous. It's a beauty spot. There are the sixteenth-century almshouses, and a Norman church, and all that" (83). Cosser's response shows his inability to see the point Mark has raised. Association with the N.I.C.E. has made Cosser's view of any subject myopic. The only relevance he perceives in Mark's comment is its immediate relevance to the plan to divert the river and the report they must make on the village: "It ought to be pretty easy. If it's a beauty spot, you can bet it's insanitary. That's the first point to stress" (83). Cosser's reply is illuminating on two levels. First, his interest in the sanitary conditions of the village relates to the N.I.C.E.'s vague goals: progress and, ostensibly, the preservation of humanity. But to place sanitation above the aesthetic value of the town offers a sterile and rootless argument for the liquidation of the village. Calling the village's shortcomings "anachronisms" frames value only in terms of the same sort of purposeless forward movement adopted by Bracton's Progressive Element. On the second level, Cosser's claim that Cure Hardy is "insanitary" is only a pretext for achieving the immediate goal of diverting the Wynd—the ultimate goal of which Cosser and Mark are completely ignorant. The dystopian future the N.I.C.E. offers is clean but barren, supportive of life but stripped of the beauty that allows people to think about anything but the task at hand. As Lewis argues in *The Abolition of Man*, the focus of humans in making instruments of nature finally makes instruments of humans themselves.

As Mark and Cosser travel to Cure Hardy, the link between one's diminished aesthetic capacities and reductive pragmatism becomes clearer. Mark contrasts with Cosser in this respect, as their time at Cure Hardy shows. During their visit, Mark is moved at several moments by the beauty of the village. The quality of this emotion in Mark is significant; he is spurred to contemplation and reflection and thus drawn away from his immediate purpose in the village. Mark cannot help but exclaim, "How nice it is!" as he descends into the valley in which Cure Hardy lies. The narrator remarks, "Mark was not as a rule very sensitive to beauty, but Jane and his love for Jane had already awakened him a little in this respect" (84). In this passage, the narrator connects Mark's aesthetic awareness to his love for his wife, Jane. Even though Mark has hitherto failed to be the sort of husband Jane needs, his relationship to her nevertheless draws his attention away from himself and his immediate goals and toward her as the object of his love. In the same way that a lover contemplates the beloved, Mark is given to contemplate the village as a thing separate from himself and a thing to which he is compelled to attend. The passage in which Mark reflects on Cure Hardy's landscape serves to reinforce that Mark is here being drawn out of his focus on himself, his career, and the petty goals that might effect his own advancement:

> The earth and the sky had the look of things recently washed. The brown fields looked as if they would be good to eat, and those in grass set off the curves of the little hills as close as clipped hair sets off the body of a horse. The sky looked further away than usual, but also clearer, so that the long slender streaks of cloud (dark slate colour against the pale blue) had edges as clear as if they were cut out of cardboard. Every little copse was black and bristling as a hairbrush, and when the car stopped in Cure Hardy itself the silence that followed the turning off of the engine was filled with the noise of rooks that seemed to be calling "Wake! Wake!" [84–85].

Mark encounters the village as something apart from himself and separate from his purpose in traveling there in the first place. In describing the sky and the fields, Lewis evokes the pleasantness of sumptuous foods and the beauty of horses—perhaps his own attempt at rendering just value to the creatures Orbilius in Lewis' *The Abolition of Man* debunks. Mark's observations of the distance of the sky and the crispness of the clouds offer a striking visual rejoinder to the short-sightedness and the obfuscation of the N.I.C.E., which is given physical expression in the fog that settles over Edgestow as the N.I.C.E. begins to take hold of the land (118). Here in Cure Hardy Mark enjoys clarity and vastness, things that have been assaulted during his time at Belbury. In the morning stillness, Mark communes even with the rooks. The cry of the rooks is not an unintelligible animal function, but something Mark interprets as addressing him and partaking in the morning ritual of waking sleepers.

Cosser, by contrast, engages with the village only insofar as it pertains to his objective. In the call of the rooks, he hears only cacophony, a distraction from his task: "Bloody awful noise those birds make" (85). Later that day, when he and Mark take their lunch at a nearby pub, Mark tries to speak to Cosser about the beauty he has observed, and Cosser proves impervious to any discussion that does not relate to their report. Cosser even turns a banal remark about the weather toward some use: "Yes, it *is* a fine morning. Makes a real difference to one's health, a bit of sunlight" (86). Cosser seems unable even to understand the pleasantness of beer and company apart from their utility: "Haven't much use for alcohol myself (read the Miller Report) but if people have got to have their stimulants, I'd like to see them administered in a more hygienic way" (86). To this Mark offers a half-hearted reply, saying, "I don't know that the stimulant is quite the whole point" (86). Mark thinks of Cure Hardy, the pub, even the beer in terms of values that cannot be derived from utility. Rather, the value Mark finds through reflection is more akin to aesthetic judgment—the knowledge of things derived by contemplation and through which subject and object cooperate to forge meaning: "The whole scene was reminding [Mark] of drinks and talks long ago—of laughter and arguments in undergraduate days" (86). Cosser, however, proves incapable of remarking upon anything not directly related to his field. In response to Mark's comment about the value of beer, he can only reply, "Nutrition isn't my subject." And when Mark ventures to address what he seems to feel is the aesthetic value of the village, Cosser is completely uninterested: "'Oh, architecture and all that,' said Cosser. 'Well, that's hardly my line, you know" (86). An excess of use has made Cosser useless for anything other than his rigidly defined area of expertise. It is at this point that Mark's estimation of Cosser approaches something like real insight: "All at once it came to Mark what a terrible bore this little man was, and in the same moment he felt utterly sick of the N.I.C.E." (86). Mark's ability, nascent though it may be, to perceive and acknowledge aesthetic value gives him a glimpse into the banality of what once seemed to him to be the lofty goals of a very important organization, and, later in the novel, it will be aesthetic value once again that induces Mark to make his final break with the group and the dystopic future it represents.

After the N.I.C.E. police have detained Mark, he is kept in a cell and receives infrequent visits from Deputy Director Wither. His aim is to coerce Mark into revealing Jane's whereabouts so she may be brought to Belbury and used for her uncanny ability to have visions of the future. In an effort to seduce Mark by bringing him into the deepest secrets of the organization, Wither reveals that the Head of the N.I.C.E. is literally the severed head of François Alcasan, a French scientist executed for the murder of his wife and artificially kept alive through machinery. In addition to revealing the Head of the N.I.C.E., Professor Frost, another high-ranking member of the Institute, brings Mark into a peculiar room in the hopes of severing once and for all his ties with objective truth. The result, Frost believes, will be Mark's complete inculcation into the N.I.C.E. Mark's ability to make aesthetic judgments is all that prevents this result.

Prior to entering the room, Mark and Frost engage in a conversation about how actions may be "justified or condemned" given the N.I.C.E.'s dismissal of objective value (292). Frost insists that such a question has no meaning for a society in which "existence is its own justification" (292). He objects to Mark's question on the grounds that it "presupposes a means-and-ends pattern of thought" (293). Frost goes on to say that "motives are not the causes of action but its by-products. [...] When you have attained real objectivity you will recognize, not *some* motives, but *all* motives as merely animal, subjective epiphenomena. You will then have no motives and you will find that you do not need them. [...] So far from being impoverished your action will become much more efficient" (293). Here the dislocated philosophy of the Institute is laid bare—the motivations typically considered to drive behavior stem not from just appraisal of objects but from chemical processes occurring solely within the subject.

Frost's final line articulates the goal of the N.I.C.E.'s educational program: without values people are free to be efficient. But this efficiency is of a peculiar kind. It is at once oriented toward some immediate goal while simultaneously being untethered from the larger end that aesthetic values might arouse. Such a notion seems paradoxical: it is directionless direction, purposeless progress, focused movement oriented toward nothing. Indeed, Lewis remarks on the absence of substance at the core of groups such as the N.I.C.E. in his sermon "The Inner Ring." In that text, he compares one's gradual inclusion into deeper and deeper levels of confidence to peeling an onion: "[I]f you succeed there will be nothing left" (Lewis, "The Inner Ring" 154; Downing 93).

The final stage of Mark's initiation is to enter a room in which one's sense of proportion and aesthetic judgment are subtly frustrated. The narrator describes it as follows: "A man of trained sensibility would have seen at once that the room was ill-proportioned, not grotesquely so, but sufficiently to produce dislike. It was too high and too narrow. Mark felt the effect without analysing the cause and the effect grew on him as time passed. Sitting staring about him he next noticed the door—and thought at first that he was the victim of some optical illusion" (294). It does not take Mark long to determine the specific causes of the disquiet he experiences in the room. Upon closer inspection, he notices many elements of the room that deviate from his sensory expectations: "The point of the arch was not in the centre: the whole thing was lop-sided" (294). Central to Mark's feelings of unease is the suggestion of order that cannot be confirmed upon investigation. This is clear also from the spots he observes on the ceiling and upon the table: "[T]heir arrangement seemed to hover on the verge of regularity. They suggested some kind of pattern. Their peculiar ugliness consisted in the very fact that they kept on suggesting it and then frustrating the expectation thus aroused" (295). There is a certain kind of horror present in this room. As I have discussed above, the kind of aesthetic judgment Kant describes in his Third Critique depends on the assumption that the world operates according to rules and that our minds are fitted to perceive those rules among the particulars of our experience. The horror of this room is the horror of finding out that the order one always suspected to undergird the world is a lie. There is no sense that can be made from experience—no larger concept to grasp from the appearance of nature. The horror present here is the mind as severed from the world as Alcasan's head is severed from his body.

This idea plays out on specifically aesthetic grounds as Mark observes the pictures hanging on the wall within the room. These paintings are absurdities: a young woman whose mouth is "thickly overgrown with hair," "a giant mantis playing a fiddle while being eaten by another mantis, a man with corkscrews instead of arms bathing in a flat" (295). Other paintings are less absurd, but deviate from expectation only so much as to raise certain unsettling questions: "[W]ho was that person standing between the Christ and Lazarus? And why were there so many beetles under the table in the Last Supper?" (295–96). Of these pictures, Mark observes that their "apparent ordinariness [...] became their supreme menace—like the ominous surface innocence at the beginning of certain dreams. Every fold of drapery, every piece of architecture, had a meaning one could not grasp but which withered the mind" (296). The philosophy of usefulness is present even in the way the N.I.C.E. utilize this peculiar room. Frost claims that sitting in the room is how one begins to develop true objectivity, but even this goal is shrouded in the language of usefulness, as becoming wholly objective is "the process whereby all specifically human reactions were killed in a man so that he might become fit for the fastidious society of the Macrobes" (296). Killing off one's "specifically human reactions," among which is the reaction of aesthetic judgment, makes people "fit" for use by the higher powers seeking to take hold of the earth in *That Hideous Strength*.

The result in Mark, however, demonstrates the great power of aesthetic judgments to make a person not only more human but a more just human. In his case, exposure to the room only makes him more keenly aware of the "room's opposite" (296). The room kindles Mark's affection for things that defy the N.I.C.E.'s doctrine of usefulness and reaffirms his belief in the connection between himself and the objects in the world. Lewis' term, "the Normal," is a somewhat unfortunate signifier for what Mark aligns himself with in the room. And surely the normal as defined by dominant culture and behavioral practices hallowed by repetition can hardly be what Lewis means to describe here. Instead, Lewis' "Normal" refers to a tradition of thought in which objects and subjects participate in the production of meaning and significance together. Lewis describes Mark's sense of the Normal in just these terms: it is "solid, massive, with a shape of its own, almost like something you could touch, or eat, or fall in love with. It was mixed up with Jane and fried eggs and soap and sunlight and the rooks cawing at Cure Hardy and the thought that, somewhere outside, daylight was going on at that moment" (296–97). All these things are objects Mark conceives of as things to attend, not things to use. These associations are things to be related to, to contemplate or reflect upon as things different from himself and his desires but nevertheless as things with which he shares a relationship. It is not the vitamin D in the sunlight Mark is considering, nor the protein in the eggs, but the utterly useless pleasure of both. Even as Frost continues in his efforts to initiate Mark, his affection for the Normal strengthens and is, for Mark, "something which obviously existed quite independently of himself and had hard rock surfaces which would not give, surfaces he could cling to" (307). Here again the durability of aesthetic value preserves Mark against Frost's adamant attempts to destroy his aesthetic judgments. He is related to these values; he is not the source of them. They have their own shape, and it is precisely in observing and attending to this shape that Mark finds he is able to cling to them. In accepting the objects as things outside of himself, Mark breaks the chains of usefulness. He reorients the direction of his own engagement with these objects; they do not come to him as objects to be used, he goes to them as objects to be contemplated and reflected upon.

Aesthetic Uselessness and Justice

Lewis' dystopian vision is one in which no meaningful relationship exists between people and the objects and individuals that surround them. It is a vision in which all interactions are reduced to use. The world toward which the N.I.C.E. strives is one in which all objects are instruments and in which even those who wield the instruments have become tools themselves. While the concept of objective truth is undoubtedly fundamental to the remedy Lewis proposes, I have endeavored to show that his rejoinder to such dystopian philosophies engages significantly with value derived through aesthetic judgment. The link between perception and the objects one perceives is a hallmark of Kant's reflecting judgment, a method of knowledge acquisition in which one's mind contemplates an object's appearance in nature in a process of organizing and understanding the larger concept to which that object adheres. This process allows for our values and judgments to be rooted in the form we encounter with our senses, and the reflection one offers these objects is wholly without the sort of pragmatic interest that defines the N.I.C.E.'s engagement with everyone and everything. Aesthetic value gives Mark the ground from which to resist his initiation into the Institute, a prospect that has grave implications for his own well-being and moral status. Therefore, I argue, Mark's aesthetic judgments have enabled him to act morally despite the threat his connection with the N.I.C.E. represents. But the question of precisely how aesthetic judgments might foster just behavior remains. In answer to this, Elaine Scarry offers some insight.

In developing her argument for the relationship of beauty and justice, Scarry is directly opposing the political complaints against beauty. These arguments claim that the gaze of the one perceiving beauty may either bring harm to the object being regarded or else cause harm to society because preoccupation with beauty causes us to be inattentive to its ills (58). Scarry's rebuttal is that beauty serves to "intensif[y] the pressure we feel to repair existing injuries" (57). Just as Lewis speaks of just, ordinate, and appropriate appraisals in *The Abolition of* Man, Scarry also affirms the "continuity between beauty and its beholder" (88). Scarry describes this continuity as "a compact, or contract between the beautiful being (a person or thing) and the perceiver" in which perceiver and perceived greet each other (90). As I have shown, the idea that aesthetic judgment requires the perceiver to consider objects as things apart from oneself runs through much of *That Hideous Strength*. As Scarry concludes her argument, she offers an explanation of why this encounter with objects should lead to just behavior. Scarry writes, "At the moment we see something beautiful, we undergo a radical decentering" (111). In this process, the perceiver undergoes a shift of consciousness. The perceiver moves out of the central position of his or her experience and lets the beautiful object take his or her place. Scarry continues, "It is not that we cease to stand at the center of the world, for we never stood there. It is that we cease to stand even at the center of our own world. We willingly cede our ground to the thing that stands before us" (112). Thus, the aesthetic dimension of *That Hideous Strength* suggests a similar process of decentering. Mark's ability to render aesthetic judgments allows him to maintain his ties to the objects that surround him in the world and serves as an antidote to the dystopic utility that has reduced the N.I.C.E. and all its members to mere instruments.

Aesthetic judgment, then, attains to justice in precisely the ways Lewis suggests in *The Abolition of Man* through his anecdote of Coleridge at the waterfall. The connection between subject and object and the uselessness with which the subject regards that object makes the values upon which just behavior rests possible, but these things also make love possible. In one of his conversations with Jane, Ransom acknowledges that these capacities distinguish those at St. Anne's from the members of the N.I.C.E.: "In fighting those who serve devils one always has this on one's side; their Masters hate them as much as they hate us. The moment we disable the human pawns enough to make them useless to Hell, their own Masters finish the work for us. They break their tools" (Lewis, *That Hideous Strength* 314). As Ransom here suggests, the ability to regard the world without respect for how we can use or incorporate it distinguishes us from devils. This ability helps Mark to perceive, address, and resist the dystopian organization that aims to dehumanize him, the citizens of England, and, indeed, the citizens of the world. In both *The Abolition of Man* and *That Hideous Strength*, aesthetic value is essential to justice and conscientious citizenship. The decentering qualities of aesthetic judgment may remove us from the center of our own world, but they keep us firmly rooted to the world in which all things share in relationship to one another. As Lewis puts it in another text, rootedness between subject and object is linked not only to justice but to love. After all, "Nothing but a *Thou* can be loved and a *Thou* can exist only for an *I*" (Lewis, "A Reply to Professor Haldane" 78).

In a review of Lewis' novel, Orwell criticized *That Hideous Strength* on the grounds that supernatural interventions can hardly be counted on by those of us who, in this world, face similar totalitarian threats (Mackay 31). But the aesthetic reading of the novel allows us to see that its resolution is no *deus ex machina*. On the contrary, the supernatural elements Lewis makes responsible for the supreme rootedness of value judgments set the terms for a world in which an organization like the N.I.C.E. cannot possibly thrive for long. Just as the Head of the N.I.C.E. is a literal disembodied head through which the organizations leaders speak, the philosophy of utility the group espouses is headless in its own right. Without acknowledging the aesthetic rootedness of value judgments, the philosophies of the N.I.C.E. hang suspended by nothing, and it is under the weight of its own overgrown head that the organization inevitably topples.

Notes

1. For more on Lewis' reading of Augustine in the context of dystopian fiction, see Mark D. Sadler's "The Failure of Men Without Chests in *Blade Runner*."

2. For Lewis, as we have seen, traditional judgments of value are only authoritative because they claim to be rooted in the objects they judge. The second tourist's appraisal of the waterfall is better than the first's because he claims his judgment as being rooted in the form or appearance of the waterfall itself. For Kant, this is why judgments of taste have a different status than statements concerning that which is "agreeable" or "pleasant" (Kant 95). The objectivity of predicates of value is for Kant a far more complex problem than it appears to be for Lewis in *The Abolition of Man*. For one thing, Kant's purpose in writing his third critique is to address a gap in the process of cognition left between his first critique, *A Critique of Pure Reason*, and his second critique, *A Critique of Practical Reason*. I would suggest that in seeking a discussion of Lewis' objective value in Kant, one consider his remarks on what he terms "intersubjectivity"—the notion that subjective judgments can be shared based on mental processes common to all minds (Guyer xvii).

Works Cited

Augustine. *The City of God*. Trans. Marcus Dods. New York: The Modern Library, 1950. Print.
Brew, Kelli. "Facing the Truth on the Road to Salvation: An Analysis of *That Hideous Strength* and *Till We Have Faces*." *The Lamp-Post* 22.1 (1998): 10–12. Print.
Downing, David C. *Planets in Peril: A Critical Study of C.S. Lewis' Ransom Trilogy*. Amherst: University of Massachusetts Press, 1992. Print.
Green, Roger Lancelyn, and Walter Hooper. *C.S. Lewis: A Biography*. New York: Harcourt Brace Jovanovich, 1974. Print.
Guyer, Paul. "Editor's Introduction." *Critique of the Power of Judgment*. By Immanuel Kant. 1790. Ed. Paul Guyer. Trans. Paul Guyer and Eric Matthews. Cambridge: Cambridge University Press, 2000. ix–lii. Print.
Kant, Immanuel. *Critique of the Power of Judgment*. 1790. Ed. Paul Guyer. Trans. Paul Guyer and Eric Matthews. Cambridge: Cambridge University Press, 2000.
Lewis, C.S. *The Abolition of Man or Reflections on Education with Special Reference to the Teaching of English in the Upper Forms of Schools*. 1 943. New York: Macmillan, 1965. Print.
_____. "The Inner Ring." *The Weight of Glory*. New York: HarperCollins, 2001. 141–57. Print.
_____. *Letters of C.S. Lewis*. Ed. Walter Hooper. New York: Harcourt, 1993. Print.
_____. "A Reply to Professor Haldane." *On Stories*. New York: Harcourt, 1982. Print.
_____. *That Hideous Strength: A Modern Fairy-Tale for Grown-Ups*. 1945. New York: Charles Scribner's Sons, 2003. Print.
MacKay, Marina. "Anti-State Fantasy and the Fiction of the 1940s." *Literature & History* 24.2 (Spring 2015): 27–40. Print.
Monick, Stanley. "C.S. Lewis: An Approach to Christian Myth." *Lantern* 27.3 (April 1978): 62–69. Print.
Sadler, Mark D. "The Failure of Men Without Chests in *Blade Runner*." *Science Fiction and the Abolition of Man*. Eds. Mark J. Boone and Kevin C. Neece. Eugene: Pickwick Publications, 2017. 121–33.
Scarry, Elaine. *On Beauty and Being Just*. Princeton: Princeton University Press, 2001. Print.
Schakel, Peter J. "That 'Hideous Strength' in Lewis and Orwell: A Comparison and Contrast." *Mythlore* 13.4 (Summer 1987): 36–40. Print.
Shippey, Tom. *The Road to Middle-Earth*. New York: Houghton Mifflin, 2003. Print.
Thorpe, Lucas. *The Kant Dictionary*. London: Bloomsbury, 2015. Print.

The Creation of the Future from Remnants of the Past
Order from Disorder in William Gibson's All Tomorrow's Parties *and* Neal Stephenson's Snow Crash

MELANIE A. MAROTTA

Contained within the works of two heralded science fiction writers is the notion that utopian constructions can originate from dystopian conditions. In response to environmental instability, William Gibson's and Neal Stephenson's main characters create a stable environment, specifically an enclosure that allows for the formation of a community. It is this community that ensures the characters' survival. In Gibson's *All Tomorrow's Parties* (1999) and Stephenson's *Snow Crash* (1992), an environmental disaster leads to the diasporic displacement of the inhabitants of various communities. In an attempt to restore order to an otherwise chaotic society, many characters in the aforementioned texts create and/or reside in self-contained environments. These enclosed structures—for example, Gibson's Bay Bridge housing and Cardboard City, and Stephenson's burbclaves and U-Stor-It—have been created in response to dystopic conditions.

In *All Tomorrow's Parties*, the third novel in his Bridge trilogy, Gibson's two main characters, Colin Laney and Chevette Washington, reside in makeshift homes. When the novel opens, Laney, who has previously been seen as a wandering figure, is living in what is known as Cardboard City, which has been created by the homeless in Shinjuku Station. Chevette, who lives on the Bay Bridge in Gibson's *Virtual Light*, returns to her previous home to escape her past and ensure her survival. Stephenson's Hiro Protagonist resides in a California that has suffered, along with the rest of the United

States, an economic disaster. California has been split into privatized burb-claves where one must be a citizen to enter and, if warranted, to receive protection. In each of the texts, the concept of place and its impact on identity formation is critical to the readers' understanding of the characters. Even though these environments promise to be hazardous to Gibson's and Stephenson's characters' survival, they make the conscious choice to reside there because of what they have to offer. For Chevette and Hiro, these locales offer freedom of self-expression, community, and safety. While these places may appear dystopic, they actually offer the characters what the outside areas lack.

The bridge, even though it was constructed as a means of transportation between Oakland and San Francisco, has had its purpose altered by a major environmental disaster, the earthquake known as Little Grande, and the economic conditions in No-Cal. Contained within *Virtual Light* is Skinner's story of how the people ended up living on the bridge, turning the bridge into a community after Little Grande has ensured it could no longer be used for travel. Skinner tells Yamazaki, "In the cities, lot of people, no place to go," and as a result, one night the displaced stormed the bridge and those that survived created a stable community (Gibson, *Virtual* 102). The bridge no longer stands as only a space; Michael Dear and Steven Flutsy note that "[m]ost world cities have an instantly identifiable signature: think of the boulevards of Paris, the skyscrapers of New York, or the churches of Rome" (64). The landmark that identifies Gibson's San Francisco and even all of No-Cal is the Bay Bridge. Through the adoption of the bridge as a home rather than a means of transport, the residents of the bridge alter the bridge's meaning while simultaneously creating a protective community upon it (Buell, *Future of* 72).

While science fiction (sf) writers are able to place their characters anywhere, the United States, or a fragmented form of it, tends to be a common and significant locale. Throughout history, the U.S. appears as a utopic site offering its inhabitants everything from fame to fortune to a new beginning. Mircea Eliade, in *The Quest: History and Meaning in Religion*, elaborates on the reasons why Europeans ventured to America, and many of these motives appear in the aforementioned sf works, specifically the desire for a utopic space (89–90). Gibson's Chevette is notable as she is frequently shown as the pioneer on the American frontier, one of the many characters in Gibson's and Stephenson's texts who seek a new beginning. This character's first appearance is in Gibson's *Virtual Light* when she resides in a makeshift room on the Bay Bridge with Skinner, her friend and father figure. In *All Tomorrow's Parties*, Chevette has left her bridge community in favor of a relationship with Carson; once this fails, she makes multiple attempts to locate that which she has previously relinquished: a community. Ross Farnell, in a discussion of *Virtual Light* and *Idoru* (the first two novels in the bridge trilogy), observes that "Gibson's recurrent theme of place, space and architecture in posthuman topologies comes to the fore in these two 'Hak Nam' inspired novels"; significantly, Farnell calls attention to societal construction, particularly focusing on the poverty-stricken section (459). In many of Gibson's texts that are set in California, this space has been split into No-Cal and So-Cal. The division of a formerly unified space due to this environmental disaster is a symbol not only of the lack of community that exists in Gibson's *All Tomorrow's Parties* and *Virtual Light*, but also of the emphasis on individualization and the preservation thereof.

Chevette is featured in the opening of *All Tomorrow's Parties* residing in what Gibson calls a "sharehouse" in Malibu and is later shown returning to her former home on the bridge (32). According to Gibson's narrator, "Interstitial meant in between things" and both of the aforementioned locations can be classified as "interstitial communities" (33). The sharehouse cannot, however, be considered a paradisical community. Eliade observes that the reason why Europeans came to the Americas, particularly the area that is now the U.S., and populated said locations is that they were seeking Paradise, the Garden of Eden (89–90). While Gibson does not focus his novel on any religion in particular, the universal archetype of paradise does permeate his writing. What many of the characters, including Chevette, want above all else is a utopia, a place of acceptance and of safety. Eliade states, "The colonization of the two Americas began under an eschatological sign: people believed that the time had come to renew the Christian world, and the true renewal was the return to the Earthly Paradise [...]" (91). In Gibson's text, the United States is no longer a unified entity; it is, however, a space categorized by disorder which tends to be caused by materialism and self-interest. Eliade continues, "[B]oth the first colonists and the later European immigrants journeyed to America as *the country where they might be born anew*, that is, begin a new life" (98; Eliade's italics). In *All Tomorrow's Parties*, the United States has already undergone a cataclysmic event and the American identity, the notion of patriotic unity, has been destroyed, and its aftereffects are being felt throughout California. The state has been split, and the beach, a feature that traditionally defines California's identity, has been subject to the Spill. According to the narrator, "Nobody knew exactly what it was that has spilled, because the government wasn't telling. [...] The government was using nanobots to clean it up though; everybody agreed on that, and that was why they said you shouldn't walk out there" (Gibson, *Parties* 32–33). While some characters revel in the chaos, others like Chevette are looking for that which has been lost—the community.

When Chevette moves away from the bridge, she does not just depart from a place of safety, she also leaves behind a group of people with a common interest. It is this type of collective that she attempts to find in the sharehouse.

When examining Chevette and her America through the lens of Eliade's theory, it can be inferred that within the sharehouse Chevette hopes to find what she has lost, that which she believes is Eden. For Chevette, an ideal place is one that offers safety and relationships with people who have common behavioral traits. Sherryl Vint comments, "There is a tendency in some postmodern theory to speak of the body as an obsolete relic, no longer necessary in a world of virtual communication and technological augmentation" (8). As Vint notes, the body cannot be forgotten; in Gibson's collected works, the focus is not only on body modification, but also on its need for protection from harm. The desire for paradise and the need for protection tend to bond people and create a community. On one hand, for Chevette the community on the bridge is paradise. On the other hand, the Malibu sharehouse community is a figurative wasteland. It is a false paradise. Tessa describes the space's conditions to Chevette: "Leave a house empty in Malibu, Tessa told Chevette, and you get the kind of people come down from the hills and barbecue dogs in your fireplace" (32). This community is unsuccessful because, while the other inhabitants have attributes in common, Chevette appears as an outsider.

The other characters are not drawn together because of a desire for survival, nor to act as a unit. The sharehouse residents are there because they are media students, and after the Spill they are the only ones who want to reside in the Malibu houses. Gibson's narrator continues the previous observation regarding the inhabitants of the Malibu beach properties: "Hard to get rid of, those kind of people, and locks wouldn't keep them out. That was why the people who used to live here, before the Spill, were willing to rent them out to students" (32). The narrator is describing the people from the hills, while simultaneously implying that this is the reason why students are able to live in residences belonging to the affluent. The students in the sharehouse have no wish to become a community, instead preferring their own interests. They take the form of renters—the students are not there because they desire to work together as a unit, but are instead driven by money and self-interest.

The students are disguised as Others. Chevette is there in the sharehouse because she met Tessa, a student in documentary filmmaking, at a party. In order to escape from her abusive partner Carson, Chevette goes to live at the sharehouse with Tessa. Chevette is the Other: she resides in a closet in the sharehouse and observes that she has neither an income or a job. Chevette requires safety in her community, a place where she may both be free of Carson and retain her individuality. Even though it looks like Tessa is offering Chevette a protective community, she is misleading in her motives. She wants to use Chevette to star in her documentary about the community on the bridge, and when she appears to be offering Chevette a safe haven she is actually herding Chevette back towards her former home and closer to the culmination of Tessa's ambition. According to Eliade, America was not only seen as a utopic space, but "For many new immigrants, the New World represented a desert haunted by demonic beings" (94). While the sharehouse seems like an in-between space much like the bridge, it only offers temptation away from the true paradise. Eliade continues, "[T]hey [the settlers] were told in sermons that the present miseries were but a moral and spiritual trial before arriving at the earthly Paradise that had been promised to them" (94). Tessa's constant efforts to lure Chevette back to the bridge and her fear of Carson's abuse cause her to retreat within herself and become submissive to Tessa; however, this type of behavior only lasts until the duo reach the bridge.

Once Chevette and Tessa near the bridge, Chevette's behavior alters and she becomes more sure of herself. Chevette reasserts the confidence that is shown in *Virtual Light*, but this behavior is only revealed once she reaches her paradise. Chevette's "trial" has been completed, and she is now permitted to re-enter the community of the bridge (Eliade 94). Once she reinserts herself into her "place," an area and a community that she has an emotional attachment to, she becomes mentally stronger and her fear lessens (Buell, *Future of* 72). Instead of relying on Tessa to save her from Carson, it is she who must protect Tessa from the dangers of the bridge. For example, it is Chevette who has Boomzilla, a bridge inhabitant, watch the van so it is not stolen, and who warns Tessa about venturing on the wrong path on the bridge. Significantly, Chevette also stands up to Tessa in the bar Dirty Is God. While the two eat, Tessa informs Chevette that she wants her to be the center of her documentary. Not only does Chevette object to being in the film, but also she walks out of the bar, leaving Tessa behind. In *Virtual Light*, Chevette notes, "[W]here she felt best was on the suspension bridge, all wrapped in it, all the people hanging and hustling and doing what they did, and the way the whole thing grew a little, changed a little, every day" (Gibson 150). Chevette shows that to her, the bridge community and the bridge itself offer her security; it is a place of comfort amidst chaos.

Like Gibson, Stephenson creates a community that resides in a structure created for another purpose; in this case, it is a U-Stor-It in Southern California. In his examination of the living conditions in the Los Angeles area, Mike Davis breaks down what he calls "a few simple facts of life about Los Angeles' single-family suburbs" while simultaneously exposing suburb living as less than idyllic (153). Notably, Davis centers his attention on three traits: "property values," "'Community,'" and "neighborhood exclusivity," that appear as characteristics of Stephenson's dystopian burbclaves (Davis 153). These traits define the burbclaves of the present and make them threats to society at large. Stephenson constructs two communal groupings in *Snow Crash*: the burbclave communities and the Other communities. The latter communities are those that house the underprivileged and the people wish to retain their individuality. Interestingly, Davis cites consistent construction of the space and the conformity of the people as identifying marks of the Los Angeles suburbs (153). To wit, Davis notes that "'Community' in Los Angeles means homogeneity of race, class and especially, home values" (153). Reyner Banham states that even though migrants converged upon Los Angeles, some with discriminatory behavioral traits, "Miraculously the city's extremes include an excessive tolerance. Partly this is that indifference which is Los Angeles' most publicized vice, but it is also a heritage from the extraordinary cultural mixture with which the city began" (7). Journalist John Buntin, however, agrees with Davis, citing prejudiced practices as existing in early twentieth-century Los Angeles. According to Buntin, to attract residents to Los Angeles, the formerly Spanish space "was reenvisioned as 'the white spot of America'" (12). Like the real Los Angeles, Stephenson's text has been separated into two spaces: exclusionary (the burbclaves) and inclusionary (the Other communities).

In response to a chaotic yet financially driven society, corporations have produced the burbclave, the self-contained environment featured in Stephenson's *Snow Crash*. Often in this novel Hiro mentions he retains citizenship in Mr. Lee's Greater Hong Kong franchise, which is one of the more prevalent burbclaves; holding a passport to the franchise enables him to enter any of Mr. Lee's burbclaves in times of crisis when seeking protection from outside forces. Citizenship also ensures that only a select group of people is permitted entrance to the community. While documenting conditions in the new Southern California, which is the location of both Hiro's Deliverator job and residence, the narrator observes, "Now a Burbclave, that's the place to live. A city-state with its own constitution, a border, laws, cops, everything" (Stephenson 6). In Hiro's second-wave cyberpunk society, the United States has been reduced to a small area of space—federal buildings only—and California is primarily constructed of freeways and seemingly idyllic burbclaves. California has been engulfed by the stereotypical characteristics known to symbolize the Los Angeles area (Banham 7). According to Banham, "Out of it [Los Angeles] comes a cultural situation where only the extreme is normal, and the Middle Way is just the unused reservation down the centre of the Freeway"—concepts clearly identified in Hiro's society (7). There is a definite division in Hiro's California and, as Baynam observes, the freeway exists as in-between space—a neutral ground. It is here that the reader first witnesses Hiro (7). When Hiro is shown, he is racing down the freeway in a car on his way to a burbclave to make a pizza delivery for Cosa Nostra Pizza. Symbolically, Hiro appears in this location as he is one of the few in California who can traverse restrictive spaces. Stephenson has created the burbclave and its inhabitants, groups of people attempting to shelter themselves from the dangers of the outside world. Significantly, these dangers include nonconformity to the selected group ideal. Stephenson also includes the individualists: it is to this Other group that the protagonist belongs. The Other in Stephenson's text also exists as a space for those that rebel against the accepted conventions of society.

Instead of living in a burbclave, Hiro elects to reside with the musician Vitaly Chernobyl, in a U-Stor-It. Brian McHale describes what he terms the "typical cyberpunk microworld": "Where space-stations and space-colonies of traditional SF are glamorous showcases of high technology [...] those of cyberpunk SF are likely to be orbiting slums—shabby, neglected, unsuccessful, technologically outdated, as in Gibson and Sterling's 'Red Star, Winter Orbit' [...]" (8). Whereas the burbclaves are elitist and embrace capitalism, the U-Stor-It is impoverished, isolated, and technologically disadvantaged (McHale 8). Both societal conformity and nonconformity appear as a benchmark of the cyberpunk novel; Stephenson has created these two communal spaces for his characters, thereby contrasting the human condition in each. Banham observes that with human migration to Southern California—particularly Los Angeles—came discriminatory behavioral practices, specifically "the prejudices, motivations, and ambitions of the central heartland of the USA" (7), ideas reflected in the burbclaves' formation. On the surface, the burbclave appears to be a privatized residential living space that exists to make the lives of its residents simpler and safer. Even though Banham has observed that the "extremes" in Los Angeles "contrive to co-exist with only sporadic flares of violence" (7), in Hiro's society, this is not the case. When the narrator describes Hiro and Vitaly's U-Stor-It living conditions, their proximity to potential danger is documented. In fact, the narrator expressly states that the duo is not subjected to any immediate criminal behavior not only because "neither one of them is important enough to kill, kidnap, or interrogate," but also because they do not have any valuable material possessions (Stephenson 19). While the U-Stor-It should be seen as a space of instability for its inhabitants, it is actually the society that exists outside of the U-Stor-It that is detrimental to Hiro's life and lifestyle. It is this U-Stor-It in which Hiro has built a life that exists as a safe haven for him. Even though the burbclaves appear to be protecting people, insulating them from exterior dangers, this is rarely the case as it is they who exist as an inherent threat to society due to their inhabitants' need for segregation.

Throughout first and second wave cyberpunk genres, the voluntary separation of monetarily privileged groups from the chaos of the masses is a reoccurring element. For example, in both Marge Piercy's *He, She, It* and Gibson's Bridge trilogy, self-contained habitats (Piercy's corporate enclaves) exist near large unregulated areas (the Glop, the Sprawl). The protagonists are also seen consciously separating themselves from the regulated communities, favoring instead a flawed, inclusionary society like that of the Bridge or the U-Stor-It. Stephenson uses this model to construct his novel and has done so while acknowledging past and current Southern Californian communal constructs. In a discussion of the slow-growth movements in Northern and Southern California, Davis identifies the environmental component of this movement in Northern California (the Bay area) as that of protection while in Southern California "Environmentalism is a congenial discourse to the extent that it is congruent with a vision of eternally rising property values in secure bastions of white privilege" (159). Rather than protecting the stability of the area, Stephenson's burbclaves revolve around self-interest and regulation of personal conduct (Davis 159). In order to show the progression in terms of construction of the burbclaves, Stephenson presents both the burbclaves of the past and those of the present. Interestingly, in terms of appearance, the more modern instillations seem to be an improvement on the old; however, Stephenson asserts that while the technological advances in construction have been achieved, the detrimental societal aspects of the past have been strengthened.

In what appears to be the original burbclaves, the danger is immediately visible to the viewer rather than being hidden beneath an attractive exterior. First, as Hiro drives to Cosa Nostra Pizza #3569, the narrator takes note of the condition and layout of the roads, which have resulted from privatization. Contained within commentary about the environmental destruction caused by the paving companies are the perceived inadequacies of some of the first burbclaves. As the narrator lists the services that the older spaces lack, this description also includes the oppression that the newer burbclaves offer. In reference to the older burbclaves, the narrator explains that they "[d]on't have their own police force—no immigration control—undesirables can walk right in without being frisked or even harassed" (Stephenson 6). Because they see the outside world as a danger to their existence, those who reside in the burbclaves use technology and material resources to distance themselves from what they see as a threat, thereby gaining a sense of security from doing so. Ursula K. Heise analyzes the impact that various dangers, particularly environmental, have on real and literary societies. Heise observes that "[e]xperts [...] often tend to evaluate and prioritize risks quite differently from the way the general public does" (124). She continues to note that, for example, while the former find nuclear power plants to have a low probability of danger, the public sees them as having a high probability (125). The freedom of movement inherent within the non-walled early burbclaves make them a threat to Hiro's societal structure; therefore, the masses deem them irredeemable. The narrator's ironic tone during the passage communicates the idea that the restrictive nature of the burbclaves makes them the actual threat to personal liberties.

According to utopian theorist Ruth Levitas, the U.S. has historically been invested in the recreation of the elusive utopia (180). As seen by Buntin, in the early twentieth century a great deal of effort was focused on the West, namely the formation of Los Angeles. Like Stephenson's fictional account of the Los Angeles area, the real city was split into enclaves bordered by definitive boundaries. Whereas Stephenson's fictional constructions are separated from the general public—the outside world—by both physical and socially constructed partitions, the actual city is divided by discriminatory practices and invisible lines. For Hiro, his U-Stor-It living quarters are in Inglewood, an urban space near Los Angeles. To create Inglewood, Stephenson amalgamates traits from the dominant urban space, Los Angeles, and segregates it outside of the city as one of the Other communities. Buell notes, "To understand fully what it means to inhabit place is therefore not only to bear in mind the (dis)connections between one's primary places but also the tenticular radiations from each one" (*Writing* 66). For Hiro, Vitaly, and the other residents, this space is a place of refuge from the intolerance that exists within the burbclaves. In the U-Stor-It, each resident has a unit where that person may behave as he or she sees fit. The narrator observes, "These are slum housing, 5-by-10s and 10-by-10s where Yanoama tribespersons cook beans and parboil fistfuls of coca leaves over burning lottery tickets" (Stephenson 19). Here, individuality is revered rather than thwarted by a socially and corporately constructed ideal. According to Buell, "Place entails spatial location, entails a spatial container of some sort" (*Future of* 63). Vitaly, a musician who Hiro discovered, uses the space to practice his music. Hiro spends his time goggled into the Metaverse, a seemingly utopic space that he is primarily responsible for creating. Timothy Leary observes that "Cyber means 'pilot.' A 'Cyberperson' is one who pilots his/her own life" (135). While the construct of the burbclave appears to offer its inhabitants freedom and safety, the over-regulated environment actually stifles personal growth.

As noted by Leary, one who exists immersed in cyberculture prefers self-control over the domination by another entity—personal choice reigns superior over all else (135). As Hiro is on his way to deliver a pizza the narrator states, "TMAWH [The Mews at Windsor Heights] all have the same layout. When creating a new Burbclave, TMAWH Development Corporation will chop down any mountain ranges and divert the course of any mighty rivers that threaten to interrupt this street plan—ergonomically designed to encourage driving safety" (12). Joel Garreau documents the occurrence of what he terms the edge city in Southern California (ch. 8). On the one hand, Garreau relates the comments made about the suburbs from John Nielson, son of the developer of Irvine, California (ch. 8). Nielson asserts that even though there is a constructional sameness about the suburbs, community is, in fact, possible (ch. 8). On the other hand, Garreau highlights the fear of the cookie-cutter suburb; notably, the existence of such a place appears in Stephenson's novel and, unless it is employed as a means to an end, it is avoided at all costs (ch. 8). When Hiro discovers that he may not have enough time to deliver a pizza—which will lead to the Mafia killing him—he races to a TMAWH burbclave in order to take a shortcut. While driving, Hiro misjudges the layout of the burbclaves and crashes his car in a pool. While he is in great peril in the pool, the only person who comes to his aid is Y.T., an adolescent female Kourier. Both characters appear practical here as they are prepared for the impending danger resulting from Hiro violating the rules of their society. While Hiro is angry that Y.T. is partially responsible for his accident because she pooned (harpooned) his car, he still begrudgingly accepts her help with the pizza delivery. Both characters wordlessly acknowledge that a late pizza delivery is more detrimental to Hiro's life than the car accident, so they join together and become a community. Hiro and Y.T. retain their individuality through the novel—they both are part of non-conformist communities—and assist each other in his or her time of need.

Stephenson creates a mirror image of the Los Angeles area in *Snow Crash* in order for it to appear realistic and to reflect both the ideologies of the time and the cyberpunk genre: Mark Bould and Sherryl Vint highlight the crossover of sf into 1980s popular culture and vice versa (147). The theorists, when discussing Stephenson's text, document a passage in which the narrator compares "'the franchise and the virus,'" noting that they are copies of one another and, as a result, "franchises [can be considered] a form of social disease" (156). In the description of the U-Stor-It, the narrator notes, "As the sun sets, its red light is supplanted by the light of many neon logos emanating from the franchise ghetto that constitutes this U-Stor-It's natural habitat" (Stephenson 20). While conveying the image of the Other community's environment, the narrator also implies that the community is being oppressed by the ubiquitous burbclave. In effect, it is the individuality offered by the Other communities which overshadows the sameness of the burbclave. In a scathing diatribe of the burbclave, the narrator labels them "vast house farms out in the loglo wilderness, a culture medium for a medium culture" (Stephenson 191). The narrator documents the changing face of America, noting that while difference in space was appreciated in the past, the mentality of the populace alters and uniformity of appearance and experience becomes the focal point. "'No surprises' is the motto of the franchise ghetto [...]" except for those who choose to live separately or refuse to conform to its ideals (Stephenson 191).

Katherine Harrison asserts, "Cyberpunk explicitly sets out to upset preconceived notions of identity and 'a good life' by proffering values which highlight alternative ways of being, coupled with an anarchic disrespect for authority associated with the punk ethos" (212). As Buntin documents, the authentic Los Angeles started as a Spanish pueblo; when the wealthy elite chose to recreate Los Angeles in their ideal image, this act was countered with chaos (12). According to Buntin, "There was just one problem with this picture of Anglo-Saxon virtue. It wasn't true. Far from being a paragon of virtue, by the early 1920s, Los Angeles had become a Shangri-la of vice" (12). Significantly, Buntin calls attention to the fact that non–Caucasians had their own sections of Los Angeles and that the majority of Angelenos came to these areas to immerse themselves in a chaotic, unauthorized environment (12–13). As Harrison observes, what is now considered the norm is oppressive and even those who reside in the burbclaves are removing themselves in an effort to find individuality (212).

For example, when Y.T. ventures into the Sacrifice Zone she examines the space and notes, "Young men blasted out of their minds must have some place to do their idiotic coming-of-age rituals. They come in from Burbclaves all over the area in their four-wheel-drive trucks and tear across the open ground [...]" (Stephenson 235). In a desperate act of escapism, many burbclave residents venture out to non-regulated spaces to immerse themselves in chaos and, in some cases, to experience freedom. For example, Y.T. resides in the Blooming Greens burbclave with her mother, but she works as a skateboarding Kourier who is able to traverse in and out of both types of communities at will. Before she reenters Blooming Greens, she changes out of her Kourier uniform and totes her skateboard because "it's legal to carry them but not to put them on the 'crete'" (Stephenson 101). Y.T. and Hiro can freely move between physical spaces. As the cyberpunk protagonist, however, Hiro is also able to move from the physical plane to the virtual one, and the Metaverse is essential to his identity. Like the quintessential cyberpunk protagonist, Norman Spinrad gives Gibson's case as an example here: Hiro willingly immerses himself in the cyberverse (111). As with the classic cyberpunk character, Hiro would prefer to live his life on his own terms, and that means existing as a powerful member of the Metaverse. Until the introduction of Snow Crash, Hiro believes his safety in the Metaverse is assured. In actuality, it is the non-conformist community that he forms in the outside world that aids in protecting him.

When Y.T., the Kourier who assists Hiro in delivering a pizza, needs help escaping from the Clink, she calls Hiro and they steal a taxi together. As the pair flees the parking lot of the Clink (franchised jail), they are chased by other taxis and must quickly locate a space in which to safely hide. While Y.T. drives, she contemplates the spaces in which they may seek refuge, simultaneously noting the characteristics and locale of each burbclave. Like edge cities, each burbclave is located near the freeway or a road; therefore, it is easily accessible by its patrons. As a Kourier, Y.T. must be able to make her deliveries, so she has a visa to each of the burbclaves, which is displayed on her outerwear in the form of barcodes. This character, like Hiro, has access to many of the burbclaves due to her job. As a Deliverator, Hiro has unlimited access, but once he is fired from his position after crashing his vehicle into a pool, he loses this capability. These characters are able to navigate both spaces, the burbclaves and the Other. Spatially, the burbclaves are described as being near freeways, the space that signifies fluidity, and are routinely traversed by both characters. Like Buntin's Los Angeles, the burbclaves are privatized and discriminatory (12); there is no freedom of movement unless one holds a passport.

In her chapter, "Cyberpunk and the City," Dani Cavallaro documents the methods in which cyberpunk writers create urban spaces (138). Referencing Emily Martin's method of documenting the construction of urban spaces, Cavallero observes that western space is divided into "the *citadels*, the *rhizome* and the *string figure*" (138). Whereas the burbclaves appear as a representation of the "citadel," the remainder of Hiro's society is that of the "rhizome" (138). Stephenson's America contains both fortresses and "fluidity and openness" (138). Cavallero observes that the "citadel" model is flawed; the borders of the fortress can be penetrated in the name of science (138). For Stephenson's burbclaves, technology exists to keep people out, thereby helping to create a segregated society, one that is reminiscent of early twentieth-century Los Angeles (Cavallero 138; Buntin 22–25). Whereas Nielson observes that actual suburbs have communal capabilities (Garreau ch. 8), in Stephenson's burbclaves there is no communal spirit, only communal fear of the deregulation of behavior that exists outside of the gates. Stephenson's creations are a hybridization of the edge city and the corporate enclave (ch. 8).

During their high-speed chase, Y.T. contemplates the various burbclaves nearby, wondering which one would suit their need for protection. Y.T. considers New South Africa, but the narrator states, "Scratch that; Hiro is black, or at least part black. Can't take him into New South Africa. And because Y.T. is a Cauc, they can't go to Metazania" (Stephenson 83). The narrator continuously shows that the burbclaves are discriminatory in some form or another. Hiro informs Y.T. that he may enter Mr. Lee's because he is a citizen of this particular burbclave; once inside they are scanned and permitted legal access. The intruders, however, are not and are violently expelled through the use of technology, specifically the Rat Thing. Dear and Flotsy quote Jennifer Wolch who observes, "In edge cities, 'community' is scarce, occurring not through propinquity but via telephone, fax and private mail service. The walls that typically surround such neighborhoods are social boundaries, but they act as community 'recognizers,' not community 'organizers'" (67). The communities in Gibson's and Sterling's texts consisted of people who wished to remain alone and retain their individualism while simultaneously desiring the protection of a community. Stephenson's burbclaves are virtually carbon copies of one another, much like their citizens; there is no room for sustained individualization. Hiro is a citizen of Mr. Lee's, but lives in a U-Stor-It. This character values his independence and individuality, so he chooses to live away from his burbclave; however, if at any time Hiro is in danger, he may enter any area owned by Mr. Lee's. Due to the chaotic state of Hiro's society, burbclaves have been created to protect some members of society, but to exclude others. Leary observes, "Cyberpunks use all available data-input to think for themselves" (136). Even though the burbclave offers protection to its community members, Hiro elects to use it only in his time of need, preferring instead to reside in a place that offers both the constant threat of danger and personal latitude.

According to James Patrick Kelly and John Kessel, "In the beginning, the stereotypical cyberpunk protagonist was a disaffected loner from outside the cultural mainstream" (xi). Gibson's and Stephenson's texts revolve around a protagonist who prefers to live her or his life as an individual but, at the same time, belongs to an unconventional community. The original cyberpunk concept noted by Kelly and Kessel has been altered (xi); the lone wolf figure does not exist in the aforementioned texts for long—rather, the saving grace for these figures is the human connection found in the Other—the nonconforming—community. When Andrew Taylor asks Gibson about the possibility that reality's technology is "catching up" with that of cyberpunk, Gibson responds in the negative, noting, "It's just that other people are starting to realize that it's already here" (Gibson and Sterling 2). In the case of the Other communities in Gibson's and Stephenson's texts, they are just that—they are "already here" and it is humanity that is beginning to take notice of their existence (2). While writing *Virtual Light*, Gibson discusses his work in process, noting, "I think LA slipped over the Fault into the 21st century about eight years ago, maybe even before that" (Gibson and Sterling 4). In his statement, Gibson captures the chaotic and technologically-advanced state of LA, which is deftly created in both *Virtual Light* and *All Tomorrow's Parties* (4). Traditionally, both the cyberpunk and postcyberpunk novel are dystopic in nature; in reference to the latter, M. Keith Booker and Anne-Marie Thomas state that "much of postcyberpunk appears hopeful about the future" (118), thereby noting an alteration to the novel's structure. Like the Bay Bridge and the U-Stor-It, if people are necessitous they will adapt to their surroundings in order to survive. In the aforementioned texts, it is this alternative community which both protects the protagonist from harm and ensures that his or her identity remains intact.

WORKS CITED

Banham, Reyner. *Los Angeles: The Architecture of Four Ecologies*. Berkeley: University of California Press, 2001. Print.

Booker, M. Keith, and Anne-Marie Thomas. *The Science Fiction Handbook*. Hoboken, NJ: Wiley-Blackwell, 2009. Print.
Bould, Mark, and Sherryl Vint. *The Routledge Concise History of Science Fiction*. New York: Routledge, 2011. Print.
Buell, Lawrence. *The Future of Environmental Criticism: Environmental Crisis and Literary Imagination*. Hoboken, NJ: Wiley-Blackwell, 2005. Print.
_____. *Writing for an Endangered World: Literature, Culture, and Environment in the U.S. and Beyond*. Cambridge, MA: Belknap Press, 2001. Print.
Buntin, John. *L.A. Noir: The Struggle for the Soul of America's Most Seductive City*. New York: Three Rivers Press, 2009. Print.
Cavallaro, Dani. *Cyberpunk and Cyberculture*. London: Athlone Press, 2000. Print.
Davis, Mike. *City of Quartz: Excavating the Future of Los Angeles*. 1990. London: Verso, 2006. Print.
Dear, Michael, and Steven Flutsy. "The Postmodern Urban Condition." *Spaces of Culture: City, Nation, World*. Ed. Mike Featherstone and Scott Lash. Thousand Oaks, CA: SAGE, 1999. 64–85. Print.
Eliade, Mircea. *The Quest: History and Meaning in Religion*. 1969. Chicago: University of Chicago Press, 1984. Print.
Farnell, Ross. "Posthuman Topologies: William Gibson's 'Architexture' in *Virtual Light* and *Idoru*." *Science Fiction Studies* 25.3 (1998): 459–80. Web. 14 May 2017. <http://www.jstor.org/stable/4240725>.
Garreau, Joel. *Edge City: Life on the New Frontier*. New York: Anchor Books, 1991. Kindle file.
Gibson, William. *All Tomorrow's Parties*. 1999. New York: Ace, 2000. Print.
_____. *Virtual Light*. 1993. New York: Bantam Books, 1994. Print.
Gibson, William, and Bruce Sterling. "'The Charisma Leak': A Conversation with William Gibson and Bruce Sterling." Interview with Daniel Fischlin, Veronica Hollinger, and Andrew Taylor. *Science Fiction Studies* 189.1 (1992): 1–16. Web. 4 May 2017. <http://www.jstor.org/stable/4240117>.
Harrison, Katherine. "Gender Resistance: Interrogating the 'Punk' in Cyberpunk." *At the Interface/Probing the Boundaries* 85 (2012): 209–27. Web. 14 May 2017. <http://web.b.ebscohost.com/>.
Heise, Ursula K. *Sense of Place and Sense of Planet: The Environmental Imagination of the Global*. Oxford: Oxford University Press, 2008. Print.
Kelly, James Patrick, and John Kessel. "Hacking Cyberpunk." *Rewired: The Post-Cyberpunk Anthology*. Ed. James Patrick Kelly and John Kessel. San Francisco: Tachyon, 2007. vii–xv. Print.
Leary, Timothy. *CyberPunks CyberFreedom: Change Reality Screens*. Oakland, CA: Ronin, 2008. Print.
Levitas, Ruth. *The Concept of Utopia*. Bern, Switzerland: Peter Lang, 2010. Print.
McHale, Brian. "Towards a Poetics of Cyberpunk." *Beyond Cyberpunk: New Critical Perspectives*. Ed. Graham J. Murphy and Sherryl Vint. New York: Routledge, 2010. 3–28. Print.
Piercy, Marge. *He, She, It*. 1991. New York: Ballantine Books, 1993. Print.
Spinrad, Norman. *Science Fiction in the Real World*. Carbondale: Southern Illinois University Press, 1990. Print.
Stephenson, Neal. *Snow Crash*. New York: Bantam Books, 2008. Print.
Vint, Sherryl. *Bodies of Tomorrow: Technology, Subjectivity, Science Fiction*. Toronto: University of Toronto Press, 2007. Kindle file.

The Future Is White, the Future Is Undead
Reframing the American Vampire Dystopia in Guillermo del Toro and Chuck Hogan's The Strain Trilogy

SIMON BACON

Introduction

At first glance, *The Strain Trilogy* by Guillermo del Toro and Chuck Hogan is just another dystopian vampire apocalypse of the type first seen in Richard Matheson's novel from 1954, *I Am Legend*, where mankind's hubris—disregard of the consequences of its actions—causes the destruction of humanity. However, *The Strain Trilogy*'s purposeful referencing of past texts and historical events progressively reframes this reading as a narrative about current racial politics and immigration, revealing the true dystopian future to be an all-consuming whiteness as epitomized in twenty-first-century America. This essay examines the ways in which *The Strain* reframes the vampire narratives of Bram Stoker and Richard Matheson so that the undead monsters are configured to embody the dominant forces of white purity in contemporary America that desires to reproduce the world in its own image. The point of danger—but also hope—in this dystopian present is the otherness of the immigrant which offers the last and only form of resistance to racial and cultural homogenization. As such, del Toro and Hogan's novel, not unlike Octavia Butler's *Fledgling* (2005),[1] suggests that the true dystopias in the twenty-first century are nations that close their borders to otherness and blindly reproduce their own identity until it becomes undead and monstrous, and that the world's only hope is to embrace difference and individuality whenever and wherever it can.

Set in modern day New York, *The Strain*, the first book in the series, begins with the arrival of a "ghost" plane at JFK airport, carrying the vampire contagion into America, prefiguring an undead apocalypse that will spread across the nation and eventually the world. The novel appears to suggest that the vampire, invited in by corporate America, embodies unbridled consumerism as many other apocalyptic vampire/zombie tales do, but this changes dramatically as the story is progressively reframed. Primarily, *The Strain Trilogy* references Stoker's seminal vampire text, *Dracula*, which connects the two stories but also links the ideological anxieties of the earlier narrative to the later one. These, according to theorists such as Stephen Arata, reveal the vampire as the embodiment of a fear of reverse colonialism and miscegenation (108); however, del Toro and Hogan reframe this fear of outside invasion by correlating events in the narrative to historical and contemporary events. First, to Nazi Germany and the Holocaust, which reconfigures the vampire to embody a form of racial purity which makes everyone the same and exterminates all those who are different. Second, the text is further reframed by the Master vampire having his lair in the sewers beneath Ground Zero, linking it to 9/11 and the subsequent War on Terror—an event which itself has been correlated to the Holocaust by certain commentators and then U.S. President George W. Bush. Rather than embodying the extremists coming from outside, the vampire's destructive incursion into New York can be seen to configure white corporate/governmental America trying to control the population—a point made when the Master and his familiars take control of all forms of communication, mirroring the extreme policies of U.S. Homeland security.

While such a dystopian vision of America finds its only real resistance in a group of Hispanic and European immigrants who configure humanity's new beginning, the series of reframings that the novel undergoes further suggest that this is not just a vision of the future but something else.

Carter Kaplan explains that the word dystopia means a "bad" or "abnormal" place,[2] meaning that dystopian literature "tells stories about bad places; specifically, it is literature about possible future or near-future societies that will result if current or hypothetical political, environmental, and technological trends are amplified by history into overarching principles of social organization" (93). While this encapsulates the surface reading of *The Strain Trilogy* fairly well, its links both to past novels and historical events, as will be discussed below, reveal it to be not just a dark vision of contemporary or future worlds but the undying resurrection/continuation of past ones.

Invitations

The Strain Trilogy consists of *The Strain* (2009), *The Fall* (2010) and *The Night Eternal* (2011), and the three volumes tell the tale of modern day

America descending into a never-ending dystopian future where it is literally consumed by a vampire apocalypse. It begins with a flight from Berlin landing at JFK Airport whose passengers and crew are seemingly dead from an unknown cause. Fearing some form of unknown contagion or biological weapon, the Centers for Disease Control (CDC) are called in. The lead investigator of the CDC, Dr. Ephraim (Eph) Goodweather and his partner, Dr. Nora Martinez, can find no known cause—just as there was no specific cause cited for the vampire apocalypse in Matheson's *I Am Legend*—but discover three passengers and one crew member showing signs of life. They also discover a large ornately carved box filled with earth in the hold of the plane that does not appear on the flight's cargo log. The passengers and crewmember revive and insist on being released, and the box mysteriously disappears from the airport. At this point, the story spins out of control. The passengers and crewmember revive as vampires and begin infecting all those they come into contact with. The box, it is discovered, contained the body of the Master, one of seven "Ancients" (part fallen angel and part vampire), who has created a lair in Manhattan and is conspiring with a human accomplice (since he needed to be "invited" into the country by a human) to take control of the United States and eventually the world. This accomplice is none other than Eldritch Palmer, who owns a global corporation and who himself wants to become a vampire as a cure to the lifelong debilitating diseases from which he suffers. He also wants to turn the United States into a series of human processing plants to provide food for the army of vampires under the control of the Master. The King Vampire himself maintains a telepathic link and some control over all vampires that are from his "blood-line."

Arrayed against the forces of the vampire apocalypse are an unlikely band of vampire-hunters led by Abraham Setrakian, a Holocaust survivor who owns a pawnshop in Spanish Harlem and has previously encountered the Master. With him come Eph and Nora, Augustus "Gus" Elizalde, a Hispanic gang member whose mother and brother are turned into vampires, and Vasily Fet, an immigrant of Ukrainian decent who is a pest exterminator. The vampire-hunters are also aided by Mr. Quinlan, who is the son of the Master, and other representatives of the surviving "Ancients," who want to stop the Master from further diminishing their number and return to some kind of order.

Initially, the vampire-hunters' attempts fail. After a struggle with the Master, Gus and Setrakian are killed, but not before the King Vampire initiates a nuclear winter. This means that it is effectively nighttime for 20 hours a day, allowing the vampires to move freely. They create a vampiric police state to control the humans that are still alive—those too weak to be used as slaves are sent to the processing camps. Meanwhile, the remaining hunters have procured an ancient book, the Occido Lumen, which explains how to destroy the Master, and once they translate it, they discover that they need to destroy the site of the vampire's "birth," which is an island on Lake Ontario.³ They manage to get a nuclear device on the island, but in dispatching the King Vampire, Eph, Zach, and Mr. Quinlan are also killed. However, the death of the Master disintegrates all the vampires that are part of his "strain," leaving society free to slowly rebuild itself. The narrative ends with Fet and Nora together, living in Vermont and raising their two children, a girl called Mariela, after Nora's mother, and a boy named Eph.

As previously mentioned, *The Strain Trilogy* owes much to Matheson's earlier tale of a vampire apocalypse, where the unknown contagion is probably caused by some form of nuclear testing/mutation. It is human (military/scientific) hubris that is cited as being at fault, as noted by Elizabeth Abele in her essay "Last Man Standing" (190). Humanity is once again seen at fault here, but science and the military are under the auspices of economics, and the hubris in del Toro and Hogan's work is the belief that money can buy anyone and anything, even life itself. Consequently, much of the narrative of the books can be read as a metaphor for consumerism: Eldritch, as the third richest man in America, represents the ultimate consumer, with private jets and penthouse suites. He is shown to quite literally own people, not just through bribery and coercion, but through the many organ transplants he undergoes. For Eldritch everything has a price and is something to consume—even his own life, which he hopes to "buy back" by inviting the vampire into America. The Master manifests the very essence of consumerism and is driven to continually consume. As Franco Moretti says of that other well-known vampire consumer, "Dracula is impelled towards continuous growth, an unlimited expansion of his domain: accumulation is inherent in his nature" (91). And so he seeks not only to take control of Manhattan, but of the United States and the rest of the world as well. In facilitating this, humans are shown for the consumerist "objects" they have become, being divided into those who consume or those who are, literally, consumed—what lives they have in the dystopian vampire future are totally dependent on these two actions. Interestingly, it is possible to read into the start of the first novel that this consumerist apocalypse is allowed to happen by contemporary American society, which is already too busy consuming to realize what is going on when the contagion begins to spread.

A correlation to Matheson's apocalyptic novel, which can be read as the anxiety of a society that has no grasp of the ideological ramifications of the nuclear/cold-war era that it was entering, sees del Toro and Hogan's narrative revealing the fears of a world controlled by the ideology of consumerism where everything and everyone is a commodity to be bought and sold. However, *The Strain Trilogy* is further reframed when considered in relation to Stoker's seminal vampire text and certain historical events that the story takes pains to make connections to.

Shadow of "the" Vampire

Almost inevitably, since its publication in 1897, the shadow of Stoker's *Dracula* hangs heavily over any text featuring vampires. As Erik Butler observes, "The literary Dracula is a singularly virulent vampire" (108), and del Toro and Hogan's vampire is no exception; in fact, they go to great lengths to make that connection to subsequently reframe the meaning of their characters and environments.

As mentioned above, *The Strain* begins with the vampire landing in New York on a ghost plane, an arrival that purposely mirrors Dracula's arrival in Britain on the deserted ship, The Demeter. It later transpires that the vampire was hidden aboard the plane and was then secretly removed and installed in his new residence in New York under the ruins of the Twin Towers, just as Dracula was transported to his English residence in the ruins of Carfax Abbey. Consequently, it makes a direct connection between the original Vampire King and the Master, so that the latter contains traces of the former. As explained by Judith Halberstam, "The monster, in its otherworldly form, its supernatural shape, wears the traces of its own construction" (349), which speaks not just of the times in which that monster was created, but also each time it is reborn or resurrected in the future. Consequently, the "traces" of gothic monsters of the Victorian period, Dracula in particular, that were created from the racist/anti–Semitic and homophobic/sexual anxieties of the age, are carried into the future with them as each generation adapts these traces to their own purposes. As such, the Master carries these scars of the past within him, and indeed, many parts of *The Strain Trilogy* demonstrate these prejudices in relation to the figure of the vampire, not least as seen in its overt, almost hyper whiteness. Transgressive sexuality is shown explicitly in Stoker's vampires, not just because of their provocative behavior and ruby-red "voluptuous lips" (Stoker 41) but in same-sex desire, as seen in Dracula's pursuit of Jonathan Harker, not just directly but also through the possession of his wife, Mina.

The Strain Trilogy appears to play down this aspect and this would seem to be confirmed by the character named Gabriel Bolivar, formerly a womanizing rock star whose body becomes a host for the Master—the King Vampire here exists as something of a parasitic spirit that inhabits the bodies of others. As the musician slowly transforms into a vampire his penis withers and falls off, along with all his bodily hair, leaving him as a totally non-sexual figure. Yet even here, the transgressive sexuality of Dracula lives on with the Master controlling Eph's ex-wife Kelly, who is now a vampire, to constantly trail him as well as exhibiting an uncontrollable fascination with Eph's son, Zach— both actions re-enacting something of Dracula's fascination with Harker. This queering of sexuality is used in the construction of transgressive ethnicity that explicitly posits the Master as a dangerous Other. This is seen partly in flashbacks where Abraham Setrakian first meets the Master in the Treblinka concentration camp, where the vampire is feeding on sick and/or weak Jewish prisoners. It is then reinforced in *The Fall* when it is shown that the vampire turned the camp's commandant, Thomas Eichhorst, into one of the undead so that he might run the human processing plants in the King Vampire's "New Order." This anxiety around anti–Semitism does not only perceive the Master as an embodiment of the spirit of racial purity but, like Dracula before him, also constructs him as the object of it and can be seen to contain elements of derogatory Jewish representation. While this is not specifically part of del Toro's or Hogan's intention in their creation of the vampire, it is carried in the traces of the undead precursor they use to partly model the Master on.

Howard L. Malchow observes in *Gothic Images of Race in 19th Century Britain* that "[the] argument for seeing Stoker's Count Dracula as the eternal Jew seems obvious and compelling" (153) while the later interpretation of the vampire from F.W. Murnau's 1922 *Nosferatu: Symphony of Terror* makes this connection explicit. Here the King Vampire is far more feral and anti–Semitic in nature, as observed by Brenda S. Gardenour Walter in *Our Old Monsters*:

> As he emerges from the shadows of his ruined castle, the vampire's frail and crooked frame, bundled beneath layers of dusty black wool, reveals a familiar physiognomy: that of the melancholic Jew. His pallid skin, desiccated flesh, and baldness signify his lack of male vital heat rendering him cold and feminine. Perverting an already horrid visage, the vampire's dark sunken eyes, enormous beaked nose, and pointy ears mark him as a foul and poisonous creature [155].

Walter further notes his "rat-like teeth" and consuming greed that also link him to "a corrupting foreign plague" and "the stereotype of the grasping, usurious Jew embedded in Christian Western culture since the Middle Ages" (155). The Master, whilst conforming to del Toro's wish to "go back to something old" (del Toro 2011), meaning the more folkloric or mythical aspects of the undead, takes much from Murnau's adaptation of Stoker's vampire, as seen in this description of him from *The Strain*:

> The head was hairless and colorless. Its eyes, lips, and mouth were all without hue, worn and washed out, like threadbare linen. Its nose was worn back like that of a weathered statue, a mere bump made of two black holes. Its throat throbbed in a hungry pantomime of breathing. Its skin was so pale that it was translucent. Visible beneath the flesh, like a blurry map to an ancient, ruined land, were veins that no longer carried blood. Veins that pulsed with red. The circulating blood worms. Capillary parasites coursing beneath the Master's pellucid flesh [435].

The Master then manifests the same anti–Semitic fears over contamination and miscegenation that Murnau's Orlok does, embodying the very thing that his "New Order," wishes to kill. This he achieves by turning people into vampires as his victims quite literally become death and become part of him. Richard Dyer explores this link between whiteness, the vampire, and death in his book *White* and explains it thus:

> the vampires' whiteness conveys their own deadness, so too their bringing of death is signaled by whiteness. [...] In the act of vampirism, white society (the vampire) feeds off itself (his/her victims) and threatens to destroy itself. All of this is so menacing that it is often ascribed to those who are not mainstream whites—the Jews [210].[4]

The "Jewish" body of the Master is then used by white society to kill everyone so that they become undead copies of itself. *The Strain Trilogy* shows this as all of the vampire contagion victims slowly transform into versions of the Master, translucently white, hairless and sexless—in fact, perfect clones.[5] Consequently, correlating the Master to Stoker's Dracula reframes del Toro and Hogan's vampire from a foreign threat from outside the nation into the undead embodiment of that same nation's wealthy, white elite who want to recreate the world in its own image. The same process of reframing has similar, if not more drastic, effects on the defenders of the nation—the self-styled vampire hunters, or crew of light, who try to repel the encroaching forces of darkness from their homeland.

The vampire in Stoker's novel is meant to represent all that is alien and most threatening to the British Empire—i.e., everything it is not—and the vampire hunters are symbolic of all that is good or desired of it. As described by William Hughes, the construction of Stoker's group of vampire hunters is meticulous in its choice of its members' "individual abilities, social origins and national identities" (74), and who are also "altruistic and self-sacrificing" (74) which sees them as embodying "not merely a source of Light to oppose and correct the Count's Darkness, but a collective West to counter his individual East" (74). As such, the band of six hunters opposed to Count Dracula—Professor Abraham Van Helsing, Arthur Holmwood (Lord Godalming), Dr. John Seward, Quincey Morris, and Jonathan and Mina Harker—are signifiers of the nation and how it sees itself developing from the past and into the future. Subsequently, being the end of the nineteenth century, most of its members are from the aspiring middle classes—only Holmwood was born into wealth—and all are prepared to work together for the sake of an ideal.

Van Helsing and Holmwood can be seen as representative of Imperialist Empires—the Dutch and British, respectively—that are on the wane and who will be steered into a commercial future by the professional and middle classes—as represented by Dr. Seward and the Harkers[6]—or even superseded by a new modern Empire—America—as represented by Morris. This is qualified by the various skills of each of the members—Van Helsing is familiar with European vampires and their associated lore, whilst Seward, a former pupil of the Professor, has the medical skills to perform blood transfusions, which will save Mina's life. Holmwood, whose fiancée Lucy was a victim of the vampire, is happy to support the new order despite being representative of the old order and their money. Quincey Morris also has huge wealth but is also shown to possess a surfeit of bravado—a commodity as valuable as money in the eyes of Stoker. The Harkers are slightly different in that although Jonathan was the first to encounter Dracula and effectively facilitate his entry into Britain, he plays little part in what ensues, whilst his wife is far more central. Even though the men of the crew keep her away from all major decisions, she is the focal point of the Count's attentions and she has a special bond with him. Mina is also the one who collects and collates all the various pieces of written material—diaries, transcripts, newspaper clippings, telegrams—that constitute the final narrative of the book. Mina, as Jennifer Wicke notes, "occupies unclear territory" (484) portraying both the future of the Empire—being shown as a mother at the end of the novel but also the destroyer of Dracula—while signaling its impending downfall by embodying the New Woman of the late Victorian period (Lorrah 32) and bonding with the undead vampire in a way that changes her forever.[7]

The defenders of the Empire in *The Strain Trilogy* are a very different, yet oddly similar, collection of members of contemporary American society. Setrakian is almost a direct copy of Van Helsing, being both a professor (with Abraham as a first name) and the most knowledgeable of the group in terms of vampire lore, but his construction as a Holocaust survivor emphasizes the connection of the Master to racial purity and Fascism. Furthermore, as a survivor of the concentration camps of the Second World War, he also corresponds to the large number of European immigrants who made the same journey both before and after the conflict, which posits him simultaneously as both American and foreign, something that is true of much of the group of modern day vampire hunters.[8] Fet (Vasiliy Fetorski), like Setrakian, is also of Eastern European decent and his grandfather was a convicted Nazi (possibly a guard at Treblinka who might have known Eichorst). His job as a pest exterminator and his technical abilities frame him as equivalent to Dr. Seward, something which is further emphasized by the father/son relationship between him and the Professor, mirroring Seward's relationship with his mentor Van Helsing. Gus is second generation Mexican-American, and like Quincey Morris he is helping to fight the vampire whilst also working his own agenda. Gus and Morris are led by their bravado, and both die whilst attempting to kill the King Vampire. His correlation with Morris reframed Gus as the future of the Empire, just as the American was seen as representative of the transfer of colonial and economic power from Britain to the United States in *Dracula*. Eph is more difficult to situate, as he is a deeply conflicted character who means well but is unable to control his emotions and, more often than not, ends up putting other people in danger. He is the only member of the slayers who is configured as a "naturalized" American and his emotional problems hint at a level of self-obsession that has caused him to split with his wife Kelly, lose custody of their son, Zach, and fail at a relationship with Nora. In many ways, he correlates to Jonathan Harker in being too focused on his career to fully comprehend what is going on around him, and with both men being on the edge of a nervous breakdown—Harker spends much of his time later in the novel recovering from his encounter with Dracula.

Eph's death at the end of *The Strain Trilogy* suggests that he, as the only one of the group who is not an immigrant, is as much a part of the extreme (vampiric) whiteness that is trying to remake the world in its own image—a point further made by the vampire's obsession with Eph and his son as though, because he is of the same order as the vampire, he needs to win them over rather than just convert them. As such, he claims some of the territory previously taken by Mina Harker in being both a hunter and one of the hunted, but unlike her he can never signal the future and so is doomed to disappear with the past. The role of Mina Harker should have been taken by Nora Martinez, but the novels downplay the effectiveness of their female characters,[9] so Eph's assistant plays half of Mina while his ex-wife Kelly plays the other. Similar to Mina, Kelly, who is turned into a vampire and is used by the Master to track Eph, is used by Dracula to "penetrate" the male-dominated "crew of light," while Nora reflects the more efficient side, or the New Woman, part of Harker's semi-professional wife.

Consequently, all this sees the saviors of the nation as almost entirely made up of immigrants of one form or another—those that Stoker's crew of light were fighting to save England from—who come together to save America from the colonizing whiteness of its founding fathers, or at least those that see themselves as the true fathers of twenty-first-century America. Eph's final sacrifice to kill the Master then replicates something of an Oedipal struggle of the son killing the father, an association which is further made by Mr. Quin, the actual vampiric son of the King Vampire, being his accomplice in this final act. However, the New America requires its "first born" to be totally eliminated from its rebirth, and so Eph and his son Zach are killed whilst destroying the Master—in fact, Eph, his ex-wife, and his son Zach demonstrate the fall from grace of the all–American family, requiring it to be remade in a new image. It is therefore unsurprising that the new age is born from the new American family created by the coming together of Fet and Nora whose offspring represent both European and Hispanic immigrants, while remembering those who laid down their lives for them. *Dracula* then can be seen to dramatically shift the dynamics of this future dystopia, emphasizing the links between the vampire and the wealthy white elites of corporate (global) America. It further posits that the nation's last and only defense against these forces is that offered by America's newest inhabitants, the immigrants[10]—an interesting inversion of the anxieties of reverse colonialism that permeate Stoker's novel and sees the Empire being threatened by an outsider who is "more vigorous, more fecund, and more 'primitive'" and eventually "more 'advanced'" than "his Western antagonists" (Arata 640). However, this is further reframed in relation to events linked to the War on Terror, which posits that this view of a white dystopian future has already arrived.

History Repeating

In *The Strain Trilogy*, the arrival of the vampire into America is inextricably linked to events around September 11, 2001, a day which, as Kevin J. Wetmore notes, saw passenger planes "used as missiles to attack and destroy the Twin Towers of the World Trade Center in New York City" (4). The opening of *The Strain* showing an airplane being taken over by a foreign force that is then used to wreak destruction upon New York City inevitably links this fictional terror attack to the earlier one. This connection is emphasized by the Master setting up his lair in the "bathtub" of the fallen World Trade Center—the sewers and tunnels that exist in the footprint of the destroyed towers that once dominated the Manhattan skyline. As one of the authors, Hogan, observes,

> Horror has to go to horrible places. It has to. And Ground Zero made perfect sense to me in a way I really can't say without giving away too much. We don't exploit the tragedy at all, but only address its role in the world today—and specifically that lingering wound in the soil of lower Manhattan [Lamkin, 2009].

This is expressed in *The Strain Trilogy* by Setrakian who explains the Master's choice of location thus: "a mole hollows out a home in the dead trunk of a felled tree. Gangrene forms in a wound. He is rooted in tragedy and pain" (del Toro and Hogan, 2010a, 455). This specifically cites Ground Zero as signifying a wound in the heart of both the City and the nation; a "spectre of 9/11" (del Toro and Hogan, 2010a, 76) which has changed the way in which America relates to itself and the world around it. The September 11 attacks then become a seminal moment that, as Wetmore further notes, signifies "an event, a period, a mindset and a cultural shift" (4). After this, the "enemy" is no longer just outside but inside the nation as well, as noted by Jane Mayer in Wetmore's book: "[I]t is clear that what began on September 11, 2001, as a battle for America's security became, and continues to be, a battle for the country's soul" (327). This ongoing battle has produced the sense of ever increasing secrecy and opacity in government and in homeland security operations that, whilst meant to keep America "safe," has conversely caused a growing sense of distrust and insecurity in regard to those very bodies.

The anxiety around one's home nation's security forces has only increased since 9/11, so that by 2005 Lydia Khalil can observe,

> When surveyed, 65 percent of the American population were modestly to extremely worried that the government would instruct them to do something that was not in their best interest. Specifically, individuals were concerned that government officials would intentionally mislead the public to further their own agenda [321].

The Strain Trilogy then manifests these anxieties both through the depiction of individuals in positions of power and influence that, with malice-aforethought, bring destruction upon American society and those that are, often unbeknownst to themselves, complicit in facilitating the former.

Eldritch Palmer, as head of the Stonewall Group, is very much in the first category, being the one who uses all the vast resources available to him to facilitate the smooth passage of the Master into the United States. Once the vampire in his coffin has landed, Palmer further arranges for the ornate container to vanish from the airport—Gus is actually hired to do this, unaware of what he is stealing from the airport security hanger. The billionaire then uses a network of bribed officials and technical experts to take control of large swathes of the Internet and telecommunications networks to broadcast misinformation to help the undead contagion spread across and take control of New York City. Palmer symbolizes both the anxieties around the unseen forces of Homeland Security that control and monitor many forms of communications as well as the notion of sleeper cells that are activated and manipulated from afar. This last part is seen most clearly in the creation of new vampires. These are ordinary citizens who become "activated" through coming into contact with the undead contagion that then turns them into agents of destruction. This idea of a contagion that dramatically alters its host is one also seen in Matheson, which directly comes out of Cold War fears of ideological infections that change those affected into communist "zombies" that blindly follow the instructions of their leader. Similarly, *The Strain Trilogy*'s vampire disease is one that can be seen to alter the ideological imperative of its victims, infecting them with what might be described as the extremist views of the King Vampire.

In light of the narratives around the War on Terror, the Master is something of an extremist fanatic—from the East—that infects the population of America with his ideological contagion, and who is funded by wealthy white American capitalists. This directly connects to the anxieties not just around Al Qaeda—who were responsible for the attacks on 9/11—and its evolution into extremist fundamentalism as demonstrated by the so-called Islamic State, but also the notion that global corporations and even one's own government are somehow complicit in allowing terror attacks to continue. These ideas of a combined physical and ideological threat are further reinforced by reference to the Nazis and the Holocaust throughout the text, from the Master's links to Treblinka and its commander, Thomas Eichorst, to the human processing plants and the dystopian vampiric "final solution." Much post 9/11 political rhetoric made links between the terror attacks and the Holocaust, as then President George W. Bush said of Al Qaeda in 2001: "[T]hey follow in the path of fascism, Nazism, and totalitarianism. And they will follow that path all the way to where it ends in history's unmarked grave of discarded lies" (Bush). Del Toro and Hogan purposely create these resonances and link them directly to Eldritch Palmer to highlight the complicity of white corporate America in this dystopian vision of America under the auspices of extremist ideology—one which not only mirrors those put forward by so-called terror groups, but by white, wealthy America itself. As Eldritch himself says, "We, the over-class, have taken those basic human drives [consumption] and advanced our own selves through their exploitation. We have monetized human consumption" (del Toro and Hogan, 2010b, 218), and indeed, as the trilogy implies, humanity itself.

This final reframing, then, turns *The Strain Trilogy*'s vampiric dystopia into a vision of the twenty-first century where the real source of terror is not from forces outside of the United Stated but from those who are already part of it: hyper-wealthy white America. Deborah Mutnick notes the "widening gap between the obscenely wealthy and the rest of us [America]" (Mutnick, 2011) which also includes a widening economic gap between them, the obscenely "wealthy" and African Americans and Latinos. This economic distance translates to physical distance, which becomes total separation as seen in the character of Eldritch Palmer, but where the rich still need to consume the poor, or turn them into the kind of "undead labour" that Moretti speaks about, referencing Karl Marx, where "their [everyone but the rich] strength becomes his strength" (91). The Master embodies this kind of economic and physical vampirism where those he infects become his "slaves" who add to his strength while simultaneously providing him sustenance. The King Vampire's extreme whiteness then portrays him as the projection of hyper-wealthy white America that literally brings him forth from their insatiable desire to own, possess, and consume the world around them. The vampire contagion manifests the global consumerist ideology that infects the world as it simultaneously consumes, replicating itself endlessly until there is nothing but itself left. *The Strain Trilogy*, then, does not show the vision of a future vampire dystopia as it initially seems to, but rather forms a critique of contemporary America that can be seen to be, quite literally, consuming itself into extinction.

Conclusion

The Strain Trilogy, at first appearance, can be read as another early twenty-first-century apocalyptic/post-apocalyptic narrative of a world so self-indulgent that it invites destruction to rain down upon it—a consumerist utopia that becomes its own dystopia. However, the various reframings the text undergoes through the earlier works and the historical events it references see it recast not just as a teleological inevitability, but also as a continual repeating of the past. One of the trilogy's authors, Guillermo del Toro, stated that he wrote the narrative with the intention of going back to the vampire's roots to create, in his own words, "a very scary vampire story, none of these romantic, languid young men sucking the necks of beautiful people" (del Toro: 2011). For del Toro, this takes form in a desire to return to a time before Stephenie Meyer and *Twilight*, before Anne Rice and *Interview with the Vampire*, and even before Hammer's Christopher Lee films,[11] when vampires were not sexy but were creatures of myth and legend that spread contagion and a plague of anxiety over change and reason.

This finds expression at the starts of *The Strain Trilogy* when Eph and Nora discover the seemingly dead bodies on the plane and think that the cause of the mysterious event is "something new [...] or something very, very old" (del Toro and Hogan, 2010, 164). Of course, as discussed above, it is both—in being the newest repetition of something very old; the contagion of power and greed that sees nothing but its own satiation above all else and despises difference, otherness and anything that it cannot use to make itself stronger. The figure of the vampire suits such a situation very well—the Master is a creature that is seemingly immortal and exists before mankind and yet his vampire victims are almost memoryless. Eph's ex-wife seems to have only residual memories of her life as a human. This bears strong resemblance to J.G. Ballard's view of consumerism, as noted by Daniel Cojocaru, where "[t]he eternal retail present of the shopping mall erases historical memory and thus the Metro-Centre is condemned to repeat history both as tragedy and as farce. Consumerism is revealed as a soft-fascist world in which 'everything good has a barcode'" (179). However, *The Strain Trilogy*'s vision of a consumerist dystopia sees a far more hardline fascism emerge, one where everybody and everything is a commodity; where its individuality and authenticity are also subsequently consumed, seeing memory and even history as something which loses its validity. Ultimately, this is the final battleground of the narrative, commodification versus authenticity, the mass versus the individual.

And *The Strain Trilogy* ends exemplifying this tension with two contrasting views of the world after the demise of the Master. One sees the new leader of the vampire hunters trying to restore authenticity to the past in an attempt to bring a halt to its continual repetitions: "Fet's lifelong project became the tracing of the Ancient's influence over the course of history. He wanted to know the mistakes we had collectively made and devoted himself to avoiding there ever being repeated again" (2011, 370). In contrast, the world around Fet is still infected with the contagion of consumerism where history is easily forgotten and replaced by commodified memory:

> In due time, others claimed to have taken down the *strigoi* [vampire]. A biologist claimed to have released a vaccine into the water system, a few gang members exhibited assorted trophies claiming to have killed the Master, and, in the strangest twist, a large group of skeptics began to deny that the plague itself ever occurred. They attributed it all to a huge new-world-order plot, calling the entire event a manufactured coup [2011, 370–71].

This sees the world after the demise of the vampiric dystopia as anything but a return to peace and creates one final correlation to Stoker's narrative. *Dracula* ends with an air of unease where it is "almost impossible to believe the things which we had seen with our own eyes and heard with our own ears were living truths" and as proof of what had actually occurred "there is hardly one authentic document! nothing but a mass of typewriting" (Stoker 411). The vampire has become a commodity,[12] the mass of typewriting which can be copied and disseminated just as its spirit can be seen to live on in Mina Harker's child—after all, the vampire and Mina shared both their blood and their minds during the narrative. *The Strain Trilogy* ends on a similar note: the ideologies that allowed the vampire to enter America are not destroyed and his project of commodification lives on, finding far greater purchase in the post-apocalyptic world than Fet's quest for authentication. Even the naming of Fet and Nora's child after Eph—just as Mina and Jonathan named their child after Quincey—suggests that the vampire dystopia will not be the last and that the tragedy and farce of repetition have not ended.

Notes

1. Butler's *Fledging* uses the figure of a young African American girl to embody the vampire/human hybridity that will ensure the safety of both species.
2. *Dys* being Latin for "bad" or "abnormal" and *topos* being Greek for "place."
3. This is a somewhat confusing part of the narrative as the Master was actually born in the Americas but travelled to Europe, but then requires an invitation to return to his home. Stoker's Dracula needed no such invitation to return to Transylvania, though the vampire travels by land rather than by sea, possibly inferring that it is crossing water that necessitates an invite.
4. See Ken Gelder *Reading the Vampire* (New York: Routledge, 2001), 13–17.
5. This idea is explicitly shown in an earlier movie adaptation of Matheson's *I Am Legend*, called *The Omega Man* (Segal: 1971), where all members of the steadily growing vampire horde are turned white when they become infected. Even black members of the human resistance slowly get more and more pale as they turn into one of the undead.
6. Jonathan is a solicitor and Mina a secretary.
7. The New Woman was a feminist ideal at the end of the nineteenth century. Marking the desire for greater autonomy in the highly patriarchal Late Victorian society, it saw larger numbers of women seeking advances in education, the arts, and professions such as industry,

law, and medicine. This happened alongside the push for female suffrage and was seen by many (men) as degenerative and against the principles that established the British Empire.

   8. Interestingly, the numbers of immigrants from Europe to America was actually far greater before the war than after it; see Dennis Wepman's *American Experience: Immigration* (New York: Facts On File, 2002), 285.

   9. The recent television adaption of the novels, *The Strain*, does much to reverse this.

   10. It is worth noting that whilst *The Trilogy* makes much of the European and Latino migrants to America, the African American community, whilst seen to combat the vampires, is kept separate and never included within the main band of vampire-hunters. Equally, Middle-Eastern, Far Eastern, and Asian immigrants play no part in del Toro and Hogan's vision of the future, nor do Native Americans.

   11. *Twilight* was released in 2008, *Interview with the Vampire* in 1976, and the first Hammer film featuring Christopher Lee as Dracula came out in 1958.

   12. See Jennifer Wicke, "Vampiric Typewriting: Dracula and Its Media," *ELH* 59/2 (Summer, 1992), 467–493.

WORKS CITED

Abele, Elizabeth. "Last Man Standing: Will Smith as the Obsolete Patriarchal Male." Ed. Elizabeth Abele and John A. Gronbeck-Tedesco. *Screening Images of American Masculinity in the Age of Postfeminism*. Lanham, MD: Lexington Books, 2016. 187–202. Print.
Arata, Stephen, D. "The Occidental Tourist: 'Dracula' and the Anxiety of Reverse Colonization." *Victorian Studies* 33.4 (Summer, 1990): 621–45. Print.
Bush, George W. "Address to Congress." 20 Sept. 2001. Web. 28 Sept. 2015.
Butler, Erik. *Metamorphoses of the Vampire in Literature and Film: Cultural Transformations in Europe, 1732–1933*. Rochester: Camden House, 2010. Print.
Cojocaru, Daniel. *Violence and Dystopia: Mimesis and Sacrifice in Contemporary Western Dystopian Narratives*. Newcastle-upon-Tyne: Cambridge Scholars, 2015. Print.
del Toro, Guilermo. "Guilermo del Toro: The Strain Trilogy." YouTube, Available at http://www.youtube.com/watch?v=4-uVSGbQRIE. Web. 1 March, 2011.
del Toro, Guillermo, and Chuck Hogan. *The Fall*. London: Harper, 2010b. Print.
_____. *The Night Eternal*. London: Harper, 2011. Print.
_____. *The Strain*. London: Harper, 2010a (2009). Print.
Gardenour Walter, Brenda S. *Our Old Monsters: Witches, Werewolves and Vampires from Medieval Theology to Horror Cinema*. Jefferson, NC: McFarland, 2015. Print.
Gelder, Ken. *Reading the Vampire*. New York: Routledge, 2001. Print.
Halberstam, Judith. "Technologies of Monstrosity: Bram Stoker's Dracula." *Victorian Studies* 36.3 (1993): 333–52. Print.
Hughes, William. *Bram Stoker's Dracula: A Reader's Guide*. London: Continuum, 2009. Print.
Kaplan, Carter. "Dystopian Literature." *Literature and Politics Today: The Political Nature of Modern Fiction, Poetry, and Drama*. Ed. Keith M. Booker. Santa Barbara: ABC-CLIO, 2015. 93–95. Print.
Lamkin, Elaine. Interview. *Dread Central* 4 July 2009. Web. 2 Oct. 2015.
Lorrah, Jean. "Dracula Meets the New Woman." *The Blood Is the Life: Vampires in Literature*. Ed. Leonard G. Heldreth and Mary Pharr. Bowling Green: Bowling Green State University Popular Press, 1999. 31–442. Print.
Malchow, Harold L. *Gothic Images of Race in Nineteenth-Century Britain*. Stanford: Stanford University Press, 1996. Print.
Matheson, Richard. *I Am Legend*. 1954. London: Gollanz, 2007. Print.
Moretti, Franco. *Signs Taken for Wonders: Essays in the Sociology of Forms*. Trans. Susan Fischer, David Forgacs, and David Miller. London: Verso, 1988. Print.
Stoker, Bram. *Dracula*. 1897. London: Signet Classics, 1996. Print.
Wepman, Dennis. *American Experience: Immigration*. New York: Facts On File, 202. Print.
Wetmore, Kevin J. *Post-9/11 Horror in American Cinema*. London: Continuum, 2012. Print.
Wicke, Jennifer. "Vampiric Typewriting: Dracula and Its Media." *ELH* 59.2 (Summer 1992): 467–493. Print.

Here's Looking at You, Kids
The Urgency of Dystopian Texts in the Secondary Classroom

Michael A. Soares

As a secondary English teacher for over twenty years, I have had a front row seat for sweeping cultural and institutional changes affecting contemporary high school students. Situations frequently become more dire, and in the building where I teach there has been no lack of troubling incidents. Last spring, students endured several instances of "lockdown" as weapons were either brought to the high school or threats were made to do so. Security was intensified in the building (teachers were even compelled to participate in locker searches with law enforcement) resulting in a very unsettling set of circumstances for everyone involved, but particularly for the students. If the headlines are any indication, incidents such as these show no sign of slowing down, and circumstances demand that teachers make curriculum decisions to coexist with actual events. From my vantage, I have come to realize the necessity of using dystopian text as a tool to mediate these circumstances in the secondary classroom. According to Henry A. Giroux in *On Critical Pedagogy*,

> At this moment in history, it is more necessary than ever to register youth as a central theoretical, moral and political concern. Doing so reminds adults of their ethical and political responsibility to future generations and will further legitimate what it means to invest in youth as a symbol for nurturing civic imagination and collective resistance in response to the suffering of others [99].

In my classroom, I insist that dystopian texts be tied to the headlines, asking students to concurrently interact with both in-text and real-life circumstances. Although dystopian texts—by virtue of their nature—address the ills (or speculated future ills) of society, my work urges the "immediacy" of the text, necessitating that teachers adopt the role of navigator even as they overcome possible objections of the institution (in my case, the secondary school). Unfortunately, in my experience, agents of the institution (such as administrators) can be combative in response to students' resistance to security tactics in the building and to the teaching of texts informing students in my classroom. Likewise, the students themselves may become roadblocks as they resist the text, particularly in the face of recognizing the unpleasant reality of the dystopian qualities of their immediate surroundings.

The pedagogical stakes are high for students as they enter into the brave new world of the high school English classroom, and the exigency of dystopian texts in the curriculum has never been more apparent. Almost thirty years ago, Thomas W. Cooper wrote, "[I]t has never been more appropriate to consider *1984* as a warning" in his "Fictional *1984* and factual 1984," recognizing that "Orwell warns of the darker tendencies present within the human species, tendencies increasing serviced by global communications systems" as well as "overkill weaponry" (83). The trend has not slowed and current situations are even more complicated, demanding that English teachers not only employ dystopian text that is comprised of elements that position it to enhance the complex objectives of teaching literature, but recognize that in the early twenty-first century *dystopian text is urgently needed in the secondary classroom*. My argument promotes a belief that teachers, using innovative and theory-inspired curriculum design expedited through the use of dystopian text, can empower students to experience "the opening of a wider world of culture" (Scholes, *English After the Fall* 35). In 2017, teachers and students are entering new territory as the headlines reflect our dystopian fiction, making it imperative to remind ourselves that "our role and our subject are not cleanly detached from the world, but messily entangled with it" (Showalter 140). The foundation of this argument is organized and supported by a multi-pronged approach that addresses the immediacy of the text in relation to the specific circumstances of the secondary English classroom, the fulfillment of standards and curricular objectives put forth by agencies such as a school district and/or the Common Core, and the resistances encountered from both the institutional forces at hand (school administration, community, and so on) and from each individual student toward the text as he or she confronts the often unpleasant realities of life in the twenty-first century.

Secondary Students and Dystopian Text

On a gloomy morning in 2016, faculty, staff, and police officers greeted students at the various entrances of the high school building; for the first time in the school's history, a systematic bag check was to take place. Faculty and staff wore gloves while law enforcement officials wielded metal-detecting wands. Earlier that week, a scientific calculator had been found in a classroom with a typed message threatening to commit violence in the building. The school's initial response had been to hold an emergency staff meeting informing us of the circumstances of the threat; during the meeting, teachers were instructed to assist administrators and police as they searched lockers immediately after the students left the building for the day. During that time, lockers were opened, and teachers, without touching any of the lockers' contents, performed a visual screening for weapons. In addition, teachers were asked to volunteer to assist in the bag searches the next morning as students entered the building. Not surprisingly, the measures sent waves of reactions throughout the school community and hundreds of students called in or just stayed away from the building. The situation came a few weeks after another unsettling incident shook the school community: a case of online harassment had escalated, resulting in three students being arrested and charged for planning to bring a gun into the building. Although the students' plan never came to fruition, the matter generated negative headlines and contributed significantly to a sense of unrest in the building that, combined with the anonymous threat on the calculator, prompted the searches. While the two situations were not necessarily related, the high-profile events set off a series of reactions that provided a unique opportunity for the students to apply the critical analysis of dystopian texts and issues to immediate, real-world circumstances.

Elaine Showalter's "Teaching During Dark Times" essay in *Teaching Literature* offers a fascinating glimpse into the possibilities of introducing certain texts during tumultuous events. Showalter begins by describing how Louise Rosenblatt wrote *Literature as Exploration* in the "shadow of fascism" (132); she advises us that, when our interactions with students are "overtaken" by public events "terrible and historic," the event "produces the desire to communicate, and insofar as we are able, we should go with that desire and facilitate it [...]" (139). Dystopian fiction is a conduit to this type of communication, despite confirming Showalter's contention that "[o]ne of the most shattering discoveries of teaching in tragedy is that literature does not invariably offer the solace and the wisdom we claim for it" (138). Teachers and students are entering new territory as the headlines imitate our dystopian texts. I certainly will never forget trying to teach, and later simply tossing out lesson plans, to just be with students on September 11, 2001, the same way my junior high teacher spent the day discussing the bravery of the Challenger crew with us on January 28, 1986. However, I do not just interpret "dark times" to be singular events; I anticipate dark days ahead for our privacy as it slips away in the digital age, whether it is due to the internet, facial recognition technology in cameras on every street corner, GPS transmitters in our cell phones, or the NSA or any other agency collecting our personal information. Headlines decry the narrative of authoritarianism that informs much of the dystopian genre, and the students so far have instant and unlimited access to this media. Secondary English teachers therefore have a responsibility to harness the power of dystopian narratives to convey their messages in the hopes that "[t]he call to action that would force them to change their culture may be an alluring one despite the despair of the narrative" (Ostry 111).

My characterization of dystopian texts relies on M. Keith Booker's research; his work details genre features of dystopian texts that include futuristic totalitarian states functioning to reflect current social, political, and, in particular, technological, concerns. Booker writes,

> To be dystopian, a work needs to foreground the oppressive society in which it is set, using that setting as an opportunity to comment in some critical way on some other society, typically that of the author or the audience. In other worlds, the bleak dystopian world should encourage the reader or viewer to think critically about it, then transfer this critical thinking to his or her own world ["On Dystopia" 5].

In his introduction to *Dystopian Literature: A Theory and Research Guide*, Booker writes of dystopian literature as a "warning against the potential negative consequences of arrant utopianism" and "a critique of existing social conditions of political systems, or through the critical examination of the utopian premises upon which those conditions and systems are based or through the imaginative extension of those conditions and systems into different contexts that more clearly reveal their flaws and contradictions" (3). The dystopian text carries a gravitas of content that reflects the seriousness of the act of critical analysis, a complex achievement of focus for students who themselves are experiencing the defamiliarizing effects of adolescence. Adolescents are in the midst of establishing themselves as individuals and are drawn to dystopian texts where the "concept of the individual" is ultimately at stake; students developing their own individuality in society would no doubt experience a vicarious sense of autonomy in the resistance to the textual power of a fictional dystopian culture "seeking to strip everyone of it" (Soares 29). In this quest for individuality and agency, dystopian texts can be used to help facilitate the development of students' critical analysis skills.

The dystopian text anticipates "where we go wrong"; clearly, cultural and technological shifts have influenced how we interpret the world, and high school students at the doorstep of adulthood are among the most fundamentally exposed. In "Engaging 'Apolitical' Adolescents: Analyzing Popularity and Educational Potential of Dystopian Literature Post-9/11," Melissa Ames writes,

> Regardless of who or what deserves credit for rejuvenating this profitable subset of young adult literature, teenagers are reading these texts and are, therefore, sustaining

the market. Their enthusiastic engagement with these novels calls for revaluating the claims that this generation is apathetic when it comes to national and global issues [8].

The dystopian text is uniquely poised to facilitate this engagement for students; in fact, according to Balaka Basu, Katherine R. Broad and Carrie Hintz in their introduction to *Contemporary Dystopian Fiction for Yong Adults: Brave New Teenagers*, "YA dystopias are a vivid snapshot of contemporary cultural anxieties: what individuals and even the human species as a whole might have to fear in the future" (13). Based on the current appetite for dystopian texts and their advantageous topical conflation with headlines, the convergence of student willingness and critical thought is certainly primed for success in contemporary secondary classrooms, as they are "marked by their ambitious treatment of serious themes" (Basu et al 4). Furthermore, teachers should not be impeded by the "popularity" of a dystopian work. Jesse Stallings, in "Pop Pedagogy," urges us to "[e]mbrace and integrate popular works because they can enrich and enliven the English classroom, can solidify the connection between the literary analyses and devices and the 'real-world' in the students' minds, and can lead to a lifelong analyses of culture (high and low) by our students" (14).

The Defamiliarized Zone

Booker writes, "The principal technique of dystopian fiction is defamiliarization: by focusing their critiques of society on spatially or temporally distant settings, dystopian fictions provide fresh perspectives on problematic social and political practices that might otherwise be taken for granted or considered natural and inevitable" (*Impulse* 19). Envisioned through Booker's lens, dystopian works are ideal vehicles towards moving students out of their comfort zones and promoting sophisticated critical analysis in the secondary classroom. Booker continues, "The dystopian genre thus serves as a locus for valuable dialogues among literature, popular culture, and social criticism that indicates the value of considering these discourses together and potentially sheds new light on all of them" (*Impulse* 174). Maria Varsam, in "Concrete Dystopia: Slavery and its Others," explains, "Applied to dystopian fiction, defamiliarization makes us see the world anew, not as it is but as it *could* be; it shows the world in sharp focus in order to bring out conditions that exist already but which, as a result of our duller perception, we can no longer see" (206). As described, the defamiliarizing elements of a dystopian text positions it to enhance the complex objectives of teaching literature in the secondary classroom, carrying a sobriety of content that reflects the seriousness of the act of critical analysis by students in the midst of their own quests for individuality and agency.

The immediacy of the dystopian text is further perpetuated by the steady stream of additions to the YA dystopian text "canon" similar to popular series such as *The Hunger Games* and *Divergent* that are aimed at contemporary readers and designed to be read in the context of society's current issues. In "Teaching Dystopian Literature to a Consumer Class," Rachel Wilkinson suggests, "Dystopian visions can help students deconstruct their contexts, which is crucial now more than ever" (25). Sally Emmons writes similarly about her curriculum in "We're Not in Kansas Anymore": "My goal is to challenge students to examine human experience by looking at the human condition through literature and to recognize that our past is not understood in isolation, but in the context of broader trends and developments" (75). Emmons begins many of her courses with less complicated dystopian texts such as Ray Bradbury's *Fahrenheit 451* and *The Matrix* films, scaffolding dystopian characteristics and concerns into more complex, and not necessarily YA, texts such as *1984* and Alan Moore's *The Watchmen*. She observes that the texts share "one common thread" in their "presentation of dystopic societies in which characters are controlled through fear, propaganda, media, commercialism, religion, science and government" (75). As the popularity of YA dystopian text continues, the choices for secondary English teachers have expanded vastly. Emmons examines each to match the needs of the students, explaining, "What leads to the dystopia is different in each society, and this is where our in-class discussions begin. My methodology in designing our class discussions revolves around classic forms of artistic, historic, literary, and philosophic inquiry" (75).

Another aspect of dystopian text that promotes enriched reading experiences is its interdisciplinary nature; under the direction of a skilled teacher, dystopian text creates an environment in which students can participate in "content-specific expert groups engaged in deepening conversations about their subject's standards and brainstormed events from the novel that could support the teaching of a standard" (Saunders 44). For example, in an essay entitled "What *The Hunger Games* Can Teach Us about Disciplinary Literacy," Saunders describes the multiple disciplines intersecting within the text: "Among these were probability, ratios, and drawings of the arena (math); comparison between Panem and the United States; attributes of the civilization like laws, tools, and society (social studies); character analyses, writing alternate endings, comparing the book to other dystopic novels (language arts); and ecology and the environment, adaptation, categorizing species (science)" (44). The multiplicity of skills, perspectives, genres, and all other variables in the reading of dystopian text make the probability of strong connections for students more likely; the variety and timeliness of dystopian text, as technology and its implications for humanity reverberate in our media and in our daily lives, make its impact impossible for teachers and their students to ignore. Robert Scholes, in *Textual Power*, writes, "At some level we accept the truth of the ivory tower and secretly despise our own activities as trivial unless we can link them to a 'reality' outside of academic life" (5). My argument remains that curriculum must be shaped to accommodate this reality; likewise, theory and classroom practice must be symbiotic to mediate it.

Role of the Teacher

Clearly, great responsibility lies with the teacher in the effective facilitation of dystopian text; the most important role a teacher can play is providing opportunities to interact with the text in ways that promote students towards positive social and political change and/or action. For the high school educator making pedagogical and curricular decisions (while also navigating the often shifting political and social climate of the institution at hand), student familiarity with dystopian text can both inform and complicate decisions as to which dystopian texts should be selected for classroom use, what qualities these texts should possess, and the text's potential for the facilitation of critical analysis. I argue that high school teachers need to, in a sense, model the "heroics" of dystopian texts' protagonists for their students, with emphasis on students being aware of what is transpiring. Students, whether they like it or not, are invested in the system, even if they choose not to participate in the process. Teachers are betting that at least some students will rise to the challenge and that, "[b]leak though the future may be, young readers who may feel underpowered in the present can rehearse the role of liberator, saving the world from the maelstrom of destruction adults have set in motion" (Hill 101). High school students, at that critical juncture in life when they are discovering and setting into motion the adults they will become, clearly have much to gain from interaction with dystopian text.

Crag Hill, in "Dystopian Novels: What Imagined Futures Tell Young Readers about the Present and Future," writes, "Studying these novels will not only tap into what students are independently reading by the ream, but also engage adolescents in the core of their beings at a time when they are just beginning to envisage ways to live a meaningful life" (114). For many of these students, they will soon be on their way to institutions of higher learning, and dystopian texts can give them a head start; ultimately, the stakes for teachers arrive at the very soul of teaching: making the lives of our students, and therefore the world, better through education. Beach et al.'s *Teaching Literature to Adolescents* includes a compelling section that discusses "teacher roles in facilitating discussion" (88). As a secondary English teacher, I made connection to quotes that posited, "Post–September 11, 2001, literacy teachers need to be mindful of what is 'central to the literary process'" and "We need to help them read the world" (183). I believe in a democratic classroom where the teacher acts as a guide and the students are encouraged to discuss the results of their critical analysis not just of the text, but also with what informs their reading. In short, students are attempting "to read the world' as they grapple with text from a variety of sources and modes. 9/11 remains an important date for these students, even if they do not personally remember it, because it punctuated the post-modern tendency towards simultaneous consideration of multiple perspectives, not just in printed or digital text, but in an event which can also be "read." As students learn to read the world, teachers need to guide them as they reconcile readings into "a range of critical lenses for analyzing texts and interrogating the beliefs, attitudes, and ideological perspectives encountered in literature" (Beach et al., *Teaching Literature* back cover).

I agree with Ames that, "Many feel that young adult dystopias are written by authors in the hope that their messages will spark action amongst their teenage readers" (16). Likewise, Elaine Ostry, in "The Role of Young Adult Culture in Environmental Degradation," argues, "Writers call upon young adults to prevent the fictional futures from becoming a reality" (110). In the secondary classroom, teachers should document participants' viewpoints of a variety of social and political issues after studying dystopian text, identifying those "actions" that emerge in resistance to grim visions of a bleak future. While it is impossible to document participants' activities beyond the classroom walls, curriculum should call for teachers to ask students about their expected actions beyond the semester and in reaction to specific issues encountered in dystopian text, leading into their reactions in relation to current news items with dystopia-related headlines or subtext. Also under consideration could be any documentable evidence of emerging inclinations towards social or political activism, from online activity to community activity inside or outside of the school. Furthermore, since issues of technology are so prevalent in dystopian text, an examination of the trajectory of participants' relationships to technology both prior and subsequent to encountering particular texts, documenting any demonstrable shifts, is an important aspect to consider, and ironically easy to accomplish using standard classroom technology such as Blackboard or Moodle.

Brave New Pedagogy in the Secondary Classroom

Michael DeCesare, in "Casting a Critical Glance at teaching 'Critical Thinking,'" writes, "Critical thinking skills, as well as the abilities to read and write critically, are cornerstone ideals—if not demonstrable realities—of schooling" (73). He examines the Greek roots of the word *critic* and discusses how *kritikos* means "skilled in judging" or "able to make judgments and or discern," concluding that teachers wish "to teach our students the value of reason, empirical evidence, of logic, of thoughtfulness" (77). In *1984*, these same values are questioned, particularly as the protagonist, Winston Smith, endures the interrogation of Inner Party member O'Brien in Room 101, where the empirical evidence of two plus two, if Big Brother demands it, equals five. In the process of determining the qualities of critical thinking, DeCesare suggests that "teaching critical thinking skills is not a one-way street" because it requires consent as well as "a certain degree of willingness" (74). He further muses, "Maybe we can most effectively teach critical thinking skills by requiring students to analyze current stories" (77). The increasing appetite for dystopian text in all forms, including novels, films, video games, comics, and even concept albums to name a few, suggests that this willingness exists in abundance.

The role of the teacher is crucial, as secondary students need guidance to make critical analysis from among other perspectives, but also to see "discourse structures themselves in all their fullness and their power" (Scholes, *Textual Power* 144). Richard Beach, Amanda Haertling Thein, and Allen Webb discuss the distinction of "critical engagement" that "combines critical distance with immersion and emotional investment" (*Teaching to Exceed* 138). Critical engagement from this pedagogical perspective is vital because it encompasses much of the other frameworks available to students, such as those focusing on content, skills, processes/strategies, literacy practices and formalist activities (Beach et al., *Teaching to Exceed* 78): "Once students identify a problem or issue, you can help them contextualize or frame that issue in terms of the larger institutional, cultural, psychological, or economic forces" (Beach et al., *Teaching to Exceed* 140). Paulo Freire, in *Education for Critical Consciousness*, calls for "the special contribution of the educator" that results in "critical education which could help to form critical attitudes" (22). The effect of such new awareness compounds upon itself as students develop their "level of awareness of reality" that "touched upon other aspects of reality, which comes to be perceived in an increasingly critical manner" (Freire, *Pedagogy* 104). Teachers are instrumental in facilitating these transactions, identified by Booker as "a locus for valuable dialogues among literature, popular culture, and social criticism that indicates the value of considering these discourses together and potentially sheds new light on all of them" (*Impulse* 174).

English teachers must also have a sense of what is current to remain relevant to secondary students. Showalter writes, "Graduate training for the PhD should include training in pedagogy, and also in acting, performance and writing. Teachers should read contemporary literature, go to the theater and movies, watch television, write in all forms, and reflect on how all these activities contribute to what we do in class" (viii). She advocates a competency that includes multiple literacies to meet the pedagogical challenges of contemporary students. Complicit in this process is the explicit instruction of literary theory and metacognitive awareness of process in the secondary classroom. The dystopian text, by its very complex nature, necessitates the symbiosis of theory and practice leading students to critical analysis. By structuring curriculum to address these concerns, teachers can create a framework that allows them to effectively "stop teaching literature and start studying texts" (Scholes, *Textual Power* 16). Deborah Appleman, in *Critical Encounters in High School English*, addresses the concept of "text" by challenging teachers to view the idea of "adolescence" itself as a type of text. An "adolescents as text" metaphor presses teachers to be particularly concerned with the transaction of reader response and the pitfalls in relying on the "oversimplified" student response. Appleman writes that "[...] by recontextualizing reader response within a multi-theoretical framework, we can create a critical and comparative context that can help us use what is best about the lens of reader response and, at the same time, guard against its excesses by not having it be the only way we encourage students to respond to texts" (49).

Teaching Literature to Adolescents weighs in by embracing "Sociocultural Learning Theory" which focuses on "collective activity based on a shared goal" (9). Through practices such as posing questions, problem solving, and rereading, teachers and students can work collaboratively as they "grapple with difficulties in text" (15). The practices are explored as tools which are defined by "purpose and outcome" of which shareholders must achieve practical awareness (Beach et al. 17). The authors point out than as "Vygotsky (1978) argued, without a sense of its social purpose, a tool has no meaning" (17); therefore, teachers are prompted to develop curriculum with methodological context for their students. Furthermore, the authors promote discussion on understanding the "developing identities of students," particularly in relation to the challenges of adolescence (24). An important aspect of this task includes providing "safe" classrooms for students to explore "challenging" curriculum created by teachers who are invested in students developing "trust" (25). As students mature in their "stance," they will likely become more capable of rendering sophisticated analysis while reading, requiring the teachers to think boldly about what they are going to teach.

Ames writes, "Although it seems logical to assume that the popularity of these novels implies that their teenage readers are interested in the social commentary they build upon, this is a hard assumption to verify" (17). The impetus is therefore on capable and informed instructors to maximize the potential of dystopian text for secondary students because "strategic instruction often increases their overall impact" (Ames 16). For example, Ostry discusses how dystopian texts can signal a call to action for readers: "Hope primarily resides not in the books themselves, but in how profoundly young readers learn their environmental lessons" (110). Raffaella Baccolini and Tom Moylan, in their introduction to *Dark Horizons: Science Fiction and the Dystopian Imagination*, describe a recent trend towards "critical dystopia" that allows readers to "hope by resisting closure" in a space of "contestation and opposition" (7). My interest lies in the trajectory of the students' resistance from reading and critical analysis to action; in other words, how they demonstrate the impact of learning from dystopian text through their spaces of contestation and opposition and the resulting activities.

Rachel Wilkinson demonstrates this trajectory in "Teaching Dystopian Literature to a Consumer Class" when the author poses "discussion starters" for Aldous Huxley's *Brave New World* and M.T. Anderson's *Feed*, both novels which depict the unfettered purchasing power of its subjects, and seeks to elicit responses from students concerning the pitfalls of unbridled consumerism in our culture. Questions such as, "Is life easy for us today? Is it too easy? Is our nation too focused on consumerism?" and invitations such as "Give examples of how people escape. Is it necessary to do so? Why or why not?" cut to several core themes of dystopian texts' most important work (25). In my classroom, issues related to both technology and literacy are also frequently analyzed through the lens of dystopian text. Kristi McDuffie, in "Technology and Models of Literacy in Young Adult Dystopian Fiction," writes, "Productive approaches to technology and literacy include both old and new literacies and respect young adults as valued citizens and agents of change capable of mastering a variety of forms of communication and technology" (155). Ultimately, in the critical selection of dystopian text, I regard it essential that the dystopian texts under consideration for use in the secondary classroom be subject to a rigorous examination of how effectively it facilitates content—or how it can be used to facilitate content—to students.

In *Textual Power*, Scholes writes, "Literary theory and classroom practice are related as any 'pure' or theoretical study is related to applications in the same field" (18). While theory and practice can often seem divorced, particularly in a typical secondary English classroom, Scholes asserts, "I would argue that practice is never natural or neutral; there is always a theory in place, so that the first job of any teacher of criticism is to bring the assumptions that are in place out in the open for scrutiny" (*Textual Power* x–xi). Integral to his argument is the explicit instruction of criticism and his emphasis that it is important to "bring poetry, painting, and advertising into the same frame of reference, in order to discover their shared repertory of techniques and to expose whatever ideological complicity exists among them [...]" (*Textual Power* 76–77). "Ideological complicity" is important for theorizing about classroom application of dystopian texts, especially given their reliance on tropes such as authoritarian imagery and propaganda. As students encounter dystopian text, they are, as Scholes suggests, negotiating between their established ideologies and the power of the text to complicate their understandings towards critically rich textual experiences.

While Scholes uses Hemingway extensively to position theory, in my work I use Orwell to examine the dystopian text. For example, when Scholes writes about teaching an author like Hemingway who is "unsettling and repellent to women scholars as well as undergraduate women," he suggests making Hemingway's "sexual bias" a part of the study (*Textual Power* 59). Likewise, the dystopian text is by nature "unsettling" as its very framework is designed to present "repellent" political and social situations. Using Scholes' tactic, a teacher could explore the biases of Orwell, or, if focusing on adolescent dystopian literature, that of Lois Lowry (*The Giver*) or Suzanne Collins (*The Hunger Games*). He continues the question of whether to teach Hemingway at all if he is "offensive or uninteresting to women," answering, "school is the one place where our major concern is to study what we don't know, to confront Otherness rather than to ignore it [sic] but if we do confront and scrutinize this Otherness, we must criticize it" (59). Therefore, a study of dystopian text—that is, text that relies on its construction of calculated affronts to humanity—can facilitate the scrutiny of many "others" both in their representation in the text and how they are interpreted through a dystopian lens. Scholes adds, "[...] [W]hat the student needs from the teacher is help in seeing discourse structures themselves in all their fullness and their power" (*Textual Power* 144). By focusing on this synergy of textual knowledge and textual skills, the ideological complexity of the dystopian text can readily accomplish what Scholes offers as a solution: "the way to see one discourse is to see more than one" (*Textual Power* 144).

The ability to see discourses is contingent upon student knowledge, and according to Freire, "Knowledge is built up in the relations between human beings and the world, relations of transformation, and perfects itself in the critical problematization of those relations" (*Education* 96). For example, if students are "oppressed" by the system, as Freire's subjects were oppressed in his native Brazil, Freire demands, "The oppressed must see examples of the vulnerability of the oppressor so that a contrary conviction can begin to grow within them" (46). Giroux writes in *Theory and Resistance in Education: Towards a Pedagogy for the Opposition*, "The notion of ideology becomes a critical pedagogical tool when it is used to interrogate the relationship between the dominant school culture and the contradictory, lived experiences that mediate the texture of school life" (67). Such a transaction may not come without its detractions, as Emmons observed when her students "pushed themselves to think about the relationship of these texts to humanity today and it scared them" (80). One way to overcome this student resistance is by decentering authority, a process that can be difficult for students who have spent more than a decade adhering to the often strict social and political structures of the public school system. In *Teaching to Transgress*, bell hooks approaches the process by calling for "a cultural climate where biases can be challenged and changed, all border crossings must be seen as valid and legitimate" (131). She describes a classroom scenario where students "accept the shift in locus of representation but resist shifting ways they think about ideas. That is threatening" (144). hooks insists that through "critical interrogation," even with its risks, that "the crossings of the powerful into the terrains of the powerless will not perpetuate existing structures" (144).

Let Them Eat Tests

When adolescent students are studying dystopian texts, they are considering issues as complex as "'Can society survive without basic freedoms and emotions?' or 'Is culture so constantly redefining what is necessary that we must slow down and take account of our lives?'" (Soares 29). Frankly, these issues for most students, whether they realize it or not, are evident in their classrooms. In "*1984* and Education as Commodity Spectacle," Attick argues that "our current education policy promotes a narrowly defined idea of education" that "increasingly confines and disempowers teachers and students within a strictly controlled public education system" (202). For both teachers and students, the cruel irony is that an increasingly totalitarian climate of education is an opposing force to the objectives of dystopian text. Attick continues, "These current policies and initiatives undermine individual autonomy and agency thorough an institutionalized focus on standardization, accountability, and bureaucratic control" (202). Perhaps not so ironically, "standardization" is a common concern in many dystopian texts. David J. Lorenzo, in *Cities at the End of the World,* relates standardization to "impoverishment" in *1984,* suggesting that Orwell saw such uniformity of Oceania's citizens as condemning them to a "physically impoverished existence," making them easier to control (165).

Peter Mclaren, in *Life in Schools: An Introduction to Critical Pedagogy in the Foundations of Education,* agrees with Giroux that "a critical and affirming pedagogy has to be constructed around the stories that people tell, the ways in which students and teachers author meaning, and the possibilities that underlie the experiences that shape their voices" (244). However, Giroux also addresses the "hidden curriculum" and the ideology inherent in mandated curriculum that pushes back against teachers' autonomy in making pedagogical choices; this is apparent in the contradictions of selecting dystopian texts which challenge "dominant culture" (*Theory and Resistance in Education* 66). The author suggests, "The notion of ideology becomes a critical pedagogical tool when it is used to interrogate the relationship between the dominant school culture and the contradictory, lived experiences that mediate the texture of school life" (*Theory and Resistance in Education* 67). My argument is that this "interrogation" must also examine the ulterior corporate motives of the standardization of public education.

In his chapter titled "The Corporate Assault on Education," McLaren illuminates the commodification of learning and its influence on the public school system, resulting in "school success" determined by students' scores in high-stakes standardized testing; furthermore, there has been a demonstrable "unwillingness of many administrators to fight against" such testing (50). Likewise, in *Teaching to Exceed Common Core*, the authors acknowledge that English teachers are facing a mandated increase in non-fictional, workplace-type reading and writing, as well as the ties of the Common Core State Standards (CCSS) to the textbook industry and the unfortunate (for both teachers and students) connections to standardized testing (the "let them eat tests" mentality) (16). The authors pair theory to practice in ways to meet the standards, ranging from reclaiming "literacy" back from those who envision it as merely standardized test practice, to the importance of teaching students to be competent in multiple literacies. While they acknowledge that "you may need to adopt your school's curriculum mandates tied to the Common Core State Standards," teachers can still "develop innovative ways of teaching that curriculum by framing the construction of your classroom affinity space as itself the curriculum" (7). The authors describe how choosing texts is fundamental to the success of a particular classroom, critiquing that while the CCSS is designed to push students toward more complex text, "complexity" is ill-defined and there may be little to no articulation between "bands" or "grade-levels" of the standards (87). In addition, they discuss the distinction of "critical engagement" which "combines critical distance with immersion and emotional investment" (38). The role of the teacher in this transaction is this: "Once students identify a problem or issue, you can help them contextualize or frame that issue in terms of the larger institutional, cultural, psychological, or economic forces" (140).

Integral to this text choosing is evaluating the needs of the students; in my practice, I immediately think of *1984* or *Brave New World*, texts which are accessible to my secondary students, but also can be read on a multitude of levels of increasing complexity as the unit progresses. These texts also easily build upon the students' prior knowledge of dystopian texts, capitalizing thematically on novels such as Lois Lowry's *The Giver* or *The Hunger Games*, texts that are a force to "foster the literacy practices" of "identifying issues" and "critiquing systems" (90). Furthermore, the texts lend themselves to critically engaging activities and projects that encourage students to reflect on their own identities and inject their reading transactions into text of their own construction. As a veteran high school teacher, I can think of no better advice than to at least attempt to stay relevant with students. Although teachers are clearly not always going to have their fingers on the pulse of what students are "into," having at least some context provides opportunities to connect whatever students are learning with what they already know. Jane M. Saunders, in "What *The Hunger Games* Can Teach Us about Disciplinary Literacy," after noticing that students were obsessively reading *The Hunger Games* surreptitiously in class, observes that "we have a moral imperative to pursue different avenues for making some of these complex concepts more accessible to students, so they can realize their potential in an era of standardized testing" (47). Likewise, Giroux insists that "educators at all levels of schooling should be addressed as public individuals willing to connect pedagogy with the problems of public life, a commitment to civic courage, and the demands of social responsibility" (*On Critical Pedagogy* 6).

Wayne Au, in *Critical Curriculum Studies: Education, Consciousness, and the Politics of Knowing*, demonstrates how curriculum can, in fact, repress segments of the student population and how it can in turn be restructured to achieve the opposite effect. A former social studies and language arts teacher, Au brings to the table a vast experience of opposites: integrated versus non-integrated curriculum, privileged versus marginalized students, actual secondary classroom practice versus ivory tower theory. Working from frameworks of epistemology and standpoint theory, Au presents an academic study of the politics of curriculum, analyzing both its application in the classroom and the forces that shape its creation. Following the trajectory of a "curriculum of the oppressed" (3), he investigates curriculum study from the "consciousness" of critical reflection and how it informs praxis. Au quotes Freire who suggests that there is a concrete relationship between critical reflection and "education for freedom," emphasizing curriculum which recognizes "relationships with the world" (24). These components are essential to framing concerns with "how meaning is communicated and who has control over what happens in classroom discourse" (43).

Big Brother Is Watching

Unfortunately, if not predictably at this point, the secondary educational system is often suspicious of the progressive pedagogy involved in teaching dystopian text. Kerry Freedman, in "An Aesthetic of Horror in Education: Schools as Dystopian Environments," describes the dilemmas:

> The dystopian educational system of constricted curriculum, mechanistic learning, and standardized assessments are supported by the dystopian visual and kinesthetic environment in school. Without opportunities to create, what chance do students have to imagine alternative worlds? How are they to create better futures? [11].

The situation is so dire that Showalter feels moved to explain, "[A]s teachers, we are not in competition with each other" (9); unfortunately, I have to disagree with that statement for secondary teachers in public school systems, as one of the legacies of No Child Left Behind is the restructuring of the profession to put teachers in direct competition with each other in respects to high stakes testing and performance evaluations reliant upon those scores. New evaluations in Illinois based upon the Danielson model rank teachers in a system used when determining which employee to lay off in a reduction-of-force situation. While tenure previously protected teachers, these evaluations have effectively eradicated seniority, and those of us who have been in a school system for years and have become expensive should watch out.

I measure the changes wrought by No Child Left Behind and its successor Race to the Top against two decades of experience in the classroom, watching with morbid curiosity at what continued havoc the proposed Every Child Achieves Act might create for my curriculum and, more importantly, my students. However, instead of simply bemoaning the state of affairs and teaching in secret, I use the political ebb and flow of education policy to invigorate my teaching of dystopian texts. Attick also makes this connection when he asserts, "Education policy today can be understood as a convergence of Orwellian notions of control (bureaucrats rely on various forms of surveillance to monitor student and teacher performance via testing)" (205). He couples bureaucratic control with the idea of spectacle, writing, "These initiatives demonstrate the essence of using language in forging political spectacle, or in this case, an educational spectacle" (207). When discussing Race to the Top, Attick draws attention to issues of language and propaganda—central themes in texts like *1984*, arguing,

> Within these federal initiatives are phrases such as "meeting benchmarks," "showing continuous improvement," and the behavioral and performance characteristics of "good" teachers verses "bad" teachers. All of these terms are laden with standardizing images of what it means to learn, to teach, to be validated within education. All of these terms are also ambiguous, and each is used to forge the education spectacle [208].

Secondary teachers watching the spectacle unfold have the choice to either placidly allow the autonomy of their classrooms to dissipate, or to demonstrate the intellectual pushback advocated by dystopian texts (the same responses we hope for in our students) by illuminating for them the dystopian thread in the system and how it relates to the classroom texts. Consider this statement from Attick: "Through the use of technologies such as standardized testing instruments and data-driven teacher assessment tools, our current education policies force teachers and students into Orwellian educational landscape not unlike the administered environment Winston Smith rebels against throughout *1984*" (209). Explaining arguments such as these, in the context of a novel such as *1984* or a graphic novel/film like *V for Vendetta*, could be a very powerful pedagogical tool indeed.

In "Against Schooling: Education and Social Class," Aronowitz addresses pedagogical applications of media and popular culture which has "called into question the separation of the public and private spheres" and challenges "the notion that autonomous private life any longer exists" (12). He acknowledges a contemporary sense of "Big Brother" when "the government now announces openly its intention to subject every telephone and computer to surveillance" and warns that "it is difficult to avoid the conclusion that media are a crucial source of education and may, in comparison to schools, exercise a greater influence on children and youth" (12). Giroux also warns, "The crisis of youth is symptomatic of the crisis of democracy, and as such it hails us as much for the threat that it poses as for the challenges and possibilities it invokes" (*On Critical Pedagogy* 99). The challenge, therefore, is for progressive educators to harness the power of media to serve classroom purposes, which may be an uphill battle in school districts where teachers have little autonomy and where curriculum may be under a Big Brother–ish system of its own.

Without question, our secondary students face unprecedented levels of uncertainty about the world around them, and our end goal is to equip them with the critical thinking skills to both understand and contend with the dystopian challenges they will face. Secondary teachers, in response, can inspire students' action through the dystopian text in spite of authoritarian systems. Nevertheless, Moylan cautions, "The emancipated future, however, will not be reached by utopian dreaming alone. The way forward involves personal and collective effort" (204). As I enter my third decade of teaching English as a committed instructor of dystopian text, I remain inspired by Hill, who advocates, "As teachers, we must understand why students are fascinated with these stories, helping them find ways to think through the issues they raise. What can I do to prevent such a world? How can we survive? How can we remain human?" (101).

Works Cited

Ames, Melissa. "Engaging 'Apolitical' Adolescents: Analyzing the Popularity and Educational Potential of Dystopian Literature Post-9/11." *The High School Journal* 97.1 (2013): 3–20. Print.

Appleman, Deborah. *Critical Encounters in High School English* 2nd ed. New York: Teachers College P, 2009. Print.

Aronowitz, Stanley. "Against Schooling: Education and Social Class." *Social Text* (2004): 13–36. British Library Document Supply Centre Inside Serials & Conference Proceedings. Web. 12 Nov. 2017. Print.

Attick, Dennis. "Orwell's *1984* and Education as Commodity Spectacle." *Dystopia & Education: Insights into Theory, Praxis and Policy in an Age of Utopia-Gone-Wrong*. Eds. Jessica A. Heybach and Eric. C. Sheffield. Charlotte, NC: Information Age Publishing, 2013. 201–212. Print.

Au, Wayne. *Critical Curriculum Studies Education, Consciousness, and the Politics of Knowing*. New York: Taylor & Francis, 2012. Print.

Baccolini, Raffaella, and Tom Moylon. "Introduction." *Dark Horizons: Science Fiction and the Dystopian Imagination*. Ed. Raffaella Baccolini and Tom Moylon. New York: Routledge, 2003. 1–12. Print.

Basu, Balaka, Katherine R. Broad, and Carrie Hintz. "Introduction." *Contemporary Dystopian Fiction for Young Adults: Brave New Teenagers*. New York: Routledge, 2013. 1–15. Print.

Beach, Richard, Amanda Haertling Thein, and Allen Webb. *Teaching to Exceed the English Language Arts Common Core State Standards*. New York: Routledge, 2012. Print.

Beach, Richard, et al. *Teaching Literature to Adolescents*. New York: Routledge, 2006. Print.

Booker, M. Keith. *The Dystopian Impulse in Modern Literature: Fiction as Social Criticism*. Westport, CT: Praeger, 1994. Print.

_____. *Dystopian Literature: A Theory and Research Guide*. Westport, CT: Greenwood Press, 1994. Print.

_____. "On Dystopia." *Critical Insights: Dystopia*. Ed. M. Keith Booker. Ipswich, MA: Salem Press, 2013. 1–15. Print.

Cooper, Thomas W. "Fictional *1984* and Factual *1984*." *The Orwellian Moment: Hindsight and Foresight in the Post-1984 World*. Ed. Robert L. Savage, James Combs, and Dan Nimmo. Fayetteville: University of Arkansas Press, 1989. Print.

DeCesare, Michael. "Casting a Critical Glance at Teaching Critical Thinking." *Pedagogy and the Human Sciences* 1.1 (2009): 73–77. Print.

Emmons, Sally. "We're Not in Kansas Anymore." *Fantasy Media in the Classroom*. Ed. Emily Dial-Driver, Sally Emmons, and Jim Ford. Jefferson, N.C.: McFarland, 2012. 74–87. Print.

Freedman, Kerry. "An Aesthetic of Horror in Education: Schools as Dystopian Environments." *Dystopia & Education: Insights into Theory, Praxis and Policy in an Age of Utopia-Gone-Wrong*. Eds. Jessica A. Heybach and Eric. C. Sheffield. Charlotte, N.C.: Information Age Publishing, 2013. 3–14. Print.

Freire, Paulo. *Education for Critical Consciousness*. London: Bloomsbury, 2013. Print.

_____. *Pedagogy of the Oppressed*. New York: Penguin, 1996. Print.

Giroux, Henry A. *On Critical Pedagogy*. New York: Continuum, 2011. Print.

_____. *Theory and Resistance in Education: Towards a Pedagogy for the Opposition*. Westport, CT: Bergin & Garvey, 2001. Print.

Hill, Crag. "Dystopian Novels: What Imagined Futures Tell Young Readers About the Present and Future." *Teaching Young Adult Literature Today*. Ed. Judith A. Hayn and Jeffrey S. Kaplan. Lanham, MD: Rowman and Littlefield, 2012. 99–116. Print.

hooks, bell. *Teaching to Transgress*. New York: Routledge, 1994. Print.

Lorenzo, David J. *Cities at the End of the World: Using Utopian and Dystopian Stories to Reflect Critically on Our Political Beliefs, Communities, and Ways of Life*. London: Bloomsberry Academic, 2014. Print.

McDuffie, Kristi. "Technology and Models of Literacy in Young Adult Dystopian Fiction." *Contemporary Dystopian Fiction for Young Adults: Brave New Teenagers*. Ed. Balaka Basu, Katherine R. Broad, and Carrie Hintz. New York: Routledge, 2013. 189–201. Print.

McLaren, Peter. *Life in Schools: An Introduction to Critical Pedagogy in the Foundations of Education*. 5th ed. Boston: Pearson, 2007. Print.

Moylan, Tom. "Conclusion." *Demand the Impossible: Science Fiction and the Utopian Imagination*. New York: Methuen, 1986. 196–213. Print.

Ostry, Elaine. "The Role of Young Adult Culture in Environmental Degradation." *Contemporary Dystopian Fiction for Young Adults: Brave New Teenagers*. Ed. Balaka Basu, Katherine R. Broad, and Carrie Hintz. New York: Routledge, 2013. 101–114. Print.

Saunders, Jane M. "What *The Hunger Games* Can Teach Us About Disciplinary Literacy." *English Journal* 103.3 (2014): 41–47. Print.

Scholes, Robert. *English After the Fall.* Iowa City: University of Iowa Press, 2011. Print.
_____. *Textual Power: Literary Theory and the Teaching of English.* New Haven: Yale University Press, 1985. Print.
Showalter, Elaine. *Teaching Literature.* New York: Wiley-Blackwell, 2003. Print.
Soares, Michael. "Grim Visions in the Classroom: Dystopian Texts and Adolescent Readers." *SIGNAL Journal* 36.2 (Fall 2012/Winter 2013): 27–30. Print.
Stallings, Jesse. "Pop Pedagogy." *Fantasy Media in the Classroom.* Ed. Emily Dial-Driver, Sally Emmons and Jim Ford. Jefferson, N.C.: McFarland, 2012. 74–87. Print.
Varsam, Maria. "Concrete Dystopia: Slavery and Its Others." *Dark Horizons: Science Fiction and the Dystopian Imagination.* Ed. Raffaella Baccolini and Tom Moylan. New York: Routledge, 2003. 203–24. Print.
Wilkinson, Rachel. "Teaching Dystopian Literature to a Consumer Class." *English Journal* 93.3 (2010): 22–26.

About the Contributors

Ashley G. **Anthony** is an associate instructor of English at Maryville University in Missouri. She earned her MA in English from the University of Missouri–St. Louis. She has published numerous articles and book reviews and presented at conferences around the Midwest. Her research interests are dystopian fiction, Frederick Douglass and Victorian women's literature.

Simon **Bacon** is an independent scholar based in Poznan, Poland. He has coedited books on various subjects, including *Undead Memory* and *Little Horrors*. His monograph, *Becoming Vampire*, came out in 2016, and he is editing the forthcoming volume *A Gothic Reader*.

Matthew **Bardowell** received his Ph.D. from Saint Louis University and is an assistant professor of English at Missouri Baptist University. His research interests include Old Norse and Old English poetry as well as the works of J.R.R. Tolkien, C.S. Lewis and their literary circle. His work has appeared in *Renascence*, *Journal of the Fantastic in the Arts* and *Mythlore*.

Jane **Beal** is an associate professor of English at the University of La Verne in California. She earned her Ph.D. from the University of California, Davis. She is the author of *The Signifying Power of Pearl* and *John Trevisa and the English Polychronicon*, editor of *Illuminating Moses*, and coeditor of *Translating the Past* and *Approaches to Teaching the Middle English Pearl*.

Alissa **Burger** is an assistant professor of English and director of Writing Across the Curriculum at Culver-Stockton College in Missouri, where she teaches courses in research, writing, and literature. She is the author of *The Wizard of Oz as American Myth* and editor of *The Television World of Pushing Daisies*.

Harold K. **Bush** is a professor of English at Saint Louis University and the author of *The Hemingway Files* and *Continuing Bonds with the Dead*. He is also the editor of *The Letters of Mark Twain and Joseph H. Twichell*.

Megan E. **Cannella** is a doctoral student at the University of Nevada, Reno. She has published several scholarly essays, including "Do Androids Dream of Derrida's Cat?," "The Pain and Prison of Post–9/11 Parenting in Jonathan Franzen's *Freedom*," and "Unreliable Physical Places and Memories as Posthuman Narration in Ishiguro's *Never Let Me Go*."

About the Contributors

Jillian L. **Canode** earned her Ph.D. from Purdue University and teaches philosophy at Owens Community College in Ohio. Her research focuses on popular culture, feminism, Marxism, speculative young adult literature and philosophy for children. She has published on *Supernatural* and *Sherlock*, as well as the *Divergent* trilogy.

Deirdre **Flynn** earned her Ph.D. from Mary Immaculate College and is a Teaching Fellow in modern drama in the school of English, drama and film at University College Dublin. She has lectured at the undergraduate and postgraduate levels in English literature and in drama and theatre studies.

Andrew **Hammond** is a senior lecturer in English literature at the University of Brighton in England. His research interests include Cold War literature, post–1945 British fiction, postcolonial writing and theory and cross-cultural representation. He has authored over thirty academic articles and eight books, including *British Fiction and the Cold War*.

John J. **Han** is a professor of English and creative writing and chair of the humanities division at Missouri Baptist University in St. Louis. He earned his Ph.D. from the University of Nebraska–Lincoln. He is the author, editor, coeditor or translator of 18 books, including *Wise Blood*, *The Final Crossing* and *Maple-Colored Moon*, and his poems have appeared in numerous journals and anthologies.

Melanie A. **Marotta** is a lecturer in the Department of English and Language Arts at Morgan State University in Maryland, where she earned her Ph.D. in English. Her research interests include science fiction, the American West, contemporary African American literature and ecocriticism.

Robyn N. **Rowley** is a doctoral student in English literary and cultural studies at Carnegie Mellon University in Pennsylvania. She writes about contemporary fiction, film, pop culture, and digital media and gender and sexuality. She has presented on topics ranging from the Riot grrrl movement to the Joss Whedon series *Firefly*.

Michael A. **Soares** is a Ph.D. candidate in English at Illinois State University and has taught in high school and college classrooms for over 20 years. His dissertation focuses on the urgency and impact of dystopian texts in the secondary classroom. Other research interests include the rhetoric and globalization of superheroes.

C. Clark **Triplett** is the vice president of graduate studies and academic program review, as well as a professor of psychology/sociology at Missouri Baptist University. He earned his Ph.D. from Saint Louis University. He is coeditor of *The Final Crossing* and has published numerous articles and book reviews. His haiku have appeared in the *Asahi Haikuist Network* and *Fireflies' Light*.

Natasha W. **Vashisht** is an assistant professor of English at St. Stephen's College, University of Delhi, India. She received her Ph.D. from Punjab University and specializes in modern European drama and twentieth-century British literature. Her interests include European comic traditions and contemporary humor studies.

Wes **Yeary** is a graduate teaching assistant at the University of South Dakota, where he teaches composition and literature where he earned MA. His research interests include familial and theological elements in contemporary American literature. He is working on his Ph.D. dissertation, and this essay is his first publication.

Index

aggression 41–42, 47, 50–51, 53–54, 80; *see also* violence
Aldridge, Alexandra 83*n*5, 84
alliance 123, 129–130
Alter, Alexandra 1, 13
alternates 17–18, 20, 22, 153
Ames, Melissa 228–229, 232, 234–235, 241
Anderson, M.T. 10, 139–140, 143, 149, 164, 166–169, 171–173, 176, 177, 235
anti-Semitism 214–215
apocalypse, apocalyptic 8, 11, 42, 63, 88–90, 95, 97–99, 105, 150, 210–213, 222–223; *see also* post-apocalyptic
archery 125
Artemis, Artemisian 125, 134, 136–137*n*10
Athens 125
Atwood, Margaret 1, 4–5, 7, 12, 15–27, 30, 135*n*3
audience 5, 15, 23, 37, 112, 131, 135*n*3, 140, 148–149, 150–153, 157–161, 166, 171, 175, 228
Augustine, St. 3, 92, 98, 181, 195
authoritarianism 42, 47, 228, 236, 241

Baccolini, Raffaella 14, 17, 22, 27, 235, 242, 243
Bachman, Richard 10, 150–151, 155–156, 159–161
bad guys 89–90; *see also* good guys
Barry, Kevin 8, 12, 56–68
Beelzebub 48, 50–51, 55
Berry, Wendell 102, 109
Beville, Maria 60, 64, 68
Big Brother 67, 233, 239, 241
body 9, 33, 50, 52, 61, 94, 123, 132, 136*n*8, 145–146, 168, 185, 188, 191, 199, 212, 214, 216
Booker, M. Keith 12, 14, 71, 85, 151, 161, 208, 209, 224, 228–229, 233, 242

"Bread and circuses" 124, 129
"Bread and roses" 129–130, 136*n*7
British Empire 216, 224
brother's keeper 90–91, 93, 97–98

California 12, 196–204
capitalism 12, 40, 69, 77, 139–140, 142–148, 164, 166, 170, 173, 202; *see also* communism
Cavalcanti, Ildney 6, 14
choice 17, 24, 25, 31, 35, 40–41, 48, 58, 68, 81, 84*n*14, 104, 111, 116, 118–119, 127, 134, 142, 144, 145, 146, 153, 156, 167, 175, 184, 197, 204, 205, 208, 216, 219, 230, 231, 237, 240
Christian ethics 9, 122–124, 127; *see also* ethics
cityscape 56, 63, 65, 67–68
class 6, 13, 58, 63–64, 72, 74–75, 77, 79, 82, 83*n*8, 84*n*13, 85, 86, 128, 130, 132, 134, 142, 146, 159, 174, 201, 216, 221, 241
classical learning 9, 122–124
Cojocaru, Daniel 222, 224
Coliseum 124–125, 132
Collins, Suzanne 1, 9, 12, 122–137, 151, 236
colonization 42–44, 57, 62, 79, 198, 211, 217–219; *see also* postcolonization; reverse colonization
communication 15, 21, 57, 68, 120, 129, 164, 166–172, 173, 199, 211, 220, 226–227, 235
communism 12, 13*n*1, 47, 50, 69, 72, 149, 220; *see also* capitalism
community 15–18, 20, 22, 26, 46, 73, 76, 81–82, 107, 111–112, 115–121, 148, 154, 157–158, 161, 179, 196–201, 204–208, 224*n*10, 226–227, 232
competition 10, 126, 150–157, 159–160, 161*n*3, 176, 240

Index

Consilience, Consilience-Positron 7, 15–26
consumerism, consumption 8, 10, 16, 71, 73, 79–80, 82, 139–144, 146–147, 148–149, 155, 164, 166–167, 171, 213, 221–223, 235
contagion 211–214, 216, 220–223
control 2, 4, 7, 13n1, 16–18, 20–25, 29–35, 37–38, 45, 48, 51, 53–54, 59, 96, 116–117, 119–120, 128, 140, 145–146, 152, 155–156, 158, 160, 178, 180, 185, 203–204, 211–214, 217, 220, 230, 237, 240
critical analysis 9, 227–229, 231–235
curriculum design 13n1, 225–226, 230–232, 234, 237–241, 242
cyberpunk 8, 11, 56, 58, 201–202, 205–209; see also postcyberpunk

darkness 24, 44–45, 49–50, 54, 58, 59, 60, 61, 62, 100, 102, 103, 136, 142, 147, 152, 153, 155, 156, 160, 161, 162, 172, 178, 188, 211, 215, 216, 226, 227, 235, 242, 243
Darwin, Charles 40–41, 52, 55
deception 9, 21, 111–112, 119, 122, 130
decolonization 79
defamiliarization 228–229
del Toro, Guillermo 11–12, 210–211, 213, 214–216, 219, 221–222, 224
democracy 47, 69, 241
Derdiger, Paula 8, 72–73, 78, 83n7, 85
despair 15, 41, 48, 105, 160, 228; see also hope; hopelessness
Dev, Amiya 49, 55
digital dystopia, digital dystopian 10, 12, 163–173, 175–176
digital labor 164, 167–168, 177
digital technology 164–176
Dimopoulos, Elaine 10, 139, 142–143, 149
disaster 2, 4, 74, 98, 196–198
discovery of a new world 9, 40, 89, 122–124
District 12 124–125, 127, 130, 133
domestic 15–16, 19, 52
doppelgänger 61, 66–67
"double action" 6–7, 113–114
dystopic femininity 15–16, 18–19, 22–23, 26, 125, 134, 136–137

Eggers, Dave 10, 164, 166–168, 171–174, 176–177
Elliott, Robert C. 83n4, 85
emojis 171, 177
empathy 10, 38, 92–93, 98, 131–132, 139, 147–149, 154, 157
empire 42, 84–87, 216–217, 219, 224
environment 2, 11, 58, 73, 104, 122–123, 135n2, 140, 148, 156, 163, 196–198, 201, 203–204, 206, 209, 211, 214, 230, 232, 235, 239, 241, 242
ethics 9, 30–31, 42, 83n3, 97, 122–124, 127, 162; see also Christian ethics
evil 22, 41, 48, 50–51, 54, 65, 111, 158, 161n4
evolution 40, 42–43, 220

Fand, Roxanne J. 26, 27
fantasy 36, 60, 71, 79, 83, 95–96, 136–137, 141, 144, 168, 178, 195, 242, 243
fashion 60, 79, 140, 142–143
Felski, Rita 9, 105, 108–109, 112, 114–115, 120–121
feminism, feminist 6, 9, 13n2, 16–19, 22–23, 26, 27, 122–128, 135n2, 135n3, 137, 215, 223n7, 224
feminist dystopian fiction 9, 122–123, 127, 135n3
Ferns, Chris 72, 85
flaneur 64–66
forgiveness 131, 136, 138
freedom 2, 9, 16, 31–32, 40, 73, 101, 118–121, 123, 125, 128, 132, 172, 197, 203–204, 206–207, 209, 237, 239
Freud, Sigmund 40–41, 43, 45–47, 53–55, 64, 110, 112–113, 121
Fromm, Erich 42, 48, 50, 53, 55

game show 57, 153, 156, 161
gender 7, 13, 16–17, 19, 25–27, 85, 209
genre 3, 9–13, 17, 26, 27, 59–60, 70–72, 78, 83n4, 85, 86, 122, 124, 127, 148, 151, 163–166, 169, 171, 176–178, 202, 205, 228–230
Gibson, William 11, 196–200, 202, 206–208, 209
gladiator 124–127, 137
Glissant, Édouard 19–21, 27
God, god 3, 8–9, 34, 40, 43, 51, 88–97, 100–101, 104, 108, 109, 110, 125, 126, 127–128, 136n6, 181, 195, 200; see also Messiah, Messianic, Messianism; religion
Golding, William 8, 12, 40–45, 48, 50, 52, 54–55, 178
good guys 89–92; see also bad guys
gothic 56–57, 60–61, 64–68, 161, 214–215, 224
Gottlieb, Erika 71, 85, 155, 161, 166, 177
Graedon, Alena 10, 164, 166–168, 170–171, 173, 175–177
greed 37, 148, 164, 168, 172–173, 215, 222

Haymitch 126, 129, 132–134
Hermeneutic of suspicion 9, 108, 111–115, 119–121
Hicks, Jeff 56, 58, 68

Hogan, Chuck 11–12, 210–211, 213–216, 219, 221–222, 224n10
Holocaust 42, 211–212, 217, 221
homogenization 77, 83, 201, 210
hope 4, 9–10, 12, 13n1, 17, 23–24, 26, 36–37, 82, 88–92, 94–95, 97–98, 102, 104–106, 108–109, 110, 123–124, 135–136n5, 136n8, 137, 139, 143, 147–149, 158, 164, 190, 199, 208, 210, 213, 228, 232, 235, 240; *see also* despair; hopelessness
hopelessness 15, 25, 91, 97; *see also* despair; hope
human *Humanae vitae* 33, 38, 39
human condition 42, 202, 230
human depravity 8, 40–41
human rights 9, 123, 128, 132
hybrid(izing) 8, 16, 57, 60, 67, 122, 124, 127, 207, 223n1

identity 5, 8, 11, 18–25, 27, 32–34, 57, 60, 67, 68, 75–77, 79–80, 84n14, 84n15, 84n17, 85, 94, 97, 118, 142, 144, 148, 149, 197–198, 205–206, 208, 210
immigrants 81, 83, 170, 177, 198, 200, 210–212, 217–219, 224n8, 224n10
internet 165–168, 171, 177, 220, 227
irrational, irrational will 43, 48

James, William 104–106, 110
Jameson, Fredric 6, 14, 70, 83n4, 85
Joan of Arc 127, 131
journey 9, 11, 66, 72–73, 91, 101, 105, 109, 123, 131, 198, 217
Judeo-Christian ethics 127
Judeo-Christian morality 122
justice 3, 69, 73, 77, 80, 122–123, 128, 133, 152, 155, 158–159, 174–175, 179–182, 192–194
Juvenal 124, 137

Kant, Immanuel 11, 182–185, 191, 193, 195n2
King, Stephen 10, 150–153, 159, 160–162
Kumar, Krishan 83n3, 85

labyrinth 59, 65, 125
LaCapra, Dominick 95, 99
Latham, Rob 56, 58, 68
Lewis, Arthur O. 83n5, 86
Lewis, C.S. 11–12, 71, 86, 178–186, 188–190, 192–195
linguistic disintegration 168–171
literacy 85, 161, 177, 230–231, 233, 235, 238–239, 242
London, Alexander 10, 139, 144, 146–147, 149
Low, Gail 79, 84n16, 86

Lowry, Lois 2, 5, 9, 12, 111, 115, 117–121, 236, 238
Luddism 164, 173
Lyotard, Jean-François 8, 56, 64, 68, 104

MacInnes, Colin 8, 69–70, 72–76, 78–79, 81–86
maps 9, 99, 100–109
martyr, martyrdom 36, 125–127, 131, 138
Marx, Marxism 19, 40, 78, 112, 140, 149, 167, 221
McCarthy, Cormac 1, 4, 8, 9, 88–89, 91, 98, 99, 100–101, 103, 106, 109
meme phenomena 167, 171, 173, 175
memory, cultural memory 9, 52–53, 65, 115, 119, 129, 133–134, 139–140, 142, 149, 222–223
Messiah, Messianic, Messianism 8–9, 88–90, 93–95, 97–98, 166, 168, 171, 173; *see also* God, god; religion
Minos 125
Minotaur 125
mockingjays 126, 129–130, 134, 137
Mohr, Dunja M. 7, 16–17, 19, 27
More, Thomas 3, 9, 13n1, 70–71, 75, 86, 122, 124, 127, 134–135n1, 135n2, 137
Morson, Gary Saul 70, 83n5, 86
Moylan, Tom 6, 12, 14, 235, 241, 242, 243

Nietzsche, Friedrich Wilhelm 40–41, 112
nostalgia 13, 56, 60–66, 68, 144

oppression 2, 18–19, 26, 29, 48, 58, 105, 132, 142, 151–152, 154, 179, 203, 206, 228
Orwell, George 1, 3–5, 12, 72, 86, 120, 121, 172, 178–179, 194, 195, 226, 236–237, 240–241, 242
Orwellian 172, 240–242

Panem 124–126, 128–129, 132–134, 230
paradise 44, 78, 198–200
patriarchal, patriarchy 7, 16–21, 24, 26, 125, 135, 223–224
patriarchal dystopia 16–17
pedagogical, pedagogy 101, 104, 226, 229, 231–234, 236–239, 241–243
Philomela, Philomelan 125, 134, 136–137
phoenix 129, 131
Phúc, Phan Thị Kim 131–132, 136n8, 138
Plato 3, 122, 135
Pomponius 126
post-apocalyptic 8, 15–16, 27, 88–90, 95, 97, 99, 150, 222, 223; *see also* apocalypse, apocalyptic
postcolonization 19, 57, 62, 84n18, 86; *see also* colonization; reverse colonization

Index

postcyberpunk 11, 208, 209; *see also* cyberpunk
postmodern 4, 8, 12, 56–62, 64–65, 67–68, 76, 84n14, 85, 101, 104, 107–109, 112, 114, 123, 199, 209
postsecular 9, 95, 100–106, 108–109, 110
post-traumatic stress disorder (PTSD) 8, 16, 27, 28, 128, 134
post-war Britain 8, 50, 73, 79, 82
power 4–5, 7, 12, 13n1, 16–19, 26, 29, 43, 45–51, 54, 55, 63, 67, 70, 72–73, 78, 91, 99, 103, 107–108, 114, 122–123, 132, 135, 136n2, 146, 153, 155, 161n4, 164, 167, 169, 171, 173–174, 182–183, 185, 192, 195, 217, 220, 222, 228, 231, 233–237, 241, 243
pragmatism 105, 135n2, 179, 186–188, 193
primitivism 13n1, 41, 46, 155, 157, 219
prison 15–18, 21–23, 26n3, 43, 91, 125–126, 206, 215
privacy 10, 13n1, 164, 167, 171–172, 174–175, 227
propaganda 30, 71–72, 155, 230, 236, 240

race 13n1, 40, 75, 79–81, 84n12, 85, 187, 201, 215, 224
Rao, Eleonora 18–19, 25, 27
Ray, Karen 111, 121
reality television 10, 124, 131, 150–152, 154, 155, 156, 157, 161–162
religion 98, 103, 106, 108–109, 127, 136, 155, 197–198, 209, 230; *see also* God, god; Messiah, Messianic, Messianism
resistance 2, 18, 19, 22–23, 47, 49, 65, 75, 77, 80–81, 92, 122, 132, 141, 142, 144, 145, 146, 149, 159, 168, 172, 176, 185, 193, 194, 209, 210–211, 223n5, 225–226, 228, 232, 235–238, 242
reverse colonization 211, 219, 224; *see also* colonization; postcolonization
revolution 10, 35–37, 42–43, 72, 75, 78–79, 139, 143, 148, 160, 179
Ricœur, Paul 9, 105–106, 110, 112–115, 119–121
right to life 9, 123
Rome 126, 132, 138, 197

Salvation, salvational 91, 94, 97–98, 195
Saturus 125–126
Schneiderman, Rose 130, 138
science fiction 6, 12, 14, 17, 38, 83n4, 85, 86, 152, 163, 195, 196–197, 209, 235, 242, 243
secondary classroom 11, 13n1, 225–241
self-determination 9, 123, 128, 132
September 11 (9/11) attacks 219, 227, 231
sexuality 22, 31–34, 38, 67, 74–75, 214
Shakespeare, William 125

Sisk, David W. 26, 27
Snyder, Katherine V. 16–17, 27
Spartacus 124–125
spirituality, spiritual 8, 9, 40, 42, 48, 50, 88, 98, 106–107, 109, 200
steampunk 8, 56, 58–59, 67
Stephenson, Neal 11, 196–197, 200–208, 209
Stevick, Philip 71, 86
Stoker, Bram 60, 210–211, 213–219, 223–224

Taylor, Charles 101–103, 105–107, 110
technology 2, 4, 8, 10–11, 13n1, 36, 38, 40, 56, 58, 67, 73, 112, 155, 159–160, 163–177, 199, 202–203, 207–209, 224, 227–228, 230, 232, 235, 240, 242
technophilia 164, 173–174
Thistleton, Anthony 114, 121
totalitarian, totalitarianism 2, 12–13, 47, 117, 120, 152, 155, 172, 178–179, 194, 221, 228, 237
trajectory 6, 119, 123, 128, 151, 166, 232, 235, 239

United States 9–11, 13n1, 14, 34, 37, 53, 56–57, 65, 70, 79–80, 84n15, 86, 100–103, 106–107, 130–134, 135n4, 140, 142, 149, 151–152, 157–161, 164, 196–202, 205, 207, 210–213, 216–221, 223–224, 230
utility 11, 178, 185, 187, 189, 194
utopia, utopian, utopianism 1, 3–9, 11–14, 16–17, 20, 22–25, 43, 50, 56, 58, 63–67, 69–83, 85–87, 111–112, 115–117, 119, 122–124, 127, 134–135, 137–138, 172, 196, 198, 204, 209, 222, 228, 241–242

vampire 11, 143, 210–224
Varsam, Maria 229, 243
Vietnam 53, 130–132, 134, 137
Vietnam War 53, 131–132, 134, 136n9, 137
violence 3, 8, 16, 19, 32, 37, 41, 43, 47, 48, 50, 54, 56–60, 63, 67, 72, 80–81, 105, 116–117, 122, 126–127, 130–132, 134, 140, 141–143, 147, 149, 152, 158, 202, 224, 227; *see also* aggression
Vonnegut, Kurt 7–8, 28–38, 166, 177, 178
voyeur, voyeuristic 67, 131, 151

Wambu, Onyekachi 79, 84n16, 86
war 1–4, 8–10, 12, 28–29, 36–39, 40–44, 47–51, 53, 55, 58, 69–70, 72–73, 79–80, 82–83, 85–86, 91, 107, 116, 124, 130, 131–132, 134, 136n8, 136n9, 137, 141–142, 152, 178–179, 211, 213, 217, 219–220, 224
War on Terror 4, 211, 219–221
Weldon, Fay 72, 87

Wells, H.G. 14, 71, 87
Westerfeld, Scott 10, 139, 144–145, 149
whiteness 210, 214, 216, 218, 221
Wolfreys, Julian 64–65, 68

young adult dystopian fiction 2, 4–7, 10, 12, 14, 29, 135n3, 137, 139, 144, 148–149, 228–230, 232, 235, 242
youth culture 73–77, 82, 83n9, 84n15

Žižek, Slavoj 94–96, 99
zombie 15, 105, 143, 150, 211, 220

www.ingramcontent.com/pod-product-compliance
Lightning Source LLC
Chambersburg PA
CBHW051217300426
44116CB00006B/606